Multicultural Literacy

Mirroring the Reality of the Classroom

Barbara J. Diamond
Eastern Michigan University

Margaret A. Moore
Eastern Michigan University

 **Longman** *Publishers USA*

**MULTICULTURAL LITERACY: MIRRORING
THE REALITY OF THE CLASSROOM**

Copyright © 1995 by Longman Publishers USA.
All rights reserved.
No part of this publication may be reproduced,
stored in a retrieval system, or transmitted
in any form or by any means, electronic, mechanical,
photocopying, recording, or otherwise,
without the prior permission of the publisher.

Longman, 10 Bank Street, White Plains, N.Y. 10606

Associated companies:
Longman Group Ltd., London
Longman Cheshire Pty., Melbourne
Longman Paul Pty., Auckland
Copp Clark Longman Ltd., Toronto

Senior acquisitions editor: Laura McKenna
Development editor: Virginia L. Blanford
Production editor: Dee Josephson
Cover design: Joseph dePinho
Cover illustration/photo: Betty Ann Booker
Text art: Fine Line
Production supervisor: Richard Bretan

Library of Congress Cataloging-in-Publication Data

Diamond, Barbara J.
    Multicultural literacy : mirroring the reality of the classroom /
Barbara J. Diamond and Margaret A. Moore.
        p.   cm.
Includes bibliographical references and index.
    ISBN 0-8013-1141-1
    1. Multicultural education—United States.   I. Moore, Margaret A.
II. Title.
LC1099.3.D53   1995
370.19'6'0973—dc20   94-27767
                                                        CIP

2 3 4 5 6 7 8 9 10-MA-98979695

In memory of my parents, Ernest and Lenora Baylor,
who taught me to look for the best in people of all races and cultures,
and to be the best that I could be.

B.J.D.

In memory of my grandmother, Hattye Campbell, and my grandfather,
Dwight Campbell, who taught me to care for all students and whose love
still surrounds me with the "strength of blue horses."

M.A.M.

To all students that educators might celebrate and affirm
their cultural heritages and traditions, who they are,
and who they may become.

Contents

Foreword

Images and Identity

Pat Mora*

Barbara Diamond and Margaret Moore wrote *Multicultural Literacy: Mirroring the Reality of the Classroom* to help committed professionals confront and overcome cultural biases in their classrooms and beyond. They assert that parents and educators share a commitment to prepare their youngsters to become both academically and culturally competent within a pluralistic society with democratic ideals. They, like I, believe that our youth need to become aware of cultural bias and cultural differences and recognize that our national cultural diversity—languages, art, music, customs, literature—is our common wealth.

Issues treated in this book—diversity, translation, and the nonstatic nature of cultures—are complex and require careful analysis and discussion. The authors underscore this point, emphasizing that "teachers need additional cultural and social knowledge as they work with increasing numbers of students from varied cultural and linguistic backgrounds." They understand that educators—be they writers, illustrators, publishers, editors, reviewers, scholars, teachers, or librarians—need to be willing to explore their own culture and values, as well as to study and seek to understand a culture before attempting to convey or share or edit or evaluate a description of it. The editor who does not understand that Puerto Ricans are not Cubans and not Mexican Americans, for example, might want a manuscript that will produce a "generic Hispanic book," which will not authentically convey the partic-

---

* Pat Mora is the author of Latino picture books, including *A Birthday Basket for Tia* (1992), *Listen to the Desert: Oye al desierto* (1994), and *Pablo's Tree*. She has also written the poetry collections *Chants* (1984) and *Borders* (1986) and the nonfiction book, *Nepantla: Essays from the Land in the Middle* (1992). Pat has a particular interest in the accurate and authentic portrayal of Latina/o protagonists. According to her, young people need and deserve freedom from invisibility and isolation. Unfortunately, to date, few books are written and illustrated by Latinas even though 25 million Latinos live in this country.

ularities, including particularities of terms in Spanish, accurate for each group. The teacher who has not educated himself about attitudes toward family in Latino communities may lead his students to draw false conclusions about family closeness as antithetical to the fostering of personal independence.

We are busy people. With a sigh we may be tempted to ask, do we have the energy to learn what we need to know? Are we willing to confront the psychological needs of the young people we serve? Are we willing to create allies who will help us explore the injustices that bias perpetuates, even in the seemingly comforting area of children's literature? We need, in the words of Anita Silvey in *The Horn Book,* "varied carolers" writing our varied experiences and traditions so that Teresa in inner-city Chicago, Monica in the suburbs of Florida, and Eduardo in the Barrio of San Antonio might see themselves when they open their picture books. If not, these children might conclude that there is something the matter with who they are, their skin color, their language, or their family customs and values. If we believe in the power of words and of books, how can we not believe that this invisibility in books can produce psychological scarring?

In our schools and homes we must further resist the multicultural reductionism that defines cultures as the 4F's: food, fashion, festival, and folklore. Serving rice and using chopsticks is not the most appropriate way to honor Japanese culture. We need to ask whether the curriculum and teaching practices in the schools are perpetuating or challenging narrow cultural views. Similarly, we need to ask if the media that we view and discuss with the young are perpetuating or challenging narrow cultural views. Moving beyond these superficial aspects of culture, Diamond and Moore illustrate ways to highlight the values, beliefs, and varied interactional patterns of people from diverse groups in authentic ways.

A poster says that every child has the right to be cherished. I go further. Every child has the right to have all she is cherished, the color of her skin, the texture of his hair. Incorporating and valuing picture books from diverse cultures is but one concrete strategy for truly integrating our pluralism into our curriculum, specifically into the lives of the vulnerable child beginning to discover book-joy. This book offers teachers specific guidelines for selecting and reviewing appropriate and authentic books that preserve each child's right to have all she is cherished. The multitude of personalized and contextualized teaching strategies to use with multicultural books further enable teachers to integrate multicultural themes and cultural issues across the curriculum.

Books preserve the cultural values and traditions that a young person has a right to know and understand. Individually and collectively, we all have a right to our cultural heritage. Native language is part of that right. In knowing our full heritage, we can decide what to take forward. *Multicultural Literacy: Mirroring the Reality of the Classroom* shows how teachers can use students' natural and cultural heritages and languages as catalysts for speaking and writing. In this way, a child's past can be a source of creativity, while highlighting aspects of his or her uniqueness.

And what a resource cultural knowledge and understanding can be for the teacher of geography, history, art, and literature! The classroom vignettes, interspersed throughout the text, illustrate how teachers can integrate themes with these subjects in order to enhance student literacy and cultural appreciation.

I believe in the power of the word. I believe in the power of books not only to reflect but to create reality. Our global challenges are significant, and we humans, our collective talent, are the hope of this planet we call home. **We are all needed.** Libraries, schools, and professional organizations, then, need to be vibrant and vital inclusive communities for us all. In a multicultural society, we can settle for no less than multicultural education and multicultural literature that enriches us all.

REFERENCES

Mora, P. (1994). *Listen to the desert: Oye al desierto.* New York: Clarion Books.

Mora, P. (1994). *Pablo's tree.* New York: Macmillan.

Mora, P. (1992). *A birthday basket for Tia.* New York: Macmillan.

Mora, P. (1992). *Nepantla: Essays from the land in the middle.* Albuquerque: University of New Mexico Press.

Mora, P. (1986). *Borders.* Houston, TX: Arte Publico Press.

Preface

This book describes our personal journey with multicultural literacy. It reflects four years of our work with teachers and students in culturally and linguistically diverse classroom settings in kindergarten through eighth grade. We are excited about sharing *Multicultural Literacy: Mirroring the New Reality of the Classroom* with preservice and inservice teachers, administrators, and other educators who are interested in multicultural education. We address the critical issues of literacy for culturally and linguistically diverse students and multicultural appreciation and understanding for students of all cultures.

Our classrooms are becoming a rich tapestry, interwoven with people of diverse cultures and ethnic groups that shape and strengthen our nation. Even though the nature of our schools is changing, current curricula primarily mirror the dominant European American culture. This transmits a hidden message to students from varied cultures and ethnic backgrounds—a message that their histories, traditions, and heritages are not valued and validated. In response to these issues, many educators advocate developing a curriculum that reflects the varied cultures comprising our nation. They see the need for a curriculum that provides our students with the understanding, knowledge, skills, and attitudes critical for functioning and interacting with people from diverse cultures and backgrounds throughout the world.

Our journey was initially driven by our belief that children of color would view themselves as valued members of society and achieve greater academic success if their life experiences, histories, and language were reflected in what they read, discuss, and write. We further believed that *all* children need to learn about their own and other cultures. To address these issues, we implemented a multicultural literacy program and investigated its effects on literacy and cultural awareness in three culturally diverse school districts. Perhaps it was fortuitous that on the afternoon of the first inservice for participants, we received a phone call from the Office of Fund for the Reform of Schools and Teaching (FIRST), U.S. Department of Education, to inform us that our project had been funded.

Since that first inservice, we have listened, learned, shared, facilitated, observed, and documented our findings, working to combine our knowledge of culture and literacy with the wisdom and knowledge of the practitioner. Our journey was made easier by a series of guides—teachers, students, and administrators. The rewards have been many, not the least of which is this book, which provides a source for educators who wish to make multicultural literacy an integral part of their curriculum.

Our backgrounds as former elementary classroom teachers and professors of reading and language arts education grounds the text in theory and practice. We bring the added perspectives of different racial and cultural backgrounds—Barbara, from an African American experience, and Margaret, from a European American experience—with different voices and world views. In our writing and deliberations, we engaged in dialogues almost daily. We challenged our assumptions and confronted our biases. We became introspective, angry, weary, energized, and hopeful. Above all we learned not to just *share* our views, but to *listen* and to *hear* each other. In fact, we feel that our personal experiences, sensitive interactions, and thoughtful deliberations opened avenues to understanding that otherwise might have remained closed. Through these experiences, we feel we have provided a richer text for the reader. For change to occur among people of diverse cultures, there is a need to be sensitive to the views of others, to listen, to hear, and to act.

The book, which emerges from the longitudinal study implemented within these three school districts, integrates our research and our experiences with the multicultural literacy program and its effect on learning. Thus, our extensive research and our experiences in these multicultural settings during the last four years provide the theoretical underpinnings of our text.

To help our readers perceive these multicultural perspectives and issues, and their role in the learning process of all students, the first section of our book, "Theoretical Perspectives of a Multicultural Literacy Program," lays the foundation and rationale for multicultural literacy. After establishing these theoretical perspectives, the second section, "Strategies for Enhancing Multicultural Understanding and Appreciation throughout the Curriculum," presents innovative, practical strategies— with detailed directions and samples of students' writing—for making multicultural literacy an integral part of the curriculum. The final section, "Organizing and Managing a Successful Multicultural Literacy Program," provides teachers and administrators with strategies for organizing, managing, and monitoring a successful multicultural program by giving in-depth descriptions of the components of a successful staff development program, describing techniques for fostering parent and community involvement, and suggesting ways to organize and manage the program at the classroom and school levels.

Many of our fellow educators at other universities have expressed an interest in offering a course on multicultural literacy. Others are also concerned about the need to prepare their preservice teachers for teaching in multicultural settings; they are looking for a multicultural literacy text to supplement their language arts, literature, or reading methods courses. Our book, which is designed for preservice and inservice teachers who work with students in kindergarten through eighth grade, can be used for a multicultural literacy course or as a supplementary text for reading, writing, literature, or language arts courses. Teachers and administrators who participate in inservice workshops will find this book an invaluable resource as well. Whether used as a primary, supplementary, or resource text, our book will serve the needs of many educators.

The following are special features that increase the book's usability:

- **A strong theoretical research base** grounded in real-life practices and providing an understanding of the connections among language, culture, and literacy, as well as the sociocultural perspective of learning.
- **Specific teaching strategies** that model and demonstrate how to infuse multicultural literature across the curriculum. Detailed directions will enable teachers to perceive how to implement these strategies successfully within their own classrooms.
- **Vignettes** that demonstrate how to implement the strategies in the classroom. The names of teachers and students are included for authenticity as well as to acknowledge the teachers' expertise and willingness to share their students and classrooms with us.
- **Samples of students' work,** in particular samples of students' writing, which show responses that are possible when using these teaching strategies.
- **Comments and quotations** from teachers and students that illustrate their viewpoints and perspectives.
- **Figures, tables, and graphic organizers** which help readers perceive the theoretical and practical issues of teaching, as well as highlight information.
- **Questions teachers frequently ask** and responses to these questions, which help teachers and administrators implement the program, at the conclusion of the text.
- **Overviews and summaries,** which help readers follow the text more easily, for each chapter.

To facilitate implementation of a multicultural literacy program, an Instructor's Manual of multicultural inservice activities is an added feature of the text. This supplement is organized to assist professors, administrators, and teachers who are providing inservices for personnel in a school district. The supplement begins with a brief description of a multicultural literacy program, the goals and objectives of the program, and a rationale for the program. Following this overview, the content, format, and organization of eight inservice sessions, as well as additional multicultural lessons, are described. These inservice sessions serve as a foundation for a staff development program that integrates multicultural literature across the curriculum. Finally, the supplement includes a database of multicultural books that can be used with a multicultural program.

To meet the needs of the varied populations in our schools and to introduce students to the many cultures in the world, a hypertext program, *Multicultural Links,* developed by Martha Irwin, has been designed to accompany the text for an additional fee. *Multicultural Links,* which will enhance a multicultural program, is a resource bank of materials, including textual information about people throughout the world and their cultures, maps, pictures, music, and familiar phrases in different languages. Teachers and students will be able to quickly and easily access a larger array of multicultural materials. In today's society, it is difficult to keep up with the rapid pace of knowledge expansion and its impact on society. Books, materials, and resources about other cultures remain limited; moreover, the sources available are often no longer current. *Multicultural Links,* which both correlates with the goals and objectives of a multicultural literacy program and enhances learning, is an invaluable current resource for teachers and students. (See Chapter 8.)

In an attempt to be sensitive and appropriate in our use of language, we have selected specific words or terms that currently identify the cultural populations we address. We realize that these terms are not universally preferred or accepted, but we have chosen them based on the opinions and recommendations of colleagues, researchers, authors, and people to whom the terms refer. Just as our language is tentative, so are the choices we have made. New terms may evolve. What remains important are the people behind the labels and the lives that they should be able to live.

Our use of the term *multicultural* encompasses individuals of color whose national and linguistic backgrounds originated outside of the United States and/or who have been excluded and marginalized by society. Therefore, in the text and our discussions we highlight Asian Americans, African Americans, Native Americans, and Hispanic Americans. Even though we realize that everyone in a pluralistic society is multicultural to some degree, we refer primarily to these groups because of our desire for teachers and students to understand the central importance that these diverse groups, which have historically been excluded, misrepresented, and marginalized, assume in society. To give equal importance to other groups—the elderly, gays and lesbians, those who have special educational needs, religious minorities, the poor, and other ethnic groups—would broaden our focus, but blur our target. Therefore, although at times we allude to the latter groups, they are not our primary focus.

Throughout the text, as we refer to African Americans, Native Americans, Asian Americans, and Hispanic Americans, we are very much aware of the diversity in values, lifestyles, and histories that exists within these groups. We therefore refer to specific subgroups rather than to the broad cultural term, when appropriate. Instead of the term *Hispanic Americans,* for example, we use *Mexican Americans* or *Puerto Ricans* as the specific subgroup under the Hispanic American umbrella. The terms, *Hispanic* and *Latino,* are also used interchangeably within our text.

We offer this book to preservice and inservice teachers, administrators, educators, and parents who are interested in multicultural education. Just as we took risks, we hope others will be risk takers, experimenting and exploring ways of integrating multicultural literacy with the curriculum. We do not mean to be condescending; we desire to provide a forum for reflection and sensitive discussions about multicultural literacy. The teachers, administrators, parents, and educators we work with are challenged to enhance literacy for all students. They, like us, are in search of ways to extend their knowledge and improve their practice to accomplish this goal. We hope this book will be a guide for others who begin their own journey, implementing similar multicultural literacy programs. What is important is to begin this journey, reflecting, listening, and discussing along the way. As our curriculum mirrors the reality of the classroom, *all* students will view themselves as valued members of society and achieve greater academic success.

ACKNOWLEDGMENTS

This book is a tribute to the many students and teachers whose voices emerge from the pages of our book. We are appreciative of the warmth and trust with which they welcomed us into their classrooms. There are many others to whom we wish to express our appreciation and gratitude: those who supported, assisted, and sustained us through the process of writing this book. We especially owe a debt of gratitude to many educators, administrators, and parents. Although the words in the text are our own, the ideas have emerged through continuous sharing, interactions, and collaborations with all these people.

We particularly wish to acknowledge the Ann Arbor, Inkster, and Ypsilanti school districts of Michigan, for their support and collaboration in the Multicultural Literacy Program. Specifically, the following administrators, teachers, and project staff have all provided their time, support, and expertise to the success of the program and the creation of this book.

Administrators

We are grateful for the support and trust of the administrators within the three school districts who gave us the freedom to take risks and discover the techniques that help all students to attain cultural knowledge and achieve academic success. They include: Edwin Ames, Jean Baker, Sharon Baskerville, Edmond Beverly, Deanna Birdyshaw, Daniel Brown, Shelley Bruder, Lana Callihan, Pauline Coleman, Pat de Rossett, Maude Forbes, Diane Geherin, Janette Jackson, Paul Kacanek, William Madsen, Mary Moss, Thelma McCollum, Rick O'Neill, Anita Parks, Ann Schmidt, Odessa Smith, Tulani Smith, Sally Stavros, Sharalene Thompson, Glenna Tringali, Nancy Voght, and Lamar Whitmore.

Teachers

The following teachers in the Ann Arbor school district generously gave their time and support by allowing us to work with them in their classrooms over the past four years. We would like to thank: Gerard Antekeier, Basil Babcock, Bonita Boyce, Beth Caldwell, Don Cody, LeeAnn Dickinson-Kelley, Ted Dorr, Pat Felipe, Sharon Greely, CaSandra Johnson, Kevin Karr, Marti Keefe, Martha Livisay, Kathryn Maurdeff, Doug McIntyre, Ben Michelson, Florida Miller, Ken Monash, Karen Mantieth, Marie Moorman, Zerilda Palmer, Jo Pattinson, Carol Peters, Elizabeth Rabkin, Janette Rucker, Cora Ssengoba, Nancy Theisen, Diane Till, Karen Valentine, and Scott Weinmann.

We are equally appreciative of the following teachers in the Inkster school district: Kim Clark, Louise Edje, Leon Flees, Mary Gilkey, Alonzo Glaze, Sharon Harris, Allean House, Shirley Howard, Ollie Hill, Ellen Jones, Lawsie Jones, Ruby Long, Bill Morgan, Opal Nolen, Marita Price, Marilyn Smith, and Evelyn Thomas.

Finally, we would like to thank the following teachers in the Ypsilanti school district: Charlotte Andrews, Novia Baran, Jack Bauer, Judy Benns, Leah Biggs, Deanna Birdyshaw, Elaine Bortz, Joan Briggs, Marlene Britton, Kay Brown, Diane Bunge, Delores Butler, Donna Carpenter, Arlene Clark, Mary Coburn, Stefanie Condoll, Barbara Cornish, Michele David, Venetia Dickerson-Sims, Barbara Dykman, Susan Fenker, Jan Fillmore, Judy Floyd, Don Garnaas, Debbie Grady, Shirley Graessley, Gary Gray, Gwen Guthrie, Merrell Harkema, Debbie Heyn, Char Holly, Gayle Hood, Alexa Hoylman, Herman Humes, Beth Hurdle, Linda Ichesco, Linda Jamieson, Betty Jessee, Eloise Johnson, Anne Johnson, Judy Jones, Lois Kamoi, Debbie Kvaran, Sharon Landrum, Marsha Lund, Bill Madden, Mary Manchester, Jeanne Medley, Kathy Micallef, Earl Morrison, Mary Mouganis, Joel Osborn, Judy Pitcher, Hazel Plummer, Lynne Raglin, Beth Ramsey, Candy Reaume, Jennifer Roland, Karen Johnston, Linda Skinner, Alicia Smith, Odessa Smith, Ruth Smith, Sue Smith, Philip Staulter, Kristine Stoelton, Bonnie Stowe, Mary Streeter, Vonnie Taylor, Jeanne Thayer, Tom Tobias, Margaret Trapp, Beverly Tyler, Karen Tzortzinis, Sharon Warring, Sue Weeks, Jennifer Wheaton, Connie Williams, and Mary Williams.

Project Staff and Reviewers

We are also grateful to the project staff for their unfailing commitment, support, and interest in completing the unending lists of tasks associated with the Multicultural Literacy Project and the writing of this book. They include: Tuhani Abboushi, Carol Baier, Jackie Bree, Joy Croel, Kenya Gilkey, Mandeep Grewal, Sallie Hardt, Alethea Helbig, Anita Holtz, Theresa Hurd, Stuart Karabenick, John Knapp, Pat Mora, Sue Moss, Marvin Pasch, Adam Riccinto, Deanna Roach, Lori Soumela, Judy Sauer, Gretchen Watson, Mary White, Terri Johnson, and Regina Winborn. We owe a special word of thanks to John Knapp, who spent endless hours on the analysis and interpretation of data, and also to Jackie Bree and Judy Sauer who gave their time, their suggestions, and feedback as we worked on the manuscript. We were especially fortunate to have Judy's talent in preparing the database of multicultural books and the Instructors' Manual. We would also like to thank the following professors for their thoughtful reviews: Linda Amspaugh, University of Cincinnati; Denise Bartolo, Plymouth State College; Nancy Bundy, Simpson College; Jesus Cortez, California State University; Donna Davenport, Texas A&M University; Jose Figueroa, Northern Illinois University; Marjorie Hancock, Kansas State University; Sandra Imdieke, Northern Michigan University; Kathryn LaFramboise, University of Southern Florida; Linda Lamme, University of Florida; Corinne Mantle Bromley, Colorado State University; Elinor Ross, Tennessee Technical University; Wayne Slater, University of Maryland; Ann Trousdale, Louisiana State University; and Addison Watanabe, San Francisco State University.

National and Local Financial Support

Without the financial support of the Department of Education and other local community businesses, the Multicultural Literacy Program would not have been possible. We wish to extend our appreciation to the Department of Education for its Grant, Funds for Improving and Restructuring Schools and Teaching, the Ann Arbor Foundation for its Grant, and the following departments, schools, and offices at Eastern Michigan University: Department of Teacher Education, Graduate School, Office of Research and Development, and Administrators. We are also appreciative of Borders, Little Professor, Francine Levine, and Kinko's for their financial support.

Publishing Process

In facilitating the publishing process, we are most appreciative of Laura McKenna, who supported us through all stages of the book. Her flexibility, knowledge, and support, and words of encouragement have been invaluable.

Students

We would also like to thank all the students who took the risk to share their reading, writing, and wonderful ideas with us. They have enriched our lives and led us down the path of successful learning so that we might share this information with others and provide others with more clues to successful learning for all students.

Family and Friends

Ultimately, we could not have completed this book without the support and love of our special friends and family. We are grateful for their love and their cheers along the way. They include Peggy's parents, John and Doris Binnion, her grandfather, Dwight Campbell, her brothers and sisters John, Ginny, and Lee, and, most of all, her three children Chad, Tiffany, and Christopher. Without their love, help, faith, patience, and belief in her, she could never have written this book and continued the many roles she serves at the same time.

They also include Barbara's husband John, her children Kim and Johnny, and her sister and brother-in-law, Pat and Pete. They were always there, always believed, listened, and cheered. Special people who helped as listeners and ardent supporters are my colleagues and friends, Aljean Bibb and Patricia Edwards.

Finally, we believe that this book is truly a collaborative effort, made possible by the talents, support, commitment, and openness of many people. To each and every one of them, we are deeply grateful. We have accomplished far more than we ever thought we could when we first began our Multicultural Literacy Program.

chapter 1

Multicultural Literacy for Today's Schools

A discussion of multicultural literacy in our schools must begin with an understanding of the diversity of children's family and community experiences in this country. Our youth form a rich mosaic of children from different cultures, ethnic groups, and races. This mosaic creates a beautiful and balanced picture, with each part making a positive and distinct contribution to the whole. But, if parts of the mosaic are chipped away, devalued, or discarded, the mosaic loses its beauty and value.

Our schools are a microcosm of society and thus are also a mosaic of children of diverse races, cultures, and ethnic groups. These children bring to school their language, values, beliefs, and ways of learning (Reyhner & Garcia, 1989; Cummins, 1986). To illuminate the natural beauty of this mosaic, our schools need to build on the "webs of meaning and value and community that students bring to school" (Holmes Group, 1990, p. 11).

In order to facilitate this illumination and to maximize learning, teachers must study their own students, learning about the cultural backgrounds and language-learning experiences within their homes and communities. Without this knowledge, the roots of failure are sown. Rather than becoming a place of learning, schools become a place where problems, poor achievement, and discontent fester.

OVERVIEW

In this chapter we present a rationale for a multicultural literacy focus in our classrooms. We lay the foundation for creating a multicultural literacy program by identifying the underlying principles and the theoretical perspectives of multicultural literacy. We focus specifically on the key aspects of a multicultural literacy program and provide a model of its components. These components include an interactive model of reading and writing, which emerges from a whole language orientation within a culturally sensitive environment.

INTRODUCTION

> "Teacher, why isn't there anyone here who looks like me? Not even the pictures in our books look like me. Teacher, are you like me? Do you eat warm frijoles when you get home? Does your family welcome you into the home with a language so sweet that you would think it was made just for lovers? Teacher, I'm not sure who I am or whether or not I belong here."
>
> (Manjarrez, 1991, p. 53)

Carlos, a young Hispanic, writes of these thoughts as an adult, thoughts that were never openly expressed to his third-grade teacher. Too often these are the thoughts and questions that children of diverse cultural groups ask, but teachers may not hear. Although it is reassuring to know that Carlos found out about his heritage, learned to love reading, and achieved academic and social success, it is unfortunate that the help and support he needed to succeed came from outside the confines of the school community. Carlos was lucky. Many students like Carlos, however, do not succeed.

The Carloses in our schools make us aware that teachers of literacy and language arts, along with all educators, are faced with a tremendous challenge today. We are challenged to meet the traditional purposes for schooling: an emphasis on academic learning, economic knowledge, and the development of informed minds for citizenship in a pluralistic democracy. In the process of meeting these purposes, we are compelled to look at our students closely and to be aware of their cultural knowledge, which influences how they view the world and, ultimately, how they respond to schooling. We must affirm and acknowledge students' cultural backgrounds, help them to develop positive self-images, and facilitate their ability to construct their own meaning from what they read and write. Educators realize that there will have to be radical changes in what and how children are taught and what they learn if we are to educate *all* children. As teachers take on new roles and adapt and refine their practices, they need to consider the factors and contexts that necessitate these modifications; they need to consider the new realities of society and the classroom. The following sections describe these factors and contexts in more detail.

A RATIONALE FOR CHANGE

Shifting School Populations

As we approach the turn of the century, we are ever reminded that the population of our nation is changing rapidly. Historically, we are a nation comprised of diverse populations, going back to the Native American tribes that lived on this land before Europeans "discovered" them and the continent (Tiedt & Tiedt, 1990, p. 2). The

FIGURE 1.1   Students work together to learn about the many countries from which their ancestors came.

people who immigrated from Europe at that time came from England, France, Germany, Italy, and Spain. Russian hunters at the same time were immigrating to Alaska. Later, Chinese, Japanese, Latin Americans, and others came to the new world, all for different reasons—religious persecution, political asylum, or economic opportunities. Unlike these immigrants, thousands of new arrivals were forcibly brought to America from Africa as slaves.

Although the European American is still the predominant majority in the United States, people of many cultural and ethnic groups are rapidly increasing in number. These dramatic shifts in population are altering the demographics of our nation's schools. In 1976, for example, 24 percent of the total school enrollment in U.S. schools was nonwhite. In 1984, this percentage had increased to 29 percent. By the year 2000, people of color will comprise one-third of all students enrolled in public schools (Hodgkinson, 1985), and authorities project that by 2020, they will comprise 46 percent of the school population (Cushner, McClelland, & Safford, 1992). It is further predicted that by the middle of the twenty-first century the "minorities" taken together will constitute the majority of the country's population (Bishop, 1992).

Of significance, this multicultural trend is not regional but is evident across the country in neighborhoods and schools that were once monocultural. These shifts in population mean that teachers who have traditionally taught students of one culture may expect to teach students who are heterogeneous in terms of language and linguistic backgrounds, degree of acculturation, country of birth, immigration experience, and socioeconomic status (Ramirez, 1988). In addition, many teachers and students do not have common cultural and social perspectives. Teachers may not have been prepared to teach children who are different from themselves and may be confused by the linguistic, racial, cultural, and social class differences they face in their classrooms (Cushner, McClelland, & Safford, 1992). Frequently, teachers unwittingly teach students as they themselves were taught, and when they discover that these teaching practices are not working for all their students, they become perplexed and confused. They often are unaware of alternative teaching strategies or knowledge sources available to them.

Such teachers need additional cultural and social knowledge to work with the increasing numbers of students from varied cultural and linguistic backgrounds. In highlighting the issue of appropriate instruction, the Holmes Group (1990, p. 30)* asserts, "It is not enough to have the same program for all children. If you as teacher don't have the cultural knowledge to have all the kids get access to the same instructional goal, then you are failing to educate those children."

Changes in the Workplace

In addition to changing demographics and their effect on teaching practices, another reality is that the workplace has changed significantly. In a society in which work is essential and a strong work ethic exists, there is a growing need for students to be able to take their place in the work force effectively. One of the overriding expectations of the workplace is that employees learn to work with people who are different from themselves. People of all racial, cultural, and ethnic backgrounds find they must work together to achieve common goals (Rogoff & Lave, 1984; Wertsch, 1985). This is true in the plants and factories where employees produce parts of a whole and in the corporate board room, where employees make decisions that influence our nation's economic health, as well as the economic health of their company. These decisions often must be made while considering the global and international effects on people all over the world. Indeed, international markets also demand that workers understand the cultures of other countries in order to communicate effectively as they travel and make important decisions regarding these countries.

Educators, then, face the need to help tomorrow's citizens acquire the knowledge, skills, and attitudes critical to functioning and interacting with people from varied cultures and backgrounds in their lives.

Conflicting Visions of What Our Society Should Be

Other harsh realities of today's society are the polarizing issues of racism, sexism, and classism. Tiedt and Tiedt (1990, p. 3) assert that "race riots, the Ku Klux Klan, anti-Semitism, rape, and child abuse are not occurrences of the past. Fear and ignorance still lead individuals or groups to perform atrocities against other human beings." People are still struggling to find the elusive formula for peaceful and fruitful existence in the United States.

---

* The Holmes Group is a consortium of nearly 100 American research universities committed to improving teacher education programs by recommending and implementing major reforms.

Even on our college campuses the debate rages over whether creating a multi-cultural campus is desirable or whether it is a denunciation of the majority population, its values, and its traditional academic view of education. In university classes of prospective teachers, we hear troubling stories from students who admit that their parents were prejudiced and that they grew up hearing racial slurs and ethnic jokes. We also hear students who have faced overt and subtle racism and prejudice in school and in their community. Often underlying these negative behaviors and views are the beliefs that people who differ from the majority in language, social class, and color have less right to share in the American dream and should have a diminished voice in shaping our world. The label *different* carries with it, in the view of some, the label *deficient.*

As educators, we cannot let these views go unnoticed or unchallenged. Our students' ways of thinking are shaped largely by what is learned and modeled in school. Teachers can help students learn about and value differing beliefs and ways of viewing the world; teachers can help students appreciate and understand other cultures and break through barriers of fear and ignorance.

Although the task appears formidable, educators are beginning to meet these challenges through innovative, modified, or refined programs and teaching practices. As teachers become motivated to address issues of learning and culture, they ask, "Where do I begin?" We believe that a focus on multicultural literacy and its role in the curriculum is a place to begin. The following sections describe the theoretical perspectives of multicultural literacy, the key components of a multicultural literacy program, and a specific model of a multicultural literacy program that we have implemented in three school districts.

MULTICULTURAL LITERACY: AN ALTERNATIVE PERSPECTIVE

In a recent conversation, a teacher who had been in the multicultural literacy program for two years shared with us her views of multiculturalism prior to becoming a part of the program. She explained that she had been hesitant about participating in the program because she thought it focused only on African American literature and issues of racism and oppression. She felt that emphasis on this cultural group was important, but that there should be a broader perspective that encompassed other cultural groups. Another teacher, in a separate conversation, questioned, "Isn't this the same thing that we used to do back in the sixties? I remember celebrating a cultural holiday each month and preparing ethnic foods for everyone to taste."

These conversations highlight many of the misconceptions that exist about multicultural literacy. They reinforce the need for a clearly articulated theoretical perspective. We offer a perspective that embodies a philosophy that *all* students can learn. *Difference* in cultural/ethnic and linguistic backgrounds does not equal *deficiency.* In contrast, difference enhances and enriches the classroom, the community, the country, and the world.

Our perspective on multicultural literacy moves beyond one cultural or ethnic group, one set of issues or isolated "cultural" activities that are "add-ons" to the curriculum. We feel that multicultural literacy includes *all* cultures. Culturally sensitive teaching practices and strategies should permeate all aspects of the curriculum, integrating content through a thematic approach to learning.

Our definition of multicultural literacy emerges from theoretical principles about culture, literacy, and learning. These principles, which lay the foundation for a multicultural literacy program, further evolve from our personal and cultural experiences, our reading, and our experiences while working with teachers and students from diverse settings during the past three years. These principles are the following:

1. **Multicultural literacy is beneficial and fundamental for *all* students, not just students of diverse cultural and linguistic backgrounds.** A commonly held misconception is that students who are in monocultural settings, particularly European American students, do not need a multicultural emphasis in the process of becoming literate. Multicultural literacy can renew and affirm cultural rights for all students by emphasizing cultural equality and respect. Multicultural literacy simultaneously enhances the self-concepts of students and teaches respect for various cultures while teaching basic skills.

2. **Schools and teachers must embrace the cultural diversity of students and affirm the cultural beliefs, views, and personal experiences they bring to the classroom.** Teachers become powerful facilitators of learning when they draw on their students' cultural capital and diversity to make learning exciting and dynamic for their students and themselves. A teaching environment that includes all cultures and celebrates all voices creates a richer classroom community.

3. **Teachers' positive attitudes and expectations of how students will perform in school have a marked effect on students' ability to achieve success.** Many students come to school with positive expectations of their ability to be successful, regardless of their cultural, linguistic, or economic background. It is critical for teachers to be aware of and discard misconceptions or stereotypes about children of diverse cultural, linguistic, or low socioeconomic backgrounds not being able to achieve with high levels of success. Teachers need to be positive, affirming, and maintain high expectations for *all* students.

4. **Teachers must empower students as individuals and learners so that they receive validation for who they are.** To foster a sense of efficacy, teachers need to design learning experiences that encourage students to explore their own desires, ideas, and perceptions of the world. They must help them identify their areas of strength, reinforce their cultural heritage, and foster positive expectations for academic achievement.

5. **Students' learning is enhanced when they can connect their personal cultural experiences with what they read and write.** Students receive information, form hypotheses, make associations, and organize and store information based on their background knowledge, which is formed from their personal and cultural experiences. When students learn to draw on these experiences and connect them to their reading and writing, they become powerful and accomplished learners.

6. **Students learn best when they take an *active* role in the acquisition of knowledge and skills.** Students who are active learners take on the responsibility for their own learning. They often go beyond the established academic curriculum, both in content and processes. They engage in active probing and exploring and ultimately construct their own meaning. Because they are actively involved, they are more likely to be able to apply their learning to their lives in and out of school.

7. **Students' learning is enhanced when they are encouraged to cooperate and collaborate, sharing and exchanging ideas, concepts, and understandings with others in the construction of knowledge.** In classrooms that foster cooperative learning, all students have equal access to learning opportunities and resources. Students of diverse cultures, ideas, and abilities engage in productive learning activities while they learn to respect the ideas of others and negotiate and resolve differences.

These principles guided us in the formation of our definition of multicultural literacy. Specifically:

Multicultural literacy is the process of linking the cultural experiences, histories, and languages that all children bring to school *with* language learning and academic learning that take place in the school.

Multicultural literacy further activates silent voices, opens closed minds, promotes academic achievement, and enables students to think and act critically in a pluralistic, democratic society.

Our views are consistent with Giroux (1992, p. 16), who asserts, "It is important that teachers learn to confirm student experiences so that students are legitimated and supported as people who matter, who can participate in their learning, and who in doing so can speak with a voice that is rooted in their sense of history and place."

MULTICULTURAL LITERACY: WHAT RESEARCH SAYS

Research on literacy, culture, and the social organization of schools has given us new knowledge from which to support and inform our perspectives. Further, the research has significant implications for teachers and teacher educators as they strive to develop curricula and practices that are compatible with students' cultural and language backgrounds while supporting academic excellence.

Connections between Culture and Achievement

Researchers suggesting that there is a link between culture and achievement emphasize that improvement in learning, including basic skills, can be expected when instruction is compatible with natal-culture patterns (Deyhle, 1983; Jordan & Tharp, 1979; Jordan, 1985; Vogt, Jordan, & Tharp, 1987). Cummins (1986) and Campos and Keatinge (1984) similarly stress that the extent to which students' language and culture are incorporated into the school program constitutes a significant predictor of academic success. In reading instruction, for example, students' life experiences and cultural background influence the degree of comprehension and memory they achieve (Lipson, 1983; Mason & Au, 1990; Steffensen, Joag-Dev, & Anderson, 1979). The essence of students' prior experience and culture—their ways of interacting, communicating, celebrating, and experiencing life—combine to form their initial understanding of the world. To facilitate learning for these students, learning needs to be compatible with and emerge from their culture, their traditions, and their heritage.

The Impact of Curricular Materials

Creating cultural compatibility requires that schools provide curricular materials that reflect the diverse racial and cultural groups in our society. Using curricular materials that only reflect the predominant European American, middle-class values exposes students to a narrow linguistic, historical, and cultural picture that (1) is not always linked to their prior experiences, and (2) is not consistent with the diverse cultural patterns of our nation. When students encounter literature that includes characters, settings, and themes that resonate with their prior experiences, however, they will attain higher levels of reading and writing performance (Bishop, 1987; Mason & Au, 1990; Diamond & Moore, 1991). Bishop (1987) further claims that multicultural reading materials improve the self-esteem of racial and ethnic minorities. These materials sharpen all students' sensitivity to the commonalities of human experience.

Introducing young learners to differing cultural viewpoints through multi-cultural literature can serve as a starting point for understanding and appreciating the varied cultures that comprise our society. As learners become aware of other cultures, their understanding and appreciation of their own culture and its relationship to other cultures is heightened (Florez & Hadaway, 1986; Norton, 1992). Simultaneously, students extend their knowledge by making connections between literature and subject areas such as history, geography, or science.

The Social Organization of Teaching, Learning, and Performance

The way students and classrooms are organized for instruction also plays an important role in the achievement of culturally and linguistically diverse students. Schools need to reconsider their traditional ways of structuring classrooms and opportunities for learning. Small group arrangements, which encourage interaction, cooperation, and group processing can improve the academic performance of many ethnically and culturally diverse students (Johnson & Johnson, 1986). Other studies (Cohen, 1986; Goodlad & Oakes, 1988; Slavin, 1987; Stevens, 1986) indicate that students achieve better in cooperative learning environments that include a mixture of ability levels. Recent studies further suggest that reading and writing instruction that permits students to collaborate in discussing and interpreting texts results in dramatic improvements in both reading and verbal intellectual abilities (Au, 1979; Mason & Au, 1990).

Despite the growing support for educators to address the achievement gap of culturally, ethnically, and linguistically diverse learners, only a few programs have been designed specifically to achieve the goals of creating curricular materials that are compatible with the cultural and linguistic backgrounds of students and promoting cultural understanding and appreciation. Our multicultural literacy program was conceptualized to address these critical issues. In the next section, we highlight the components of our program to provide a model—one way that multicultural literacy might be accomplished.

A CONCEPTUAL MODEL FOR A MULTICULTURAL LITERACY PROGRAM

Our interest in multicultural literacy was informed by the conceptualization and research of a multicultural literacy program, which was funded by a grant from the Department of Education, Funds for Improving and Restructuring Schools and Teaching (FIRST). (FIRST is still in operation under the Innovations grants.) The multicultural literacy program involved three school districts over a period of three years (1989–1992). During these three years we learned and grew professionally with the teachers and students in all three school districts. Our teaching strategies and approaches to multicultural literacy emerged from this research and our experiences in working with creative and dedicated teachers and their students. For these reasons, we feel it is important to share the nature of our program, its goals, and objectives.

Purpose

The purpose of our program was to implement a multicultural literacy program that would (1) improve the educational achievement of students, particularly culturally diverse students and "at-risk" students, (2) heighten the cultural awareness of all students, and (3) provide enrichment opportunities for all students. To achieve these goals, teachers and students engaged in practices and strategies that are briefly highlighted in the following objectives:

1. **To provide a strong alignment between the written text and the cultural background, language, and experiences of students of diverse cultures, racial groups, and linguistic backgrounds.** We use strategies that elicit an understanding of a cultural group's beliefs, values, and ways of viewing the world. In the Chinese world view, for example, man, nature, and history connect. As Chinese American children read books with themes that embody these beliefs and others, they can achieve a high level of comprehension because their experiences and the way they understand life are compatible with the stories they read.

   We further affirm the language backgrounds of children by reading stories about children who share a similar language pattern. The rich language heritage of Latino American children, for example, becomes highlighted as Spanish vocabulary is interspersed throughout stories that they read.

2. **To heighten reading comprehension, writing quality, and vocabulary of elementary students.** We teach in ways that are compatible with the child's experience, previous knowledge (including cultural knowledge), and ways of organizing learning and thought. Navajo children, for example, often learn from their elders through demonstration and observation prior to performance. Similarly, Mexican American children actively engage in dialogue as parents and older siblings demonstrate learning activities. As we tap into these multiple ways of knowing and learning, students experience increased comprehension, writing quality, and vocabulary development.

3. **To develop understanding and appreciation of one's own culture and the culture of others.** We facilitate meaningful communication and discussion about diverse cultures by highlighting specific elements of these cultures that appear in literature. As students read multicultural books, they gain new insights into the values and beliefs of their own culture and the culture of others and develop pride in their cultural heritage. All students further acquire new knowledge about the contributions of culturally diverse groups to the history and development of our nation.

   We also provide opportunities for students to interact with poets, musicians, artists, storytellers, and people skilled in crafts from the community. Many parents also have special talents to share with the students.

4. **To develop positive attitudes toward reading and writing.** We provide opportunities for students to read a wide variety of multicultural literature reflecting a range of interests and a variety of genres. Those who read widely and excel in reading find books that challenge them. Students who are less able readers find appealing books at their level that have age-appropriate content. After interactively reading the stories, students participate in creative responses to multicultural literature through the use of story and poetry writing, dramatic performances, choral reading, storytelling, reader's theater, music, and art. Finally, students are encouraged to work cooperatively as well as independently. They read together in paired reading sets or in other grouping configurations. They listen to others read in order to give critical responses that benefit both listener and reader.

These objectives, which incorporate multiple ways of knowing and learning, were used to guide us in developing our multicultural program. Just as students have different ways of learning and different instructional needs, teachers also have varied teaching styles. We believe we should respect these differences. Therefore, we emphasize key components rather than prescribe teaching strategies in our program. The following section describes how these components, if included in the program, can provide a workable *framework* for implementing a multicultural literacy program. This framework can then be tailored to match the teaching styles and individual preferences of classroom teachers, as well as the needs and interests of their students.

FIGURE 1.2   Paired reading affords students an opportunity to be both listener and reader.

Key Components of a Multicultural Literacy Program

An effective multicultural literacy program includes three major components, which are based on the theoretical and research literature cited above and our experiences in working with students and teachers. These components, illustrated in Figure 1.3 are: Multicultural Literature and Resources, A Whole Language Perspective on Learning, and a Socioculturally Sensitive Learning Environment.

Multicultural Literature

Literature serves an important function in our society, for children shape their reality about themselves and others based on much of what they read. Students' attitudes, values, and beliefs are influenced by children's literature (Aoki, 1992; Diamond & Moore, 1991; White & Parham, 1990), which has the power to develop positive self-concepts and feelings of pride and confidence in members of a given group. Multicultural literature further stimulates thinking and helps students understand the stories in their own lives. Pang, Colvin, MyLuong, and Barba (1992, p. 217) assert that "literature is the means by which all children come to understand the stories of others and learn to embrace the rich diversity of our schools."

Traditionally, students of diverse backgrounds seldom saw images of themselves in the books they read. When they did encounter characters of their cultural background, they often saw negative or stereotypical images that portrayed them as

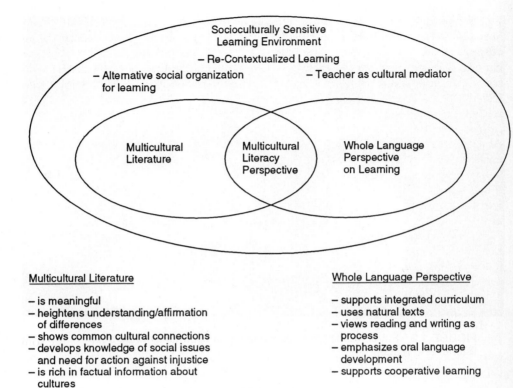

Multicultural Literature

- is meaningful
- heightens understanding/affirmation
  of differences
- shows common cultural connections
- develops knowledge of social issues
  and need for action against injustice
- is rich in factual information about
  cultures

Whole Language Perspective

- supports integrated curriculum
- uses natural texts
- views reading and writing as
  process
- emphasizes oral language
  development
- supports cooperative learning

FIGURE 1.3   A Conceptual Model of a Multicultural Literacy Program.

different from and deficient in comparison to the majority European American population. In speaking about the image of African Americans in literature, Gerald (1972) highlights a point that is applicable to children of all racial, cultural, and linguistic groups. She asserts:

> Man projects his cultural and racial images upon the universe and he derives a sense of personal worth from the reflection he sees gazing back at him. For he defines himself and the world in terms of others like him. He discovers his identity within a group. . . . We cannot judge ourselves unless we see a continuity in other people and in things and concepts. We question our very right to exist without other existences like our own.   (p. 373)

Reyhner & Garcia (1989) further stress that schools must counter "cultural discontinuity in reading materials that are dissonant with the student's home and language background." They emphasize that the curriculum should include instructional materials reflective of students' background and culture.

Consistent with these perspectives, the first component of our multicultural literacy program, demonstrated in the first concentric circle of the model in Figure

1.3, is multicultural literature—literature that mirrors the reality of the classroom. Our definition of multicultural literature is consistent with our use of the term multicultural, defined in the preface. This term encompasses individuals of color whose national and linguistic backgrounds originated outside the United States and/or who have been excluded and marginalized by society. Therefore, we highlight Asian Americans, African Americans, Native Americans, and Hispanic Americans. Although we realize that everyone in a pluralistic society is multicultural to some degree, we refer primarily to these groups because of our desire for teachers and students to understand the central importance these diverse groups, that have been historically excluded, misrepresented, and marginalized, assume in society. To give equal importance to other groups—the elderly, gays and lesbians, those who have special educational needs, religious minorities, the poor, and other ethnic groups—including European Americans—would broaden our focus, but blur our target. Although at times we allude to the latter groups, they are not our primary focus.

Multicultural literature, therefore, affirms and legitimizes a culture *and* the human race. We have found that the qualities of multicultural literature described in the following sections are significant for the teacher and student.

Multicultural literature is *meaningful literature* in that it speaks to the interests of children of diverse cultures and stimulates imaginative experiences. In an exciting and emotionally charged manner, this literature resonates with a child's magical way of thinking and his natural quest for knowledge. It captures the spirit of youth and allows children not merely to read the words superficially, but also to capture the soul of the words. Although literature that has historically reflected the European American culture—literature that was not multicultural—is also meaningful, multicultural literature has an added quality of connecting with people of diverse cultures and traditions and providing information and insight about their own lives and culture and the lives and cultures of others.

Multicultural literature further heightens understanding, respect, and affirmation of differences because it acknowledges that it is all right to be who you are. Being different from someone else is not bad but good, exciting, and desirable. This concept is significant for all children, because they learn to see and better understand themselves as they begin to see others through literature. As they travel to different "cultural sites" through literature, they learn that they are the "different" ones, as viewed through the eyes of the characters.

Literature that is multicultural *demonstrates common connections through emotions, needs, and desires.* Students often perceive differences among people more readily than they perceive similarities. Although people may have differences in behavior patterns and physical characteristics, underlying emotions, values, and needs are often similar. Multicultural literature provides a medium for understanding these connections. For example, the rite of passage to manhood for a boy from a Masai family in Africa might appear different from that of a Jewish boy's Bar Mitzvah. But as students read about these celebrations from two different cultures, they realize that both are ceremonies signaling one of life's important transitions, the passage from childhood to adulthood.

Through multicultural literature, children develop an *understanding of social issues and conflicts that create the need for social change.* The wide range of themes in historical and realistic fiction and informational children's books provides students a depth of understanding, often through characters who are their age. They identify with characters who experience "real" problems and either work to change an imperfect society or become victims of its injustice. While reading these multicultural selections, students become critical readers, who learn to view the world from multiple perspectives as they construct their version of the truth. Once students understand the harmful effects of social injustice and inequities, they can make informed and rational decisions about the most effective ways to correct injustices in their community.

Finally, multicultural literature is *rich in factual information about cultures* and is often presented in a manner that encourages students to broaden their understanding of history and geography as they visit different regions of the world through print. Multicultural literature provides a means of crossing boundaries that often exist between subjects and becomes a natural bridge between language arts and the content areas. Many of the themes of literature can be used across cultures and form the foundation for thematic learning.

We will discuss examples of multicultural literature and guidelines for selecting literature that reflects the qualities outlined above in detail in Chapter 3.

A Whole Language Perspective

The second component of a multicultural literacy program, as shown in Figure 1.3, is a whole language perspective. This perspective emphasizes that (1) learning should be rooted in students' lives and experiences and (2) acquiring the meaning of what is read and written is of paramount importance. This perspective further stresses that learning and language in the classroom should be holistic, not separated into isolated parts such as letters, combinations of letters, and phonics rules, unless as a means to aid the understanding and comprehension of meaningful text. Attempting to define whole language, Williams (1987, p. 1) asserts that it is "somewhat akin to the story of the blind men and the elephant. Some people feel the trunk and say it is the writing process. Some grab hold of a leg and say it is reading through literature. Some sense the enormous body and say it is teaching through themes. And, of course, some grab the tail and say it is no big deal and nothing new." As we see it, whole language is not the individual parts of the elephant, but rather the enormous and powerful *whole* of the beast.

The whole language perspective also includes a democratic community of learners with a curriculum grounded in the cultural and social experiences of the larger community (Goodman, Bird, & Goodman, 1991). In truth, this is the essence of how we try to accomplish the goals of a multicultural literacy program. Other common elements shared by the multicultural literacy program and the whole language perspective are the following:

- An integrated, thematic approach to curriculum
- The reading of natural texts through use of real literature
- A view of reading and writing as processes of constructing meaning, with opportunities for self-selection and choice of reading materials and writing topics

- Many opportunities for oral language use and personal expression
- Cooperative learning within a community of learners

An Integrated Thematic Curriculum.   In an integrated thematic curriculum, curricular areas are linked and thus integrated across subject areas. Children's oral and written language provides the foundation for the curriculum. Children can learn the language modes—listening, speaking, reading, and writing—by using language in meaningful situations. The traditional boundaries that separate one subject from another are permeable, so that students learn to connect their learning from one subject to another into a meaningful whole. In a thematic unit on trees, for example, students might begin by discussing the need for man to preserve trees, which is a social studies concept. This study can naturally extend to science, as children study the relationship of trees to man's physical environment, and to math, as they estimate and measure tree age. Cultural connections are made as children examine the values that some groups, such as the Native American and Chinese, place on nature and its aesthetic contributions to their lives. An example of a thematic unit plan is shown in Figure 1.4.

Several goals can be accomplished simultaneously through thematic learning. For example, students might (1) learn valuable information about natural erosion and erosion caused by human, (2) become acquainted with historic as well as scientific changes during a particular time in history, (3) increase their awareness of the variety of social values evidenced by literary characters, and (4) learn characteristics of different genres of literature. The application of the concepts of thematic learning to multicultural literacy will be discussed in detail in Chapter 6.

Reading Natural Texts.   Reading natural texts—texts that have not been abridged and distorted by controlled vocabulary for basal readers—is another important ingredient of a whole language perspective. This literature is written in natural, uncontrolled language; character and plot are well developed. Children who read natural texts make excellent progress in learning to read and write, master phonics and decoding skills as needed, and develop positive attitudes toward reading and writing (Boehnlein, 1987; Holdaway, 1982; Pinnell, 1986).

Reading and Writing as Processes of Constructing Meaning.   Reading and writing are viewed as parallel processes of constructing meaning. Tierney and Pearson (1983) hold that reading and writing are acts of constructing meaning and thinking. They are processes through which readers and writers constantly make connections with their background and cultural knowledge, make inferences, make predictions, and employ metacognitive strategies. These processes involve *planning* as readers and writers set goals and activate relevant background knowledge in order to understand the author's meaning (in the case of the reader) or to generate ideas (in the case of the writer).

The notion of *drafting* similarly applies to both reading and writing. Students are encouraged and supported in constructing meaning through a trial-and-error process. In writing, this means a first draft and subsequent drafts as students clarify their message. In reading, students arrive at an initial understanding and then refine and modify this meaning as they continue to read. As students read and write, they begin

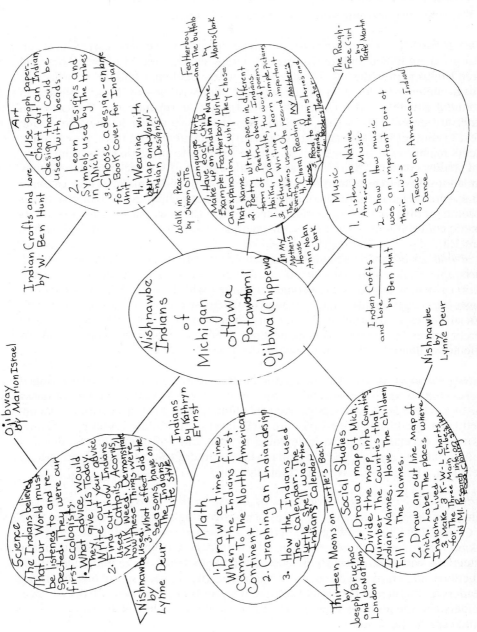

FIGURE 1.4 A teacher made a web of her plans for a thematic unit on the Native American tribes of Michigan for her class.

to develop a framework about the overall text—the setting, the characters, the events—and how they all fit together to form an interesting, intriguing plot. Along the way, they evaluate, deliberate, and reflect critically, often *revising* what they have read or written.

Finally, readers and writers often will return to their texts or drafts to refine or edit what they have read or written and to share ideas with others through oral reading or publication during the reading and writing processes. This sharing or publishing can be formal or informal—the reader or writer often chooses. The numerous connections between the reading and writing processes and multicultural literacy will be considered in detail in Chapters 4 and 5.

Oral Language Use and Personal Expression. A whole language perspective promotes oral language use and development. Children's language development is part of the whole cultural setting in which they grow up, and language is developed as they see a need for its use. Oral language development in whole language classrooms is supported by teachers' high expectations and confidence in students' ability to use language. Teachers realize that *all* students, including second-language learners and students who speak a dialect, have rich experiences, knowledge, and language skills.

In whole language classrooms, students are surrounded by oral language in meaningful contexts. They are encouraged to engage in meaningful dialogue and discussions; they are free to use their own language in expressing their ideas and experiences and in giving critical answers to questions. Ample opportunities for oral sharing of creative responses to literature occur through writing, dramatizations, choral and interpretive readings, and chants and poetry reading. These activities build on the oral traditions that are part of the heritage of many students of diverse cultures. All students' language abilities are engaged in tasks that arise from meaningful learning activities and a real need to communicate. Goodman and Goodman (1991) remind us that

> whole language implies celebrating language in all its variety. We start in whole language, as Dewey advised, where the child is. The goal is never to reject one language form and replace it with another. Rather, the goal is to expand on the base of the home dialect and to support learners as they add other dialects and registers to their repertoire. (p. 83)

Cooperative Learning. Cooperative learning is a powerful element of whole language. Teachers structure learning so that heterogeneous groups of students work together to achieve a shared goal (Sapon-Shevin & Schniedewind, 1991). The principles of cooperative learning are compatible with the principles of an effective multicultural literacy program. For example, one principle of a multicultural literacy program is that all students are valued. Similarly, in a cooperative learning situation all students are respected and have equal access to educational opportunity and resources. Students are specifically taught to help and encourage those who need help in order that all can succeed. Learning activities are structured so that each student within the group has an important task, making optimal learning possible for all students.

Another shared principle is that heterogeneity and diversity enhance learning experiences. In cooperative learning settings, students and teachers view diversity as enriching; conversely, opportunities to gain a breadth and depth of knowledge are absent when students from homogeneous backgrounds work in groups. Learning takes on new meaning when it occurs in the context of a community where students learn that all of us are smarter than any one of us (Johnson, Johnson, & Holubec, 1986; Kagan, 1988; Slavin, 1987).

As Goodman (1992, p. 196) stresses, the whole language perspective "revalues the classroom as a democratic learning community where teachers and pupils learn together and learn to live peacefully together." Goodman further emphasizes that whole language is an inclusive, coherent, and scientific perspective that has already produced profound changes in the education of Native Americans, Hispanic Americans, and African Americans as well as among the poor and disenfranchised of our society.

The Socioculturally Sensitive Environment

The third component of a multicultural literacy program is a context for learning that is sensitive to the social and cultural background of all students. We have already alluded to cooperative learning and other aspects of the whole language perspective that create an environment of inclusion, affirmation, and respect for all learners. In a multicultural literacy classroom, we extend our thinking beyond the classroom to students' families and communities. Literacy—the acquisition of oral and written language—begins in the family and community as students are socialized through everyday interactions. They learn to make sense of the world, develop cognitive structures (ways of knowing), and adapt to social interactions and the various roles they and others must play in various settings. When children come to school, they bring these socialization and cognitive frameworks with them (Schieffelin & Ochs, 1986). The child's culture, home, family, and community form the sociocultural backdrop for school learning. The classroom must be sensitive to these multiple histories, which are the ways of knowing and learning that students bring.

We feel this perspective is crucial to an effective multicultural literacy program. Figure 1.3, therefore, illustrates that the sociocultural environment encompasses the other components of the multicultural literacy program. The materials of learning, the strategies and teaching practices, and classroom organization evolve from this sociocultural environment. The sensitive sociocultural environment becomes the medium in which a multicultural literacy program flourishes and grows.

In Chapter 2, we identify three essential components of a socioculturally sensitive school environment: (1) recontextualized learning, or learning that is imbedded in functional, meaningful, and relevant experiences and situations; (2) alternative social organization structures; and (3) the teacher as cultural mediator. The critical role these components play in a multicultural literacy program are further described in depth in this chapter.

SUMMARY

We have presented a rationale for multicultural literacy, discussing the challenge educators have in responding to the needs of all students. This challenge is heightened in today's society by the shifting demographics of the schools, which are becoming increasingly diverse; the changes in the nature of the workplace; and society's conflicting views about what a democratic country should be. Educators are beginning to look for ways to meet these challenges. Implementing a multicultural literacy program, in which students value and respect all learners, is one way to meet these challenges.

After delineating six principles of literacy and learning, we defined our view of multicultural literacy as the process of linking the cultural experiences, histories, and languages that all children bring to school with language learning and academic learning that takes place in the school. Finally, we presented a conceptual model of a multicultural literacy program that was implemented in three school districts. We discussed the purpose and the three major goals of the program and explained the key components: multicultural literature, whole language, and a socioculturally sensitive environment.

REFERENCES

Aoki, E. (1992). Turning the page: Asian Pacific American children's literature. In V. Harris (Ed.), *Teaching multicultural literature in grades K-8.* (pp. 109-135). Norwood, MA: Christopher-Gordon.

Au, K. (1979). Using the experience-text-relationship method with minority children. *Reading Teacher, 32,* 677-679.

Bishop, R. S. (1987). Extending multicultural understanding through children's books. In B. Cullinan (Ed.), *Children's literature in the reading program.* (pp. 60-70). Newark, DE: International Reading Association.

Bishop, R. (1992). Extending multicultural understanding. In B. Cullinan (Ed.), *Invitation to read: More children's literature in the reading program.* (pp. 80-91). Newark, DE: International Reading Association.

Boehnlein, M. (1987). Reading intervention for high risk first-graders. *Educational Leadership, 44,* 32-37.

Campos, J., & Keatinge, B. (1984). *The Carpinteria preschool program: Title VII second year evaluation report.* Washington, D.C.: Department of Education.

Cohen, E. (1986). *Designing groupwork: Strategies for the heterogeneous classroom.* New York: Teachers College Press.

Cummins, J. (1986). Empowering minority students: A framework for intervention. *Harvard Educational Review, 56,* 18-36.

Cushner, K., McClelland, A., & Safford, P. (1992). *Human diversity in education: An integrative approach.* New York: McGraw-Hill.

Deyhle, D. (1983). Measuring success and failure in the classroom: Teacher communication about tests and the understandings of young Navajo students. *Peabody Journal of Education, 61,* 67-85.

Diamond, B. J., & Moore, M. A. (1991). *The effects of a multicultural literature-based reading approach: Year two.* Paper presented at the annual meeting of the National Reading Conference, Palm Springs, CA.

Florez, V., & Hadaway, N. (1986). Bridging linguistic and cultural differences through reading: Multiethnic literature in the classroom (Report No. CS 00692). Paper presented at the annual meeting of the Southwest Regional Conference of the International Reading Association, San Antonio, TX. (ERIC Document Reproduction Service No. ED 278059)

Gerald, C. (1972). The black writer and his role. (pp. 370–375). In A. Gayle (Ed.), *The black aesthetic.* New York: Doubleday.

Giroux, H. (1992). Critical literacy and student experience: Donald Graves' approach to literacy. In P. Shannon (Ed.), *Becoming political: Readings and writings in the politics of literacy education.* (pp. 15–20). Portsmouth, NH: Heinemann Educational Books.

Goodlad, J., & Oakes, J. (1988). We must offer equal access to knowledge. *Education Leadership, 45,* 16–22.

Goodman, K. (1992). I didn't found whole language. *Reading Teacher, 46,* 188–199.

Goodman, K. S., Bird, L. B., & Goodman, Y. M. (1991). What is whole language? In K. Goodman, L. Bird, & Y. Goodman (Eds.), (pp. 4–5). *The whole language catalog.* Santa Rosa, CA: McGraw-Hill.

Goodman, K. S., & Goodman, Y. M. (1991). As we see it: The dialects of English. In K. Goodman, L. Bird, & Y. Goodman (Eds.), *The whole language catalog.* (p. 83). Santa Rosa, CA: McGraw-Hill.

Highwater, Jamake, (1985). *The ceremony of innocence.* New York: Harper and Row.

Hodgkinson, H. L. (1985). *All one system: Demographics of education—kindergarten through graduate school.* Washington, D.C.: Institute for Educational Leadership. (Report No. ISBN-0-937846-93-7) (Eric Document No. ED 261–101).

Holdaway, D. (1982). Shared book experience: Teaching reading using favorite books. *Theory into Practice, 21,* 293–300.

Holmes Group. (1990). *Tomorrow's schools: Principles for the design of professional development schools.* East Lansing, MI: The Holmes Group.

Johnson, D., & Johnson, R. (1986). Learning together and alone: Cooperation, competition and individualization. Englewood Cliffs, NJ: Prentice-Hall.

Johnson, D., Johnson, R., & Holubec, E. J. (1986). *Circles of learning.* Edina, MN: Interaction Books.

Jordan, C. (1985). Translating culture: From ethnographic information to educational program. *Anthropology & Education Quarterly, 16,* 105–123.

Jordan C., & Tharp, R. G. (1979). Culture and education. In A. J. Marsella, R. G. Tharp, & T. Ciborowski (Eds.), *Perspectives in cross-cultural psychology.* (pp. 265–285). New York: Academic Press.

Kagan, S. (1988). *Cooperative learning: Resources for teachers.* Riverside, CA: University of California Press.

Lipson, M. (1983). The influences of religious affiliation on children's memory for text information. *Reading Research Quarterly, 18,* 448–57.

Manjarrez, C. A. (1991). Mama, they don't serve frijoles! In D. Schoem (Ed.), *Inside separate worlds: Life stories of blacks, Hispanics, and Jews.* Ann Arbor: University of Michigan Press. p. 53.

Mason, J. M., & Au, K. H. (1990). *Reading instruction for today.* Glenview, IL: Scott Foresman.

Norton, D. (1992). *Through the eyes of a child: An introduction to children's literature.* Columbus, OH: Charles Merrill.

Pang, V., Colvin, C., MyLuong, T., & Barba, R. (1992). Beyond chopsticks and dragons: Selecting Asian-American literature for children. *The Reading Teacher, 46,* 216–223.

Pinnell, G. S. (1986). *Reading recovery in Ohio 1985-86: Final report.* (Technical Report). Columbus: Ohio State University.

Ramirez, B. (1988). Culturally and linguistically diverse children. *Teaching Exceptional Children, 20,* 45-46.

Reyhner, J., & Garcia, R. (1989). Helping minorities read better: Problems and promises. *Reading Research and Instruction, 28,* 84-91.

Rogoff, B., & Lave, J. (Eds.). (1984). *Everyday cognition: Its development in social contexts.* Cambridge, MA: Harvard University Press.

Sapon-Shevin, M., & Schniedewind, N. (1991). Cooperative learning as empowering pedagogy. In C. E. Sleeter (Ed.), *Empowerment through multicultural education.* (pp. 159-178). Albany: State University of New York Press.

Schieffelin, B., & Ochs, E. (1986). Language socialization. *Annual Review of Anthropology, 15,* 163-191.

Slavin, R. (1987). Cooperative learning and the cooperative school. *Educational Leadership, 45,* 7-13.

Steffensen, M. S., Joag-Dev, C., & Anderson, R. C. (1979). A cross-cultural perspective on reading comprehension. *Reading Research Quarterly, 15,* 10-29.

Stevens, R. J. (1986). Cooperative integrated reading and composition: Two field experiments. *Reading Research Quarterly, 22,* 433-454.

Tiedt, P., & Tiedt, I. (1990). *Multicultural teaching: A handbook of activities, information, and resources.* Boston: Allyn and Bacon.

Tierney, R., & Pearson, P. (1983). Toward a composing model of reading. *Language Arts, 60,* 568-580.

Vogt, L., Jordan, C., & Tharp, R. (1987). Explaining school failure, producing school success: Two cases. *Anthropology & Education Quarterly, 18,* 276-286.

Wertsch, J. V. (1985). *Introduction to culture, communication, and cognition: Vygotskian perspectives.* New York: Cambridge University Press.

White, J. L., & Parham, T. A. (1990). *The psychology of blacks: An African-American perspective.* Englewood Cliffs, NJ: Prentice-Hall.

Williams, R. (1987). The whole elephant. *The Whole Idea, 1,* 1-3.

chapter **2**

Sociocultural Issues in Multicultural Literacy

OVERVIEW

We begin this chapter by describing family, community, and language socialization patterns of children from diverse backgrounds and detailing how these patterns can influence literacy within the school. We then view two contrasting classrooms through windows that reveal the role of cultural experiences in literacy. Finally, we focus on the school, illustrating how it can provide a learning environment that embraces and affirms the needs of *all* students through an emphasis on multicultural literacy.

EARLY SOCIALIZATION EXPERIENCES IN LITERACY

Literacy begins at an early age, as children interact with family to meet personal needs, gain self-identity, and establish behavior patterns that reflect cultural values and beliefs (Heath, 1989; Schieffelin & Ochs, 1986; Wertsch, 1991). In a country of diverse cultures, we can expect to find variations in the way children become literate, view the world, and come to understand the world. All children construct their knowledge through cultural lenses that reflect their cultural and economic backgrounds. Children from the mainstream European American culture and the middle class often experience early-language development that is replete with opportunities to interact with print in ways that approximate conventional reading and writing. Parents communicate with their children as they read stories aloud and participate in storytelling activities when the children are very young. As parents tell or read stories to their 2- or 3-year-old children, they discuss language and story concepts and relate these concepts to their children's personal experiences. They further develop story understanding while spontaneously asking questions and discussing characters, event sequences, and problem solutions (Snow & Ninio, 1986; Wells, 1986). Through these "literacy events," the child actually experiences the motives, goals, and conditions associated with literacy and its aspects of reading, writing, speaking, and listening (Teale, 1987).

Although these socialization patterns might illustrate how many European American and middle-class children become literate, different patterns evolve among many cultural groups. In their research, Scollon and Scollon (1981) document their 2-year-old daughter's early socialization to literacy and contrast it to the socialization of Athabaskan children at Fort Chipewa, Alaska. They describe Rachel's questions about how reading occurs as her mother reads to her and Rachel's interactions with her younger brother, who is unable to read because "his hands are too small to hold the book." The authors illustrate that Rachel knew several things about literacy by age 2. She knew that literacy amounted to reading at least, that it was expected of humans, and that it was as natural as growing hands that are big enough to hold a book. Scollon and Scollon (1981) state:

> Rachel's typification of literacy by two years of age was essentially the same as ours. She had her own books, letter blocks, knew the "ABC" song, and fully expected to go to school when she was older. Literacy for her included the symmetrical balance between reading and writing. Readers were writers, and writers were readers in her view. Literacy was something both assumed as a value and asserted as a right. For Rachel literacy was a central attribute and activity of human life.   (pp. 62–63)

On the other hand, literacy for the Athabaskan children at Fort Chipewa is characterized by a dialogue between a 7-year-old Athabaskan boy and his Anglo visitors. The 7-year-old inquired, "You guys sing from this?" referring to a copy of Goffman's *Asylums,* a song book used in the church. When the visitors responded that they did not sing from the song book, the Athabaskan child incredulously asked the visitors if they read the book. The young boy's astonishment reflects his culture's view of literacy, which is linked to religious contexts. Fort Chipewyan books are typically song books or prayer books used in church. People are readers or singers, not writers.

Further, there is an intense belief in the Athabaskan culture that only older people can or should read. A young child's interest in reading would not be characteristic in their culture. For example, when an Athabaskan girl, mimicking Rachel, picked up a book at Rachel's house and began reading to Rachel and her younger sister, the Athabaskan mother told her daughter, "You can't read anyway. It's too high words for you" (Scollon & Scollon, 1981, p. 63).

These two examples of literacy socialization patterns are distinctly different. Rachel's socialization to literacy is modeled in the home and prepares her to perform well in the traditional schooling of the European American and Western culture. On the other hand, Athabaskan children's socialization to literacy prepares them to perform well in the typical Athabaskan school; literacy in the Athabaskan culture is socially located in the church, secondarily in the school, but not in the home. Given the contrasting Athabaskan and traditional European American orientations to literacy, we might expect Athabaskan children to experience difficulties in literacy development if they were to attend a traditional European American school. By the same token, we might expect Rachel to face problems were she to attend school in the community of Fort Chipewa where literacy is socially grounded in the church.

THE PRIMACY OF CULTURAL EXPERIENCE IN LITERACY

These two orientations to literacy illustrate different socialization patterns that affect literacy even before children come to school. These patterns are the reflections of the deeply rooted cultural experiences and traditions of the child, his or her parents and siblings, and the community. If literacy is to emerge, instruction must first embrace and affirm the cultural experience and traditions of children (Franklin, 1986; Harste and Burke, 1978; Heath, 1983). Teachers must, therefore, become more knowledgeable about the cultural and language learning patterns of the children they teach. In the following sections, we examine more closely the cultural influences in four cultures that can affect literacy.

The African American Oral Tradition

In the culture of African Americans, we find a clear example of language learning that is deeply rooted in cultural and historical traditions and experiences. This group has a long-standing, rich oral tradition of communication, typified by rhymes, stories, music, sermons, verbal play, and call-response patterns (Smitherman, 1977; Folb, 1980). Many of these patterns of communication can be traced to the storytelling of the griot, the oral historian in African society who was responsible for memorizing and teaching the history and culture of the people and passing this knowledge down through generations (Fox, 1992).

This oral tradition was continued when African slaves, brought to the United States, created and shared folk tales as an imaginative way for oppressed people to express their fears and hopes to one another. These folk tales combined memories and habits from the old world of Africa with the new world of plantation life (Hamilton, 1985). These folk tales and later poetry recitations, songs, and chants became a reflection of historical and traditional patterns rooted in the rural life of the southeastern part of the United States, both during and after slavery.

The church and family (both nuclear and extended) played a large role in the language learning of African American children. The reading of biblical texts and Sunday School materials was an important aspect of written literacy. Occasions for reading were embedded in these meaningful contexts. Recitations, performances, and plays for major holidays in school, which were an important way of celebrating life, reflected many days of practice, with coaching from approving adults (Heath, 1989).

Even as families moved to urban areas in the North and many traditional behaviors and customs were lost, many African American children retained the ability to use words creatively. They could change forms of interaction, synthesize information from a variety of sources, and impart knowledge in a rhythmical, lyrical form with an underlying and sometimes profound message. Baugh (1983) asserts that "these uses of language—spoken and written—are wide ranging, and many represent skills that would benefit all youngsters' keen listening and observational skills, quick recognition of nuanced roles, rapid-fire dialogue, hard-driving argumentation, succinct recapitulation of an event, striking metaphors, and comparative analyses based on unexpected analogies" (p. 32). The rap music of the late 1980s and early 1990s is an example. In performing rap, writing and reading come as by-products of this verbal knowledge and power; words are written and recorded within a purposeful context to be shared and preserved for the future.

We see that an important aspect of the African American culture is the primacy of oral language in the life of the child as a way of understanding and reacting to his or her environment, which includes the family, the church, the peer group, and the extended community. This pattern of language development and learning is based primarily on an oral tradition, in which interaction, group response, and approval are an integral part of life's experiences and knowledge attainment. Reading and writing are *contextualized* and become meaningful in response to oral and real-life experiences and situations.

The Hawaiian Child Groups and Talk Story

The Hawaiian community provides another example of the influence of cultural experiences and traditions on the language-learning patterns of children. According to Jordan (1984), native Hawaiian children (descendants wholly or partly of the original Polynesian inhabitants of Hawaii), especially those who live in rural and lower-income urban families, spend a large percentage of their time in child groups. From 18 months to 2 years, these Hawaiian children are the charges of an older sibling, and then become full-fledged members of the group by age 3 or 4. Until age 9, the group generally includes members of both sexes and sometimes relatives who live nearby. These sibling groups generally share responsibility for much of the daily work of the household. The entire group, rather than individual children, is rewarded when success is attained. Adult supervision is minimal; siblings are expected to be responsible for one another, especially the older children for the younger. D'Amato (1982) reports that children have considerable "felt independence, autonomy and competence, and these are central to their sense of identity" (p. 65).

Significantly, in the home, the child group becomes an important context for learning. Students initially acquire skills for child care and housework by participating with older siblings, who serve as supervisors and models. Children are able to acquire competence by observing or through direct assistance of siblings who intervene as errors occur during ongoing performance (Jordan, 1984). As a result of these conditions, Hawaiian children tend to perform well in situations that involve peer interaction with a minimum of one-to-one adult intervention.

As one might expect, we find a language style that reflects the cultural interactions of the peer group in the low-income homes of Polynesian-Hawaiian children. An example of this language style is the group interactional dialogue called "talk story, a rambling personal experience narrative mixed with folk materials" (Watson, 1975, p. 54). In this speech event centered around the group, children cooperate in telling stories. For example, the first child begins a story, then the second child joins in by adding another event or detail to the story, and the children complete the story by taking turns, speaking back and forth to one another.

In their extensive research, Watson-Gegeo and Boggs (1977) found that Hawaiian children value performance in collaboration with others over individual performance. They use these strategies of teaching and learning from their peers, which they developed at home, in their acquisition of literacy at school. They are also skilled in utilizing a variety of people as sources of information and help (Jordan, 1984). These cultural experiences reflect a communication style that differs from the dyadic, book-centered interactions between parents and young children in the mainstream culture and middle-class homes (Kawakami & Au, 1986). Knowledge of these cultural influences on language and learning is an important consideration for school contexts and literacy.

The Hispanic American Family as a Cultural Concept

Family roles are central to cultural descriptions of Hispanic people. Among Mexican, Puerto Rican, Cuban, and Venezuelan Americans, for example, family gatherings, which are often centered in traditional events and religious holidays, symbolize and highlight the importance of the people's cultural heritage (Cintron de Esteves & Spicola, 1982; Ramirez, 1967; Ramirez & Price-Williams, 1976). The family, therefore, becomes the "keeper" of the culture. By examining values and attitudes toward the family, one gains deeper insight into the rich Hispanic culture and heritage.

The centrality of family is evident in studies showing that achievement is often "sought within a context and for the purpose of family and peer group solidarity and identification, rather than for individual and independent attainment" (Tharp, 1989, p. 354). Within the family there is a sense of acceptance and belonging—a sense of being there for one another. Valdez (1991), for example, talks about her family in the midst of an "angered" barrio. She recounts:

> Both my parents worked hard for the things we needed and even for those extra things we did not need. I always felt that my family came through when I needed them. My father always said, "A job is important because of the benefits and longtime security." This was instilled in my mind. He also said that an education is important. My brothers and sisters and I would get tired of listening to his lectures, but we nodded our heads to say yes to make sure he knew we were listening. My oldest sister was always making sure we paid attention.   (p. 27)

This closeness and caring extends beyond the nuclear family to grandparents, cousins, aunts, and uncles. There is a web of kinship that brings responsibility and obligations for mutual assistance and reciprocal favors. Relationships to these extended-family members are characterized by variations of roles in the immediate family of mother, father, brother, sister, son, and daughter (Brussell, 1971). According to Abi-Nader (1993), the individual family member's response to this unconditional acceptance by the family is "loyalty, service, success, and leadership in preserving and extending the life of the family" (p. 217).

The Hispanic child's sense of family can provide cultural capital for the child as he or she enters school. However, Mora (1995) reminds us that "the teacher who has not educated himself about attitudes toward family in Latino communities may lead his students to draw false conclusions about family closeness as antithetical to the fostering of personal independence" (p. 1). As we continue to learn and integrate appropriate information about the students' background into the instructional environment, we can foster a successful learning experience for Hispanic students.

Native American Interactional Styles

The interactional patterns in the Native American community, specifically the culture and languages of the Three Fires, three Native American nations in Michigan—Odawa, Ojibwa, and the Potowatomi—offer another example of how literacy and culture are bound together. Native American adult-child interactions are direct and honest. Adults speak with children as though they were adults, including them in family conversations, where their opinions are valued. Children and adults will also spend hours together without saying a word. When a child is being taught, however, adults demand and expect that the child watch the adult do a task and demonstrate intense concentration and respect as the adult models the task (Watson, 1975).

Oratory skills are highly prized in the Native American culture, as they are in the African American culture. Jamake Highwater compares the teller of Native American folk tales to a weaver whose designs present his or her personal saga, as well as the history of the weaver's people (cited in Norton, 1992). Native American storytelling styles, developed over centuries of oral tradition, vary somewhat among tribes, however. It is common for the storytelling style of Northwest Indians, for example, to be terse, staccato, and rapid. Stories are usually short, with very little description to enhance the story.

Songs, chants, and poems also play a critical role in the lives of Native Americans, who believe there is power in words. In fact, they created poetry because of this belief. Each family has at least one member who memorizes the family history and tribal stories, songs, chants, and poems. Frequently these storytellers, who are a very important facet of every Native American family and community, mingle their stories with stories from other tribes, which are then passed from one generation to the next. These traditional folk tales, poems, and songs have been a vehicle for transmitting the cultural norms, morals, and history of their culture to future generations. Many of these stories, which carry dominant Native American themes—living in harmony with nature, showing respect for the wisdom of the elderly, and emphasizing group needs rather than individual needs (Norton, 1992)—continue to be shared today through storytelling and literature.

While listening to the storyteller, Native American children are expected to be attentive and not to interrupt the storyteller, as a sign of appreciation. Being listeners first and paying attention to the speaker are characteristics that are often seen in Native American students today. The role and style of the speaker and the response of the listener become important information in understanding Native American students and their reaction to literacy (Hanson and Eisenbise, 1983; Dorris, 1979).

Threads of Similarity and Shades of Difference

In these examples, we see threads of similarity across cultural groups, but we also see shades of difference. In three of the cases, oral language is valued, but varies in its use. We also see that language learning is contextualized, and language is to be shared with others. These examples show that many children from diverse cultural backgrounds experience a language and cultural environment at home and in their community that differs from traditional learning. If these children are to succeed in school, their cultural and linguistic traditions must be understood and respected. Rather than recognizing and affirming the cultural and linguistic strengths of students from diverse backgrounds, however, schools have often considered these students to be culturally or linguistically deprived, economically disadvantaged, or educationally at risk (Ramiriz, 1988; Applebee, 1981; Goodlad, 1984). Focusing on deficit models of learning jeopardizes the fulfillment of our ultimate goals and objectives for literacy. Focusing on each student's knowledge about language, learning, and culture, in contrast, maximizes literacy by linking it to the students' cultural experiences. The materials and strategies employed for instruction and the methods of organizing learning events, moreover, should reflect the students' cultural experiences and historical traditions.

SOCIOCULTURAL CONSIDERATIONS FOR THE CLASSROOM

The school, as a community of learners, should be a place that accommodates varying orientations to literacy, because "literacy instruction is a cultural event" (Franklin, 1986, p. 51). Teachers, as primary facilitators of literacy, can guide students' construction of meaning, which is derived from their home, community, and school.

But how do we guide literacy for *all* students? A beginning point is to look at two classrooms—a traditional classroom and a student-centered classroom—to examine and attempt to understand how school socialization patterns can affect literacy for students of all cultures.

Learning in the Traditional Classroom

Looking into the window of the traditional classroom—one that maintains independent, isolated learning and a teacher-centered focus—we discover students seated in neatly arranged rows. The students come from diverse backgrounds, including a large number of European American students and a small number of African American, Chinese American, and Latino students. All the students are quietly and independently completing workbook pages and work sheets related to skills and stories in their basal readers. Several students, who appear to have completed one set of assignments, are copying a poem from the board. They are reminded to finish their work and to write neatly. When they have finished, they are encouraged to read a library book.

The teacher's attention is focused on a reading group of 10 students who are taking turns reading a story orally. After the story is read, the teacher asks questions about the story from her teacher's manual, encouraging students to raise their hands to answer. The students respond with short answers, and the teacher praises those students who answer correctly. Most surprising is the silence that prevails with 24 second-graders in a classroom!

After reading groups, the students prepare for language arts by removing soft-covered grammar books from their desks. The teacher briefly reviews with the students the importance of punctuation marks in sentences. Students then take turns reading aloud the sentences from their text, stating the type of punctuation mark to be used after each sentence. The teacher then reads the directions for their two-page assignment and asks the students if they have questions. As the teacher sees no hands raised, she tells the students they may begin, reminding them to work quietly.

Looking around the room, one spots a number of textbooks on shelves: reading, math, language arts, social studies, and science. Library books also neatly line one shelf. On the right, a colorful bulletin board displays students' work with the caption, "See Our Best Work!" One sees written reports about the first Thanksgiving, all of which are marked A or A+, displayed on the board. The penmanship is notably well formed; the reports tell about the Pilgrims and their struggles to survive and the feelings of shared joy among Native Americans and Pilgrims on the first Thanksgiving.

Another bulletin board, located by the teacher's desk, is arrayed with large and colorful punctuation signs, with their use and function described in sentences. Over to the left, there is also a table with a variety of books arranged neatly. Only one book, *The Five Chinese Brothers,* appears to have a theme or content related to a cultural group other than the mainstream European American culture. Finally, toward the back of the room is a display of science materials—a magnifying glass, rocks, sand, and layers of different types of soil—on a small table.

As we move away from the window, we reflect on this traditional classroom's lack of spontaneity and student involvement. Although the teacher is pleasant and warm, the social, cultural, and physical organization negate opportunities for students to explore interests or generate meaning in ways that are consistent with their personal and cultural experiences. Within this social context, students come to understand that language is written in books that are read orally or silently and that literacy is a passive, rather than active, experience related to language use. Students' beliefs are not affirmed because the verbal exchanges that do occur are brief, simple, and infrequent. The purpose of learning is determined by the teacher, who delivers knowledge to the students. McLaren (1988) asserts that this traditional, mainstream approach to learning too often concentrates on the sheer mechanics of reading and writing and fails to consider the learners' sociocultural context—their own social reality—from which meaning can actively be constructed.

Although this concept of literacy is changing, it still exists to varying degrees in classroom settings in urban, suburban, and rural settings throughout the country. Literacy developed in this traditional context compromises learning for all students and is often devastating to students from diverse cultural, linguistic, and economic backgrounds. As students are socialized into this setting, they "learn" how to behave in order to "succeed" in school. Some do very well, particularly middle-class students and students of European American backgrounds. Other students of varied backgrounds achieve marginal success. Unfortunately, many fail miserably (Cummins, 1986; Sleeter & Grant, 1991).

Students who succeed become appropriately socialized, accepting that learning to read and write is an individual matter and that meaning is gained through neatly completed work sheets and short, precise, correct responses to questions. Students who fail are frequently from diverse cultural backgrounds or from low-income homes and communities. Problems emerge for many of these students, such as the African

Americans and Hawaiian Americans described earlier who learned and used language at home by interacting with peers, sharing ideas, posing questions, and manipulating words and language in creative ways. They perceive the classroom as a place where language that is used in ways familiar to them is devalued. Similarly, problems emerge for many Native American students, whose interactional patterns at home include affirmation of children's ideas and opinions. How can these students succeed in an environment where they are unable to express opinions and interact in cooperative ways with their peers and adults?

Learning in a Culturally Sensitive Classroom

A view into the window of a culturally sensitive classroom reveals alternative ways that learning and socialization patterns might be developed. The fourth-grade class is a cross section of racial and ethnic groups, including a large number of African American and European American students, two Chinese American students, three Korean American students, and one Native American student. Students are seated in small, heterogeneous groups, spaced across the room.

The "reading class" for this day begins with the teacher reading *The Black Snowman,* by Phil Mendez. The story is about a poor, unhappy boy from the city who has a low self-image and feels he is powerless to change his life until he is taken off into a dream world about his African heritage. In his dream world, he learns about the power of the kente—a beautiful, brightly colored African cloth—and the magic it brought to the Ashanti people. As he awakens, he is moved by the dream, which marks the beginning of his personal restoration. The story concludes with the boy, Jacob, after an act of heroism, believing in himself.

The themes in the story—about low self-image, poverty, and parental love—become springboards for lively discussion guided by the teacher. As Mrs. Long reads the story with her students interactively, she encourages students to share times when they could not have a fancy jacket or a bike that they wanted, times when they felt unhappy with the way they looked or acted. As she asks questions and discusses the story's meaning, the African American students in the class contribute frequently to the discussion. They explain language expressions that are familiar to them and share additional information about their African heritage and traditions. Language takes on meaning as it is related to the background experiences of the students within the social context of the classroom.

Following this discussion, the members of the class are encouraged to reread the book with a partner during their morning language arts time, which follows reading. Mrs. Long establishes a purpose for reading by asking the students to reread the story, identifying possible themes. After rereading the story, the students regroup to share their themes, which Mrs. Long records on large chart paper. Within minutes, the chart paper is filled; all ideas are accepted. Her main focus—to have her students construct meaning for the story through their own personal experiences—is accomplished.

At the end of the morning, she announces that tomorrow they will write in their response journals about their favorite part of the story, telling why it was their favorite. After recording their ideas in their journal, students will then share their entries with a partner, a small group, or the whole class.

In subsequent classes, her students made a class kente cloth. Mrs. Long gave her students a rectangular piece of cloth, which they designed and decorated to symbolize an incident, an event, a person, or a possession that was special or held a significant place in their lives. After the rectangular pieces were stitched together, students wrote about their piece of the cloth, explaining its significance. These writings were then shared with their peers and displayed on the bulletin board below the very long, but attractive class kente. Everyone's cloth and writing were featured.

Glancing about the classroom, we further see that desks are arranged in clusters of four. A colorfully decorated bulletin board includes samples of students' writing underneath the caption, "Columbus's Exploration." The compositions, which are marked with statements from the teacher—"Good comments," "Good thoughts," "Interesting point of view,"—express a range of ideas about Columbus's journey to America and what his exploration meant to the Spaniards and Native Americans. Another bulletin board, near the teacher's desk, features Barry, who is "Student of the Week." Photographs, drawings, and a "BioPoem" about Barry are clustered around his name. Just below the bulletin board, a small rectangular table displays books, hats, trophies, posters, and other trinkets that are special to Barry.

In the Library Corner, an array of books highlighting stories and information from several cultures are displayed. Biographical sketches about Columbus are clustered at one end of a long table near the back of the room. Books about Columbus and the Tainos—the people who inhabited the land when Columbus arrived—are scattered at the other end of the table. In another corner of the room, seeds, plants, a magnifying glass, a terrarium, and related informational books are arranged on the science table. Paper, pencils, and cards for students to measure, graph, and describe the growth patterns of the plants are also available.

As we come away from the window on this class, we see that the social organization of the class offers many opportunities for group discussion and interaction. Literacy includes many forms: students listening to stories, discussing story meanings and their relationship to their own personal lives, reading silently and orally, setting purposes for their own reading and writing, responding to literature through reading and writing activities, and integrating math, art, and science with their reading and writing in meaningful ways. The cultural knowledge that African American students bring to the classroom is affirmed through class discussion and a variety of activities. Further, all students are given opportunities to interact, to share knowledge, and to extend their appreciation and understanding of other cultures and experiences. Learning is contextualized not only by using culturally diverse materials, but also by engaging students in social reading, by sharing experiences, and by providing many opportunities for students to construct their own knowledge.

Alternative methods of instruction can have a significant effect on all students' learning and, specifically, on students from diverse linguistic and cultural backgrounds. There is evidence that when cultural literacy and social organization patterns are reflected in classroom practices, student participation and enthusiasm increases and school achievement improves (Au, 1980; Au & Jordan, 1981). The Holmes Group (1990) clearly supports the need for schools and teachers to rethink the way they go about their craft. They state:

> Schools need to do a much better job of building on students' own cultural capital. Teachers will have to become closer students of their own students. A pluralistic democracy whose schools are full of immigrant children and

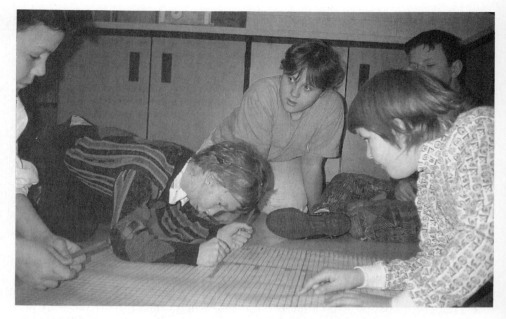

FIGURE 2.1   Learning is contextualized as students graph information about their likes and dislikes.

children from many peoples and races requires teachers prepared to become more thoughtful about "culture" in another sense: cherishing and building on the webs of meaning and value and community that students bring to school.   (p. 11)

Indeed, to provide a learning environment for all children, the learning contexts and social interaction requirements of the classroom should mirror, at least in some ways, the contexts and cultural backgrounds of the children.

A SOCIOCULTURAL PERSPECTIVE ON LITERACY

In the preceding sections we attempted to provide an understanding of the social organization of the classroom and how its content and curricular materials become important determinants of success for all students. Classrooms are most appropriate when they are sensitive to and driven by sociocultural factors. To further show how schools can maximize learning for all students, we have identified three essential components of a socioculturally sensitive school environment, which builds on the knowledge of children of diverse cultural backgrounds and how they learn most effectively. These components are (1) recontextualized learning, (2) alternative social structures, and (3) the teacher as cultural mediator.

Recontextualized Learning

In schools where traditional classrooms are prevalent, learning has become decontextualized. That is, learning is not grounded in real-life situations or purposeful, meaningful activities that are part of the child's home and cultural experiences. Rather, learning is abstract and deals with experiences and knowledge that are sometimes far removed from the student's own background.

Contrast the traditional classroom with the culturally sensitive classroom, which fosters multicultural literacy. This classroom recontextualizes learning in order to empower students to read and write as they incorporate their own cultural experiences and background with the text. Tharp (1989) outlines three levels of contextualization that are useful to our discussion. These three levels are highlighted in the following sections.

Technical Level.   At this level, students engage in the reading material by using their conceptual understandings, knowledge, experiences, attitudes, values, and skills. Ogle's (1986) KWL strategy exemplifies such an approach. Students first brainstorm everything they know about a topic and then formulate questions about what they *want* to know before they begin reading. This strategy encourages students to bring forth any knowledge or information they have, stimulating them to think about and share their personal knowledge, experiences, and attitudes related to the topic. Learning is contextualized as students interact with others, sharing information and listening. Through these interactive experiences, students personalize new knowledge to correspond with their prior understandings and experiences.

Curriculum Level.   Materials and experiences that are meaningful and culturally relevant are used at the curriculum level. In a school setting of diverse cultures, instructional materials reflect a variety of cultures in order to provide (1) the foundation for literacy development and (2) a vehicle for acquiring reading and writing skills. The use of real books, rather than traditional basal readers, and specifically multicultural literature, is most suitable for accomplishing this level of contextualization. Multicultural literature promotes an understanding of self in a cultural context and provides connections between the self and other cultures through emotions, needs, and desires (Bishop, 1987). The interest and motivation generated fosters the development of literacy skills and enhances academic achievement.

Multicultural literature is also a powerful mechanism for integrating learning across the curriculum. Halliday (1980) reminds us that students use language to learn in all areas of the curriculum. Multicultural literature, therefore, serves as a launching point for language and a vehicle for creating linkages to other content areas, such as social studies, science, art, or music. Multicultural literature and its use in a multicultural literacy program will be discussed further in Chapter 3.

Policy Level.   A third level of contextualization is the policy level. The entire community comes together to produce community-controlled schools that reflect the culture of the students they serve. A major tenet of this third aspect of contextualization is that learning is a social process that affects and is affected by the entire community (Tharp, 1988). School programs in Alaska, for example, strive to create a context for learning that fosters a strong sense of Inuit identity by merging cultural and academic skills (Gardner, 1986; Harrison, 1986). Similarly, there has been a movement in some African American communities to modify the curriculum and classroom contexts so that they are more closely aligned to an African-centered perspective. Those who support this approach believe that such a perspective—that is, finding patterns in African American history and culture that create a foundation from which learning can evolve—will produce a strong sense of self-identity and esteem in African American students. Others emphasize that this approach enhances cultural understanding while developing academic skills (Asante, 1991; Kunjufu, 1984).

Alternative Social Structures for Learning

Earlier, we focused on the traditional classroom, which is arranged in neat rows, limiting social interactions. This classroom contrasts sharply with the culturally sensitive classroom, which includes a variety of grouping configurations—students working within whole-class arrangements, in heterogeneous cooperative learning groups, in ability groups, and in pairs, or individually. Many opportunities for social interactions evolve within this second classroom. Indeed, social group structures within the classroom can influence motivation, attitudes toward learning, and academic achievement.

Creating Social Group Structures.   The Kamehamaha Early Education Program (KEEP) (Jordan, 1984; Tharp, 1982), developed to improve the educational achievement of Native Hawaiian children, is one example of how social group structure can be responsive to students' cultural needs and how students learn. In the study, researchers investigated ways to make classroom organization and instructional methods compatible with the social organization of Native Hawaiian children's homes. Using information from the study, which revealed that Native Hawaiian students worked cooperatively with their siblings and were often taken care of by older children, educators then modified the learning environment and social interaction configurations of the Native Hawaiian classroom. They developed learning contexts that were compatible with the cultural and social contexts of the community (Jordan, 1984). Thus, independent learning centers, peer interaction opportunities, and peer tutoring became an integral part of the learning environment. Other aspects of the classroom setting that were changed to be more compatible with the students' culture were comprehension-oriented reading instruction linked to the students' culture and language development activities that included multiple opportunities to use language and increase general cognitive/linguistic skills (Jordan, 1984).

Creating Structured Cooperative Learning Groups.   Similarly, structured cooperative learning groups can be used to help achieve social equity and justice, as well as improve student motivation and academic achievement (Sapon-Shevin & Schniedewind, 1991). Cooperative learning is an instructional approach in which the classroom is structured in small heterogeneous groups where individuals work together to accomplish a shared learning goal. Positive interdependence and individual accountability are emphasized as the groups strive to accomplish their goals (Johnson, Johnson, & Holubec, 1986; Kagan, 1988; Slavin, 1983).

The following principles, inherent in cooperative learning, are also appropriate for a multicultural perspective: (1) Cultural diversity and heterogeneity are valued and affirmed in cooperative learning groups, (2) students in such groups take responsibility for themselves and others, (3) such groups are democratic, and (4) students learn about people from different cultural backgrounds as they work together (Tiedt & Tiedt, 1990; Slavin, 1983). Chapter 11 describes methods of implementing cooperative learning strategies and other alternative grouping configurations in more detail.

Using a Variety of Social Organizations for Learning.   The implications of the KEEP project are far-reaching and significant, for although its focus was on a monocultural setting, its premise—that the social context for learning should be related to the social relationships and contexts of the culture of the home—holds true for all settings, monocultural or multicultural. In a multicultural setting, however, one would provide a variety of social organizations for learning, including students working independently on a project and students working in pairs, small groups, or whole-group configurations.

The Teacher as Cultural Mediator

The social organization of the classroom involves more than alternative social groupings and interactional patterns. Social well-being in a classroom is created by teachers who facilitate expression of ideas and knowledge in a variety of ways. In a real sense, the teacher's role is changing from that of the keeper of all knowledge and the deliverer of knowledge to children, to a person who facilitates students' acquisition of knowledge, enabling them to take ownership of their learning (Goodman, 1986; Graves, 1986; Shannon, 1989). According to Diaz, Moll, & Mehan (1986), teachers are responsible for creating the culture of the classroom and inviting students to co-participate in this effort. Teachers' roles, therefore, become more challenging as they become (1) cultural organizers who facilitate strategic ways of accomplishing tasks so that the learning process involves varied ways of knowing, experiencing, thinking, and behaving; (2) cultural mediators who create opportunities for critical dialogue and expression among all students as they pursue knowledge and understanding; and (3) orchestrators of social contexts who provide several learning configurations that include interpersonal *and* intrapersonal opportunities for seeking, accessing, and evaluating knowledge.

As **cultural organizers,** teachers must first recognize and understand the culture in the classroom, including the experiences and everyday ways of behaving that students bring to the classroom. For this culture to emerge so that learning can thrive, teachers must create an atmosphere that acknowledges all students' diversity, while fostering shared norms of behavior and expectations. Teachers must structure and mold opportunities for personal and cultural expression in order that the voices of all students may be heard and considered. Further, the teacher builds in support for diverse language experiences, realizing that students may not always succeed and can make mistakes without fear of embarrassment. Through the teacher's careful guidance, students acquire social responsibility, as they learn to discuss the consequences of their personal actions for their own well-being and the well-being of others.

FIGURE 2.2 The teacher, acting as the cultural mediator, facilitates students' examination of their cultural identity through group interactions.

Teachers as **cultural mediators** explore and clarify their own ethnic and cultural identity and that of their students. As teachers do this, they perceive ways to guide cultural awareness and understanding of their students so that positive relationships can evolve. Through dialogues, teachers guide students' identity quest so that students may become effective and able learners who value society's heterogeneity. They further help students to analyze their values and assumptions critically, so that prejudices, stereotypes, and misconceptions may be minimized. As teachers unite different knowledge and backgrounds within a community of learners, diversity is celebrated and affirmed so that one culture does not dominate and sacrifice the ideas of another. Feelings of powerlessness and oppression dissipate; feelings of liberation and empowerment evolve.

Teachers who **orchestrate social contexts** recognize that learning is influenced by students' cultural backgrounds and that learning is enhanced in socioculturally compatible contexts. Students are encouraged to experiment and take risks as they build their own knowledge in varied learning environments that include opportunities for social interactions, collaborations, and cooperation. Students work together on tasks, discuss, adjust, and adapt decisions they make. These varied learning configurations include whole-class and small cooperative learning groups, ability groups, dyads, and individualized learning.

Thus, the teacher's role has a special significance in a democratic, multicultural classroom, where all must find their voice. For teachers to create a community of learners who celebrate and affirm diversity and work toward consensus and shared understanding, they must become reflective decision-makers, using past experiences to shape future actions in the recurrent cycle of planning, implementing, evaluating, and modifying learning.

SUMMARY

We have focused on the need to consider students' early experiences with literacy in the home and community and the various ways in which students' socialization toward literacy emerges. We began this chapter with a discussion of children's early socialization experiences as they acquire literacy and use their learning within the home and community before entering school. We asserted that acknowledging and affirming varied cultural traditions and patterns of social interactions are critical if students are to acquire, extend, and broaden literacy skills in the school. Furthermore, the organization and context of the classroom need to reflect these traditions and patterns of social interaction. When this does not occur, discontinuity develops between learning at home and at school. Learning becomes difficult, if not impossible, for many young students.

By contrasting the traditional classroom and the culturally sensitive classroom, we illustrated how the classroom context can reflect the dominant culture, with few opportunities for meaningful verbal interactions, purposeful reading and writing experiences, and shared learning encounters that are linked to all subjects in the curriculum. We illustrated how the classroom can mirror student diversity through development of a culturally sensitive environment. Student diversity is celebrated and affirmed through this multicultural literacy perspective.

We also detailed the three key elements of this multicultural perspective on literacy, beginning with the recontextualization of learning, and demonstrated how to ground learning in students' personal and meaningful cultural experiences. The second element, alternative social organization, fosters opportunities for students to work together in large, small, or whole-class groupings, as well as individually. The third element, the teacher as cultural mediator, emerges as the teacher guides the activities and experiences that help students learn in a culturally sensitive classroom.

REFERENCES

Abi-Nader, J. (1993). Meeting the needs of multicultural classrooms: Family values and the motivation of minority students. In M. O'Hair & S. Odell (Eds.), *Diversity and teaching: Teacher education yearbook I.* (pp. 212–228). Orlando, FL: Harcourt Brace Jovanovich College Publishers.

Applebee, A. (1981). *Writing in the secondary school: English and the content areas.* Urbana, IL: National Council of Teachers of English.

Asante, M. K. (1991). The Afrocentric idea in education. *Journal of Negro Education, 60,* 170–180.

Au, K. H. (1980). Participation structures in a reading lesson with Hawaiian children: Analysis of a culturally appropriate and instructional event. *Anthropology and Education Quarterly, 11,* 91–115.

Au, K. H., & Jordan, C. (1980). Teaching reading to Hawaiian children: Finding a culturally appropriate solution. In H. T. Trueba, G. P. Guthrie, & K. H. Au (Eds.), *Culture and the bilingual classroom: Studies in classroom ethnography* (pp. 139–152). Rowley, MA: Newbury House.

Baugh, J. (1983). *Black street speech: Its history, structure, and survival.* Austin: University of Texas Press.

Bishop, R. (1987). Extending multicultural understanding through children's books. In B. Cullinan (Ed.), *Children's literature in the reading program.* (pp. 60-70). Newark, DE: International Reading Association.

Brussell, C. (1971). Social characteristics and problems of the Spanish-speaking atomistic society. In J. C. Stone & D. P. DeNevi (Eds.), *Five heritages: Teaching multicultural populations.* (pp. 169-196). New York: Van Nostrand Reinhold.

Cintron de Esteves, C., & Spicola, R. (1982). *Four Hispanic groups: Oral and social traditions, education and play implications for educators* (Report No. RC013872). Chicago, IL: International Reading Association. (ERIC Document Reproduction Services No. ED 226 897)

Cummins, James J. (1986). Empowering minority students: A framework for intervention. *Harvard Educational Review, 56,* 28-45.

D'Amato, J. (1982). *Contests and confrontations among Hawaiian school children.* Paper presented at the meeting of the American Anthropological Association, Washington, D.C.

Diaz, S., Moll, L., & Mehan, H. (1986). Sociological resources in instruction: A context-specific approach. In *Beyond language: Social and cultural factors in schooling language minority students* (pp. 187-230). Los Angeles: Evaluation, Dissemination and Assessment Center.

Dorris, M. (1979). Native American literature in an ethnohistorical context. *College English, 41,* 147-162.

Folb, E. A. (1980). *Runnin' down some lines: The language and culture of black teenagers.* Cambridge, MA: Harvard University Press.

Fox, R. (1992). The Oral Tradition: The African literary tradition. In *African American Traditions: Voices in a Tradition.* (pp. 83-89). Chicago: Holt Rinehart and Winston.

Franklin, E. (1986). Literary instruction for LES children. *Language Arts, 63,* 51-54.

Gardner, E. B. (1986). Unique features of a band-controlled school: The Seabird Island Community school. *Canadian Journal of Native Education, 13,* 15-32.

Goodlad, J. (1984). *A place called school: Prospects for the future.* New York: McGraw-Hill.

Goodman, K. (1986). *What's whole in whole language.* Portsmouth, NH: Heinemann.

Graves, D. (1986). *Writing: Students and teachers at work.* Portsmouth, NH: Heinemann.

Halliday, M. A. K. (1980). Three aspects of children's language development: Learning language, learning through language, learning about language. In Y. M. Goodman, M. M. Hausler, & D. S. Strickland (Eds.), *Oral and written language development research: Impact on the schools* (pp. 7-19). *Proceedings from the 1979 and 1980 IMPACT conferences sponsored by the International Reading Association and the National Council of Teachers of English.*

Hamilton, V. (1985). *The people could fly.* New York: Albert A. Knopf.

Hanson, W., & Eisenbise, M. (1983). *Human behavior and American Indians.* Rockville, MD: National Institute of Mental Health. (ERIC Document Reproduction No. ED 231 589)

Harrison, B. (1986). Manokotak: A study of school adaptation. *Anthropology & Education Quarterly, 17,* 100-110.

Harste, J., & Burke, C. (1978). Toward a socio-psycholinguistic model of reading comprehension. *Viewpoints in Teaching and Learning, 54,* 9-34.

Heath, S. B. (1983). *Ways with Words.* Cambridge, England: Cambridge University Press.

Heath, S. B. (1989). Oral and literate traditions among black Americans living in poverty. *American Psychologist, 14,* 367-373.

Holmes Group. (1990). *Tomorrow's Schools: Principles for the Design of Professional Development Schools.* East Lansing: Michigan State University.

Johnson, D., Johnson, R., and Holubec, E. J. (1986). *Circles of Learning*. Edina, MN: Interaction Books.

Jordan C. (1984). Cultural compatibility and the education of ethnic minority children. *Educational Research Quarterly, 8,* 59-71.

Kagan, S. (1988). *Cooperative learning: Resources for teachers*. University of California Press, Riverside, CA.

Kunjufu, J. (1984). *Developing positive self-images in blacks*. Chicago, IL: African American Images.

Mora, P. (1995). Forward. In B. Diamond & M. Moore. *Multicultural literacy: Mirroring the reality of the classroom*. White Plains, NY: Longman.

McLaren, P. L. (1988). Culture or cannon? Critical pedagogy and the politics of literacy. *Harvard Educational Review, 58,* 2.

Norton, D. (1992). *Through the eyes of a child: An introduction to children's literature*. Columbus, OH: Charles Merrill.

Ogle, D. M. (1986). K-W-L: A teaching model that develops active reading of expository text. *The Reading Teacher, 39,* 564-570.

Ramiriz, B. (1988). Culturally and linguistically diverse children. *Teaching Exceptional Children, 20,* 45-46.

Ramirez, M., III, & Price-Williams, D. (1976). Achievement motivation in children of three ethnic groups. *Journal of Cross-Cultural Psychology, 7,* 49-60.

Ramirez, M., III (1967). Identification with Mexican family values and authoritarianism in Mexican-Americans. *The Journal of Social Psychology, 73,* 3-11.

Sapon-Shevin, M., & Schniedewind, N. (1991). Cooperative learning as empowering pedagogy. In C. E. Sleeter (Ed.), *Empowerment through Multicultural Education*. Albany: State University of New York Press. 159-178.

Schieffelin, B., & Ochs, E. (1986). Language socialization. *Annual Review of Anthropology, 15,* 163-191.

Scollon, R., & Scollon, S. (1981). *Narrative, literacy and race in interethnic communication*. Norwood, NJ: Ablex.

Shannon, P. (1989). The struggle to control literacy lessons. *Language Arts, 66,* 625-634.

Slavin, R. (1983). *Student team learning*. Washington, D.C.: National Education Association.

Sleeter, C., & Grant, C. (1991). Mapping terrains of power: Student cultural knowledge versus classroom knowledge. In C. Sleeter (Ed.), *Empowerment through multicultural education*. Albany, NY: State University of New York Press.

Smitherman, G. (1977). *Talkin' and testifyin: The language of Black America*. Boston: Houghton Mifflin.

Snow, C., & Ninio, A. (1986). The contribution of reading books with children to their linguistic and cognitive development. In W. Teale & E. Sulzby (Eds.), *Emergent literacy: Writing and reading*. Norwood, NJ: Ablex.

Steffensen, M., Joag-Dev, C., & Anderson, R. A cross-cultural perspective on reading comprehension. *Reading Research Quarterly, 1,* 10-29.

Teale, W. (1987). Emergent literacy: Reading and writing development in early childhood. In J. Readance & R. Baldwin (Eds.), *Research in literacy: Merging perspectives: Thirty-sixth yearbook of the National Reading Conference* (pp. 45-74). Rochester, NY: National Reading Conference.

Tharp, R. G. (1982). The effective instruction of comprehension: Results and descriptions of the Kamehameha Early Education Program. *Reading Research Quarterly, 18,* 287-298.

Tharp, R. G. (1989). Psychological variables and constants: Effects on teaching and learning in schools. *American Psychologist, 2,* 349-359.

Tiedt, L., & Tiedt, I. (1990). *Multicultural literacy: A handbook of activities, information and resources.* Needham Heights, MA: Simon & Schuster.

Valdez, A. (1991). Surviving in the barrio. In D. Schoem (Ed.), *Inside separate worlds: Life stories of Blacks, Hispanics, and Jews.* Ann Arbor: University of Michigan Press.

Watson, K. (1975). Transferable communicative routines: Strategies and group identity in two speech events. *Language and Society, 4,* 53–72.

Watson-Gegeo, K., & Boggs, S. (1977). From verbal play to talk story: The role of routines in speech events among Hawaiian children. In S. Ervin-Tripp & C. Mitchell-Kernan (Eds.). *Child discourse* (pp. 67–90). New York: Academic Press.

Wells, G. (1986). *Language development in the preschool years.* New York: Cambridge University Press.

Wertsch, J. V. (1991). *Voices of the mind: A sociocultural approach to mediated action.* Cambridge, MA: Harvard University Press.

chapter 3

Evaluating and Selecting Multicultural Literature for Children

OVERVIEW

In this chapter we present standards for selecting multicultural literature that will enable children to recognize and appreciate good literature, understand themselves and others, acquire knowledge of their heritage, and gain enjoyment from reading. In selecting multicultural literature it is particularly appropriate to identify literature that fosters a heightened understanding and appreciation of cultures and an attitude of respect for all people. After presenting a definition of multicultural literature, we will detail specific literary and sociological elements that should be present in literature if it is to authentically represent the values and contributions of people of diverse cultures. Realizing the formidable task that teachers and librarians face as they consider literature choices, we will share selected literature from the African American, Asian American, Hispanic American, and Native American cultures that we have used in our multicultural literature program and that meets our standards.

We include discussion of students' selections of favorite books in this chapter because of the importance of students' voices as critics in the selection of what they read. Quotations and comments from students who freely, enthusiastically, and honestly shared their feelings add interest and credibility to our selection process.

INTRODUCTION

Instead of saying "oooh, you're eating gross stuff," I mean . . . I've learned from the multicultural books that a lot of cultures are different and have different beliefs, but they're all wonderful and they're neat to read about.
(Eric, sixth grade).

These books have helped me realize that not everybody is the same . . . all over the world and even in this country. If you don't know that, you might treat somebody in a way they don't like.

(Shannon, fourth grade).

The multicultural books, they let us know more about where we (African Americans) came from, about our history and what happened during times we weren't born.

(Lakeesha, third grade).

These comments, shared in interviews we conducted, reassure us that reading about other cultures through multicultural literature can have a positive impact on students. The responses underscore the need for a body of children's literature that provides authentic information and affirms people of all cultural groups. These words tell us that students of color, like all students, seek an image of themselves that tells them they are important and their ideas, feelings, customs and beliefs are worthwhile.

In a multicultural literacy program, the teacher plays a pivotal role in the identification and use of literature that enables all children to appreciate and understand their culture and the culture of others. Because of this role, it is important that teachers make *informed* decisions in selecting literature. Purists suggest that chil-

FIGURE 3.1   Students share favorite books they have read.

dren's literature should be judged on literary merit alone. For teachers to look at multicultural literature from this perspective only diminishes their ability to develop social responsibility in their students. Sims (1982) maintains that the literature we choose helps to socialize our children and transmit our values to them. Teachers must, therefore, become familiar with the available multicultural literature and develop a sensitivity to the messages the literature conveys.

MULTICULTURAL LITERATURE: A DEFINITION

Several definitions have been offered for multicultural literature. In the United States, the term *multicultural literature* is most often used to refer to literature by and about members of groups considered to be outside the sociopolitical mainstream of this country (Bishop, 1992). According to Bishop, "Most frequently the term *multicultural literature* refers to books about people of color in this country—African Americans, Asian Americans, Native Americans, Hispanics" (p. 39). Similarly, Norton (1991, p. 531) states that "multicultural literature is literature about racial or ethnic minority groups that are culturally and socially different from the white Anglo-Saxon majority in the United States, whose largely middle-class values and customs are most represented in American literature."

We define multicultural literature as literature that focuses on specific cultures by highlighting and celebrating their cultural and historical perspectives, traditions and heritage, language and dialects, and experiences and lifestyles. Included in these *specific cultures* are all people of color in the United States. We emphasize the literature of these cultural groups, whose values and customs are not typically represented in children's literature. Further, our multicultural literature selections include the literature of diverse cultures outside the United States, from which the people of color in this nation claim ancestral heritage. Our literature selections also include books about religious minorities and regional groups that have often been devalued, misunderstood, or ignored (i.e., Jewish, Amish, Appalachian).

Therefore, in this chapter we highlight literature about Africans and African Americans; Asians and Asian Americans, including the Chinese, Japanese, Korean, Vietnamese, and Hmong cultures; Hispanic Americans, including Mexican Americans and Puerto Ricans; and Native Americans, including regional nations of the Plains, Great Lakes region, the Canadian North, and Hawaiian Americans. We realize these groups do not represent the entire population of people of color in this country. Within the text, however, we include literature and literacy activities of other diverse groups, such as Arabs and East Indians. Further, the database included with our Instructors' Manual will be a useful and more comprehensive reference.

STANDARDS FOR EVALUATING
MULTICULTURAL LITERATURE

The criteria for evaluating multicultural literature for children is consistent with the literary standards applied to any fine children's literature. Typically, literature has been evaluated on the basis of literary elements and literary criticism, social issues and concerns, developmental and psychological appropriateness, and popularity (Lindgren, 1991; Norton, 1991). The evaluators of children's literature are literary critics, teachers, librarians, parents, publishers, citizens of diverse cultures, and children, themselves. For example, there are groups of adults who select books for awards based primarily on literary merit, such as the Newbery Medal, Caldecott Medal, Notable Children's Books, and Boston Globe-Horn Book Award. There are other adult groups who evaluate books for their aesthetic standards, cultural pluralism, and social concerns for equality and justice (i.e., Council on Interracial Books for Children; the Children's Literature Review Board; the Association of Women Psychologists). Children, who are the ultimate critics of what they read, have been represented through lists of children's favorites. Among these are lists compiled by the joint project of the International Reading Association and the Children's Book Council, which allows 10,000 children from around the United States to evaluate children's books published during a given year. These "Children's Choices" are published each year in the October issue of *The Reading Teacher.*

However, because multicultural literature is about groups who are typically underrepresented and often inaccurately or negatively portrayed in literature, we recommend that multicultural literature be evaluated carefully for authentic and accurate images of the cultures it represents.

Many teachers lack confidence in their ability to make informed choices, fearing they do not have the necessary cultural knowledge to select literature that does not foster stereotypical images of a particular group. To counter this uncertainty, we recommend that teachers choose a variety of literature about a cultural group, to allow for more portrayals of characters in diverse occupations, lifestyles, and economic conditions. Teachers can train themselves to evaluate literature from multiple perspectives, including perspectives other than traditional European American aesthetic standards (Bishop, 1992). Through wide reading of the literature over time, teachers will gradually develop cultural sensibilities that will inform and guide their decision making. They can further develop their expertise by seeking opportunities to interact with people of diverse cultures and backgrounds.

We hope this chapter will help teachers make informed and sensitive choices of multicultural literature. Although multicultural literature includes informational books, our primary emphasis is on poetry, biography, realistic fiction, folk tales, and picture books in this chapter. Chapter 6 includes more informational books and biographies. To evaluate and analyze multicultural literature, we have drawn on our experiences and information from other resources (Bishop, 1992; Council on Interracial Books for Children, 1974; Harris, 1991; Norton, 1991; Rudman, 1984; Pang, 1991). On that basis we look for the following characteristics in multicultural literature:

1. **Characters who authentically reflect the distinct cultural experiences, realities, and world view of a specific group.** Characters exhibit a unique perspective on the world, based on everyday experiences and specific details of language style, family interaction, religious practice, and other qualities that reflect the cultural behaviors of a group. For example, a story about a contemporary Ojibway girl in Minnesota might include her visit to a shopping mall, attendance in an American Indian language class at school, and experiences with her grandmother as she makes beadwork for a powwow.

2. **Character representations portrayed in a true-to-life and balanced manner.** Characters represent a balanced portrayal of good and evil, as well as a variety of physical, social, and emotional attributes. Cultural differences within the groups are clearly recognizable, although there are common cultural frames of reference and collective experiences. Therefore, to reflect authentic treatment, individuals within a group have their own thoughts, emotions, and behaviors.

   However, characters are not to be overglorified or touted as the "exception," which might occur if authors, attempting to cast characters in a positive light, give them qualities that are unnaturally positive. To attribute high intellect, athletic prowess, physical beauty, and a warm, charming personality to one character is to make the character unbelievable.

3. **Settings representative of an environment consistent with a historical/contemporary time, place, or situation of the specific culture.** A historical selection accurately and authentically mirrors the situations of the time from the diverse perspectives of the specific cultural group involved. For example, if the book is about the Chinese emigrant experiences in the early 1900s, it should clearly present Chinese Americans' life experiences and world view.

   Factual information is accurate in detail. If the selection is contemporary, it will describe current situations of a given cultural group. The author maintains compatibility of setting and characters. A story set in a Puerto Rican home in a large city has characteristics consistent with the actions, values, and beliefs of Puerto Ricans in that context.

4. **Themes developed within the story or selection that are consistent with the values and beliefs, customs and traditions, needs, and conflicts of the specific culture.** If strong family relationships and respect for elders are important values in a cultural group, for example, the themes advanced in the literature about the cultural group should reflect these values. If the author chooses to develop themes that conflict with these values, they should be reflected as the exception, not the norm. It is also important that social issues, problems, and conflicts related to cultural group status be treated frankly, realistically, accurately, and without oversimplification.

5. **Informational literature presented in a detailed and accurate manner.** Biographies about figures of a specific culture are consistent with the historical settings and events of the time. Sources of information clearly reflect events from the perspective of the given cultural group. If more than one cultural group is reflected in the events described, the multiple perspectives are presented without favoring or valuing one group above the other.

6. **Language characteristic of the distinctive vocabulary, style, patterns, and rhythm of speech of the specific cultural group.** The language used is natural and blends with the story line and characterizations. Dialect has a legitimate purpose consistent with the character and story line. In cases where grandparents are talking to grandchildren, for example, differences in language style and usage often exist and should be reflected in the language. Dialect is not viewed as an example of substandard

English. When words from languages other than English are incorporated in the text, they are spelled and used correctly.

7. **Literature that is free of stereotypes in language, illustrations, behavior, and character traits.** The language is not exaggerated or used in unlikely contexts, but is treated with respect. Characters also reflect a range of socioeconomic conditions, educational levels, and occupations. The characteristic behaviors and traits should be both positive and negative.

   Illustrations and pictures reflect the physical diversity that exists in cultural and racial groups. Features are depicted as they exist in the culture, not as caricatures or in illustrations in which all the characters look alike. The illustrations should show characters who are readily recognized as representative of the cultural group, not simply as darker painted versions of Caucasian-featured people.

8. **Language that reflects a sensibility to the people of the culture; offensive, negative, or degrading vocabulary in descriptions of characters, their customs, and lifestyles is absent.** Characters are not depersonalized or given names that compare them to animals, unless it is consistent with the traditions of the culture. Sacred ceremonies, traditions, and artifacts are described in respectful, not disparaging terms. Traditional dress is not referred to as "costumes."

9. **Gender roles within the culture portrayed accurately and authentically reflecting the changing status and roles of women and men in many cultures.** Women are portrayed in active as well as passive roles as appropriate to the specific culture. Both male and female characters are free to express a wide range of feelings and interests where culturally appropriate. Females are cast in a variety of roles beyond that of subservience.

Using these criteria reassures us that children of all cultures, when seeing themselves in print, will derive a sense of personal worth from the images they see. Moreover, children of cultures other than those depicted will be not be misinformed or develop a sense of superiority based on uneven, distorted views. In the following sections we examine the literature of specific cultural groups.

AFRICAN AMERICAN LITERATURE

The image of African Americans in children's literature has historically been a negative one (Broderick, 1973; Banfield, 1985; Sims, 1982). For many years blacks were nearly invisible in children's books. In a study that looked at children's books published over a three-year period in the 1960s, Larrick (1965) reports that there was a notable absence of children of color in these books. Her report, *The All-White World of Children's Books,* points out that of the 5,206 children's books published in the three years, only 6.7 percent (349) had a single black child in the text or illustrations. More recently Broderick (1973), in her review of analyzed children's literature published between 1827 and 1967, asserts that several stereotypes are perpetuated, including: black people are not physically attractive; black people are musical; and black people depend on white people for the positive things they want to attain. Sims (1982) found that by the late 1960s and early 1970s the negative images of blacks in children's literature were more subtle, focusing on stereotypes that Sims said included the matriarchal family and the "super Negro."

But there is a body of literature written by and about African American children that is culturally conscious (Sims, 1982), reflecting the African American heritage, traditions, and world view. These books, according to Sims, are set in African American communities, the main characters are black, the language reflects the black rhetorical styles, and the story highlights an African world view. Harris (1992) reports that African American authors have emerged to create a body of literature notable for its literary and artistic excellence and its ability to, in the words of Eloise Greenfield (1975), "take effect."

The books we will discuss are those we identify as culturally authentic, enlightening, and enjoyable; they will inform children of all cultures about the African American experience of joy, struggle, perseverance, and hope. We share some books that have the potential to become classics—works of enduring excellence—because of their message, plot, and author's style. We also highlight books that are more recent publications.

Traditional Folk Literature

Traditional folk literature, the tales handed down through centuries of storytelling, reflects the African American oral tradition and dates back to the griot (*greo*), the highly regarded oral storyteller in West African societies. Storytellers in African communities were not simply entertainers; they were chroniclers of tradition, custodians of history, and guardians of their society's beliefs and values (Holt, Rinehart, and Winston, 1992). Children were educated about their customs and traditions through these stories. Today they are used to help children celebrate, appreciate, and reinforce their connections with the past.

The traditional folk literature of the African American traveled from Africa to the New World in the oral tradition with slaves on the "middle passage," the route from West Africa across the Atlantic to the West Indies and America. The slaves combined the memories of the past with the contacts and relationships on the plantations to form a body of literature about themselves and their experiences on the plantation and in their new world. This traditional literature can be categorized into (1) tales that are indigenous to countries in Africa, (2) folklore of the Caribbean, and (3) the African American folklore of the United States.

African Folk Tales.   Many African folk tales, notably the *Ananse* tales, involve animals indigenous to the continent. Anansi*, the Spider, is a trickster hero, a type of character often present in folklore of different lands. In Virginia Hamilton's *In the Beginning: Creation Stories from around the World,* Ananse appears in "Spider Ananse Finds Something: Wulbari the Creator." This delightfully amusing creation myth from the Krachi people of Togo in West Africa details how Ananse, the sup-

---

* Variant spellings (*Ananse, Anansi, Anansy*) exist for this character.

posedly weak spider, overcomes Wulbari, the strong sky god who is all-powerful. Ananse uses his wit and trickery in finding the darkness, moon, and sun that Wulbari requests. Ananse outsmarts God Wulbari and thereby proves that the weak can indeed conquer the strong. Another Ananse folk tale, Gerald McDermott's *Anansi the Spider: A Tale from the Ashanti,* places the god Nyame, god of all things, in a role of aiding Anansi as he places the moon in the sky for all to see. In Gail E. Haley's *A Story, A Story,* Ananse attempts to get stories from the all-powerful sky god, stories that belong only to the god. Again in this Ananse story, Ananse outwits the sky god by bringing unlikely gifts to the god: the "leopard-of-the-terrible-teeth"; Mmboro, the hornet who stings like fire; and Mmoatia, the fairy whom people never see. The sky god rewards Ananse by giving him the stories he so desired.

Although these Ananse tales have their origin in Africa, they are also among the most popular tales in the West Indies and have been told and retold there for many years. Ananse's character is the embodiment of how the weak, with their intelligence and cunning, can outsmart and overpower the strong. The stories have symbolized hope for people who were enslaved and oppressed, which is why they are popular with West Indians and Africans, even today.

In *The Origin of Life on Earth: An African Creation Myth,* David Anderson builds on the Yoruba religion to underscore the myth about Olorun, god Almighty, who lives in the sky with many assistants. This myth, which includes outstanding illustrations, details how Orisha Obatala was sent by Olorun to make earth and the first people.

Traditional African tales often describe interdependence of humans and nature and the need for them to coexist. It also addresses social customs and lifestyles. Two books by Ann Grifalconi are illustrative. In *The Village of Round and Square Houses,* the entire village of Tos, in Cameroon West Africa, is destroyed by a volcanic eruption. The spirit of the volcano, Mother Naka, directs the villagers to change their lifestyles dramatically and rebuild the village. She tells men to live in square houses and women and children in round ones in order that they have a "place to be apart and a time to be together." This tale speaks of respect for privacy and the power of nature. It also provides the reader with an appreciation of the language and storytelling tradition of the people of West Africa. *Osa's Pride* is also set in the Cameroons; the women are in the round houses, and Osa's grandmother, through a special storytelling time, teaches Osa a lesson about the importance of humility.

In Verna Aardema's *Bringing the Rain to Kapiti Plain,* the Masais' dependence on nature is highlighted. In this humorous folk tale, a Masai herdsman punctures the rain cloud with his bow and arrow, bringing rain to the Kapiti plain of East Africa. This feat makes it possible for the cycle of the rainy and dry seasons to continue. The theme is consistent with the Masai people's beliefs in the spirituality of nature.

Mufaro's Beautiful Daughters, a popular folk tale by John Steptoe, addresses the themes of the triumph of humility over vanity, good over evil, and generosity over selfishness. The book, beautifully illustrated by the author, reveals the true character of the two daughters—one ill-tempered and vain, the other kind and generous—as they journey to appear before the king, who is choosing a wife. The story setting is an ancient walled city in Zimbabwe built by the Bantus between the 11th and 18th centuries. The ruins of this city are still standing, reinforcing the authenticity of the text.

These folk tales are but a small sample of those available. (See database in

FIGURE 3.2   Students proudly display their artistic representations of *Bringing the Rain to Kapiti Plain* by Verna Aardema.

Instructor's Manual.) They represent stories and tales that authentically present African folklore and the values and beliefs of a people. These tales present underlying themes of cooperation, generosity toward others, respect for privacy, and perseverance in attaining peace and harmony with nature. They also evoke an appreciation of the oral tradition and the richness of the languages. Above all, they instill in African American children pride and pleasure in their rich cultural heritage.

African American Tales.   Black folk tales were originally recorded in the late 19th century (Hamilton, 1985). These tales are a unique blend of the slaves' life in North and South America and the Caribbean, and their memories and habits of Africa. The folk tales became the slaves' voices through various animals such as the rabbit, fox, bear, wolf, turtle, snake, and possum (Hamilton, 1985). One of the most notable of these animals, Brer Rabbit, assumes the exploits of the trickster figure. Although generally considered helpless when compared to larger animals, the rabbit is smart, tricky, and clever in the slaves' stories. Andrews (1992, p. 141) notes that "spirit of Brer Rabbit lived in every slave who deceived his master with a smile of loyalty while stealing from his storehouse and making plans for an escape." Although the tales were created out of sorrow, the "hearts and minds of the black people who formed them, expanded them, and passed them on to us were full of love and hope. We must look on the tales as a celebration of the human spirit" (Hamilton, 1985, p. xii).

Hamilton's *The People Could Fly* is a significant volume of African American folk tales. It is divided into four parts and gives readers an opportunity to enjoy (1) animal tales, particularly the witty trickster tales; (2) tall tales, with their fanciful humorous twists; (3) scary tales of witches, devils and ghosts; and (4) slave tales, including true slave narratives and stories about slaves' quest for freedom. Hamilton uses "moderate colloquialisms," which render the tales understandable and readable. In some of the tales, she uses the repetition of the language and African words and sayings to demonstrate the connections of Africa to America. An example is *A Wolf and Little Daughter,* a fanciful tale that can be appreciated more when read aloud because of the repetition of words, especially in the song fragment that Little Daughter sings: "Tray-bla, tray-bla, cum qua, kimo." (p. 63) The tales also provide opportunities for discussions about the use of symbolism, as in the Brer Rabbit tales and the trickster tales, and themes that can be connected to historical fiction. The strikingly beautiful illustrations by Leo and Diane Dillon enhance the beauty and spirit of these stories.

Robert D. San Souci's *The Talking Eggs,* a folk tale of two sisters from the American South, is unforgettable in its magical surprises, as the honesty and obedience of the kind and gentle sister bring her wealth and reward. The mean, selfish sister, in contrast, becomes miserable and unfulfilled because of her evil ways. This tale, adapted from a Creole folk tale, with similarities to the Cinderella of European tales, reminds us that people in all parts of the world have gathered around the storyteller to hear captivating stories. The theme of good prevailing over evil is predictable in this folk tale, lending itself to comparisons with folk tales of other cultures with similar themes.

Turtle Knows Your Name, by author and illustrator Ashley Bryan, is a humorous retelling of a West Indian tale. A young boy, Upsilimana Tumpalerado, has a difficult time remembering his name. When he finally remembers, he is rewarded with a special *name dance* with Granny. However, another problem, that of finding Granny's name, arises, presenting an even greater challenge for the young boy. Bryan skillfully weaves the rest of the story, detailing how Upsilimana Tumpalerado meets his new challenge. The colorful, rhythmic language, the appealing food, and the humor are elements that authentically reflect the West Indian culture.

In the same tradition, *Flossie & the Fox,* by Patricia McKissack, has similarities to Little Red Riding Hood of European folk tales. McKissack highlights the importance of storytelling in the lives of African Americans as she relates to her audience how her grandfather used rich and colorful language of the South in telling his stories. " 'Did I ever tell you 'bout the time lil' Flossie Finley come out the Piney Woods heeling a fox?' I'd snuggle up beside him in the big porch swing, then he'd begin his tale. . ." (p. 3).

African American and Caribbean Songs and Poems

In chapter 2 we discussed how poetry recitations, songs, and chants are historically a part of the African American culture. Several poetry books and books of chants have been published that continue this tradition. Eloise Greenfield's *Honey, I Love* has maintained its appeal for young readers since its publication in 1978. The author includes 16 poems about everyday experiences that connect with both boy and girl readers. In the poem "I Look Pretty," for example, Greenfield shares the feelings of a little girl dressed in her Mama's shiny purple coat. Another selection emphasizes the frustration of a young girl who has lost her brother to basketball:

It's summertime
And Reggie doesn't live here anymore
He lives across the street
Spends his time with the round ball
Jump, turn, shoot
Through the hoop . . .

Greenfield's *Under the Sunday Tree* (1988) captures life in the Bahamas and provides children with a glimpse of island life. The poems about everyday life and relationships on the island, along with the vividly rich paintings by Amos Ferguson mirroring the colorful life of the Bahamas, are a lovely and meaningful introduction to a little-known world.

Arnold Adoff's story-poem for young children, *Black is Brown is Tan,* is the author's true story about an interracial family who finds harmony in living and sharing their lives. Here is a sample of the rhythm and rhyme:

black is brown is tan
is girl is boy
is nose is face
is all the colors
of the race.

Lynn Joseph's *Coconut Kind of Day* is a colorful glimpse of the island of Trinidad through the eyes of a young girl, and Sandra Speidel's lush paintings capture the vibrant spirit of the island. The author draws on her own experiences to create the sights and sounds of the island: the coconut drives with Daddy, the snail races, the All

FIGURE 3.3 A sample sketch about the Caribbean Islands, written by a school child 9 years of age.

THE CARIBBEAN ISLANDS

APRIL 28, 1992   BY DARRELL PASCO

The Caribbean is like one big chain that boarders the Caribbean Sea. They lie in something that looks like a big curve at the western end of the Atlantic Ocean. To the north are a lot of little islands. These islands make up the Bahamas.

The Caribbean is a hot spot for the people to tour the place. Among these islands are Cubs, Jamaica, Puerto Rico and the islands of Hispaniola.

The people of the Caribbean are mostly blacks.

The education area is good. The Caribbean government makes sure that they get a good education.

The food is wonderful with great fruits and good dinner dishes.

JAMAICA

Jamaica is and Island nation in the West Indies. It lies about 780 miles south of Florida and is the third largest Island in the Caribbean Sea. Jamaicas pleasant climate and its beautiful beaches and mountains attract more than 700,000 tourist yearly. But the Jamaican economy does not depend chiefly on tourists.

Star boys' cricket games, and buying ices from the "palet man." Young readers will be intrigued by the differences and similarities of this culture compared to their own. Natives of Trinidad will read about their beautiful island with pride.

Fiction

There are numerous outstanding, realistic fiction selections in which African Americans are featured as main characters. Sims (1982, pp. 15–16) classifies these realistic fiction offerings as the (1) *social conscience books,* which are about blacks but essentially educate white audiences to the conditions of "their fellow humans"; (2) *melting pot books,* written for white and black audiences, which carry the message that all children are essentially the same except for their physical features; and (3) the *culturally conscious books,* written from the perspective of the African American and highlighting "both the uniqueness and the universal humanness of that experience." The literature we have used in our program is most similar to the culturally conscious books. These tend to cluster into three general categories, dealing with (1) social issues and problems, (2) family values and family relationships, and (3) self-esteem building and issues of pride. Although some of the themes are universal, the qualities that were identified earlier for evaluating authenticity in the literature of specific cultures are present in these books.

Social Issues.   These books tend to be written for middle school students as the primary audience. Mildred Taylor has written a series of books about the Logan Family: *Roll of Thunder, Hear My Cry; Let the Circle Be Unbroken;* and *The Road to Memphis.* In these books, set in the South, she tells the story of a black family's struggle for survival against racism and of the love that permeates the family's relationships as they seek a resolution to the problem. In *Mississippi Bridge,* Taylor continues the saga of the Logan family in a story based on a tale that her father told her about his childhood. This story centers around Jeremy Simms, a 10-year-old white boy, neighbor, and would-be friend of the Logan children. The drama unfolds as a bus driver orders all the black passengers off a crowded bus to make room for white passengers who arrive late. This compelling story brings social inequity to the fore and provides a bridge to an examination of problems faced by people of color.

Walter Dean Myers's books have wide and much-needed appeal to male readers, particularly African Americans, who seldom find themselves portrayed in the literature. *Scorpions* has believable characters faced with growing up in a social environment in which staying on "the right path" is sometimes not a matter of will but of chance. In this very sober book, Jamal and his best friend, Tito, a Puerto Rican, struggle to resist gang membership, but when they are unwillingly drawn into the Scorpions, they are faced with an event and possible consequences that could change their lives forever. The pervasiveness of gangs, their destructiveness, and their drain on society are effectively underscored in this selection.

Family Relationships.   Many books with themes about how families learn to live and grow together are available for all age groups. The characteristics that make these books unique to the black experience are language usage and style—nicknames, words used to address one another—and the characters' perspectives on life. A book

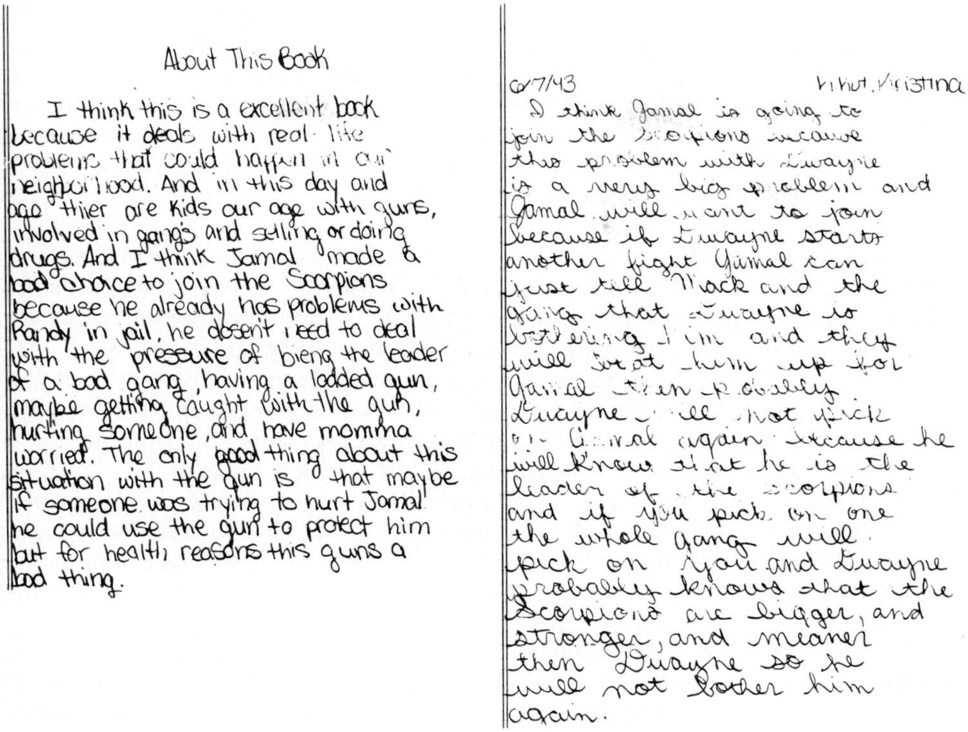

About This Book

I think this is a excellent book because it deals with real life problems that could happen in our neighborhood. And in this day and age their are kids our age with guns, involved in gangs and selling or doing drugs. And I think Jamal made a bad choice to join the Scorpions because he already has problems with Randy in jail, he doesn't need to deal with the pressure of bieng the leader of a bad gang, having a loaded gun, maybe getting caught with the gun, hurting someone, and have momma worried. The only good thing about this situation with the gun is that maybe if someone was trying to hurt Jamal he could use the gun to protect him but for health reasons this guns a bad thing.

6/7/43   Kihut, Kristina

I think Jamal is going to join the Scorpions because the problem with Dwayne is a very big problem and Jamal will want to join because if Dwayne started another fight Jamal can just tell Mack and the gang that Dwayne is bothering him and they will beat him up for Jamal then probably Dwayne will not pick on Jamal again because he will know that he is the leader of the Scorpions and if you pick on one the whole gang will pick on you and Dwayne probably knows that the Scorpions are bigger, and stronger, and meaner then Dwayne so he will not bother him again.

FIGURE 3.4 Through writing in their literature response logs, students learn the value of reflection on their lives. Here are two students' thoughts on *Scorpions,* by Walter Dean Myers.

that highlights family relationships as well as the richness of African American traditions is Camille Yarbrough's *Cornrows.* This book authentically presents three generations, as Great Grandma and Mother share how the hairstyle of cornrows, an African symbol since ancient times, can symbolize the courage of African Americans today. The dialect, the bond between grandparent and children, and the lyrical, rhythmical language make this book a pleasure to read aloud and perform in a choral reading (See chapter 4.)

A special relationship between a young boy, Michael, and his great-great-aunt is similarly shared in Sharon Bell Mathis's *The Hundred Penny Box.* The author brings together advanced age and childhood as she tells the story of Michael's attempt to try to save the hundred penny box that hold all the stories of Aunt Dew's 100 years.

The Patchwork Quilt, by Valerie Flournoy, is a story of a family who learns the art of quilting from Grandmother, who lives with them. The story portrays the extended family that often characterizes the African American population. As Tanya and her grandmother work on the quilt, memories surface and the bond between them grows stronger. As grandmother falls ill, Tanya lovingly takes up the project her grandmother started.

In *Tar Beach,* another book in which quilting is prominent, Faith Ringgold creatively highlights family relationships. The book was inspired by the author's story quilt, which combines autobiography, fictional narrative, painting, and quilt making in one art form. It details the author's memories of childhood in Harlem and the hot summer nights the family spent together on the roof. The page border replicates the original story quilt, and the background material for the text is printed on the canvas paper that Ringgold used in her paintings.

Understanding Self/Self-Esteem. Many outstanding realistic fiction selections deal with African American children's quest for who they are and who their ancestors are. The characters in these books grow to understand themselves better and to see what they have to do to cope with the problems of growing up.

Phil Mendez's *The Black Snowman* combines contemporary realism with fantasy through the story of Jacob, who learns to deal with self-doubt and poverty with the help of a dream that puts him in touch with his ancestors and the power of a kente cloth. Like Jacob, the imaginative young girl, Geeder, in Hamilton's *Zeely,* is swept up in a fantasy. Sparked by Zeely's resemblance to a woman in a magazine, Geeder fantasizes that Zeely is an African queen. Through her friendship with Zeely, Geeder realizes that each person has the power to be something special as long as she loves and respects herself and her way of viewing the world. She shares these insights with her brother and Uncle Ross: "It's not what a person stoops to do—oh, No, it's not! It's what's inside you when you dare swim in a dark lake with nobody to help if something should happen. . ." (p. 120). This book is particularly notable for its positive portrayal of the Watutsi people of Africa. As Harris (1992, p. 68) relates, "Zeeley contains no images of Africa as the dark continent peopled by uncivilized hordes unlike the popular Tarzan series. Instead, the Watutsi are depicted as regal, proud people with a complex culture."

Two books for younger students are Eloise Greenfield's *Nathaniel Talking* and Mary Hoffman's *Amazing Grace. Nathaniel Talking,* a masterpiece of a story-rap/poem, portrays Nathaniel as a philosopher who shares his intellect and his beliefs through raps and rhymes about his family life, his friends, and his future. His musings and understanding about life make him appear far wiser than his nine years. The exciting black and white illustrations help to make this book a unique expression of the African American child's experience of the soul that all can appreciate.

Amazing Grace is a lighthearted story about a young girl, Grace, of many talents. Although she is confident in her ability to portray Peter Pan in a school play, she discovers that her peers see limitations because of her race and gender. Grace, helped by her mother and grandmother, soon has her confidence restored. She subsequently wins the part, regaining her confidence and learning in the process that hard work can help her to attain most of her goals. Both stories can lead naturally to discussions of problems children face as they mature and possible solutions for those problems.

Informational Picture Books

There are many excellent informational books about the African culture that can help instill pride in African American students and provide information to students of other cultures. These books help to dispel myths frequently perpetuated about the

African continent. Margaret Musgrove's *Ashanti to Zulu,* illustrated by Leo and Diane Dillon, provides an authentic and detailed portrait of 26 African tribes. The strikingly beautiful artwork gives readers a glimpse of the diversity among African tribes and the vitality in their lifestyles.

Kwanzaa has become an important holiday in the lives of many African Americans, and its celebration increases each year. As the holiday is relatively new (established in 1966), teachers and students frequently have questions about it. Two books that young children will find informative and fun to read are Deborah Chocolate's *My First Kwanzaa Book* and Sundaira Morninghouse's *Habari Gani? What's the News? A Kwanzaa Story.* The former book, although written in narrative form, takes children through the seven principles of the Kwanzaa celebration with a young African American child. The afterword includes more detailed explanations of the seven principles and definitions of the symbols and words used during Kwanzaa. *Habari Gani? What's the News? A Kwanzaa Story* similarly describes how Kia and her family celebrate each day of Kwanzaa.

Through art, young people learn something about the history and traditions of a country. *African Crafts,* by Judith Corwin, offers ideas and directions for making masks, dolls, sculptures, jewelry, and designs. The directions are clear and simple so that students can make attractive crafts. The ideas presented might also spark students to create their own projects.

ASIAN AMERICAN LITERATURE

Our experiences with student responses to using Asian American literature in the multicultural literacy project are similar to those of Aoki (1992, p. 112), who asserts, "As I share the few Asian Pacific American books with Asian Pacific American children, their identification is so spontaneous that they immediately develop a linkage with the characters." We have observed the Asian American students' excitement and willingness to share ways that their personal experiences are connected with story events and characters in Asian American literature. We note with disappointment the dearth of quality children's literature about Asian Americans. In 1976, the Asian Children's Books Project was commissioned to identify books currently in print that depicted Asian Americans and to analyze these books for accuracy and authenticity. They identified 66 books with Asian American central characters that were published between 1945 and 1975. These books were primarily about Japanese and Chinese Americans. They were also found to present stereotypical portrayals of the physical appearances, living conditions, and customs of the Asian Americans. Although there has been some improvement, the availability of authentic Asian American literature is still limited. According to Aoki (1992), Asian American authors report a lack of support from publishing houses for their work, primarily because they are looking for major sales markets and not the limited market they perceive characterizes Asian American literature. Further confounding the problem is Aoki's assertion that many educators view Asian American literature as appropriate only for a small population of students. Apparently, until economic concerns become less of a factor, Asian American authors will continue to be challenged to find ways to bring Asian American literature to all students.

As with a study of African American literature, we recommend that teachers begin a study of Asian American literature by using traditional folk literature. This practice reinforces the students' understanding of the power of the oral tradition in transmitting the beliefs and values of the people. Traditional folk literature also mirrors aspects of the culture in many ways. Many of the books, because they are written by Asian authors, help to bring the insider's perspective and help others appreciate traditional values, beliefs, and life experiences of Asian people.

Chinese Traditional Folk Literature

Many of the folk tales used in our project grew out of China's ancient history. This is clearly true of two traditional folk tales: Demi's *Liang and the Magic Paintbrush* and Robert San Souci's *The Enchanted Tapestry*. In the former tale, based on an ancient Chinese legend, Liang uses his magic paintbrush to help the poor and eventually destroy the evil emperor. Demi reinforces the traditional theme of good over evil and the importance of art in the lives of the Chinese people through his retelling of the tale and his softly alluring pictures. Similarly, art plays an important role in *The Enchanted Tapestry,* the story of a widow who raised her three sons by the gold that she received from weaving a beautiful tapestry. The widow painstakingly wove her hopes and dreams into the tapestry, before it was taken away by the Sorceress. The sons' attempts to recapture the tapestry, and the obstacles they encounter, round out this intriguing tale. The subtle, muted earth tones of László Gál's artwork highlight the flora and fuana of the region and add to the charm and geographical authenticity of this tale.

Another folk tale, *The Sleeper,* by David Day, is based on the traditions and history of China. It highlights the importance of books to the Chinese nation, as the main character, Wu, becomes a hero when he restores peace and the recorded Chinese history to the land. The book, which is enhanced by its bright watercolor illustrations, is useful as a catalyst for further study because of its linkage with Chinese history.

Ed Young's Chinese tale of *Lon Po Po,* Granny Wolf, like the European tale of Little Red Riding Hood (with some similarity to the African American tale of *Flossie and the Fox*), comes from an ancient oral tradition and is thought to be over a thousand years old. The story's language, the names of the children, the setting (the gingko tree), and the soft pastels of the Chinese panel art will captivate the reader. When contrasted with the European tale of Little Red Riding Hood, the tale's uniquely Chinese features can be highlighted.

Another Chinese folk tale, *Yeh Shen, A Cinderella Story from China,* by Ai-Ling Louie, is thought to predate the European tale of Cinderella by at least a thousand years. The reader develops an appreciation for the ancient history of the Chinese people, as the book features a reprint of the block-printed story from the Ch'ing dynasty (1644–1912). The original story appears in the *Miscellaneous Record of Yu Yang,* a book that dates back to the T'ang dynasty (618–907 A.D.) (Louie, 1982) and is most likely the original story that we know as "Cinderella."

Dragon's Pearl, by Julie Lawson, is significant not only because of its appealing story about a dutiful son who finds a magic pearl, but because it highlights the significance of dragons in the Chinese culture. The author asserts, "From the most ancient times in China, the dragon was considered the emblem of royalty and the symbol of greatness . . . . A man of great ability or courage was said to be like a dragon. There was no greater honor than to have the dragon's name associated with one's own." Lawson, also the illustrator, traveled to China to research the setting and characters for the story, which are authentically and strikingly represented by muted paintings, bordered by a distinctive Chinese design.

Modern-day Chinese tales are found in the work of Laurence Yep, a prolific writer of Chinese American literature, who has lived the Chinese American experience in San Francisco. In Yep's volume *The Rainbow People,* we find a collection of folk tales told by the Chinese people who made their home in Oakland, California, during the 1930s. Yep's books help students understand the experiences of Chinese immigrants in America.

Chinese Fiction and Informational Literature

Pang, Colvin, MyLuong, and Barba (1992) suggest that teachers identify Asian American books that present a bicultural perspective, showing Asian children who retain their Asian heritage while embracing the American culture. This means that in addition to the traditional folk literature, book selections should include literature that reflects the experience of Asians in America. In *Dragonwings,* Yep does a masterful job of telling the story of 8-year-old Moon Shadow and his experiences in America. The author details Moon Shadow's initial impression of the "Gold Mountain," his introduction to the Tang men, and his chance to join his father in his dream to build an airplane, Dragonwings. Yep provides cultural authenticity as he sensitively shares the realities of life for Chinese immigrants.

Other books by Yep poignantly present conflicts faced by Chinese American children growing up in the United States and their attempts to develop a bicultural identity. In *Child of the Owl,* for example, Casey, who moves to San Francisco to live with her grandmother, comes to realize that she has a lot to learn about her Chinese heritage. Living in Chinatown, Casey gradually comes to learn about herself and her heritage. In Yep's *Sea Glass,* the protagonist, Craig, has to learn to live in a non-Chinese community after leaving Chinatown, where he has lived all of his life. He is faced with his father's expectations for him, the rejection of friends, and the rejection of the old Chinese in his neighborhood. Even though confronted with these problems, Craig is able to find his identity and self-esteem with the help of "Uncle Quail."

Paul Yee's *Tales from the Gold Mountain: Stories of the Chinese in the New World* is a collection of eight original stories based on the history of Chinese immigrants during the time of the California Gold Rush, the building of the transcontinental railway, and the settling of the West Coast in the nineteenth century. It is interesting to compare this book with Yep's *Dragonwings,* which is also set in California during this tumultuous time in Chinese American history. Through reading and discussing the successes, conflicts, and everyday experiences of the characters presented in these books, readers of Chinese origin can revisit the past and experience intense satisfaction in the perseverance of their ancestors.

Modern China is brought to life in Virginia McLean's, *Chasing the Moon to China,* which is a book about her travels in China. The book has special appeal to students because the information is presented from a child's perspective as a young girl tours China. Photographs, paintings, and the phonograph record that is part of the book make this a fun-filled learning experience.

Another book, a true story told from the perspective of a very young child, is Kate Water's and Madeline Slovenz-Low's *Lion Dancer: Ernie Wan's Chinese New Year.* The story, set in New York, describes a young boy's passion for the Lion Dance tradition. The author captures the hard work, the joy, and the spirit of preparation for the Lion Dance. Another true story, Allen Say's *El Chino,* is a narrative about the life of Bong Way, "Billy" Wong, who was the first Chinese bullfighter. Billy Wong, a Chinese American, grew up in Arizona. His story is about the pursuit of a dream that bridges two cultures—Chinese and Spanish—in a way that provides insight into some of the history and traditions of each.

Japanese Traditional Folk Literature

As with Chinese American literature, the numbers of children's books about Japanese Americans are few when compared to the number of children's books published yearly. We have found, however, that several of those that are published are of high quality and authentic in their characterization of the people and culture of Japan.

The traditional Japanese literature is distinct in the manner in which the art and text are interrelated and integrated. Katherine Paterson's *The Tale of the Mandarin Ducks,* illustrated by Leo and Diane Dillon, uses brilliant watercolor and pastel paintings in the style of 18th-century Japanese woodcuts. The traditional tale pits the greedy and covetous lord against a wild drake and a loving couple. The drake and the couple create an interesting and surprising outcome to this story.

A modern fable, Claude Cle'ment's *The Painter and the Wild Swan,* is another example of the integration of art and text. In fact, the tale was inspired by the pictures of swans taken by the Japanese photographer Teiji Saga. The story details the life of a Japanese painter who is so enthralled by the beauty of a flock of swans that he sets out on a quest to capture their beauty in his painting. The delicate and serene art by Cle'ment provides an unforgettable visual experience. The unpredictable story line creates the opportunity for meaningful discussion about Japanese values and beliefs.

Japanese Fiction and Informational Literature

Two examples of stories about the Japanese and Japanese American experiences are Eleanor Coerr's *Sadako and the Thousand Paper Cranes* and Sheila Hamanaka's *The Journey: Japanese Americans, Racism, and Renewal,* respectively. In *Sadako and the Thousand Paper Cranes,* the reader learns firsthand about the tragedy of war through the life and bravery of Sadako, who lived in Hiroshima, Japan, from 1943 to 1955. The spirited Sadako is a memorable character as she fights for life, receiving support from her family and her friends. The reader becomes a part of the struggle and hope when Chizuko, Sadako's friend, tells her about the paper crane.

> It's supposed to live for a thousand years. If a sick person folds one thousand paper cranes, the Gods will grant her wish and make her healthy again. (pp. 34–35)

This tenderly told story conveys an important message about the cruel effects of war and provides students with useful information about the beliefs, values, and traditions of the Japanese people. In another serious rendering, Hamanaka's illustrations and text *The Journey: Japanese Americans, Racism, and Renewal* carries a strong message about the cruel effects of racism. The book, inspired by the author's vivid 25-foot mural, depicts her family's experience in America. The story is a dramatic historical rendition of a progression of scenes portraying the early farmers in the United States, the concentration camps and the war years, and finally the protests of the 1980s by the fourth generation of Japanese Americans. Unlike the tenderly told story of *Sadako, The Journey* is bold in depicting the harsh reality of injustice. In her final statement of pain and hope, Hamanaka asserts:

> As I write, the Japanese American community still works to see that reparations are actually paid: half of the camp survivors have already died. In the painting's final panel, one man's shirt bears swallows, a symbol of the repayment of debt; a boy's T-shirt, a wave—symbol of power and resilience. And floating before us, a carp, the symbol of renewal.   (p. 37)

Faithful Elephants, by Yukio Tsuchiya, is yet another book that tells the sad story of war. This story is about three performing elephants at the Ueno Zoo who had to be killed to protect citizens from the possibility that animals might run wild in a direct bomb attack on the zoo. This gripping story, which is historically authentic, is read aloud on Japanese radio each year to mark the anniversary of Japan's surrender in World War II and to remind people of the horrors of war.

Yoshiko Uchida's *A Jar of Dreams* is the first of a trilogy that chronicles events in the life of Rinko, the main character, as she deals with the internal struggle of finding acceptance while being true to her Japanese heritage. The second book, *The Best Bad Thing*, finds Rinko on summer vacation with a widow, Mrs. Halta. The events that occur during that summer—both the bad and the positive things—make Rinko feel that her summer was indeed the "best bad thing" that ever happened to her. *The Happiest Ending,* which completes the trilogy, shows the conflict that can arise when there are differences in values between the traditional Japanese culture and the Japanese American culture. Uchida recounts the story with sensitivity, helping the reader to understand and appreciate the cultural conflict that may exist for people of Japanese heritage.

Allen Say tells the story of his first Christmas in *Tree of Cranes,* a beautifully illustrated selection set in Japan. The book brings the traditions of the Japanese and Americans together as Mama, a native Californian of Japanese descent, shares with her son the tradition of the decorated Christmas tree. In this story, Say fondly remembers her explanation that the day of peace and love is symbolized by that tree. He also remembers, with excitement, the samurai kite that he received.

Vietnamese, Laotian, and Cambodian Literature

The children in our program, except for those of Vietnamese background, had little knowledge or appreciation of the Vietnamese culture. Jeanne Lee's *Ba-Nam* is based on the author's childhood experiences in South Vietnam. This book gives the reader information about the special Vietnamese Thanh-Minh Day, which honors one's ancestors. The story further describes a young girl and her experiences with the gravekeeper, "an ugly, old woman" whose name is Ba-Nam. This authentic story has a universal theme—outward appearance often belies inner beauty.

A second book, Eva Boholm-Olsson's *Tuan,* is set in northern Vietnam and provides information about daily life in Vietnam, the work of the people, the rice fields, and the festivals. It is also a story of a boy's fight for survival after suffering a bite by a rabid dog. The story line helps children understand the joys and struggles of people who live in countries in which widespread poverty is often a part of their daily existence.

The Brocaded Slipper, by Lynette Vuong, is a volume of five folk tales, rich in cultural details that highlight the fact that "we are each uniquely individual, with rich ethnic identities, yet bound together by a common humanity" (Vuong, 1982, p. xi). Following the tales are explanatory notes from the author and a guide to the pronunciation of Vietnamese names.

A delightful folk tale from the Hmong people of Laos, written for younger children, is *Nine-In-One Grr! Grr!,* by Blia Xiong and Cathy Spagnoli. The forgetful tiger returns from the great god Shao, happily singing the song "Nine-in-one Grr! Grr!" to help her remember that she will have nine cubs each year. Bird feels that there would be too many tigers on earth and tricks Tiger into forgetting her song. Thanks to Bird, Tiger ends up singing, "One-in-Nine, Grr! Grr!" "And that is why, the Hmong people say, we don't have too many tigers on the earth today!" Nancy Hom illustrates the folk tale in a style that recreates the embroidered story cloths that are the Hmong's unique way of recording their history and legends. Due to its repetitive language, this appealing tale about the balance of nature is enjoyed most when read aloud. Children especially enjoy the repetition when it is read chorally.

Another folk tale, Jeanne Lee's *Silent Lotus,* is the story of a beautiful young Cambodian girl, Lotus, who could not hear or speak. Lotus finds a way to express herself, however, through dance—the thousand-year-old tradition of the Cambodian Court Ballet. Lee's vivid watercolors and drawings engage readers in the story. The inspiration for the artwork comes from the decorations on the 12th-century temple at Angkor Wat in Cambodia.

We feel strongly that if children are to learn about the cultural heritage, traditions, and contributions of Asian American people, more literature of quality and authenticity is needed. It is also true that it is through reading, discussing, and responding to the quality of culturally authentic literature that children are able to discover the similarities and differences between Asian and non-Asian Americans, understand the differences within the Asian population, and understand the work that must be done to eliminate existing social inequities.

HISPANIC AMERICAN LITERATURE

Hispanics in the United States comprise a large and diverse population. As they are the fastest growing ethnic group in the country, (Banks, 1991; Nieto, 1992), it would be appropriate if the body of children's literature paralleled this growth. However, consistent with Barrera, Liguori, and Salas (1992), and Shon (1988), we have found that relatively few children's books have been written about Hispanics. Further, when books are published, they often present romantic images or stereotypes that run counter to the traditions and cultural experiences of the Latino population (Nieto, 1992). In fact, very little has changed since Shon (1981) reported that many of the books at that time repeated the same stereotypes and misconceptions that were prevalent in the books of the 1960s and 1970s. These books contained themes about the poverty of Mexicans, a Cuban girl's embarrassment about her background, or exaggerated and/or simplistic discussions of serious problems of Latin America. Today, more than ever, partly because of the rapidly increasing Hispanic population, there is a need to present a range of images that define and highlight the complexity of the Hispanic experiences in the United States.

Before discussing selected literature about Hispanics, it is useful to preface our discussion with a brief explanation of the term Hispanic, which is often a source of confusion. Hispanic is used as an umbrella term to describe Mexican Americans, Puerto Ricans, and Cuban Americans, who comprise the three major Hispanic groups in the United States. Other groups from Central and South America are also referred to as Hispanics, including populations from Nicaragua, El Salvador, Guatemala, Colombia, Guyana, and Ecuador. Although Hispanics may share a past that is influenced significantly by Spain, there are wide ranging historical, racial, cultural, and ethnic differences among them (Banks, 1991; Barrera, Liguori, and Salas (1992); Ramirez-Krodel and Vazquez (1987).

Hispanic Traditional Literature

The traditional Hispanic folk literature of Central and South America incorporates pre-Spanish tales of the Aztecs, Maya, and the Incas. Many of the themes are universal and similar to those found in folk tales of other cultures — virtuous living and good works are rewarded while vanity is punished. Others, however, highlight themes about the connection of all life on earth — that is, everything in nature is closely related to the objects around it; each action produces a reaction.

The *Legend of the Food Mountain,* by Harriet Rohmer, is a creation myth from Mexico that has survived over the centuries. It is a tale adapted from the Chimalopopocatl Codice, one of several picture-writing manuscripts recorded by native priests after the Spanish conquest of Mexico. Significantly, many of the symbols used by the illustrator came directly from the old codices. Rohmer states of her adaptation:

> It is a story of origins: how the present human race was created from the bones of the ancestors and how the Gods and Goddesses discovered that corn could feed the people. It is also a drama of the conflict between the civilizing God, Quetzalcoatl, and the warlike rain God, Tlaloc. (p. 24)

Children will learn from the theme, which survives in the Native American cultures of today, that an important aspect of the culture of Mexicans is respect for the earth as the nurturer of food; we must care for the earth if the people and animals are to survive. The book is beautifully illustrated by Graciela Carrillo and has a bilingual Spanish and English text.

Another creation story, adapted by Harriet Rohmer and Mary Anchondo, is *How*

We Came to the Fifth World. This is an original story from ancient Mexico with a bilingual text and illustrations based on the original Indian picture writings. The Aztec gods, who believe that our world has been created four times, became angered because the people are selfish and ignore their gods. According to the Aztec elders, if people learn to live in harmony and peace, the fifth world can be saved.

A magical tale, *The Invisible Hunters,* by Rohmer, is a story from the oral tradition of Nicaragua. Again, Rohmer aptly explains the value of this tale for children of all cultures. The story documents initial contact between the outside world and an indigenous culture. Although this story takes place in the Miskito Indian Village of Ul in northern Nicaragua, it is also a metaphor for what has happened to traditional cultures in many other parts of the world. The authenticity of the story is validated by the author's account of how she came upon the story in fragments as she traveled several times to Nicaragua. Made even more compelling with its vivid contemporary illustrations by Joe Sam, the story is written in both English and Spanish and begs to be read aloud.

Beatrice Vidal's tale, *The Legend of El Dorado,* is a retelling of the Chibcha Indian legend of how the treasure of El Dorado came to be. The legend relates, through vibrant illustrations, a tale of sadness and happiness. After the disappearance of his wife and daughter in the deep waters of Lake Guatavita, the king, El Dorado, becomes despondent. El Dorado and the people, in order to appease the serpent of the sea, create a ceremony in which golden dust and treasures are left for the serpent each year. El Dorado ultimately is reunited with his loved ones in the sea. This legend has been so widely told that it has reportedly driven generations of men into the jungles of the Amazon in search of gold. Vidal offers this thought about the legend:

> Paradoxically, the mysterious El Dorado was indeed found . . . but the Span-iards never knew it. It was found in the enormous amounts of gold that the Indians extracted from the earth and shaped with the most admirable sense of aesthetics. It was found in the beliefs and the sacredness of the Indian's way of life.

Pura Belpre's *The Rainbow-colored Horse* is a Puerto Rican tale about two brothers who cannot solve the problem of the trampled fields. In the story, one brother is tempted to forsake his honesty when there is a possibility that he might marry the princess. However, his honesty prevails. The universal theme is similar to themes found in European, African, and Asian tales. The language, phrases, and Spanish names authentically reflect the culture of the Puerto Rican people.

Hispanic Historical and Contemporary Realistic Fiction

The images of Hispanic Americans in historical and contemporary realistic fiction are often flawed by lack of authenticity and misconceptions and confusion about the Hispanic American experience (Garcia, Hadaway & Beal, 1988; Norton, 1991). As noted earlier, Hispanics have lamented the lack of literature that portrays Hispanic characters, traditions, and customs in a positive light. The following examples of books about the Mexican American experience and the Puerto Rican American experience present accurate, authentic portrayals of these cultures.

The Mexican American Experience.   Carmen Garza's *Family Pictures* is an album of the author's memories as she grew up in Kingsville, Texas, near the Mexican border. This book is notable because of its descriptions of important events in the life of a Mexican American child, the richly detailed images of family life, and its bilingual text. The author invites the reader to a family outing on the Gulf of Mexico, a cakewalk in the center of town, and a visit to her grandparents' home, where the family enjoys many activities together. The description of the healing ritual by the *curandura,* a healer, provides cultural insights about Mexican life experiences. The final picture, for example, takes the readers onto the rooftop, where Garza shares her dream of becoming an artist. Garza (1990) recalls,

> I knew since I was 13 years old that I wanted to be an artist. And all those things that I dreamed of doing as an artist, I'm finally doing now. My mother was the one who inspired me to be an artist. She made up our beds to sleep in and have regular dreams, but she also laid out the bed for our dreams of the future.   (p. 30)

Muriel Stanek's *I Speak English for My Mom* chronicles the experience of Lupe, a school-age child, and her mother, who immigrated to the United States after the death of Lupe's father. The story depicts the warm relationship and strong bond that exists between Lupe, who speaks English, and her mother, as Lupe helps her mother learn the English language. Stanek shares how, with Lupe's help, her mother overcomes her anxiety about enrolling in an English class, which she needs in order to prepare for future employment. The illustrations, especially the Aztec-motif border, enhance the text and provide the reader with the flavor of the culture.

Josey Krumgold's *. . . and Now Miguel,* based on the Chavez family of New Mexico, relates Miguel's strong desire to go with the older family members to herd sheep in the Sangre de Cristo mountains. Through the intercession of San Ysidro, the patron saint of farmers, Miguel works hard to impress his family so that he will be allowed to go with his elders. This story is told in a manner that enhances the appreciation of family traditions and portrays the mutual cooperation that exists within many Mexican American families today.

Tricia Brown's *Hello, Amigos!* is a story about a day in the life of young Frankie Valdez, a Mexican American boy who is celebrating his birthday. The story is notable for its portrayal of a child who speaks two languages, lives in two cultures, and seems to be content and happy with his life. Large black and white photographs by Ortiz relay Frankie's excitement and vitality as he prepares for and enjoys this special day. Frankie's birthday, in this selection, inspires students to reflect on their own birthday celebrations.

In *A Birthday Basket for Tia,* Pat Mora, drawing on her personal experiences, highlights the warm relationship that exists between Cecilia, a young Mexican American child, and her great-aunt, Tia. As Cecilia plans for Tia's 90th birthday, she has a grand time with her cat, Chica, recalling special activities that she has shared with her great-aunt. This delightful book authentically shares a slice of Mexican American family life. Students will be able to draw parallels between the birthday celebration for Tia and the party for Frankie Valdez in *Hello Amigos!*

Another appealing selection that portrays the richness of the Hispanic heritage is *Abuela,* by Arthur Dorros. The story details the imaginings of Rosalba, a young Hispanic girl, as she visits the park with her abuela. Rosalba imagines that she and Abuela are flying over city streets, factories, trains, and airports to unfamiliar and familiar places. They return to the park energized after their spirited journey. The Spanish words and phrases throughout the text, and the vibrant collage illustrations provide cultural grounding for the delightful story.

Diego, by Jonah Winter and illustrated by Jeanette Winter, is the true story of Mexican-born Diego Rivera. The story describes Diego's early days as a sick child and the help he received as the Indian Antonio nursed him to health. The book recounts Diego's passion for real life, his devotion to helping poor people, and his desire to make his art public. His art form is entirely Mexican, and each vibrant illustration is delicately framed. These illustrations help the reader appreciate Diego's passion and commitment to his painting and his people.

The Puerto Rican Experience.   The setting for Nicholasa Mohr's *Felita* contrasts with . . . *And Now Miguel.* This authentic story is about a Puerto Rican girl, Felita, who grows up in a Puerto Rican neighborhood in New York City. Felita is forced to move when her father decides that she will have more opportunities in a neighborhood with "better" schools and no gangs. Felita experiences ugly name-calling and abusive acts from European American children, who tell her to move away. Felita and her family are ultimately forced to move back to the old neighborhood, where Felita regains her self-esteem. Mohr's book raises issues of racism and helps the reader realize the inner strength that children of diverse cultures often need.

Interestingly, in Mohr's *Going Home* a conflict from within the culture provides other experiences for Felita. When she revisits relatives in Puerto Rico, Felita is verbally attacked and not accepted by her own people because she is the gringa (a foreigner, especially of U.S. or English descent). The manner in which Felita resolves this problem provides a lesson for readers of all cultures.

Cruz Martel's *Yagua Days* is an opportunity for children to travel to Puerto Rico along with a young boy who visits there. His experiences are highlighted by "yagua days" — days after rainstorms when children slide down the hills on the yagua leaves.

Lula Delacre's childhood memories kindled her desire to write *Vejigante: Masquerader,* a fictionalized story of the *vejigantes* (devillike masqueraders) in Puerto Rico. Ramon, the main character, fulfills his secret desire to be a *vejigante,* but problems develop when his *vejigante* costume is destroyed. In this warmly touching story, Delacre, with bilingual text and vivid illustrations, captures the rich traditions of a Puerto Rican family and community.

Central and South American Experiences.   Many students have not had an opportunity to read stories about Central and South American children in their age range. Two books can provide this opportunity. Patricia Markun's *The Little Painter of Sabana Grande* is a true story set in the mountains of Panama. Fernando, who makes his own paints from the natural surroundings, is eager to paint during his vacation from school. Because he has no paper, his parents give him permission to paint his adobe house. His creativity attracts the neighbors, who marvel at his work and ask him to paint their houses as well. Students will appreciate Fernando's zestful artistry.

A second book, *Amazon Boy,* written and illustrated by Ted Lewin, details the experiences of Paulo's travels down the Amazon with his father. In his journey, Paulo gets to see the many treasures of the Amazon and learns a valuable lesson about the preservation of these great gifts. Young readers will become aware that environmental protection is not a local issue, but a worldwide one.

Informational Books

Aztec Indians, by Patricia McKissack, a book in the New True Book series (Children's Press, Chicago), highlights the rich culture of the Aztec Indians and its influence on the people of Mexico today. The book also chronicles the arrival of the Spaniards, their influence on the people, and the ultimate survival of some Aztec Indians. The reader learns about the contributions of the Aztec Indians to the arts, sciences, and culture of Mexico.

Two books are noteworthy because they present the social life and customs of contemporary Mexican families. The book *Mexico* a part of the Children of the World series, shares important aspects of a young girl's life in Guadalajara, Mexico. The reader sees, through the young girl, Maria, the diversity of life and the richness of the culture in a city that is both ancient and modern. Connections are sure to be made between the visible remnants of the ancient Aztec culture and the city of Guadalajara as it is today. The book contains colorful photographs and a comprehensive reference section with information about the country's demographics, education, culture, and natural resources.

A Family in Mexico, by Tom Moran, looks at Mexico through the eyes of yet another family. It describes the life and activities of 9-year-old Paula Maria. Paula Maria's father, a businessman who sells art and craft items, traces many of the craft techniques to artisans many, many generations ago. A trip to the rodeo, a Mexican folk dancing celebration, and a graduation celebration are some of the events Paula Maria attends. As in *Mexico,* the pictures are colorful photographs that capture the reader's interest and imagination. Moreover, both of these books help students make connections between the traditions of "old" Mexico and contemporary Mexican American life.

June Behrens's *Fiesta* is a book for young readers that provides information about Cinco de Mayo, a Mexican American holiday that is celebrated on May 5. In simple, descriptive language, the author shares the historical importance of the holiday. It is on this day that the Mexican army won a great victory over the French army. Behrens (p. 12) asserts, "The victory helped to drive foreigners out of North America. No foreign power has invaded North America since."

Kids Explore America's Hispanic Heritage, by Westridge Young Writer's Workshop, is a book written by 82 student authors, grades 3 through 7. The book details the history of Hispanics in America: the people, the food, the festivals, and the activities of daily life of Hispanics in America today. Although the book is factual, it is readable and appealing, with student illustrations and photographs.

The books we have discussed and those included in the bibliography are merely a beginning for providing students with an appreciation of the cultural traditions of the Hispanic people. As mentioned earlier, Hispanic literature makes up a very small part of the body of children's literature in the United States. Along with Barrera, Liguori, and Salas (1992), we recommend that teachers broaden their perceptions of multicultural literature to encompass the oral tradition and language of the Hispanic culture. The poems that are recited, the stories that are told, the chants and rhymes that are recanted during informal times are important stories of a culture, as well. Barrera et al., in addressing this issue, emphasize:

> Sometimes, because literature in the schools has been defined only as (a) written, (b) in English, and (c) commercially-produced, diverse literary expressions and forms not fitting that description have been ignored. Until, and even after, Mexican-American children's literature is more plentiful within U.S. children's literature, the community's oral literature is an important resource for school literature and literacy instruction.   (p. 234)

NATIVE AMERICAN LITERATURE

Native Americans, who are believed to be the original settlers of the United States and Canada, have a rich and historic culture to share. Their values, language, foods, clothing, music, art, and recreation have been talked and written about for many years. According to Mary Byler (cited in Norton, 1991), however,

> There are too many books featuring painted, whooping, befeathered Indians closing in on too many forts, maliciously attacking 'peaceful' settlers or simply leering menacingly from the background, too many books in which white benevolence is the only thing that saves the day for the incompetent childlike Indian, too many stories setting forth what is 'best' for American Indians.   (p. 533)

We are learning to be diligent in our selection and evaluation of Native American literature, exactly because of the points Byler makes. Consequently, we have identified Native American literature of high quality that is free of stereotypes. The books that we have found, however, are primarily traditional folk tales written since the 1970s. These selections are written with sensitivity and frequently reflect the oral tradition of the Native American nations. Realistic fiction offerings, however, as Byler asserts, are few in number and often contain stereotypical information about Native Americans in terms of language, physical features, beliefs, and behavior.

Traditional Native American Folk Literature

It is important to identify the tribal regions from which the Native American tales originate, because children often view Native Americans as a monolithic group who all have the same customs and way of life. Although there are traditional values that are universal to native nations, there are also important customs that are unique to each nation or tribe. We begin this discussion of authentic and recommended literature from the Native American perspective with a return to Virginia Hamilton's *In the Beginning: Creation Stories from Around the World.* Native Americans, like people from all cultures, told tales that attempted to explain the origins of the universe. Hamilton defines the myth from the Maidu Indians of California as an Earth-Diver type, in which a creature dives into water, or back to nature. The myth suggests that by plunging into the water, the old is washed away and the new creation may begin. In this tale Earth Starter is the creator who cleverly, with the help of turtle, dives into the water in search of land and thus forms the land, animals, and people. *The Woman Who Fell from the Sky* is another Earth-Diver myth, with Divine Woman as the creator. Of interest is the important role of the turtle in this creation myth, which originated with the Huron Indians, who came from the St. Lawrence Valley (Hamilton, 1988).

Paul Goble has retold many tales about the feeling of kinship between the Native Americans and animals of the Plains, particularly the buffalo and horse. In *Buffalo Woman,* a young man falls in love with a woman who is of the Buffalo nation and marries her. Because she is not accepted by the hunter's people, she returns to the Buffalo nation. Her husband follows and is transformed into a buffalo. Goble explains:

> The relationship was made between the People and the Buffalo Nation; it will last until the end of time. It will be remembered that a brave young man became a buffalo because he loved his wife and little child. In return the Buffalo People have given their flesh so that little children, and babies still unborn, will always have meat to eat. It is the Creator's wish. . . . Mitakuye oyasis . . . We are all related.

The horse, like the buffalo, is an animal that was extremely important to the Native Americans of the Plains. In *The Gift of the Sacred Dog,* Goble weaves a story of wonder as the horse first appears to the natives of the plains: "This animal is called the sacred Dog. He can do many things your dogs can do and also more."

Horses were brought to North America by the Spanish. They made an enormous change in the life of the tribes of the Great Plains because they were able to carry loads and run faster than the dogs that were used previously. Although there are horses in factual accounts, often the horse is cast in legendary tales that attribute the existence of horses to the generosity of the Great Spirit. Another Goble tale, *The Girl Who Loved Wild Horses,* reinforces Native Americans' respect for animals and their belief that man and animal must live in harmony.

A final tale from the Plains Indians is Tomie dePaola's *The Legend of the Indian Paintbrush.* This book chronicles the life of Little Gopher as he follows his destiny, which comes to him in a Dream Vision. He is told that he will become an artist for his people. He struggles to live up to his destiny, but always seems to fall short. Eventually, however, because of his dedication and perseverance, he is able to bring the colors of the sunset down to earth in the form of the lovely red, orange, and yellow flowers known as the Indian Paintbrush. Other tales, such as dePaola's *The Legend of the Bluebonnet,* have a similar theme.

Native American tales from the western Great Lakes region are characterized by

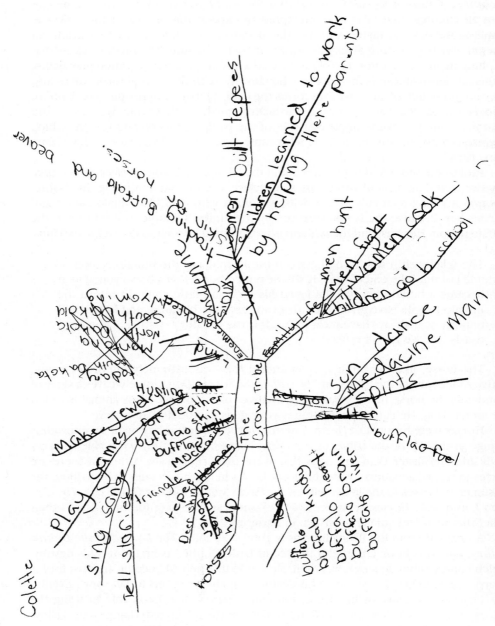

FIGURE 3.5 As students web the information they research about Native American tribes, they begin to see similarities and differences among the tribes more clearly.

the Ojibway tale *Star Maiden,* by Barbara Esbensen. In this beautifully illustrated tale, Star Maiden and her sisters leave their home in the sky and become the beautiful star-shaped water lilies. This tale, which fits into the "setting the world in order" category described by Bierhorst (1976), suggests that the world is created out of or fashioned from the chaos of nature. Other Ojibway tales, found in Sheila Dailey's *The Land of Sky Blue Water,* explain the formation of the Great Lakes.

Two outstanding selections from the Canadian North, particularly Saskatchewan, were orignally written by Cree-speaking students. Freda Ahenakew's *How the Birch Tree Got Its Stripes,* is illustrated by George Littlechild. Whitstone relates, in an uncluttered and dramatic fashion, how Wisahkecahk, who was held by the birch trees against his will, punished them by spanking them with willow branches, leaving marks that birch trees have to this day. A second legend, *How the Mouse Got Brown Teeth,* by Freda Ahenakew, explains how a young Cree boy set a snare in the tree to capture an animal. Instead, he captures the sun, which now cannot provide daylight. After appealing to all the animals of the Plains, the boy finally finds that the mouse can free the sun by chewing through the snare. However, in the process, the mouse burns his teeth; thus the mouse will have brown teeth forever.

Another outstanding legend of the Canadian North is Elizabeth Cleaver's, *The Enchanted Caribou.* This is written as a "threshold tale," defined by Bierhorst (1976) as a tale in which transformations allow characters to go into and out of the animal world. In this tale, Cleaver describes how Tyla was tricked and transformed into a white caribou. A young caribou hunter later rescues Tyla by skill and magic. Cleaver tells of the bond between the Inuit and the white caribou in these words: "And ever since, when hunters meet a white caribou they treat it kindly and do not kill it, for it might be enchanted." This book can be compared to other transformation tales, such as Goble's retelling of Buffalo Woman. Cleaver illustrated her book with pictures of characters that can be used for a shadow theater. She includes instructions for making shadow figures and a theater for this and other stories at the end of the book.

Poetry and Story Poems

The beauty and charm of traditional Native American literature is matched only by the songs, chants, poems, and story poems that are a part of the various tribes. Through *Dancing Teepees,* author Virginia Driving Hawk Sneve shares the oral tradition of the North American Indians and contemporary tribal poets, as well as three of her own poems. The poems begin with a theme of life's cycle from birth to young adulthood. The first poem, for example, describes a man's life cycle:

> The life of a man is a circle from childhood to childhood, and so it is in everything where power moves. Our teepees were round like the nests of the birds, and these were always set in a circle, the nation's hoop, a nest of many nests, where the Great Spirit meant for us to hatch our children.
> (p. 8)   Black Elk, Lakota Sioux

An illustration of "the nation's hoop, a nest of many nests" exemplifies the way the text and illustrations work together throughout the book. Other selections eloquently describe birth, babies, and the events of youth. After listening to these poems, many students are inspired to write their own (See Figure 3.6.)

The works of Byrd Baylor reflect her respect and love for the Native American people of the Southwest. Several of her books are outstanding in their ability to capture the spirit and beauty of Native Americans and the land they inhabit. In *I'm in Charge of Celebrations,* Baylor relates some of the special experiences in the Southwest desert country—for example, "The Time of Falling Stars," in the middle of August, when "every time a streak of light goes shooting through the darkness, I feel my heart shoot out of me." Reading the story aloud helps students to appreciate the poetic, metaphorical language.

When Clay Sings traces the daily life and customs of prehistoric Southwest Native American tribes from the designs on the remains of their pottery. The original work was done by ancient potters of the Anasazi, Mogollon, Hohokam, and Mimbres cultures. Baylor skillfully and artistically bridges two worlds: "When they find a bowl that isn't broken the children can pretend that they've just eaten from it and that they're sitting by some campfire on a deerskin blanket and it's then not now and they speak an older language."

In a second selection, Susan Jeffers illustrates Henry Wadsworth Longfellow's *Song of Hiawatha,* illuminating some of the poem's most lyrical verses as she depicts Hiawatha's boyhood. The illustrations and text are gloriously intertwined so that they become one. The beat and sounds of this poem compel the reader to hear the beat of Native American drums as they echo and re-echo from line to line. This book can be enjoyed for both its visual and auditory experience.

Contemporary Realistic Fiction

Jack Crowder's *Tonibah and the Rainbow* provides a glimpse into a Navajo family's life in the Southwest. He develops the theme of community cooperation and strong family relationships as the family has to rebuild their hogan after a fire. An illustrated alphabet of the language of the Navajo people, a noun glossary, and a bilingual English and Navajo text present an accurate and enlightening depiction of Navajo culture.

Sandra King's *Shannon: An Ojibway Dancer* provides an "insider's" view of the Ojibway people of today. Shannon, a 13 year old, lives in Minneapolis with her grandmother, two sisters, and two cousins. The book describes everyday occurrences in Shannon's life, which are like those of most teenagers, but focuses on her preparation for the powwow, a traditional social event featuring drumming and dancing, through her eyes. Readers learn about the traditions of beadwork, shawl making, and dance. They also gain insight into the powwow and into Shannon's love for dancing. The color photographs add warmth and intimacy.

In a book for older students, Jamake Highwater's *Legend Days,* readers are challenged by the symbolism and tribal customs described in detail. The inner conflicts that Amana experiences are because she is both a warrior and a woman. Highwater carries Amana's story into the present in *The Ceremony of Innocence* and *I Wear the Morning Star,* parts two and three of Highwater's Ghost Horse Cycle.

Issues of bias are raised in Barbara Girion's *Indian Summer,* when a 10-year-old white child, Joni, and her 5-year-old brother spend a summer with an Iroquois family. Both children hold biases toward Native Americans, but the brothers are more bla-

BURNINGEAGLE

I was stalking over a corn field for a mouse, for a rabbit, for food. I saw something with black hair, brown eyes, brown skin. Something shot at me and it was not alive so I soared up and up. All of the sudden my wings started burning. It was the God of the earth. He would not let me out. Then one of those things struck me and I was burning and falling and burning and falling. All of the animals watched like the beaver and my cousins, the birds, and hit the ground. And I have a feeling I was the supper of the animal with black hair, brown eyes, and brown skin.

THEEND

FIGURE 3.6 A poem written by a young author after listening to several Native American folk tales and poems.

tant. The book deals effectively with the issue of how stereotypical images are perpetuated and their negative effect on children's perceptions and understanding of a group of people, in this case the Iroquois.

HAWAIIAN LITERATURE

Hawaiians are a unique group because they are indigenous to one area of the United States. We have found, however, that many students have little knowledge of the rich culture of the people of the Hawaiian Islands. Several books can provide an introduction to the islands and the people.

Hawaii Is a Rainbow, by Stephanie Feeney, is a picture book that introduces early readers to colors, people, places, plants, and animals of Hawaii. It captures the rich variety and beauty of the islands through its colorful photographs by Jeff Reese. When the color word *red* is introduced, four full-page photographs of flowers, dancers, chopsticks, and leis—all highlighted in red—follow. Each color is similarly presented. The final section of the book explains how the book can be shared with children, with detailed information on the island mountains and volcanoes, plants and animals, and people. The book has appeal for people of all ages.

Another exciting informational book is *Kidding Around the Hawaiian Islands: A Young Reader's Guide,* by Sarah Lovett. The book takes the reader on a journey to six of the eight islands in the Hawaiian archipelago. This book is particularly appealing because it can be enjoyed by fourth- and fifth-grade students and middle school students. Highlights of the islands are presented in a lighthearted, sometimes humorous narrative, with lively pictures that entice youngsters to read more. The book is an excellent resource for students engaged in reading and writing activities in the content areas.

Fay Stanley's *The Last Princess: The Story of Princess Ka'iulani of Hawaii* is an illustrated biography that provides readers with historical and political information about Hawaii, as well as interesting facts about the Princess Ka'iulani. The book details the princess's journey to school in London and her years of happiness there. It also covers the period in which missionaries and foreigners from Britain, France, Russia, and the United States sought to influence and in some cases run the government. The princess's struggle to preserve the freedom of her people with dignity is a moving and bittersweet story.

How Maui Slowed the Sun, by Tune Ching, is a delightful and authentic tale that chronicles how Maui, a Polynesian deity, is able to slow the sun's path across the sky through his magical powers. This, of course, is not easy to accomplish, especially when the sun resists. However, Maui prevails, and as a result, "Men have time to catch fish. Farmers have time to plant their crops. Women have time to dry their tapa. And children, like Maui, have time to play."

The Power of the Word

In reading these books, teachers and students will be ever reminded of the power of the word. One student in our program stated, "I never knew that books could just open up your eyes. I see so many new things, now." Another student said, "I get to travel and stuff with these books. Well, it kind of feels like I'm in the book or something." Similarly, teachers say, "These books have changed all our lives." There *is* power in the word. Our hope is that more authentic multicultural books will be published so that students and teachers will continue to have their eyes opened.

In the final section of this chapter we identify books that children in our program select as their favorites and include their comments.

STUDENTS' SELECTIONS

As we worked with students over a three-year period, it became clear that many books were special to them. In an interview in which we asked students several open-ended questions about the multicultural program, we included the question, "What books did you enjoy?" We would like to share these student selections with you (See Figure 3.8). The books have been reviewed or used with strategies in the text. The reasons for their choices are summarized below the books. These responses indicate that characterization was important to the students. If the characters were appealing, the book was appealing, as well. Illustrations were also mentioned frequently. This is noteworthy because the students were primarily third-, fourth-, fifth- and sixth graders. Many question whether students of this age like picture books. Our experiences suggest that they do.

Finally, several of the comments appeared to be the result of instructional em-

FIGURE 3.7   Without hesitation, Stephanie selects one of her favorite books—*Mufaro's Beautiful Daughters,* by John Steptoe.

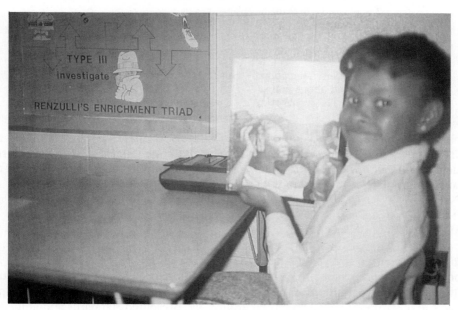

The Black Snowman
- The characters Joseph and Pee Wee
- The way Joseph changed and began to like himself and his family
- The magical snowman coming to life
- Learning about the Kente cloth

Flossie and the Fox
- The character, Flossie; her wit
- The dialect, the way she talked
- The humor, the things she said to outsmart the fox
- The reader's theater activity

Knots on a Counting Rope
- The boy and the Grandfather, the way they talked together
- The author's descriptions of what happened; the blue curtain over his eyes
- Reading the story like a choral reading
- The action in the race
- The illustrations

Mufaro's Beautiful Daughters
- The problems Manyara had to overcome
- The opposite personalities of the two sisters
- The illustrations
- The story line; the way the story was told

Village of Round and Square Houses
- The explosion of the volcano; the excitement
- The decisions of the men and women after the volcano exploded
- The illustrations

Dancing Teepees
- The poems were made by children like us
- The pictures were great
- The book helped us write poems
- The things we learned from the poems

FIGURE 3.8 Student selections of their favorite multicultural books and what they especially liked about them.

phasis. For example, the kente cloth in *The Black Snowman* was researched and discussed in much more depth after reading the book. Similarly, the metaphorical language in *Knots on a Counting Rope* was emphasized by the teacher and used as a launching point for further study of metaphors in other literature selections.

SUMMARY

In this chapter we stressed the need to use multicultural literature in classrooms and presented several perspectives on what type of literature is considered multicultural. After giving our definition of multicultural literature and clarifying why we emphasize the literature of specific cultural groups, we presented standards and guidelines for selecting multicultural literature. We maintained that multicultural literature reflects an underrepresented population in children's literature and therefore must be evaluated for authentic, accurate images of the specific cultural group. We further emphasized that in order for teachers to gain confidence in the selection process, they need to develop the practice of viewing literature from perspectives other than just the European American world view. We then presented nine characteristics of multicultural literature that, when present, ensure that it is culturally authentic, balanced, and unbiased.

In the following sections, we discussed selected literature from the African American, Asian American, Hispanic American, and Native American cultures, using the standards we identified. We further identified specific elements from traditional folk literature, realistic fiction, songs, poetry, and informational selections that illuminate the culture in an authentic and balanced manner. Teachers who select books that have qualities similar to those discussed will provide students of the specific culture a sense of pride and all students an increased knowledge and insight into the culture.

Finally, we presented a few student selections of favorite books, as well as some of the students' reasons for their selections.

REFERENCES

Andrews, W. (1992). The beginnings of African American literature. In *African American literature: Voices in a tradition.* (pp. 133-143). Austin, TX: Holt, Rinehart and Winston.

Aoki, E. (1992). Turning the page: Asian Pacific American children's literature. In V. Harris (Ed.), *Teaching multicultural literature in grades K-8.* (pp. 109-135). Norwood, MA: Christopher-Gordon.

Asian Americans in Children's Books (1976). Council on *Interracial books for children, Bulletin 7.* New York.

Banfield, B. (1985). Racism in children's books: An Afro-American perspective. In D. MacCann & G. Woodard (Eds.), *The Black American in books for children: Readings in racism.* Metuchen, NJ: Scarecrow.

Banks, J. (1991). *Teaching strategies for ethnic studies.* Boston: Allyn and Bacon.

Barrera, R., Liguori, O., & Salas, L. (1992). Ideas a literature can grow on: Key insights for enriching and expanding children's literature about the Mexican American experience. (pp. 203-241). In V. Harris (Ed.), *Teaching multicultural literature in grades K-8.* Norwood, MA: Christopher-Gordon.

Bierhorst, J. (1976). *The red swan: Myths and tales of the American Indians.* New York: Farrar, Straus & Giroux.

Bishop, R. (1992). Multicultural literature for children: Making informed choices. In V. Harris (Ed.), *Teaching multicultural literature in grades K-8.* (pp. 37-53). Norwood, MA: Christopher-Gordon.

Broderick, D. (1973). Image of the black in children's fiction. New York: R. R. Bowker.

Council on interracial books for children (1974). *10 quick ways to analyze children's books for racism and sexism.* New York.

Garcia, J., Hadaway, N., & Beal, G. (1988). Cultural pluralism in recent nonfiction tradebooks for children. *The Social Studies, 79,* 252-255.

Greenfield, E. (1975). Something to shout about. *The Horn Book Magazine, 51,* 624-626.

Hamilton, V. (1985). *The people could fly.* New York: Albert Knopf.

Hamilton, V. (1988). *In the beginning: Creation stories from around the world.* New York: Albert Knopf.

Harris, V. (1991). Multicultural curriculum: African American children's literature. *Young Children, 46,* 37-44.

Harris, V. (1992) (Ed.), *Teaching multicultural literature in grades K-8.* Norwood, MA: Christopher-Gordon.

Holt, Rinehart & Winston (1992). The Oral Tradition. In *African American literature: Voices in a tradition.* (pp. 83-94). Austin, TX: Holt, Rinehart and Winston.

Larrick, N. (1965). The all-white world of children's books. *Saturday Review, 48,* 63-65, 84-85.

Lindgren, M. (1991) (Ed.), *The multicolored mirror: Cultural substance in literature for children and young adults.* Fort Atkinson, WI.

Louie, A. (1982). Yeh-Shen: A Cinderella story from China: New York: Philomel.

Nieto, S. (1992). We have stories to tell: A case study of Puerto Ricans in children's books. In V. Harris (Ed.), *Teaching multicultural literature in grades K-8.* (pp. 171-201). Norwood, MA: Christopher-Gordon.

Norton, D. (1991). *Through the eyes of a child: An introduction to children's literature.* Columbus, OH: Charles Merrill.

Pang, V. (1991). Teaching children about social issues. In C. Sleeter (Ed.), *Empowerment through multicultural education.* (pp. 179-197). Albany: State University of New York Press.

Pang, V., Colvin, C., MyLuong, T., & Barba, R. (1992). Beyond chopsticks and dragons: Selecting Asian-American literature for children. *Reading Teacher, 46,* 216-224.

Rohmer, H. (1982). *The legend of food mountain.* San Francisco: Children's Book Press.

Rudman, M. (1984). *Children's literature: An issues approach* (2nd ed.). New York: Longman, Inc.

Schon, I. (1981). Recent detrimental and distinguished books about Hispanic people and cultures. *Top of the news, 38,* 79-85.

Schon, I. (1988). *A Hispanic heritage, series II and III.* New Jersey: The Scarecrow Press.

Sims, R. (1982). *Shadow and substance.* Urbana, IL: National Council of Teachers of English.

Vazquez, A., & Ramirez-Krodel, A. (1987). *America's Hispanic heritage.* Programs for Equal Opportunity. Ann Arbor: University of Michigan.

chapter 4

Creating Meaning Through Reading Experiences with Multicultural Literature

OVERVIEW

In this chapter we describe aspects of our multicultural program that we have found especially effective in helping students develop communicative competence: the complementary abilities of comprehending meaning through listening and reading and of conveying meaning through talking and writing. By encouraging students to respond to texts in a variety of ways and to articulate their responses, we move beyond such traditional practices as basic sight-word vocabulary, phonics, comprehension skill sheets, and fragmented instruction. During the past four years of working with numerous teachers and students in multicultural settings, we have found that using a variety of multicultural literacy strategies along with multicultural literature is highly effective with students of all ability and grade levels. We have identified specific strategies that enable culturally and linguistically diverse students and at-risk students to become readers and writers.

We provide in this chapter practical strategies for teaching communicative competence, using vignettes and including teachers' real names to illustrate the strategies which were designed and implemented by teachers in grades 1–6. We also share student reading and writing samples. Although fostering communicative competence for students of varying cultural and ability levels remains a challenge, using these strategies opens new avenues for successful learning.

INTRODUCTION

It has been hard for me to move to another country because I do have a difficult time here. When I first came to America, I thought I would live a happy life but I was wrong. Some people would make fun of me just because I am from a different world and it is hard to live like that. Some people would think that I am Chinese just because I look like them. Just think about it. Would you like living your life in a new country with people from different worlds and going to new places? Life here is not like the life I had in the land of my birth and the land of my people.

Vangchai, Grade 5

We were in Vangchai's class the day he wrote about his experiences in a "new country with people from different worlds." Not only do students like Vangchai, whose family is from Laos, have to adjust to a new country with people from different worlds, but many seldom have opportunities to read books reflecting their way of life, cultural heritage, or history. Similarly, culturally and linguistically diverse students who were born in the United States rarely have opportunities to read books about their cultural heritage. Many students, like Carlos in Chapter 1, are asking themselves why the pictures in their books don't resemble them, their families, or their way of life. What hidden message are we giving to these students? Are we saying that their history, traditions, and heritage are not valued and validated?

The mosaic of immigrant students and students from diverse cultures, ethnic groups, and races creates a beautiful, balanced picture when all the parts positively unite to shape the richness of our schools and nation. A curriculum that supports

FIGURE 4.1   A fourth-grader learns to enjoy reading as he shares *Why Mosquitoes Buzz in People's Ears,* by Aardema, with his first-grade friend.

communicative competence must mirror the cultural heritages and traditions of *all* students. All students must feel that their cultural and linguistic roots are affirmed and respected.

As students read, write, listen, and talk about their own culture and the culture of others, perhaps more students will become successful readers and writers who are proud of their roots, traditions, and values. Vangchai later wrote (in his journal published for a Young Authors Conference):

Every time I write about this in my journal, I feel that I am concerned about my past. I had not thought much about it before and now I am concerned. I have learned from writing about my life that the human spirit is stronger than anything and it does not matter how you look, or how healthy, or how strong you are. It is the human spirit that counts. I have learned another thing. It is that dreams can come true if you hope for it and never let go of that dream.

We begin with a description of an environment that fosters cultural pride and the ability to communicate in meaningful ways.

CREATING AN ENVIRONMENT FOR COMMUNICATIVE COMPETENCE

Consistent with Martinez, Cheyney, McBroom, Hemmeter, and Teale (1989), our multicultural program strives to create a variety of literacy experiences for students in the context of a risk-free environment—an emotionally supportive environment that encourages students to explore and experiment with language. We believe all students can become effective communicators; we set high expectations for them. When we accept what our students know about language, learning, and culture, we acknowledge their self-worth (Bishop, 1987). By building on students' cultural background, language systems, and experiences (Cummins, 1986; Florez, Cousin, and Diaz, 1991), we lay a foundation for literacy and provide stepping stones for more complex learning.

By focusing on what students do know and what they are able to do (Martinez et al., 1989), we extinguish feelings of hopelessness, voicelessness, and despair and cultivate an emotionally supportive environment in our program. To broaden this nurturing environment, we organize many of our activities so that students work with partners or in cooperative learning groups. In this way, we avoid categorical programs that require labeling and separation. Rather, we create a community of learners and foster cognitive development of literacy through a social environment. Consistent with Vygotsky (1978), students have opportunities to become proficient learners by engaging in social interactions and experiences with peers and adults of mixed ability levels and varied experiences.

Once students develop more confidence and enthusiasm through these cooperative learning experiences, they also participate in independent reading and writing activities. When students realize that others value and respect their ideas and thoughts, they learn to believe they are readers and writers.

COMPREHENDING MEANING THROUGH LISTENING TO AND READING MULTICULTURAL STORIES

Consistent with whole language theory, our program includes a balance of aesthetic and efferent experiences with multicultural literature. Aesthetic literature is used for its emotional appeal through its colorful words, images, lyrical language, or emotions, and efferent literature is used for acquiring skills or information (Rosenblatt, 1985). As explained previously, whole language principles guide our instructional approach to learning; multicultural literature serves as a framework for many of our learning activities. The two major types of listening and reading experiences we offer in our program are (1) multicultural stories read aloud by the teacher and (2) multicultural stories read by students independently, with partners, or in small groups.

Sharing multicultural stories is an important way to help students enjoy literature and learn to appreciate their own culture and the culture of others (Bishop, 1987; Hadaway & Florez, 1990; Moore & Diamond, 1992). Using multicultural literature can also serve: (1) as a mirror which reflects and validates familiar cultures and experiences of students from culturally and linguistically diverse backgrounds and (2) as a window which reveals similarities and differences between one's own culture and the culture of others (Cox and Galda, 1990).

Rosen, Hoffman, and Farest (1990) advocate that all students—whether at-risk or enriched—need to experience a literacy environment that includes sharing and discussing quality literature and opportunities to respond to the literature. Reading multicultural stories aloud accomplishes these goals. Too often, however, teachers think they should stop reading aloud—particularly picture books—to their students once they begin to read independently. Hoskisson and Tompkins (1991) and Huck (1979), however, emphasize that reading aloud should be an important component of the language arts program at all grade levels. When adults read stories aloud, they bring the magic, the excitement, the drama, and the beauty of the stories to students; they awaken students' desire to read for themselves. As learners of all ages listen to their teachers read stories aloud, they perceive the connection between reading and meaning and learn to interpret the language of books. Through discussions about literature, they further learn to produce and use the language of books, which differs from day-to-day conversational language.

As teachers share multicultural stories with their students, we notice that students become more interested in books and reading. Encountering characters, settings, and themes that resonate with students' own cultural backgrounds improves their self-esteem and pride in their cultural heritage (Bishop, 1987; Hadaway & Florez, 1990; Norton, 1991) and enhances comprehension skills (Lipson, 1983; Moore & Diamond, 1991, 1992; Peregoy & Boyle, 1993). This pleasurable shared experience further motivates all students to read and reread stories independently during Sustained Silent Reading (SSR), when students and teachers choose something to read silently without interruption for a specified period or during their free time. Teachers consistently comment that students no longer feel that these books are only for younger students. Because their teachers are reading these stories aloud to their class, students begin to feel comfortable reading and rereading these stories independently. They gradually, naturally, and without pressure, become readers who *want* to read.

Similar to many educators (Cazden, 1981; Dickinson, 1989; Durkin, 1980; Fields, Spangler, & Lee, 1991; Holdaway, 1979; Hoskisson & Tompkins, 1991; Martinez et al., 1989; Morrow, 1982; Trelease, 1985, 1989; Wells, 1986), we discovered that reading aloud provides many benefits to all students. These include:

- Stimulating interest in books and reading
- Improving attitudes toward reading and writing
- Broadening interests and background experiences
- Establishing an understanding about the way ideas are communicated through print
- Extending knowledge about the form and structure of written language
- Increasing understanding of the functions and uses of written language
- Expanding language acquisition and ability
- Expanding vocabulary and sentence patterns
- Introducing students to different poetry, genres of literature, and story grammar
- Allowing opportunities to listen to literature too difficult to read
- Modeling good expression and the enjoyment of reading
- Improving reading comprehension and writing performance

Strategies to Follow When Reading Aloud

Although many teachers realize the importance of reading aloud to their students, sustaining interest and maintaining reading comprehension can be challenging. Many times students daydream, doodle, or complete other assignments while their teachers are reading aloud. We have, therefore, identified three key stylistic elements of reading aloud that seem to minimize these wanderings: (1) interactive reading and questioning techniques as the story is being read aloud; (2) student participation in the reading of the text as they respond to teachers' questions, predict words using context clues, and chime in during repetitive phrases or rhyming sequences; and (3) student prediction of coming text. Having students move to a carpeted area and gather around the teacher is also highly effective—even with students in the upper elementary grades. By using this warm, interactive approach to reading and by keeping the listening period within the limits of the students' attention span, we find that students are more actively engaged in the listening process, and comprehension is enhanced.

Once the story is read aloud, reflective discussions about the story's content and cultural context follow. Follow-up activities related to the book's theme extend interpretation and understanding of the story. We find that using multiple activities to enhance comprehension and understanding of stories enables students to improve their performance on standardized tests of reading comprehension (Moore & Diamond, 1991, 1992). In the following sections, we will describe this process of reading aloud through several vignettes.

Using the Directed Reading Listening Thinking Activity with the Story *Mufaro's Beautiful Daughters*

The Directed Reading Thinking Activity (DRTA), a procedure developed by Russell Stauffer (1975), can easily be adapted for reading aloud to students as the Directed Reading-Listening-Thinking Activity (DRLTA). As teachers read the story aloud, students listen, making predictions about the story. While continuing to listen to the story, students make new predictions, confirming and rejecting their earlier predictions.

Extending Meaning through the DRLTA.   The sequential steps (adapted from Hoskisson & Tompkins, 1991) are illustrated with the African folk tale *Mufaro's Beautiful Daughters,* by John Steptoe. This beautifully illustrated folk tale is about Mufaro and his two beautiful daughters. When the king announces that he wishes to choose the most beautiful and worthy young girl in the land for his wife, Mufaro and his daughters decide to travel to Zimbabwe in hopes one will be chosen as the bride.

Step 1. Predicting.   After building background experiences about Africa, Mrs. Livisay shows students the book's cover and title page and allows them to share their reactions and feelings about the illustrations. She also encourages students to make predictions about the story by asking questions. Typical questions might include:

- What do you think *Mufaro's Beautiful Daughters* might be about?
- Where do you think this story might take place?
- What do you think might happen in this story?
- What clues do the pictures and the title give you about what might happen in the story?

Throughout, Mrs. Livisay remembers to accept multiple answers to questions, being careful not to stop when correct responses are given. All responses are valued.

Step 2. Reasoning and Predicting from Succeeding Pages.   After students make these early predictions about the story, Mrs. Livisay begins to read part of the story, using a conversational tone and speaking slowly and distinctly. She periodically pauses to ask new questions. For example, after reading the first three pages, she might ask:

- Where does the story take place?
- Who are the main characters in the story?
- What words would you use to describe the daughter, Manyara? Nyasha? Why?
- What do you think might happen in the story now?

Students confirm or reject their previous predictions as they respond to these questions.

Continuing to read the next three pages, she stops at the point that the messenger from the city arrives, asking students to predict what the message might be. As she proceeds reading the next few pages, she asks:

- What will Manyara do when the boy asks her to give him something to eat? When the trees laugh at her?
- What will Nyasha do when she meets the boy, the old woman, the trees?
- What will Nyasha do when her sister begs her not to go to the king? What do you suppose will happen when she meets the king?
- Why do you suppose her friend the little garden snake was at the great chief's stool?

Step 3. Proving.   Throughout, as students confirm or reject their predictions, Mrs. Livisay probes, encouraging students to support their predictions by answering questions such as the following:

- Why do you think so?
- How do you know?
- What clues in the story/pictures support your prediction?
- What clues in other folk tales support your prediction?

In this way, she helps students learn strategies for making their predictions.

The DRLTA is particularly effective with books that are highly suspenseful and include a well-formed plot and striking characters. Moreover, the strategy provides opportunities to engage students actively. Teachers comment that their students become more attentive, more involved, and more interested in the story when they read interactively. They report, "I've never seen my students so motivated and involved in the story!" or "I think my students understand the story and its meaning when I use the DRLTA."

Teachers further observe that when students see themselves reflected in books, their participation in class discussions increases. Mrs. Britton, for example, remarked that her Vietnamese student, Chen Lei, who had never said a word in class, raised her hand for the first time while Mrs. Britton was reading the Vietnamese story *Ba-Nam*, by Jeanne Lee. After seeing that her peers were intrigued by the additional information she shared about her culture, Chen Lei blossomed, becoming an active participant in class activities and discussions. Needless to say, *Ba-Nam* became a book she read and reread during her free time.

Simultaneously, students are learning to take risks and develop thinking strategies as they participate in the DRLTA. All responses are accepted by our teachers. By asking students "Why do you think so?" or "How do you know?" we further help them learn to base their decisions on clues from the text. Many teachers observe that some of their reluctant readers gain recognition and respect from their peers because of their clever thinking. As they encounter these positive experiences, these reluctant readers also become more interested in rereading these stories during their free time or Sustained Silent Reading.

Extending Meaning through Cultural Activities.   Having read *Mufaro's Beautiful Daughters* aloud in this way, Mrs. Livisay revisits the story on subsequent days, highlighting the cultural elements of the story. Questions Mrs. Livisay might ask include:

- Where is Zimbabwe located? Can you locate it on a map?
- What clues do the pictures give you about the flora and fauna of this African country? About the city, Great Zimbabwe?
- What kinds of food do the people in Zimbabwe eat? How are these similar to the foods we eat today?
- How do people travel in Zimbabwe?
- How are the people in Zimbabwe similar to you? Different from you?

Emphasizing these features of the African culture helps her African American students discover more about their heritage. Mrs. Livisay reports this was the first time that some of her African American students had heard about the positive aspects of their culture and heritage; this was the first time they were able to make connections between their present life and the lives of their ancestors. Through these discussions, she adds, her African American students began to form more positive images about themselves.

Extending the Meaning through Writing Activities.   After listening to and discussing the story in these ways, teachers further foster the connection between reading and meaning through writing activities. For example, having the students create a web of words that describe each sister, Manyara and Nyasha, heightens understanding of characters. The web of Manyara, created by Mrs. Baran's class, is displayed in Figure 4.2. Although Mrs. Baran's class was a heterogeneous group, not

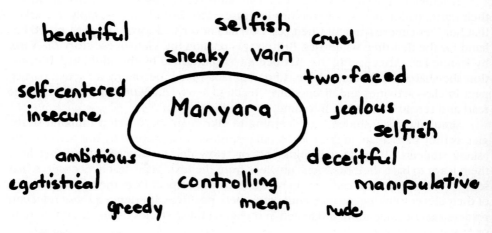

FIGURE 4.2 Webbing of words describing Manyara.

only high-ability students, one can see that the students chose sophisticated words to describe the two sisters. A friendly sort of competition to suggest a "bigger or better" word emerged as she recorded all words on the board. Many students also learned the meanings of some words unfamiliar to them. When a student shared an unusual word such as "inconsiderate," for example, Mrs. Baran asked the student to "tell us about the word *inconsiderate.*" Listening to a peer share the meaning of a word seemed to spark interest in learning new vocabulary among the others.

Once the webs were completed, Mrs. Baran's students further extended their understanding of the two characters by using the words in their webs to create "I AM" poems. The "I AM" poem is an example of a formula poem in which students choose a character and select words to describe the character from that character's point of view. The completed "I AM" poems below demonstrate students' understanding about the two sisters.

I AM

I am sweet, kind, and smart
I like to pick flowers, sing, and feed my garden.
My family and my garden are important to me.
I am good at planting flowers and singing.
I am not good at being cruel and mean and selfish.
I love flowers and songs and my garden.
I don't like it when my sister teases me and I don't like to tease her back.
This is me!
I am
Nyasha.

Mohamed, Grade 4

I AM

I am nice, beautiful, sweet and kind.
I like working in my garden.
My family and Nyoka are important to me.
I am good at being kind and polite.
I am not good at being cruel and greedy
I love my father and sister.
I don't like it when Manyara teases me
This is me I am Nyasha!

Kate, Grade 4

I AM

I am ugly, selfish and cruel.
I like my family and friends.
I am good at being mean and grouchy.
I am not good at being nice and respectful.
I love to eat.
I don't like small boys
This is me. I am! Manyara

Jack, Grade 4

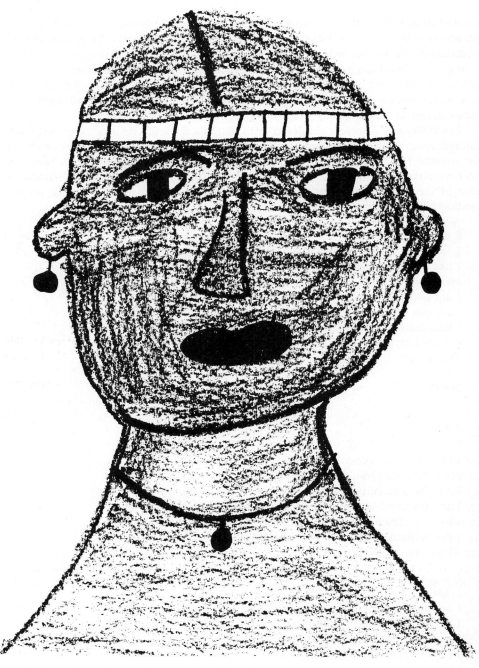

FIGURE 4.3 Students enjoy illustrating their I AM Poems.

As Mrs. Baran's students worked on their poems with partners, she discovered that some of her students began to talk about the characters' qualities and how the characters perceive themselves. Spontaneous opportunities for thinking and problem solving evolve naturally within such a social context. Mrs. Baran further observed that having the character webs displayed on the chalkboard encouraged her students to select interesting, sophisticated words to use in their own poems and eliminated their fear of misspelled words.

Interestingly, Demetrius asked if he could write a poem about the prince instead of Manyara or Nyasha. Without hesitation, Mrs. Baran encouraged him to try writing a poem about the prince. Once Demetrius finished his poem (which follows), Mrs. Baran encouraged him to share it with the whole class. After hearing his poem, two other boys decided to write one about the prince. Participating in this writing activity about Africans instilled a renewed pride in the boys' cultural heritage.

I AM
I am nice, helpful, and caring
I like my friends
My family and friends are important to me.
I am good at being king
I am not good at being mean
I love my mother
I don't like people who are mean
This is me. I am King Demetrius!

Demetrius, Grade 4

Using Story Grammar as a Read-Aloud Technique for *The Legend of Scarface*

Just as the DRLTA technique is an effective strategy to use with predictable stories, we find that using story grammar (story elements such as characters, setting, goals or problems, actions or events, and resolutions) is an alternative strategy for interactive reading. After building background knowledge about the Native Americans, one can introduce the story *The Legend of Scarface*, by Robert San Souci, a legend about a Blackfeet Native American whose kindness, persistence, honesty, and courage lead him to the Sun Lodge to release a maiden, Singing Rains, from her sacred oath. Similar to the DRLTA, the Story Grammar Reading-Thinking Activity (SGRTA) is interactive, as the teacher reads, pauses to ask questions, and continues to read.

For example, after reading the first page, Mrs. Weeks asks:

- Who is the main character of this story?
- Where is the story taking place?

After reading the next three pages, she pauses again, asking:

- Who is another main character of this story?
- What do we know about Singing Rains?

- What new things do we know about Scarface?
- What might the problem or goal in this story be?

As she reads the next few pages, students confirm or reject their predictions about Scarface's goal to reach the sun to ask him to release Singing Rains from her sacred oath. Students then begin to list the actions Scarface takes to reach the sun. To help students perceive these actions, Mrs. Weeks asks them to think about the series of actions that lead Scarface to his goal. She guides this thought process by asking the following sequential questions:

- Who are "those along the way who can guide me"?
- Why do the animals agree to help Scarface?
- How does Scarface manage to cross the great expanse of water?
- What do you think Scarface will do when he sees the quiver? Why do you think so?
- Why does Morning Star agree to help Scarface?
- Why doesn't Scarface tell the Moon the reason he came to the Lodge of the Sun? Why doesn't he tell the Sun?
- What do you think might happen as Morning Star and Scarface wander through the forest? Why?
- What will Scarface do when he sees the savage birds attack Morning Star? How do you know?
- How will the Sun show his appreciation to Scarface for saving his son?
- What do you think the resolution of the story might be? Why?
- How will Singing Rains know the sign of the Sun's will?

Reading aloud in this way helps children become familiar with the elements of story grammar and how these elements combine to form meaning. Initially, teachers ask the questions to help students figure out the author's message. Eventually, students begin to internalize these questions, using the questions to help them understand new stories and to comprehend the author's message in other stories.

Internalizing the Structure of Stories through Story Mapping.   To enable students to further internalize the structure of stories, we use story maps, similar to those displayed in Figure 4.4. Mrs. Briggs prefers to do the first story map as a class, using the overhead projector. After reading *The Legend of Scarface* by Robert San Souci aloud to her students, Mrs. Briggs makes a transparency of a story map. As students share and discuss the setting, the characters, or the goal or problem, for example, she records the information on the transparency. Once students are comfortable with the story map, she has them work as partners, interviewing one another. First, one partner interviews his teammate, asking him who the characters are and the time and place of the setting. As the partner shares the information, the teammate records the responses on the story map. The partners then switch roles—the interviewee becomes interviewer and vice-versa—and continue to work on the story map. When the story maps are complete, Mrs. Briggs has them share their

MY STORY MAP

NAME _____ DATE _____

Setting		
Characters: _____	Time: _____	Place: _____
_____	_____	_____
_____	_____	_____
_____	_____	_____

↓

The Problem _____
_____
_____
_____

↑

Action _____
_____
_____
↔
_____
_____
_____
_____
_____
_____
_____

↓

Resolution/Outcome _____
_____
_____

FIGURE 4.4 An example of a story map.

responses as a class, to clarify any misconceptions or misunderstandings. Mrs. Briggs comments that not only are all her students involved and engaged in the experience, they are also learning how to write their own stories. She observes that story maps can further be used to help students organize their ideas for writing their own stories. Mrs. Briggs is careful not to overuse story maps, realizing that overuse might detract from the meaning of the story. Students, moreover, need varied experiences in order to become successful and motivated readers and writers.

Highlighting Cultural Elements of Stories.   Just as teachers revisit the stories on subsequent days when using the DRLTA strategy, teachers share *The Legend of Scarface* a second time, highlighting the cultural elements of the story. Mrs. Briggs, a fifth-grade teacher, uses the following questions to stimulate ideas about the Blackfeet:

- Where do the Blackfeet Native Americans live? Can you locate it on a map?
- What clues do the illustrations and the text give you about the natural surroundings in this region of the United States?
- What kinds of food do the Blackfeet eat? What do you know about their clothing? What are their homes like?
- Why do you think Scarface was kind to the animals?
- What does it mean to live in harmony with nature?
- What do you know about the Blackfeet beliefs and values?
- What are some words we might use to describe Scarface? Do these words tell us more about the Blackfeet?
- How are the Blackfeet similar to you? Different from you?

After discussing these ideas with her students, Mrs. Briggs distributes a Cultural Web (see Figure 4.5) for students to complete on the Blackfeet. Working in groups of three or four students, students discuss the cultural features of the Blackfoot. As their discussion continues, someone records descriptive words around each topic heading. Once the webs are finished, each group shares one descriptive word they have chosen for each topic. Group members then add any new ideas shared by their peers to their webs.

Pooling the ideas from all the groups, Mrs. Briggs then creates a large Cultural Web, which she displays for all to see. Additional information is recorded on the chart as more stories and resources are used. To enable her students to visualize the cultural lifestyle of the Blackfeet, Mrs. Briggs also has students illustrate the large Cultural Web. Through writing, thinking, illustrating, and talking about more Native American legends, her students can similarly broaden their knowledge of other Native American nations and perceive the differences and similarities among the nations.

Inviting Guests to Share Stories

Trelease (1989) emphasizes a need to invite guests to our classrooms to share favorite literature. Inviting guests from various cultures to share their favorite literature provides an important role model for students. Mrs. Hueter, for example, invited her principal, Mrs. Baker, to her class to share some of her favorite African American

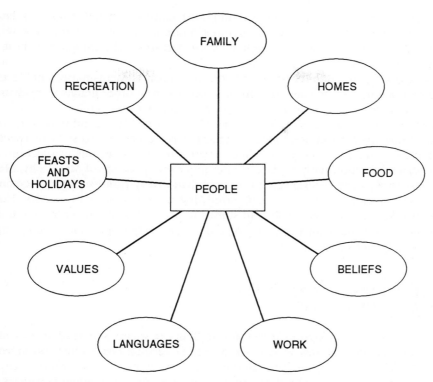

FIGURE 4.5   Students Complete a Cultural Web to Learn More about the Blackfeet.

poems. Mrs. Hueter's class was spellbound as they listened to Mrs. Baker recite these poems from memory. Using a Southern African American dialect, Mrs. Baker captured the voice of the poets. Spontaneously, the class begged her to recite the poems again. After listening to Mrs. Baker, Mrs. Hueter's students began to appreciate the dialogue between the grandmother and her granddaughter in *Patchwork Quilt* when it was read the next day.

Similarly, before working on the choral reading of *Cornrows*, by Camille Yarbrough, Mr. Bauer invited his principal, Mrs. Smith, to read this story aloud with his class. Not only did she read the story using the authentic dialect, but Mrs. Smith shared additional information about the history and traditions of the African American culture with his students. When his class performed the choral reading of *Cornrows* (see section on choral reading in this chapter), he noticed that his students began to reflect the African American dialect in their choral readings. An appreciation and interest in dialects emerged for these students through these positive encounters with language and culture.

Other teachers also enjoyed inviting parents or community members to their classes to read favorite folk tales, poems, or stories from their culture. When Mrs. Livisay asked two of her Chinese parents to visit her class (she invited two parents because they had just immigrated to America and did not yet feel fluent in the English language), the parents came dressed in traditional clothing, shared artifacts and foods of their culture, and brought slides, pictures, and photographs. What a celebration! Her students were particularly intrigued by the pictures and photographs about the Chinese New Year.

Mrs. Holly uses a different strategy: She encourages students to present literature to other students. Periodically, she invites students from other grades to read to her class. Her favorite activity, however, is to encourage her own students to select and prepare a favorite story to read to a younger class. During the second semester, one of her students, Megan, volunteered to read her favorite multicultural story to a second-grade class. After she rehearsed proper expression, voice pauses, projection, and appropriate inflection with her peers, and under the guidance of Mrs. Holly, Megan read her story to the second-grade class. She had a very positive experience and is eager to read more stories to them. After Megan's success, many of Mrs. Holly's students asked if they could also read stories to other classes. After rehearsing their stories for several days, all students—regardless of ability level—successfully shared stories with other classes.

DEVELOPING MEANING WITH MULTICULTURAL NOVELS

Providing a variety of opportunities for students to share and read stories aloud heightens students' interest in reading, and their reading comprehension increases (Shanklin & Rhodes, 1989). Through questioning strategies and appropriate expression while reading stories aloud, the teacher models effective reading behaviors that students can begin to internalize as they read independently and as they read longer books and novels. Helping students apply these reading and questioning strategies with novels is critical if they are to successfully make the transition from shorter stories to novels. The following section provides strategies teachers are using to assist young readers as they make this transition from folk tales to novels.

Using Story Grammar Frames with Novels

Just as the SGRTA reinforces comprehension of folk tales and fictional stories, story grammar frames provide an excellent means for teaching plot development in novels. Specifically, through the use of a story grammar frame, students can begin to relate the action of each chapter to the novel's overall structure (Kinney & Schmidt, 1988).

Once students are comfortable with the concept of story grammar in reading folk tales or fictional stories, Kinney and Schmidt suggest that students can easily apply these concepts to novels. To help his students make the transition from shorter stories to novels, Mr. Bauer adapted Kinney and Schmidt's use of story grammar frames with the novel *Sadako and the Thousand Paper Cranes,* by Eleanor Coerr, a moving story about a young girl who had leukemia as a result of radiation from the atom bomb dropped on Hiroshima.

Using large wall chart paper and a marker, he listed the parts of the story grammar—setting, time, characters, problems/goals, events, and reactions—along the vertical axis of the paper. Working in pairs, the students then predicted what the setting, time, characters, problems/goals, events, and reactions might be by looking at the cover of the book. They recorded these predictions on their paper during the next seven or eight minutes. Mr. Bauer then regrouped the students as a total class and asked each group to share their predictions. He recorded their ideas on the chart paper in pencil. By simultaneously interjecting information about the Japanese culture as it related to the discussion, Mr. Bauer helped his students develop their background knowledge for the story.

Seeing their predictions on the chart motivated students to begin reading the story to verify them, even before Mr. Bauer asked them to begin reading. After reading the chapter, they discussed the story and responded to Mr. Bauer's questions, which further emphasized the parts of the story grammar. These responses were recorded with a marker over the pencil predictions.

The next day, the chart served as a review component and a way to build background knowledge before reading new chapters. Referring to the chart, Mr. Bauer asked specific questions that focused on the story elements and the features of the Japanese culture. Next he asked them to work with their partner again, using these same story grammar parts to predict what would happen in the next two chapters—who the characters might be, where the action would take place, or how the problem might be solved. After Mr. Bauer recorded these predictions on the chart in pencil, students began reading the second and third chapters. While discussing the two chapters, they confirmed or rejected their predictions on the chart.

As Mr. Bauer continued this review, prediction, and summarization sequence with subsequent chapters, his students began to see how chapters were interrelated. For example, students realized that Chizuko's golden crane (chapter 5), an *attempt* to find a cure for Sadako's illness, became a *goal* for Sadako—a goal to fold one thousand paper cranes—in chapters 6 and 7.

Once the students finished reading *Sadako and the Thousand Paper Cranes,* Mr. Bauer encouraged them to view the chart holistically. While examining the chart, students quickly discovered a pattern: Chapters 1 and 2 introduced the characters and the setting; chapters 3 and 4 exposed the problem of Sadako's illness; chapters 5, 6, 7, and 8 focused on attempts to find a cure for Sadako's illness; and chapter 9 disclosed the resolution of Sadako's illness and the reactions of Sadako and the main characters to her imminent death.

Mr. Bauer was impressed with his students' understanding of plot development in a novel after using story grammar frames in this way. He observes that students are quick to perceive that authors must first introduce the characters and the setting before presenting a problem or a goal. Once the characters and setting prepare the groundwork for these story elements, students realize that actions can evolve and attempts to solve the problem or accomplish a goal can emerge naturally.

The story frame also helps students as they discuss the story and its themes about death, illness, and the horrors of war. As students read the story, suffering and exulting as Sadako learns how to cope with her illness and death, they begin to perceive new ways to view these experiences within their own lives.

Mr. Bauer says he further believes that fiction can inspire children to ask why our ancestors behaved in certain ways. After exploring the ideas surrounding the horrors of war, Mr. Bauer and his students began to seek new solutions to problems in our society. He hopes his students will be able to avoid the mistakes of our past.

Building Comprehension through Opinion/Proof Charts

To help her students begin to read critically and creatively, Mrs. Streeter often uses Opinion/Proof Charts (Santa, Dailey, & Nelson, 1985) with novels. She models the approach with the class first by drawing a line down the center of an overhead transparency and labeling the left side Opinion, and the right side Proof (See Figure 4.6). After her students read the first chapter of *Sadako and the Thousand Paper Cranes,* for example, she asks them to share an opinion they might have about one of the characters. When Mike proposes that Sadako is always in a rush, Mrs. Streeter records this statement on the left side of the transparency. Then she asks her students to come up with sentences to prove this statement. Hands quickly fly up as students share the page number of their sentence and read it aloud to the group: Akiba refers to page 10, "Rushing like a whirlwind into the kitchen Sadako cried . . ."; Jared chooses page 13, "When she jumped up, Sadako almost knocked the table over . . ."; and Kirk selects page 9, "One morning in August 1954 Sadako ran outside into the street as soon as she was dressed." As students read their proofs aloud, Mrs. Streeter writes the page numbers and the main word that proves that Mike's opinion is correct on the right side of the transparency.

FIGURE 4.6 Opinion/Proof Charts Improve Students' Inferential Skills.

SADAKO AND THE THOUSAND PAPER CRANES	
OPINION	PROOF

Similarly, Julie shares her opinion that Sadako and her family respect their ancestors. To support her opinion, Sean refers to page 11, "But I do respect Oba chan . . . I
pray for her spirit every morning . . ."; Terrence reads on page 11, "He prayed that
the spirits of their ancestors were happy and peaceful."

Once her students are comfortable with the Opinion/Proof Chart, she has them
work in cooperative groups, recording their opinions on the left side of an Opin-
ion/Proof Chart for different chapters. These charts are then exchanged with other
groups, who are to find the proof for each opinion. Working in groups, students find
sentences to prove the opinion and then record the page number and the important
words on the right side of the chart. Once the chart is completed, it is returned to the
original group for corroboration.

As her students continue to provide their opinions and proofs about various
characters or the actions of characters, Mrs. Streeter soon realizes that their understanding of the story is heightened. She also finds that the Opinion/Proof Chart
becomes a catalyst for more discussion about life experiences, cultural traditions, and
cultural heritage.

Responding to Meaning through
Reading Response Journals

Mrs. Streeter also has her students keep reading response journals when reading
longer novels. While she reads a chapter to her students from *Search for Delicious,*
by Natalie Babbitt, an adventurous story about a king's search for the meaning of the
word *delicious,* the students illustrate the characters by listening to the author's
descriptions. As they listen to the descriptions about the character in subsequent
chapters, many students add new details to their drawings. (See Figure 4.7.)

To help her students keep track of each character, she has them keep a chart on
which they record the name of each character as he or she appears in the story, their
age, their home, and their choice for "delicious." On other days, Mrs. Streeter has
them respond to questions that relate to story elements in their journal. For example,
one day she might have them write the name of their favorite characters and why
they like these characters; another day she might have them describe their favorite
part of the story, explaining why this is their favorite part; still another day, she might
have them focus on a specific character—for example, Gaylen—and have them
describe Gaylen in their journal. As her students continue working in their journals,
Mrs. Streeter always provides time for her students to share their journal entries with
the class. She has found that their entries become more elaborate because their
audience becomes their peers rather than merely their teacher.

DEVELOPING MEANING, FLUENCY,
AND AUTOMATICITY WITH CHORAL
READINGS AND READER'S THEATER

Students who read in an environment that supports oral reading become fluent
readers (Vacca, Vacca, & Gove, 1991) who view reading as communication, sharing
language and ideas, and entertaining or informing (May, 1990). Fluency and compre-

FIGURE 4.7   Kevin illustrates a Woldweller in his journal.

hension are important goals for all readers. According to Anderson, Hiebert, Scott, and Wilkinson, (1985), Allington (1983), and Dowhower (1989), emphasis on fluency is frequently a "missing ingredient" in classroom reading instruction. In her extensive review of the literature, Dowhower (1989) illustrates the use of repeated reading procedures to gain speed and accuracy, foster better phrasing and expression, and enhance recall and comprehension for readers of all ability levels. Researchers further report that comprehension gains appear to transfer to unfamiliar texts at the same reading level (Dowhower, 1987; Herman, 1985; Morgan & Lyon, 1979; Samuels, 1988).

The question remains: How does one create an environment that supports oral reading as a communication process and still emphasize meaning? We have found that creating opportunities for our students to engage in meaningful, purposeful repeated readings, coupled with a cooperative learning environment, stimulates reading as a communication process. As our readers perform in choral readings, reader's theater, dramatic readings, or "Radio City," they learn to perceive reading as a way of communicating, sharing language and ideas, and entertaining or informing themselves and others. These activities blend the cognitive and affective aspects of learning to improve communicative competence. While shaping the environment to become supportive of all readers and reducing anxiety levels of readers, teachers also foster friendly relationships among students as they read with partners or in cooperative learning groups.

The key to successful reading is practice. Without practice, students attempt to become only accurate readers who identify words they read. With practice, students become accurate, expressive, and fluent readers who comprehend the text. Developing automaticity and fluency—the ability to recognize words immediately and read smoothly and with expression—further reduces anxiety and negative attitudes toward reading. Students, in fact, enjoy reading and rereading the stories and often delight in publishing their reading by videotaping or sharing it with other classes or parents.

Using Choral Reading as a Reading Strategy

After listening to stories that include lyrical or musical language, students enjoy participating in choral reading activities, simply defined as students taking turns reading together (Hoskisson & Tompkins, 1991). Choral reading is a wonderful way to practice reading with expression—to use different pitches and pauses and to use loudness and stress to emphasize certain words the way an author might have said them. When students become actively engaged in these reading styles, they improve their fluency and comprehension while having fun.

One primary advantage of the choral reading strategy is that it lifts pressure from individual readers because students read out loud together. Teachers observe that remedial readers, in particular, feel a sense of security as they read with their peers. At the same time, they learn new expressions, new intonations, and new pausing techniques to refine their oral and silent reading. They further begin to appreciate the sounds, feelings, and magic of language. Graves (1983) explains that students will internalize language as they encounter these delightful experiences. Later, he adds, this language becomes part of their writing.

Choral Reading of Poetry.   Poetry is one of the most popular forms to use with choral reading. Traditionally, in fact, choral reading is considered to be the oral reading of poetry through various voice combinations and contrasts in order to create meaning or enhance the tonal qualities of the passage (Arbuthnot, cited in McCauley & McCauley, 1992). According to Hoskisson and Tompkins (1991), selecting and preparing a poem for presentation requires that one consider tempo (how fast or slow to read the lines), rhythm (which words to stress or say loudly), pitch (when to raise or lower the voice), and juncture (when and how long to pause). Other considerations may include sound effects, exclamatory words, crowd noises, asides, and movement (McCauley & McCauley, 1992).

In preparing for a choral reading of "All the Colors of the Race," a poem included in Arnold Adoff's book *All the Colors of the Race,* Mrs. Smith prefers to model reading the poem to her class first. Displaying the poem on the overhead projector, she reads it aloud and then asks her students to listen as she reads the poem a second time, listening to her use of pitch, loudness, stress, and pauses. To help her students focus on these features, she asks:

- What parts of the poem did I read loudly . . . softly? Why?
- Where did I pause when I read the poem? Why?
- What words did I read with more stress? Why?
- Did I change my voice as I read other parts? How? Why?

As students respond to her questions, she uses a colored transparency pen to underline words that they suggest to be read with stress, loudly, or softly. While discussing these techniques of expression, students also begin to understand the author's meaning and use of words and figurative language to convey feelings and ideas. By asking why or how, Mrs. Smith further highlights stylistic techniques poets use to express ideas. For example, in this poem, she shows the relationship between her pauses and the way Adoff arranged the words in the text. By providing spaces within the text, she explains, Adoff emphasized his feelings about the "colors of the race" behind his face and inside his head.

Following this discussion, Mrs. Smith divides the class into two groups to practice reading parts of the poem chorally. To help her students visualize their parts, Mrs. Smith distributes copies of the poem for students to read with a partner. She further marks each part with a highlighter so that there will be no confusion about their parts. (For example, Group I might be in pink; Group II might be in aqua; the refrain is not highlighted.) Illustrated below is one way the poem can be divided into two parts.

Each team practices reading its part together three times. As Mrs. Smith circulates, monitoring her students' reading, she praises various teams for reading with smoothness and expression. When teams are not using appropriate pitch, loudness, stress, or pauses, Mrs. Smith reads with the team, modeling these techniques for them. Students quickly try to adopt their teacher's expression in this nonthreatening context, which minimizes criticism and maximizes praise.

ALL THE COLORS OF THE RACE
By Arnold Adoff

Group 1:   All the colors of the race
Group 2:   are
                in my face, and just behind my face:
Group 1: Behind my eyes:
                inside my head.
Group 2:   And inside my head, I give my self a place
                at the end of a long line
Group 1: forming
                        it self into a
                        circle.
    All: And I am holding out my hands.

Usually these practice sessions last for about 15 minutes. When Mrs. Smith feels the students are ready to read the poem chorally, she chooses one class member to introduce the poem and a student from each group to lead the choral reading for the group. By reminding her students that they will need to practice reading the poem chorally as a group a few times, Mrs. Smith provides a meaningful context for repeated readings of the poem. As the entire group chorally reads the poem, she helps them acquire timing, parallel inflections, and voice quality by reading with the groups, modeling appropriate expression, and avoiding a singsong effect. With each successive reading, she reads less and less, intervening only as necessary.

As they perform the choral reading, students feel a sense of pride and success— they know all the words and they know how to read their parts with expression. While encountering the text on repeated occasions, they also begin to form new and deeper understandings of the author's message and figurative language (i.e., "Behind my eyes"). With each rereading new meanings emerge from the words. As students join hands while reading the last line together, the message of this poem, and how it relates to their own lives, is further heightened.

Teachers observe that reluctant readers especially enjoy choral readings. If they make a mistake, no one knows. Their self-esteem mounts, moreover, as they realize they can read sophisticated words successfully. These are also important experiences for second-language learners. Through the repeated readings, they learn more about the rhythm, syntax, and vocabulary of the English language. Figure 4.8 includes the names of some multicultural books of poetry, as well as multicultural stories, suitable for choral readings.

Choral Readings of Stories.   Students also delight in choral readings derived from stories that include lyrical or musical language. When selecting stories appropriate for choral readings, teachers usually prefer (1) predictable stories, such as *Chicka Chicka Boom Boom,* by Bill Martin, Jr.; (2) stories with repetitive patterns or rhyme, such as *Love You Forever,* by Robert Munsch; (3) stories with cumulative patterns, such as *Bringing the Rain to Kapiti Plain,* by Verna Aardema; and (4) stories with lyrical or musical language, such as *Cornrows,* by Camille Yarbrough, or *I'm in Charge of Celebrations,* by Byrd Baylor.

When Mrs. Taylor, a Chapter I teacher (Chapter I is a federally funded program for students at-risk, classified according to their performance on standardized tests and whether or not they receive free or reduced lunches.) and Mrs. Baran, a third-grade classroom teacher, perform choral readings, they prefer to follow a coordination process (see Chapter 11) through a combination of "pull out" (taking Chapter I students to a resource classroom to receive instruction) and "push in" (facilitating the learning of Chapter I students within their own classroom) activities. Before reading *Cornrows* to her students in the resource room, Mrs. Taylor invites, with permission of the classroom teacher, five or six additional third-graders of varying ability levels to attend the 30-minute reading sessions in her resource room for about a week. Once she interactively reads the story to this newly formed group, she divides the students into three groups—which include students of varying ability levels—to practice the choral reading (found in Figure 4.9). Inviting these additional students to her class gives her students supplementary support as they practice reading their parts in groups, learning to recognize many new words. While the students practice reading their parts in their respective groups, Mrs. Taylor circulates, monitoring and

All of the Colors of the Race	Arnold Adoff
Bringing the Rain to Kapiti Plain	Verna Aardema
The Desert is Theirs	Byrd Baylor
Everybody Needs a Rock	Byrd Baylor
Hawk, I'm Your Brother	Byrd Baylor
If You Are a Hunter of Fossils	Byrd Baylor
I'm in Charge of Celebrations	Byrd Baylor
When Clay Sings	Byrd Baylor
Shadow	Marcia Brown
The Great Kapok Tree	Lynne Cherry
Spin a Soft Black Song	Nikki Giovanni
Beyond the Ridge	Paul Goble
Brother Eagle, Sister Sky	Susan Jeffers
All of You Was Singing	Richard Lewis
Chicka Chicka Boom Boom	Bill Martin
Love You Forever	Robert Munsch
The Story of Light	Susan Roth
The Empty Pot	Robert San Souci
People	Peter Spier
Lord of the Dance	Veronique Tadjo
Cornrows	Camille Yarbrough
Shalom My Peace	Paintings and Poems by Jewish and Arab Children

FIGURE 4.8 Multicultural Poetry Books and Stories Appropriate for Choral Readings

supporting their reading, similarly to Mrs. Smith. To further reinforce word recognition and vocabulary development, when she hears students stumbling on a word Mrs. Taylor clearly pronounces the word, sometimes explaining its meaning by relating the word to their own experiences.

After working like this for two sessions, the students practice reading as a group. While learning to appreciate the sounds, the feelings, and the magic of language in this supportive atmosphere, the Chapter I students simultaneously increase their reading fluency and comprehension of the text. Before long, they gain a sense of security about themselves as readers. One student, in fact, stated, "I think my classroom teacher gives us things to read that are too easy."

Once these students are comfortable with the choral reading, Mrs. Taylor switches to the "push in" phase of coordination and arranges a time for the students to perform the choral reading in their classroom. The group presents the choral reading with such enthusiasm and eloquence that their peers are highly motivated to learn the choral reading, too. Responding to their interests, Mrs. Baran and Mrs. Taylor divide the class into small groups (four or five students of varying ability levels), assigning each group a part to read. They then assign all Chapter I students and the invited students a group to lead.

FIGURE 4.9 An Example of a Choral Reading.

CORNROWS
by Camille Yarbrough

Narrator—Shirley Ann
Group 1—Great Grammaw
Group 2—Mama

Narrator: Then Great-Grammaw put MeToo down on his little chair so she could get at his head, and she said:

Group 1: Child come and sit by my knee,
an I will tell you about your family tree.
An I will dress you
As a prince should be,
an the right name will come
to both you an me.
An I will braid your hair
an I will braid your hair. . .

Group 2: You could tell the clan, the village,
by the style of hair they wore. . .
Then the Yoruba people
were wearin thirty braids and more. . .
You would know the princess, queen, and
bride
by the number of the braid. . .
You would know the gods they worshiped
by the pattern that they made.

Narrator: Then a terrible thing happened. I said, "What, Mama?"

Group 2: The clan,
the village,
the priest,
the bride,
the royalty,
all were packed into the slaver ships
and brought across the sea. . .
where they trembled on the auction block
and on the chain-gang line. . .
where they flickered on the pyre
and while hangin from the pine. . .
And the style that once was praise
then was changed to one of shame
and forgotten was the name. . .

Narrator: MeToo asked Great-Grammaw. "Did the spirit die?" And Great-Grammaw said:

Group 1: No such thing!
If you're quiet
you can still hear the royal rhythms,
still feel the spirit in the air.

(continued)

FIGURE 4.9 (*continued*)

Look around an you will see the old, old
symbol
that we now call cornrowed hair. . .
You see, the spirit of the symbol
is not changed by time, place, class, or fame,
an not even by hate or shame,
oh noo . . . You see,
it's the spirit that makes the symbol
an the spirit goes by many names.

Narrator: Then Mama said:

Group 2: Little girl, little boy,
let's play the hair name game. . .
every day a different style,
every day a different name. . .

Narrator: MeToo said, "Me first! Me first! Where can I get a name, Great-Grammaw?" Great-Grammaw said, "She's gonna tell you. Listen to ya mother." And Mama said:

Group 2: You can name it for a river,
you can name it for a flower,
for the year, for the month,
for the day or for the hour.

Narrator: They started clappin, and Great-Grammaw said,
"Keep ya head still, boy."

Group 2: You can name it for a poem,
for a city, for a school.
You can name it for your teacher
or for the golden rule.
You can name it for a hero,
for a proverb or a fish
You can name it for a star,
for a song or for a wish. . .

Narrator: I said, "How should we braid it?"
Great-Grammaw said:

Group 1: Braid it under,
braid it over,
braid it upward,
braid it down
braid in circles,
braid in angles,
then you wear it
like a crown. . .

Narrator: I said, "How should we style it?" Great-Grammaw said:

(*continued*)

FIGURE 4.9 (*continued*)

Group 1:   Style it fancy,
           style it simple,
           style with seeds and cowry shells.
           Style with ribbons,
           style with ivory,
           style with beads and tinkly bells. . .

Narrator: MeToo said, "What should we name it, Mama?"
           Mama said:

Group 2:   Name it Robeson,
           name it Malcolm,
           you can name it Dr. King.
           Name it DuBois,
           name it Garvey
           name it something you can sing.
           Name it Tubman,
           name it Harner,
           oh, you can style a Fannie Lou.
           Name it Nzinga,
           Rosa Parks,
           and please name it Hatshepsut, too. . .

           Name it Powell,
           name it Carver,
           Richard Wright and Langston Hughes.
           Name it Belafonte,
           name it Baldwin,
           name it glory,
           name it blues. . .

           Name it Miriam,
           Katherine Dunham,
           Mary Bethune and Josephine,
           Name it Aretha
           name it Nina,
           name it priestess,
           name it queen. . .

Narrator: By that time I had some serious cornrows. So did MeToo. Great Grammaw said:

Group 1:   Little girl, little boy,
           with the cornrowed style,
           let me see your pretty face,
           let me see your handsome smile.
           Now . . . what are you goin to name it?

Narrator: I named mine after Langston Hughes, because I can say one of his poems. MeToo named
           his after Batman. Tell me, tell me . . . What are you going to name yours?

Each child should select a name . . . tell why he selected it. As an extension have the child read more about the person whose name was selected.

Once again, the two teachers circulate, monitoring and supporting their students' reading. Having the Chapter I students serve as leaders of the various groups, however, reduces the need for teachers to repeatedly model expression—all students begin to reflect their group leaders' expression. Mrs. Baran and Mrs. Taylor also observe that groups are able to read in unison more quickly under the leadership of the Chapter I students.

After about 15 minutes, the class comes together to perform the choral reading. Both teachers comment that this is a wonderful experience for the Chapter I students. In Mrs. Taylor's words, "For so long the system has made them (Chapter I students) feel as if they can't read." Through this coordination process between Chapter I teachers and classroom teachers, she explains, "They discover they really can read. Some of the words are a little sophisticated for them, so they are really thrilled that they can read them."

Mrs. Taylor further observes that some African American students are able to read the dialect more quickly and easily than many of the other students. This becomes especially rewarding to the less able readers, who begin to help their peers with the pronunciation of certain words and the rhythm and flow of the language.

Whether practicing choral readings in a resource room or the classroom, teachers need to provide time for students to practice reading the text in small groups of varying ability levels. As Mrs. Caldwell points out, "I think it is much better to have the best reader in with the poorer readers, because if you always group the poorer readers together, they never get the strategies that the good readers use." When students perform the choral reading as a class, she further explains, "All students experience the rewards of their cooperative efforts immediately."

Similarly, McCauley & McCauley (1992) emphasize the use of choral reading with second-language learners. According to these authors, choral reading promotes language acquisition and fluency, develops communication systems of reading and writing in their second language, enhances comprehension through a variety of contextual supports, reinforces language patterns, and encourages risk taking in a low-anxiety environment. By blending cognitive and affective learning activities, these authors maintain that all students will become good communicators who "use language in a form that delights and excites" (p. 532).

Selecting and Preparing Choral Readings.   Teachers and students can easily prepare choral readings. Favorite poems, songs, or stories with lyrical or rhythmic qualities are most appropriate for choral readings. When using poems or songs, one needs to decide how to arrange them for choral reading. Students can read the selection in unison or in small groups, or can independently read particular lines or stanzas. Hoskisson and Tompkins (1991) suggest four possible arrangements:

- Echoic readings—The leader reads each line and the group echoes the line.
- Refrain readings—The leader reads each stanza and the group chimes in on the refrain or the chorus in unison.
- Antiphonal—The class is divided into groups, and each group reads parts of the poem or song.

- Cumulative—As each stanza of a poem or song is read, new voices are added. One student or group might read the first stanza or line; another student or group joins in to read the successive stanza or line, continuing until the entire poem or song is read.

Once students have participated in choral readings, they enjoy deciding how to arrange a poem or song for a choral reading. They become very creative, sometimes combining all four of these reading arrangements. Having students work in small groups to determine how they would like to read a poem or song becomes an excellent problem-solving activity that promotes cooperation and social skills.

When adapting stories with lyrical or rhythmic qualities, students or teachers need to select key segments of the text for the choral readings, while preserving the language and meaning of the story. This is an important application skill, as students must understand the meaning of the story in order to select portions of the text for choral reading. After reading the story several times, they need to determine what section or sections of the story to include, making adjustments as needed. Including too much text can make the choral reading too long to hold the interest of readers; including only a part of the text might detract from the meaning of the literature. Once an adapted version has been written, teachers or students need to decide how to arrange it for the choral reading, following the four suggested arrangements. The most popular arrangements for prose are antiphonal and cumulative. The musical, lyrical prose in Byrd Baylor's books, for example, *I'm in Charge of Celebrations,* *Hawk I'm Your Brother,* or *The Desert Is Theirs,* especially lend themselves to choral readings.

Follow-up Activities for Reinforcing Concepts about Vocabulary and Symbol–Sound Relationships. To reinforce understanding of figurative language and meaning in the choral reading of *I'm in Charge of Celebrations,* Mrs. Weeks asks her students to find a word that means *beat* and a word meaning *animal;* she also asks them to look for words that describe the *whirlwinds' movements, moving* through the darkness. After practicing the choral reading and enjoying its language, students are asked to scan their choral readings to find words or phrases that answer her questions. As they listen and read along, they place their fingers underneath the words, raise their hands, and respond: ". . . your heart will *POUND,*" or "She seemed to think that I was just another *creature . . .*" or ". . . they come from far away, *moving* up from the flats, *swirling* and *swaying* and *falling* and *turning . . .*" or ". . . a streak of light goes *shooting* through the darkness."

Similarly, Mrs. Benns reinforces understanding of the symbol/sound relationships for her first-graders in the choral reading *Chicka Chicka Boom Boom,* by Bill Martin and John Archambault. After chorally reading the story and experiencing the rhythm and magic of language, her students scan their choral readings to find words that begin with certain sounds. If Mrs. Benz asks them to find a word that begins like *button,* for example, students suggest "*Beat . . .* I'll *beat* you to the top of the coconut tree," or "*Boom . . .* Chicka chicka *boom boom!*" Likewise, if she asks them to find a word that begins like *table,* they place their fingers under their example and respond: "*Tangled.* **H** is tangled up with **I**," or "*Tooth.* It's black-eyed **P, Q R S,** and loose-*tooth* **T.**" Having the students share their example first reinforces the letter sound; having the students read the word in the context of its sentence reinforces the sound in meaningful text. As her students begin to learn about ending sounds and vowels, she follows the same techniques to reinforce these symbol/sound relationships.

Both teachers, however, use these strategies sparingly, selectively deciding what meanings or sounds they wish to reinforce. As the children practice the choral readings, the meanings of the words and the understandings of the symbol/sound relationships often evolve naturally. Overuse would destroy the beauty of the language, the story, and the choral reading.

Benefits to Students.   Using choral reading enables students to experience language in many different ways. When students encounter choral readings that are similar to their family experiences, they hear their own voices and language, and they feel good about them. Moreover, their ability to understand and comprehend the message of the story and its use of figurative language improves. They can grasp the meaning and share insights about the message more easily because the story connects with their prior experiences and knowledge. These aesthetic responses to reading, when they emerge from stories reflecting students' cultural heritage, can serve as a foundation for literacy development and comprehension strategies for culturally and linguistically diverse readers.

Additional benefits students receive from choral reading (Harste, Short, & Burke, 1988; McCauley & McCauley, 1992; Sampson, Allen, & Sampson, 1991; Stewig, 1981; Templeton, 1991) include:

- Improving reading fluency and word recognition skills
- Motivating students to read
- Teaching students to experiment with oral language and expression
- Heightening reading comprehension and vocabulary development
- Internalizing language, its rhythms, patterns, and lyrical qualities
- Modeling syntactic phrasing, which fosters comprehension of passages
- Providing additional contextual supports and clues to convey meaning
- Building confidence in one's ability to read
- Encouraging cooperation, rather than competition, as students practice reading in unison
- Allowing less able readers to experience fluency in a low-anxiety setting
- Reinforcing language patterns for limited-English-speaking students
- Fostering acquisition of language through repetition for second-language learners

Using Reader's Theater as a Reading Strategy

Reader's theater, "a formalized dramatic presentation of a script by a group of readers" (Busching, 1981, p. 330), is another powerful way to share language and ideas while improving fluency and comprehension. In this dramatic presentation, students each assume the role of a character, reading the character's dialogue without using actions. As they do so, they practice using their voice and expression to communicate the plot, characterization, mood, and theme of a story (Hoskisson & Tompkins, 1991). Different from theatrical productions, reader's theater eliminates the need for memorized parts, elaborate props, costumes, and backdrops. The emphasis is on the interpretive quality of the readers' voices, simple gestures, and facial expressions (Busching, 1981; Woodbury, 1979).

Preparing Scripts for Reader's Theater.   Scripts to use with reader's theater, which is a relatively new teaching idea, are available in limited quantities. Many teachers use the play scripts found in basal reading textbooks; others use the published scripts in books such as *Plays from African Folktales,* by Carol Korty, or published plays in books such as *Take a Walk in Their Shoes,* by Glenneth Turner, or *Listen Children: An Anthology of Black Literature,* edited by Dorothy Strickland.

Teachers can also prepare their own scripts for reader's theater from multicultural stories. In deciding which stories to use for reader's theater, we look for stories that include: (1) a well-formed plot with a clear ending, (2) interesting characters, (3) lively dialogue, and (4) an appealing theme. *Flossie and the Fox,* by Patricia McKissack; *Abiyoyo,* by Pete Seeger; *Amigo,* by Byrd Baylor; or *Nine-in-One, Grr! Grr!* by Blia Xiong, are examples of stories that we have adapted for reader's theater.

After reading a story several times, we select a scene or scenes to script. Many times we preserve the dialogue of the characters and adapt the narrator's lines to bridge gaps, set the scene, or summarize actions. Once the script is completed, we reproduce it for other classrooms to enjoy.

Preparing for a Performance of Reader's Theater.   Our script for *Flossie and the Fox,* a favorite of Mrs. Manchester's class, is found in Figure 4.10. After Mrs. Manchester interactively shares the story with her class, modeling Flossie's African American dialect, she divides her students into groups of three, making sure each group includes a variety of ability levels and at least one good reader. Once the groups are formed, students each choose a part to read — Flossie, the fox, or the narrator — and begin to practice reading their parts. Just as she circulates when her students practice choral readings, Mrs. Manchester rotates among the groups, monitoring, supporting, and praising their reading of the script.

After the groups have practiced for about 20 minutes, various groups volunteer to perform their interpretations with the class. How they present their interpretations varies. Some groups prefer to stand, stepping forward as they read their parts. Some groups stand facing the blackboard and turn to face the audience as they read their parts. Others use gestures — stomping their feet, placing their hand on their hip, or circling one another as they talk — when sharing their interpretations. Throughout, emphasis is not on production quality; it is on the interpretative quality of the readers' voices and expressions. Although movement and action are limited, the audience uses its imagination and the group's oral interpretation to visualize what is happening.

After performing their interpretations before their peers, many groups express

FIGURE 4.10 An Example of a Reader's Theater.

FLOSSIE & THE FOX
Reader's Theatre
by Patricia C. McKissack
pictures by
Rachel Isadora

Narrator: Flossie commenced to skip along, when she come upon a critter she couldn't recollect ever seeing. He was sittin' 'side the road like he was expectin' somebody. Flossie skipped right up to him and nodded a greeting the way she'd been taught to do.

Fox: Top of the morning to you, Little Missy. And what is your name?

Flossie: I be Flossie Finley. I reckon I don't know who you be either.

Narrator: Slowly the animal circled around Flossie. All the time eyeing the basket of eggs.

Fox: I am a fox. (Stopping in front of Flossie, smiled as best a fox can, and bowed.) At your service.

Narrator: Flossie rocked back on her heels then up on her toes, back and forward, back and forward . . . carefully studying the creature who was claiming to be a fox.

Flossie: Nope. I just purely don't believe it.

Fox: you don't believe what? (Looking away from the basket of eggs for the first time.)

Flossie: I don't believe you a fox, that's what.

Narrator: Fox's eyes flashed anger. then he chuckled softly.

Fox: My dear child, (disgusted) of course I'm a fox. A little girl like you should be simply terrified of me. Whatever do they teach children these days?

Flossie: (Tossing her head in the air) Well, whatever you are, you sho' think a heap of yo'self.

Narrator: Flossie skipped away. The fox looked shocked.

Fox: Wait. You mean . . . you're not frightened? Not just a bit?

Flossie: (Stops and then turned) I aine never seen a fox before. So, why should I be scared of you and I don't even now know you a real fox for a fact?

Fox: (Pulled himself tall and cleared his throat) Are you saying I must offer proof that I am a fox before you will be frightened of me?

Flossie: That's just what I'm saying.

Narrator: Lil' Flossie skipped on through the piney woods while that Fox fella rushed away lookin' for whatever he needed to prove he was really who he said he was. Meanwhile Flossie stopped to rest 'side a tree. Suddenly Fox was beside her.

(*continued*)

FIGURE 4.10 (*continued*)

Fox: I have the proof. See, I have thick, luxurious fur. Feel for yourself.

Narrator: Fox leaned over for Flossie to rub his back.

Flossie: Ummm. Feels like rabbit fur to me. shucks! You aine no fox. You a rabbit, all the time trying to fool me.

Fox: Me! A rabbit! I have you know my reputation precedes me. I am the third generation of foxes who have out-smarted and out-run Mr. J. W. McCutchin's fine hunting dogs. I have raided some of the best henhouses from Franklin to Madison. Rabbit indeed! I am a fox, and you will act accordingly.

Narrator: Flossie hopped to her feet. She put her free hand on her hip and patted her foot.

Flossie: Unless you can show you a fox, I'll not accord you nothing!

Narrator: And without further ceremony she skipped away. Down the road a piece, Flossie stopped by a bubbly spring. She knelt to get a drink of water. Fox came up to her.

Fox: I have a long pointed nose. Now that should be proof enough.

Flossie: Don't prove a thing to me. (She picked some wild flowers.) Come to think of it, rats got long pointed noses. (She snapped her fingers.) That's it! You a rat trying to pass yo'self off as a fox.

Narrator: That near 'bout took Fox's breath away.

Fox: I beg your pardon (gasping),

Flossie: You can beg all you wanna (skipping on down the road). That still don't make you no fox.

Fox: I'll teach you a thing or two, young lady (calling after her). You just wait and see.

Narrator: Before long Flossie came to a clearing. A large orange tabby was sunning on a tree stump.

Flossie: Hi, pretty kitty.

Narrator: Meanwhile Fox slipped from behind a clump of bushes.

Fox: Since you won't believe me when I tell you I am a fox, perhaps you will believe that fine feline creature, toward whom you seem to have some measure of respect.

Narrator: Flossie looked at the cat and winked her eye.

Flossie: (Whispering) He sho' use a heap o' words.

Narrator: Fox beckoned for Cat to speak up. Cat jumped to a nearby log and yawned and stretched— then she answered.

Cat: This is a fox because he has sharp claws and yellow eyes.

(*continued*)

FIGURE 4.10 (*continued*)

Narrator: Fox seemed satisfied. But Flossie looked at Cat. She looked at Fox, then once more at both just to be sure.

Flossie: All due respect, Miz Cat, but both y'all got sharp claws and yellow eyes. so . . . that don't prove nothing, 'cep'n both y'all be cats.

Narrator: Fox went to howling and running around in circles. He was plum beside himself.

Fox: I am a fox and I know it. This is absurd!

Flossie: No call for you to use that kind of language (she skipped away).

Fox: Wait, wait. I just remembered something. It may be the solution to this - this horrible situation.

Flossie: Good. It's about time.

Fox: I-I-I have a bushy tail. That's right. All foxes are known for their fluffy, bushy tails. That has got to be adequate proof.

Flossie: Aine got to be. You got a bushy tail. So do squirrels.

Narrator: Flossie pointed to one overhead leaping from branch to branch in the tree tops.

Flossie: Here, have a bite of peach.

Narrator: But Fox was crying like a natural born baby.

Fox: No, no, no. If I promise you I'm a fox, won't that do?

Narrator: Flossie shook her head no.

Fox: Oh, woe is me. I may never recover my confidence.

Narrator: Flossie didn't stop walking.

Flossie: That's just what I been saying. You just an ol' confidencer. Come tellin' me you was a fox, then can't prove it. Shame on you!

Narrator: Long about that time, Flossie and the fox came out of the woods. Flossie cupped her hands over her eyes and caught sight of McCutchin Quarters and Miz Viola's cabin. Fox didn't notice a thing; he just followed behind Flossie begging to be believed.

Fox: Give me one last chance.

Flossie: Okay. but just this one more.

Narrator: Fox tried not to whimper, but his voice was real unsteady-like.

(*continued*)

FIGURE 4.10 (*continued*)

Fox: I-I have sharp teeth and I can run exceedingly fast.

Narrator: He waited for Flossie to say something. Slowly the girl rocked from heel to toe . . . back and forward.

Flossie: You know, it don't make much difference what I think anymore.

Fox: What? Why?

Flossie: Cause there's one of Mr. J. W. McCutchin's hounds behind you. He's got sharp teeth and can run fast too. And, by the way that hound's lookin', it's all over for you!

Narrator: With a quick glance back Fox dashed toward the woods.

Fox: The hound knows who I am! But I'm not worried. I sure can out-smart and out-run one of Mr. J. W. McCutchin's miserable mutts any old time of the day, because like I told you, I am a fox!

Flossie: I know, I know.

Narrator: And she turned toward Miz Viola's with the basket of eggs safety tucked under her arm.

an interest in sharing *Flossie and the Fox* with other classes, using simple costumes and props. Groups who perform for other classes receive a wonderful response. Students in other classes often want to do their own reader's theater.

Mrs. Manchester also notices that all of her students, even her reluctant readers, are enthusiastic and motivated while practicing their scripts; discipline problems vanish. She observes that all her students learn to read with expression and fluency as "better readers train readers who don't read so well." Capitalizing on her students' interest in the dialect, Mrs. Manchester explains that this dialect is appropriate for the setting of the story. She also emphasizes that dialects vary among and within groups.

Benefits to Students.   Using reader's theater with multicultural stories appears to promote the self-esteem of Mrs. Manchester's culturally diverse students. Flossie's quick wit and clever actions, for example, enable her students to see African American characters portrayed in a positive light. Consistent with Patricia McKissack's goals, they are also able to learn a little more about their folk history and traditions in a supportive environment.

Similar to choral readings, practicing reader's theater also reinforces word meanings and understanding of symbol/sound relationships as teachers have students scan their reader's theater piece for examples of words or phrases that mean the same as a certain word or that begin or end with certain sounds. Again, these techniques must be used cautiously to avoid destroying the beauty of the language, the story, and the choral reading.

The following are other benefits of using reader's theater:

- Fostering enjoyment and delight in reading
- Improving self-confidence
- Encouraging cooperation rather than competition
- Teaching students to experiment with oral language and expression
- Allowing students to take responsibility for their own learning as they make decisions about interpretation
- Extending comprehension of plot and character interpretation
- Heightening decoding abilities and vocabulary development
- Enhancing reading rate and fluency
- Internalizing language, which becomes part of their conversation and writing
- Improving their writing and script-writing abilities
- Allowing less able readers to experience fluency in a low-anxiety setting
- Reinforcing language patterns for limited-English-speaking students
- Fostering acquisition of language through repetition for second-language learners

Helping Students Prepare Their Own Scripts.   Although we have prepared most of the scripts for our reader's theater, students can also prepare their own scripts from favorite stories. Laughlin and Latrobe (cited in Hoskisson & Tompkins, 1991) suggest that students begin by reading and rereading a favorite story, thinking about its theme, characters, and plot. By following the DRLTA or SGRTA strategies, teachers can help students gain a clearer understanding of the story and its elements.

Once they have an understanding of the story, Laughlin and Latrobe suggest, students need to choose a scene or scenes to script and make copies of them in order to highlight the dialogue with felt-tip markers. Students then begin to adapt the scene by inserting narrators' lines to bridge gaps and summarize actions or plot. As students assume roles and read the scripts aloud, they continue to experiment with the text, making revisions. A final version is then typed and distributed for students to practice and perform.

Initial attempts to script for reader's theater should include short stories that are familiar to students. Certainly, teachers will need to guide and facilitate the groups' efforts.

Using Dramatic Interpretations with Reading

Dramatic interpretations, which we define as dramatic rereadings of stories, are another exciting way to help students gain reading fluency and automaticity while heightening their interest in reading. Dramatic interpretations use different pitches, pauses, loudness, and stress to convey meaning to the listener, similar to choral readings and reader's theater.

A popular story to use with dramatic interpretations is *Knots on a Counting Rope,* by Bill Martin, Jr. After interactively reading the story aloud to her students,

Mrs. Streeter discusses the author's beautiful use of language and dialogue between the grandfather and grandson to tell a story about the grandson's life. Through discussion, she also helps her students appreciate the oral traditions of Native Americans, who frequently tell stories around a campfire, tying a knot in a rope each time a story is told.

To help them experience this tradition, she distributes a card to each child, which contains one event in the grandson's life being retold by the grandfather. (Figure 4.11 shows how the dramatic interpretations are scripted.) Working with partners, students practice reading their card three times, simulating the expression the grandfather might use as he retells the story. Each partner listens to the reader, helping with unfamiliar words and sharing how the reader improved with each reading. For example, partners might comment, "I like the way you read with more expression," "I like the way you read the words *stormy night*—it sounded scary," "You are reading all the words smoothly," or "You sounded like the grandfather when you read." After the reader reads his part three times, the partners switch roles. While partners are practicing, Mrs. Streeter circulates and supports her students' reading, following the techniques she uses with choral reading and reader's theater.

Usually Mrs. Streeter allows students to practice with their partners 15 to 20 minutes. She then regroups her class and has them sit in a circle in the order the events in the grandson's life occur. To help them experience the setting for this dramatic reading of the story, she dims the lights, places logs and a paper fire in the center of the circle, and plays music from the tape *For My People,* by Brooke Medicine Eagle. Her students then assume the role of the grandfather, reading a part of his dialogue; she assumes the role of the grandson, reading his dialogue. Then, each time the group rereads the story one of the students ties a knot in a rope.

Once again, all students participate and are successful in this activity. The mood and atmosphere are inspiring; students' pride in themselves and their peers as readers is moving.

Using 'Radio City' to Enhance Comprehension and Questioning Strategies

"Radio City," a strategy which reinforces reading comprehension through oral reading and questioning strategies, is an effective cooperative learning activity to use with short stories or folk tales. To prepare her students for this activity, Mrs. Mouganis reviews with them the Question-Answer Relationships (QAR) strategy (Raphael, 1982, 1986), which sensitizes readers to different thinking patterns and demands required by various levels of questions. As she reads a few folk tales from the book *Japanese Children's Favorite Stories,* by Florence Sakadl, she encourages her students to ask three types of questions about the folk tale: right there questions, whose answers can be found right in the text; think-and-search questions, which require students to search the text for information and think about relationships; and on-my-own questions, which must come from inside the readers' heads, even though the text might help.

After practicing the QAR strategy (which Mrs. Mouganis spends several weeks on at the beginning of the year), Mrs. Mouganis selects two short folk tales from *Japanese Children's Favorite Stories* to be used with her students. After dividing the

FIGURE 4.11 An Example of a Dramatic Interpretation.

KNOTS ON A COUNTING ROPE
by Bill Martin, Jr. and John Archambault

Tell me the story again, Grandfather.
Tell me who I am.
I have told you many times, Boy,
you know the story by heart.

But it sounds better when you tell it, Grandfather.
It was a dark night,
a strange night.
Your mother and father and I
were safe in the hogan. . .
when a wild storm
came out of the mountains. . .

. . . crying, *"Boy-eeeeeeeee! Boy-eeeeeeeee!"*
and your mother said,
"I hear it in the wounded wind.
A boy child will be born tonight."

Then what happened, Grandfather?
I rode up the canyon fast,
to bring the grandmother.
It is not a good sign
for a child to be born
without a grandmother's blessing.

Was the wind still calling for me, Grandfather?
Yes, Boy, it was whipping up sand
as sharp as claws,
and crying like a bobcat,
"Boy-eeeeeeeee! Boy-eeeeeeeee!"

Then what happened, Grandfather?
Just as I was born. . .
tell me that part.
It was strange . . . strange
Just as you came forth
and made your first cry,
the wind stopped howling
and the storm was over.

. . . *And the night became as quiet*
as soft fallen snow. . .
. . . the grandmother took you up
in her arms, and said,
"He will walk in beauty
to the east, to the west,
to the north, to the south,
he will walk in beauty . . . forever."

(continued)

114

FIGURE 4.11 (*continued*)

And I was born strong,
wasn't I, Grandfather?
No, you were not strong.
You were sick and frail.
We thought you would die.

But I didn't die, did I?
Tell me about that, Grandfather.
Two great blue horses
came galloping by. . .
and you raised your arms
to the great blue horses,
and I said,
"See how the horses speak to him.
They are his brothers from. . .
beyond the dark mountains.
This child will not die.
The great blue horses have given him
the strength to live."

And that is when you named me,
isn't it, Grandfather?
After you smiled your first smile,
we had the naming ceremony.
All of the grandmothers
and grandfathers were there.
And we named you Boy-Strength-of-Blue-Horses.

And I grew strong, didn't I?
Yes, Boy-Strength-of-Blue-Horses,
and each day
you are growing stronger.
You are learning to cross
the dark mountains.

Will I always have to live in the dark, Grandfather?
Yes, Boy.
You were born with a dark curtain
in front of your eyes.

But, there are many ways to see, Grandfather.
Yes, Boy, you are learning
to see through your darkness
because you have
the strength of blue horses.

I see the horses with my hands, Grandfather,
but I cannot see the blue.
What is blue?
Blue? . . . blue?
Blue is the morning. . .

(*continued*)

115

FIGURE 4.11 (*continued*)

the sunrise. . .
the sky. . .
the song of the birds. . .

Blue! Blue! Blue is happiness, Grandfather!
I feel it . . . in my heart!
There was a sweep of blue
in the rainbow, Boy,
that morning your horse was born.
I awakened you, Boy,
during the night, remember,
just before the foal was born.

And you said to me,
"Come, Boy, Circles is ready to foal.
The colt will be yours."
It was a long night of cold rain. . .
As the sun
came through the clouds,
the foal was born.

And a rainbow danced across the sky.
It was a good sign, Boy.
And you named the little wet foal. . .
Rainbow!

Rainbow is smart, Grandfather.
Like you.
She is good at remembering.
No one thought you could teach her
to race, Boy.

But I did, Grandfather!
Everyday, day after day,
we followed you along the trail. . .
And you let me hold the reins.

You traced the trails
in your mind, Boy,
both you and Rainbow.

Yes, Grandfather, we learned the trails by heart . . .
Now tell me again about the race, Grandfather.
It was a tribal day, Boy.
You and the other boys
were at the starting line. . .
but you pulled back.

I was afraid, Grandfather,
until you called to me.
Tell me again what you said.

(*continued*)

FIGURE 4.11 (*continued*)

I said,
"Don't be afraid, Boy!
Trust your darkness!
Go like the wind!"

And I leaned forward on Rainbow's neck.
I grabbed her mane tight,
and I said, "Go, Rainbow, go!"
And the people said:
"Who is that boy riding bareback. . .
racing the race with all his heart?"

And what did you say, Grandfather?
I said, "That is Boy-Strength-of-Blue-Horses. . .
He and his horse are together like one."

But I didn't win, Grandfather.
No, but you rode like the wind.
You crossed dark mountains, Boy.

Tell me again what you told me then.
I like to hear it over and over.
I said,
"Boy-Strength-of-Blue-Horses,
you have raced darkness and won!
You now can see with your heart,
feel a part of all that surrounds you.
Your courage lights the way."

And what did the grandmothers say?
They said,
"This boy walks in beauty.
His dreams are more beautiful
than rainbows and sunsets."

Now that the story has been told,
will you tie another knot in the counting rope,
Grandfather?
Yes, Boy, and when the rope is filled with knots,
you will know the story by heart
and can tell it to yourself.

So that I will grow stronger, Grandfather?
Yes . . . stronger . . . strong enough
to cross the dark mountains.

I always feel strong when you are with me, Grandfather.
I will not always be with you, Boy,
but, you will never be alone.
My love, like the strength of blue horses,
will always surround you.

class into six groups consisting of four students of varying ability levels, she distributes copies of "The Rabbit and the Moon" or "Silly Saburo" to each group. Using colored markers, she has already divided the folk tales into four segments of text. Each group member then reads the folk tale silently and chooses one of the segments to read orally. Working in pairs, group members practice reading their parts to their partners. Group members then record two QAR questions from their segment on a sheet of paper.

Group members are now ready to begin the "radio" reading. Using handmade microphones, the reader with the beginning segment of text reads his or her section aloud, and the remaining group members listen, leaving their folk tale face down on their desks. When the segment is finished, the reader asks the group members the two questions. They place a plus sign by the name of the person responding if the answer is correct and a minus sign if incorrect. Following the same procedures, each successive group member uses the microphone to read his or her segment of text and ask questions.

Mrs. Mouganis observes that her students are hesitant to ask questions at first and that early questions are at the explicit level. With practice, however, her students begin to refine their questioning strategies, asking more think-and-search questions with each successive experience. She further notes the questions invite more discussion about the story, its meaning, and its relationship to their own experiences. According to Mrs. Mouganis, "Even the weaker reader is gaining tremendously because of the larger group discussion and the opportunity to read every day." Opportunities to question and discuss the meaning of stories increase students' interpretation and understanding of the stories and their ability to communicate meaning. Radio City further creates a literate environment in which students' voices, as well as the author's, are heard. Helping students discover their voices, however, requires numerous opportunities to read and discuss books and novels.

Paired Repeated Readings

When reading stories silently during SSR, many students love to share a picture or a passage spontaneously with a nearby friend. We like to provide a more formal structure for sharing language and ideas. Mr. Bishop, for example, encourages each of his students to choose a favorite passage from a book to share with a partner, following the guidelines for reading with partners (see Dramatic Interpretations). While sharing passages in this way, readers also discuss their stories with their partner. Through these interactive situations, students learn how to relate the story to their own experiences and personal lives. Many times listeners become interested in their partners' stories and decide to read the same book on another day.

Likewise, Mrs. Briggs enjoys having her students prepare favorite stories to read to a younger class. For example, after she shares the stories *Why Mosquitoes Buzz in People's Ears* and *Who's in Rabbit's House,* by Aardema, Mrs. Briggs allows her students to choose their favorite story to read to a first-grader. Working with partners, her students first rehearse reading their favorite story aloud for several days, practicing proper use of expression, voice pauses, and projection. While her students rehearse their stories, Mrs. Briggs circulates and monitors their reading.

Once she is sure all students are comfortable with reading the stories aloud, she and a first-grade teacher, Mrs. Fenker, pair each fourth-grader with a first-grader. In order that all students might be able to read and hear one another comfortably, Mrs. Fenker keeps half of her first-graders in her classroom to read with their fourth-grade partners and sends the remaining students to Mrs. Briggs' classroom to read with their partners. Both teachers are amazed to hear all students, regardless of reading ability, read with expression and enthusiasm. Mrs. Briggs comments that she did not realize that many of her students could even use expression when reading aloud prior to this experience. Mrs. Fenker further adds that she is impressed with the way her students listen, asking questions and spontaneously reacting to the text by chiming in when phrases or words are repeated.

Both teachers realize how well students can read and how much they enjoy reading when given a meaningful purpose and context. The activity is so positive, in fact, that both teachers continue to provide opportunities for the partners to read together monthly. Over time, the fourth-graders learn how to prepare questions to ask their partners as they read aloud and discover ways to encourage their partners to read repetitive phrases or words as the story unfolds.

DEVELOPING MEANING AND VOCABULARY WITH MULTICULTURAL STORIES

Seminal works of Davis (1944), Thurstone (1946), and Spearitt (1972) indicate that vocabulary knowledge is highly correlated with reading comprehension. Discovering strategies for improving vocabulary, however, remains a challenge for educators. Merely looking up definitions of words and memorizing their meanings seldom results in improved reading comprehension and vocabulary growth. These activities do not provide the in-depth knowledge required to increase comprehension of difficult concepts. According to Fielding, Wilson, and Anderson (1986), the amount of free reading is the best predictor of vocabulary growth between grades two and five. Similarly, Nagy (1988, 1989) indicates that reading may be the most important source of vocabulary growth. Recent research further indicates that writing (Duin & Graves, 1987; Beyersdorfer & Schauer, 1989) and discussion (Stahl, 1986; Stahl & Clark, 1987; Stahl & Kapinus, 1991) are effective strategies for increasing word knowledge and comprehension.

Our research also suggests that reading aloud to students, discussing the stories and the meanings of words, and writing promote vocabulary development and reading comprehension (Moore & Diamond, 1991). During our work with teachers and students, we have discovered four strategies that, when integrated with reading aloud and discussion of meaning, seem to enhance vocabulary growth in students: semantic mapping, Predict-O-Grams, Possible Sentences, and writing activities (writing activities will be shared in more depth in Chapter 5.)

Semantic Mapping with Multicultural Stories

Semantic mapping, or webbing, which encourages students to draw on their prior knowledge and organize information into categories, is an effective strategy to promote vocabulary development using multicultural informational stories such as *Chas-*

ing the Moon to China, by Virginia McLean; *A Weed Is a Flower,* by Aliki; *Corn Is Maize,* by Aliki; *Mummies, Tombs and Treasures,* by Lila Perl; and *Castle,* by David Macaulay. Before reading *Chasing the Moon to China* to her class, for example, Mrs. Montieth writes the word *China* in the middle of a large chart. Next, she asks her students to take a sheet of paper, to record the word China in the middle of this paper, and to brainstorm words about it, placing these words around the word China. After about five minutes, Mrs. Montieth asks her students to move into their coopera- tive learning groups (groups of three or four students) to share their words with their group members. While working in these groups, all students are encouraged to add new words to their individual lists. After about seven minutes of sharing time, she asks each group to select eight of the words they feel to be most important and place a star by them.

The class then comes together to pool their information about China on the large chart paper. Taking turns, each group volunteers two of their words to be placed on the chart. As the groups share their words, Mrs. Montieth arranges the words accord- ing to categories—such as information about food, clothing, culture, places, or homes. Once all the words are clustered on the chart paper, she has the class discuss possible category labels. These labels are then written above the clusters with a colored marking pen. Using semantic maps as well as graphs or clusters are effec- tive ways to foster language and vocabulary development for second-language learn- ers, especially when they are combined with peer interaction (Peregoy and Boyle, 1993).

To further help her students understand new and unfamiliar terms, Mrs. Mon- tieth pauses and asks students to explain these words to their peers; she occasionally elaborates on their explanations to clarify the meaning. Using small- and large-group discussion about these words enables students to build connections between their prior knowledge and the new information about China. Her students benefit not only from their own active participation in the discussion about these words and the information; they also benefit from the contributions of other class mem- bers.

Seeing the beaming faces of Mrs. Montieth's Chinese American students made this experience rewarding to us all. As they contributed additional information to the chart and compared their cultures, their peers listened avidly. The Chinese American students became more involved as their cultures were validated through these discus- sions. Interestingly, Clara, a Korean student, perceived many similarities between her culture and the Chinese culture and began to share this information with her peers. All three students felt less self-conscious about their cultural background; they began to bring clothing, artifacts, pictures, and food to class to share their heritage with their peers.

The next day, Mrs. Montieth read the story aloud to her students, who quickly realized that many of the words and concepts they discussed are included in the story, helping them acquire a better understanding of the meaning of words and the Chinese culture. With their Chinese and Korean friends to further explain these ideas, their knowledge and understanding grew. New words and concepts from *Chasing the Moon to China,* as well as other stories about China, were added to the chart. Having the words on display for several weeks motivated students to use these words with other activities, particularly in their writing.

Predict-O-Grams as a Way to Reinforce Meaning and Vocabulary

Predict-O-Grams, a strategy that heightens the ability to predict while reading, also effectively unites new knowledge with prior experiences. The strategy begins with a list of words from the story to be read aloud. When reading *The Hallowed Horse,* by Demi, Mrs. Streeter selects these target words—which include words about the characters, setting, goal or problem, actions, or resolution of problem—and places them on the chalkboard before class. Working in pairs, her students then predict whether these words should be grouped under the headings of characters, setting, goal or problem, actions, or resolution of problem on their Predict-O-Gram sheet (Figure 4.12). After her students have worked with a partner for about six minutes, she brings her class together so that teams can share their categorizations. As group members share words for setting, problems, or actions, for example, Mrs. Streeter encourages them to explain why they predicted this category. Supporting their rationale for their predictions further enables her students to realize that some words can be classified in more than one way. To help develop their vocabulary, she also has students explain the meanings of words that may be unfamiliar to some students. Words from *The Hallowed Horse* that Mrs. Streeter elaborates on include: retreat to

FIGURE 4.12 Predict-O-Gram for *The Hallowed Horse.*

The Hallowed Horse

kingdom	multiheaded snake
potter	crystal ball
trumpets blew	India
Hallowed Horse	shot out like an arrow
a long time ago	whinnied loudly
retreat to the mountains	celebrate
mountain of rubies	king

The Hallowed Horse

The setting

The characters

_____

_____

_____

_____

The goal or problem

The actions

_____

_____

_____

_____

The resolution

_____

_____

the mountains, multiheaded snake, shot out like an arrow, whinnied loudly, mountain of rubies, and celebrate.

Once these possible classifications have been explored, students use the words from their lists to complete a story frame (Figure 4.13) about *The Hallowed Horse*. After students have worked for about five minutes, Mrs. Streeter asks them to stop for a few minutes to hear how various teams have used the words in their story frames. While sharing their stories aloud, students receive praise and supportive comments from their peers, which helps them feel more comfortable about their writing. Modeling the use of praise for her learners, Mrs. Streeter also adds comments about their choice of words or their creative use of the words in their stories.

After three or four students share their writing, she encourages them to continue their story frames, adding that she will look forward to seeing how they integrate the additional words from their lists with their writing. As they continue writing, incor-

FIGURE 4.13 Predict-O-Gram/Story Frame Chart.

Predict-O-Gram/Story Frame

_____ is the main character in this

story. The story takes place _____

_____

_____

The problem is _____

_____

_____

It starts when _____

_____

_____

After that _____

_____

_____

Then _____

_____

_____

The story ends when _____

_____

_____

porating these words within their own story frames, students begin to understand the structure of stories and discover how language such as "multiheaded snake" or "shot out like an arrow" can make a story more interesting and appealing to readers. These words, moreover, become part of their vocabulary as they apply them in their stories.

As partners complete their story frames, she encourages them to share their stories with the class. By providing praise and supportive comments throughout the writing experience, Mrs. Streeter and their peers help these young authors feel more positive about their writing. Needless to say, all students are now ready to hear *The Hallowed Horse.* In fact, Mrs. Streeter says she has never seen her students so motivated and interested in a story—they wanted to hear whose predictions were similar to the actual story.

As a culminating activity, she has her students use their story frames to write their own stories about *The Hallowed Horse.* Many students modify and refine their stories, using information from the story to add new details and events. Once the revisions are complete, the partners publish their stories, using a word processor and illustrations. Here are copies of two stories.

The Hallowed Horse

Once there was a king that ruled a kingdom. In the kingdom, the king lived with his queen. The multiheaded-snake surrounded the mountain of rubies. The multiheaded-snake shot out like an arrow at the king. The king tried to race the snake to the rubies that he had hidden. The king followed the snake to where he hid the rubies. There was an enormous lion that scared the snake away and saved the kings life.

Brian and Kevin, Grade 5

The King's Crystal Ball

Once upon a time in India there was a king. He had a beautiful crystal ball that was very fragile. One day the two potter drank too much whiskey and got drunk. He started throwing pots all over. He even threw a tiny pinchpot through an open window and it hit the king's crystal ball. SMASH! There lay a crystal!

A little while later the king (who was VERY overweight!) went to the crystal ball to magic up some cookies. He was shocked! "My crystal ball! My beautiful crystal ball!" he cried. He lay down on the floor and cried. He then rolled over on the pinchpot. "I'm going to get you potter!!!! He went into town to find the potter. He didn't have to look long. There was the potter, dancing and screaming in the middle of the dusty road. He stopped every once in a while to get some more whiskey. He came to the king and started dancing around the king. The king grabbed the potter by the neck and sent him to get another crystal so that he could carve it. He put the potter down. The potter screamed and ran away. "Fine then," the king said, "I shall get it myself. He went to the crystal mountains to fetch one. A two-headed snake raced out and got the king off-guard. He ate up the fat king. And the king lived unhappily ever after in the snake's stomach.

By Matthew and Steven, Grade 5

Using Possible Sentences to Predict Word Meanings

Possible Sentences, a strategy adapted from Stahl and Kapinus (1991), is another instructional activity that develops vocabulary in informational or narrative texts. Similar to the Predict-O-Gram, this strategy further helps students see relationships among words. The teacher first chooses about six to eight target words that might be unfamiliar terms for the students. When using this strategy with *The Story of Light*, by Susan Roth, Mrs. Birdyshaw, a multicultural consultant, chooses the words *cunning, shielded, scorched, charred tail, singed fur,* and *scurried.* Then she selects an additional four to six familiar words, which can be used to help generate sentences for the target words. These words are *clever, sunlight, spark, ash,* and *rays of sun.*

After placing these words on the board, Mrs. Birdyshaw asks volunteers to share information about words they might know, extending and elaborating on their responses as needed. Next, she has each student, with a partner, write sentences that include two to three of these new words on sentence strips. Regrouping as a class, Mrs. Birdyshaw asks for teams to share their "possible sentences." As groups share their possible sentences, their sentence strips are placed on the chalk ledge for others to view. All examples, accurate and inaccurate guesses, are accepted; discussion about the sentences is postponed.

Once all teams contribute at least one of their possible sentences with the class and all words have been used in possible sentences, Mrs. Birdyshaw begins to read *The Story of Light* aloud. Following the interactive reading of the story and a discussion about its meaning, she revisits the sentences, discussing whether each word is used appropriately in the sentence and how the sentences might be modified to reflect the true meaning of the word. The meaning of the words and concepts is heightened when the class practices and performs a choral reading of the story.

Similar to semantic mapping and Predict-O-Grams, Possible Sentences draws on students' prior knowledge of words. By making predictions about the words and how they might be used in the story, students are making connections between their own experiences and the story they are about to read. Mrs. Birdyshaw further notes that her students acquire a better understanding of these words as they see and use them in their sentences, listen to the way they are incorporated in the story, and revise their sentences. Through multiple exposures to words, students are able to remember the meaning of new vocabulary words.

Enhancing Vocabulary Knowledge of Other Languages through Writing

As the numbers of immigrants continue to increase in our nation, there is a need for these students to encounter characters like themselves in the stories they read. There is also a need for them to hear and see their language in stories they read if they are to preserve strong ties to their ethnic origins. For example, Vietnamese, as well as other Asian students, delight in hearing their language in the story *Angel Child, Dragon Child,* by Michele Surat.

More and more Hispanic writers are likewise integrating Spanish words in their texts. *Abuela,* by Arthur Dorros, and *A Basket for Tia,* by Pat Mora, are two examples. If all students are to understand the meanings of these words from other languages in stories they are reading, teachers will need to develop understanding of the new words. Just as students use picture and context clues from the surrounding words to determine meanings of new words, students can use picture and context clues to find out the meanings of the Spanish words in these two stories. When Abuela says, "*El parque es lindo,*" students can use the collage illustrations and the surrounding words, "I think the park is beautiful, too" to derive the meanings of the Spanish words. Similarly, when Cecilia shares how she and Tia "like to make *bizcochos,* sugar cookies for the family," students can easily determine the meaning of *bizcochos* from the colored cut-paper illustrations and the surrounding words *sugar cookies.*

Mrs. Coleman, a Mexican-American parent, asked her daughter's teacher if she might read the story *Abuela* and do a writing activity with the second-grade class. Mrs. Coleman, who was taking a graduate-level class at the university and needed to try an instructional technique with a class as part of her course work, wanted to see how her daughter's friends might respond to hearing Spanish words in a story and how they might use these words in their own stories. Mrs. Swartz was pleased to have Mrs. Coleman model how to read the story; she wanted to learn the correct pronunciation of the Spanish words in this charming story about a young girl and her grandmother.

To build background knowledge for the story, Mrs. Coleman began the activity by asking the students if they knew any Spanish words. As students shared the words they knew, she clustered them in a web. Students quickly realized that many of the words were similar to the words in English; for example, *padre* was similar to papa and *familia* was similar to family. After students shared words they knew, Mrs. Coleman added some words to the web—*aeropuerto, momento, parque,* and *aventura*—asking them to predict the meaning of the words. She explained that they would be able to use pictures and clues from the story to learn the meanings of additional words.

Following this activity, Mrs. Coleman asked how many enjoyed going to the park, encouraging them to tell about the things they might see at the park. After a few students shared their experiences, she explained that Rosalba and Abuela, her grandmother, were going to the park in this story. As Mrs. Coleman interactively read the story to the second-graders, she paused frequently, encouraging them to talk about the story and share the meaning of the Spanish words they heard and pointing out the importance of family in the Hispanic culture.

At the conclusion of the story, Mrs. Coleman asked them to brainstorm some things Rosalba and Abuela might see on their boat ride, recording their words on the board. She also wrote the Spanish words next to each of these words. When they had a variety of words on the board, Mrs. Coleman explained they could write their own stories about Rosalba's and Abuela's adventure on the boat, using as many Spanish words as they could—just like the author of the story. Before beginning their stories, students also had a chance to ask her how to write down any other Spanish words they remembered from *Abuela.* As they began writing, she reminded them that they could use their temporary spelling to write the Spanish words, just as they do with English words.

The second-graders eagerly began writing about Rosalba's and Abuela's boat adventure. An example of one story is displayed in Figure 4.14. As one can see,

"Un Otra Adventura"

"Vamos," says Abuela,
Once we get into the middle
of the lake, Abuela says
"Vamos for a swim" because
there are no other El
bots in sight "Si" I say.
We dive down into the Aqua.
"El pescadd" says Abuela, not
thinking about the water
rushing into her mouth.
Abuela was right! Tons of
El pescado were coming
towars me and Abuela.

FIGURE 4.14 An example of a story written by a second-grader.

writing a story with Spanish words is not a problem for these second-graders. They are simultaneously learning to appreciate and understand the Spanish language. The second-graders are also applying the use of context clues, a reading strategy for determining the meaning of new words, and transferring this strategy to a new context.

CLASSROOM IMPLICATIONS

Consistent with research studies (Boehnlin, 1987; Larrick, 1987; Tunnell & Jacobs, 1989), we find that literature-based instruction is a key to literacy development and improves the reading performance of all students, including students from diverse cultural and linguistic backgrounds and with varying ability levels. Along with other researchers, we find that literature-based programs are especially effective with high-risk students (Boehnlin, 1987; Larrick, 1987), with limited-English-speaking students (Larrick, 1987; Peregoy & Boyle, 1993; Quintero & Huertera-Macias, 1990), and with disinterested and disabled readers (Tunnell, Calder, Justen, & Waldrop, 1988; Tunnell & Jacobs, 1989).

Unlike these studies, however, we stress the importance of a *multicultural* literature-based program. We find that using literature that complements the cultural background of our students improves their self-image, while validating their cultural experiences and traditions (Hadaway & Florez, 1990; Reyhner & Garcia, 1989). As Mrs. Edje said, "Instead of laughing self-consciously, they are learning more about their histories, customs, traditions, and heritage—that it is something to be proud of." Through the use of multicultural literature, instruction becomes enjoyable, engaging, and motivating to all students. These affective factors, in turn, influence reading performance (Athey, 1985; Au, 1993; Eldredge & Butterfield, 1986; Moore & Diamond, 1991, 1992; Peregoy & Boyle, 1993; Reyhner & Garcia, 1989; Shumaker & Shumaker, 1988).

Merely integrating multicultural literature with reading curricula will not produce gains in reading performance. Teachers must depart from the deficit model, which implies that some students are ill-prepared for literacy acquisition (Reyhner & Garcia, 1989); they must first believe in and have expectations for *all* their students. Teachers promote literacy development by combining their high expectations with multiple opportunities to read in a social context that integrates adult guidance with peer collaboration and effective teaching strategies. Some of the effective teaching strategies discussed include: reading aloud, DRLTA, SGRTA, choral readings, reader's theater, dramatic interpretations, Radio City, paired readings, semantic mapping, Predict-O-Grams, Possible Sentences, and various writing activities.

SUMMARY

We focused in this chapter on ways to develop communicative competence, the complementary abilities of comprehending meaning through listening and reading and transmitting meaning through talking and writing. Through the use of vignettes and samples of students' reading and writing, we strove to illustrate ways teachers might open new avenues for student learning. Our goal is for *all* students to experience success in reading and writing.

We began with a description of an emotionally supportive environment that is risk free and encourages students to explore and experiment with language. Consistent with our guiding principles, we emphasized that teachers must set high expectations for *all* students and accept their knowledge about language, learning, and culture. We further illustrated how teachers can provide a foundation for literacy and a steppingstone for more complex learning by (1) building on cultural background, language systems, and experiences and (2) creating a community of learners.

The following sections highlighted various strategies for understanding meaning through listening and reading experiences. Reading multicultural stories as the framework for many learning activities provides students with many aesthetic and efferent experiences with reading, while fostering an appreciation of their own culture and the culture of others. The next sections illustrated ways to develop meaning, fluency, and automaticity through the use of choral readings, reader's theater, dramatic interpretations, Radio City, and paired reading.

The final section of the chapter emphasized strategies that promote vocabulary growth when integrated with reading aloud, discussion of meaning, and writing. These include semantic mapping, predict-o-grams, possible sentences, and writing. We demonstrated how teachers can depart from traditional techniques for gaining knowledge of words, which are seldom associated with improved vocabulary, to introduce meaningful, purposeful activities instead.

REFERENCES

Allington, R. (1983). Fluency: The neglected reading goal. *The Reading Teacher, 36,* 556–561.

Anderson, R., Hiebert, E., Scott, J., & Wilkinson, I. (1985). *Becoming a nation of readers.* Washington, D.C.: The National Institute of Education.

Athey, I. (1985). Reading research in the affective domain. In H. Singer, & R. Ruddell (Eds.), *Theoretical models and processes of reading.* Newark, DE: International Reading Association.

Au, K. (1993). *Literacy instruction in multicultural settings.* Fort Worth, TX: Harcourt Brace Jovanovich College Publishers.

Au, K., & Jordan, C. (1981). Teaching reading to Hawaiian children: Finding a culturally appropriate solution. In H. Trueba, G. P. Gutherie, & K. H. Au (Eds.), *Culture and the bilingual classroom: Studies in classroom ethnography.* (pp. 139–152). Rowley, MA: Newbury House.

Beyersdorfer, J., & Schauer, D. (1989). Semantic analysis to writing: Connecting words, books, and writing. *Journal of Reading, 32,* 500–508.

Bishop, R. (1987). Extending multicultural understanding through children's books. In B. Cullinan (Ed.), *Children's literature in the reading program.* Newark, DE: International Reading Association.

Boehnlein, M. (1987). Reading intervention for high risk first-graders. *Educational Leadership, 44,* 32–37.

Busching, B. A. (1981). Readers theatre: An education for language and life. *Language Arts, 58,* 330–338.

Cazden, C. (Ed.). (1981). *Language in early childhood education.* Washington, DC: National Association for the Education of Young Children.

Cox, S., & Galda, L. (1990). Multicultural literature: Mirrors and windows on a global community. *The Reading Teacher, 43,* 582–589.

Cummins, J. (1986). Empowering minority students. *Harvard Education Review, 56,* 866–898.

Davis, F. (1944). Fundamental factors of comprehension in reading. *Psychometrika, 9,* 185–197.

Dickinson, D. (1989). Effects of a shared reading program on one Head Start language and literacy environment. In J. Allen, & J. Mason (Eds.), *Risk makers, risk takers, risk breakers: Reducing the risks for young literacy learners.* (pp. 125-153). Portsmouth, NH: Heineman.

Dowhower, S. (1987). Effects of repeated reading on second-grade transitional readers. *Reading Research Quarterly, 22,* 389-408.

Dowhower, S. (1989). Repeated reading: Research into practice. *The Reading Teacher, 42,* 502-506.

Duin, A., & Graves, D. (1987). Intensive vocabulary instruction as a pre-writing technique. *Reading Research Quarterly, 22,* 311-330.

Durkin, D. (1980). *Teaching young children to read.* Boston: Allyn and Bacon.

Eldredge, L., & Butterfield, D. (1986). Alternatives to traditional reading instruction. *The Reading Teacher, 40,* 32-37.

Fielding, L., Wilson, P., & Anderson, R. (1986). A new focus on free reading: The role of trade books in reading instruction. In T. Raphael (Ed.), *The contexts of school-based literacy.* New York: Random House.

Fields, M., Spangler, K., & Lee, D. (1991). *Let's begin reading right: Developmentally appropriate beginning literacy.* New York: Maxwell Macmillan International Publishing Group.

Florez, V., & Hadaway, N. (1986). *Bridging linguistic and cultural differences through reading: Multiethnic literature in the classroom.* (Report No. CS 00692). Paper presented at the Annual Meeting of the Southwest Regional Conference of the International Reading Association, San Antonio, TX. (ERIC Document Reproduction Service No. ED 278059)

Florez, B., Cousin, P., & Diaz, E. (1991). Transforming deficit myths about learning, language, and culture. *Language Arts, 68,* 369-377.

Graves, D. (1983). *Writing: Teachers and children at work.* Portsmouth, NH: Heinemann.

Hadaway, N., & Florez, V. (1990). Teaching multiethnic literature, promoting cultural pluralism. *The Dragon Lode, 8,* 7-13.

Harste, J., Short, K., & Burke, C. (1988). *Creating classrooms for authors: The reading-writing connection.* Portsmouth, NH: Heinemann.

Herman, P. (1985). The effect of repeated readings on reading rate, speech pauses, and word recognition accuracy. *Reading Research Quarterly, 20,* 553-564.

Holdaway, D. (1979). *The foundations of literacy.* Gosford, N.S.W., Australia: Ashton Scholastic.

Hoskisson, K., & Tompkins, G. (1991). *Language arts: Content and teaching strategies.* Columbus, OH: Merrill Publishing Company.

Huck, C. (1979). *Children's literature in the elementary school.* New York: Holt, Rinehart & Winston.

Kinney, M., & Schmidt, J. (1988). Relating the parts to the whole in novel reading: Using story grammars to teach plot development in novels. *Wisconsin State Reading Association Journal, 31,* 47-51.

Larrick, N. (1987). Illiteracy starts too soon. *Phi Delta Kappan, 69,* 406-408.

Lipson, M. (1983). The influences of religious affiliation on children's memory for text information. *Reading Research Quarterly, 18,* 448-457.

Martinez, M., Cheyney, M., McBroom, C., Hemmeter, A., & Teale, W. (1989). No-risk kindergarten literacy environments for at-risk children. In J. Allen & J. Mason (Eds.), *Risk makers, risk takers, risk breakers: Reducing the risks for young literacy learners.* (pp. 93-124). Portsmouth, NH: Heinemann.

May, F. (1990). *Reading as communication: An interactive approach.* Columbus, OH: Merrill Publishing Company.

McCauley, J., & McCauley, D. (1992). Using choral reading to promote language learning for ESL students. *The Reading Teacher, 45,* 526-533.

Moore, M., & Diamond, B. (1991). *A staff developmental model for promoting literacy and cultural awareness: A multicultural literature-based approach.* Paper presented at the annual meeting of the American Educational Research Association, Chicago, Illinois.

Moore, M., & Diamond, B. (1992). *Promoting teacher empowerment in a multicultural literature program.* Paper presented at the annual meeting of the American Educational Research Association, San Francisco, CA.

Morgan, R., & Lyon, E. (1979). Paired reading—A preliminary report on a technique for parental tutoring of reading-retarded children. *Journal of Child Psychology, 20,* 151-160.

Morrow, L. (1982). Relationships between literature programs, library corner designs and children's use of literature. *Journal of Educational Research, 75,* 339-344.

Nagy, W. (1988/89). *Teaching vocabulary to improve reading comprehension.* Urbana, IL: National Council of Teachers of English.

Norton, D. (1991). *Through the eyes of a child: An introduction to children's literature.* New York: Macmillan.

Peregoy, S., & Boyle, O. (1993). *Reading, writing, and learning in ESL.* New York: London.

Quintero, E., & Huetera-Macias, A. (1990). All in the family: Bilingualism and biliteracy. *The Reading Teacher, 44,* 306-312.

Raphael, T. (1982). Question-answering strategies for children. *The Reading Teacher, 36,* 186-191.

Raphael, T. (1986). Teaching question-answer relationships, revisited. *The Reading Teacher, 39,* 516-522.

Reyhner, J., & Garcia, R. (1989). Helping minorities read better: Problems and promises. *Reading Research and Instruction, 28,* 84-91.

Rosen, N., Hoffman, J., & Farest, C. (1990). Language, literacy, and at-risk children. *The Reading Teacher, 43,* 554-559.

Rosenblatt, L. M. (1978). *The reader, the text, the poem: The transactional theory of the literary work.* Carbondale: Southern Illinois University.

Rosenblatt, L. (1985). The transactional theory of the literary work: Implications for research. In C. R. Cooper (Ed.), *Researching response to literature and the teaching of literature.* (pp. 33-53). Norwood, NJ: Ablex.

Routman, R. (1991). *Invitations: Changing as teachers and learners K-12.* Portsmouth, NH: Heinemann.

Sampson, M., Allen, R., & Sampson, M. (1991). *Pathways to literacy.* Chicago: Holt, Rinehart and Winston.

Samuels, S. (1988). Decoding and automaticity. *The Reading Teacher, 41,* 756-760.

Santa, C., Dailey, S., & Nelson, M. (1985). Free response and opinion proof. A reading and writing strategy for middle grade and secondary teachers. *Journal of Reading, 28,* 346-352.

Shanklin, N., & Rhodes, L. (1989). Comprehension instruction as sharing and extending. *The Reading Teacher, 42,* 496-500.

Shumaker, M., & Shumaker, R. (1988). 3,000 paper cranes: Children's literature for remedial readers. *The Reading Teacher, 41,* 344-349.

Spearitt, D. (1972). Identification of subskills in reading comprehension by maximum likelihood factor analysis. *Reading Research Quarterly, 8,* 92-111.

Stahl, N. (1986). Three principles of effective vocabulary instruction: A model-based meta-analysis. *Review of Educational Research, 56,* 72-110.

Stahl, S., & Clark, C. (1987). The effects of participatory expectations in classroom discussion on the learning of science vocabulary. *American Educational Research Journal, 24,* 541-556.

Stahl, S., & Kapinus, B. (1991). Possible sentences: Predicting word meanings to teach content area vocabulary. *The Reading Teacher, 45,* 36–43.

Stauffer, R. (1975). *Directing in reading-thinking process.* New York: Harper & Row.

Stewig, J. (1981). Choral speaking. Who has the time? Why take the time? *Childhood Education, 58,* 25–29.

Templeton, S. (1991). *Teaching the integrated language arts.* Boston: Houghton Mifflin.

Thurstone, L. (1946). A note on a reanalysis of Davis' reading test. *Psychometrika, 11,* 185–188.

Trelease, J. (1985). *The read-aloud handbook.* New York: Viking/Penguin.

Trelease, J. (1989). *The new read-aloud handbook.* New York: Penguin.

Tunnell, M., Calder, J., Justen, J., & Waldrop, P. (1988). An affective approach to reading: Effectively teaching reading to mainstreamed handicapped children. *The Pointer, 32,* 38–40.

Tunnell, M., & Jacobs, J. (1989). Using "real" books: Research findings on literature based reading instruction. *The Reading Teacher, 42,* 470–477.

Vacca, J. A., Vacca, R., & Gove, M. (1991). *Reading and learning to read.* New York: Harper Collins.

Vygotsky, L. S. (1978). *Mind in society.* Cambridge, MA: Harvard University Press.

Wells, G. (1986). *The meaning makers: Children learning language and using language to learn.* Portsmouth, NJ: Heinemann.

Woodbury, J. (1979). Choral reading and reader's theatre: Oral interpretation of literature in the classroom. In D. L. Monson, & D. K. McClenathan (Eds.), *Developing active readers: Ideas for parents, teachers, and librarians.* (pp. 65–72). Newark, DE: International Reading Association.

chapter **5**

Generating Meaning Through Writing Experiences with Multicultural Literature

OVERVIEW

In this chapter we describe practical strategies to promote writing in a multicultural program, with the focus on process writing. By integrating research and theory about the writing process with practical teaching strategies, including detailed descriptions and samples of students' writing, we hope to furnish teachers with many instructional techniques that will enable students to convey meaning through writing. By following a process approach and using the cultural background and experiences of our students, we further hope to promote the growth and development of young writers of all ability levels. The use of multicultural literature, a key component of a multicultural program, provides a stimulus, as well as a model of language, for writing ideas for all students. Multicultural literature further becomes a natural way to integrate the reading and writing processes so that each supports and reinforces the development of the other.

We begin with an overview of the writing process, its connection to reading, and ways to facilitate written expression. This overview is followed by a variety of multicultural writing activities, which can be adapted to any grade level. Through the use of vignettes and samples of students' writing, we illustrate more clearly how to implement these writing activities.

THE WRITING PROCESS

Traycee handed us this touching poem at the end of class one day. This was the second poem Traycee wrote that day. She is learning that writing is a way to express her ideas and feelings.

Look into the future
See what is there
A bunch of sweet little children seating in there
Mama's chair waiting for her but she don't come
It is to much hissle and work to be done
She act like she don't ever care
Because if she did she would be siting in the mamma's
chair

                                                    Traycee, Grade 4

One can see that her voice flows naturally from the printed page. How did Traycee learn to express her ideas and feelings so freely? Just a short time ago she had said, "I can't write. I don't know what to write about." How did she become so comfortable with writing that she was willing to write *two* poems in a 45-minute class session? This chapter describes how to create a print-rich, socioculturally sensitive environment that stimulates young learners to become authors who, like Traycee, are enthusiastic about reading and writing.

The writing process, which involves thinking, feeling, and communication (Daiute, 1985; Graves, 1978a; 1978b), is a dynamic, complex process. Moffett (1982) suggests that writing is a discovery process as writers expand and master inner speech. While writers are actively constructing meaning, they use their knowledge and experiences to generate ideas in order to create meaning. As they transform their experiences and knowledge into written language, they make judgments about idealized readers' backgrounds; they make decisions about ways to express their ideas so that readers think or act in a certain fashion (Flower & Hayes, 1981). Throughout, writers use problem-solving strategies to plan, select, combine, arrange, monitor, and evaluate relationships between their writing and the needs of the intended audience.

Helping young writers, especially students from diverse cultures and linguistic backgrounds, discover the ideas they wish to express and what form or structure they will use to translate these ideas into written language represents a challenge to teachers. The pioneering work of Graves (1978a; 1983), Emig (1971), and Flower and Hayes (1981) confirm the importance of using a process approach to writing. This approach includes five subprocesses—the stages of composing that writers follow in order to communicate effectively. Various labels are used to describe the subprocesses of composing. For the purposes of this chapter, we apply the following five stages of the writing process: (a) prewriting, (b) drafting, (c) revising, (d) editing, and (e) sharing. Even though the labels describe the subprocesses in a linear fashion, the process is recursive as writers move back and forth among the subprocesses.

Prewriting

During the prewriting stage, writers discover their ideas while setting goals and organizing and generating content through prewriting and rehearsal activities. They transform their ideas and thoughts to written language. According to Murray (1978), 70 percent or more of writing time should be spent in prewriting or rehearsal activities. Prewriting or rehearsal activities refer to activities that prepare students for composing, as writers daydream, sketch, doodle, make lists or clusters of words, outline, read, converse, or write. While students do these things, particularly talking, they gain control over inner speech. We have observed that students who come from diverse cultural backgrounds or home environments that have an oral tradition particularly benefit from opportunities to express their ideas aloud during this stage of writing. Task-directed talk—the use of oral language for functional and meaningful purposes (Peregoy & Boyle, 1993)—further enables second-language learners to develop their own thinking and expand second-language proficiency in oral and written language.

Providing multiple opportunities for all students to expand and master inner speech becomes critical during this stage of writing. We find that many students— especially reluctant writers, students of diverse cultures and linguistic backgrounds, or students of lower ability—feel they do not know what to write about or how to express their ideas. By using several brainstorming, clustering, freewriting, webbing, or sketching activities (see Figure 5.1), these writers can more easily make connections between their own background experiences and new knowledge in order to generate written language.

Creating a risk-free environment where students experiment and explore written language further supports reluctant writers as they overcome their hesitancy to write, which is often the result of their repeated failures with writing and its conventions. Similarly, students from diverse cultural and linguistic backgrounds overcome their reluctance to write, which is often caused by their feeling that their language differences or experiential differences may not be affirmed. These informal activities enable *all* writers to gather and organize ideas for writing in an atmosphere of

FIGURE 5.1   Examples of webbing by students of various grade levels.

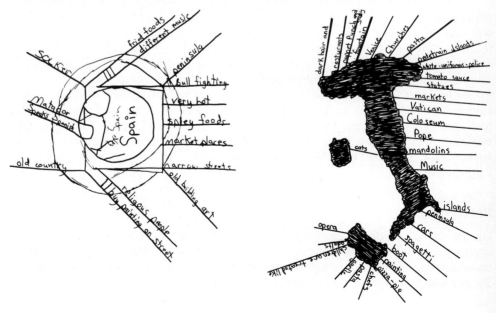

respect and acceptance. As they uncover their inner speech, they, like Traycee, soon discover they are authors who have something to say.

Young authors also need to consider function, audience, and form during this stage of writing. While gathering information, they mentally plan and organize content according to function, audience, and form of their final product. Planning and organizing content is a recursive event that includes both global (overall) planning and in-process planning (planning that occurs as writers locate their ideas while expanding their inner speech). Global and in-process planning are influenced by (a) the function of the writing piece—to entertain, to persuade, to inform, or to describe; (b) the form—a poem, story, letter, journal entry, joke, script, or cartoon; and (c) the audience—teachers, peers, younger children, pen pals, parents, grandparents, or principals.

If they are to become successful writers, students need to learn how to plan and organize information according to these three components. Teachers in our multicultural program, therefore, consistently inform students about the function, form, and audience for each writing piece. They further help young authors acquire monitoring schemes so that they might determine how to place their ideas within their text, how to emphasize certain ideas, and how to achieve their goals for expressing the ideas according to the function, form, and audience for the specific writing piece. When several prewriting and rehearsal activities are used during this stage, we find that writers are able to discover their ideas more easily and use these monitoring strategies to form a coherent text. Students further develop fluency and automaticity in their writing through these prewriting and rehearsal activities.

Nevertheless, our teachers realize that students of varied backgrounds often express their ideas in different forms, using stylistic techniques that relate to their cultural or linguistic background. Other students might alternate back and forth between their native language and English as they record their ideas on paper. As cultural organizers and mediators, teachers recognize what's important; they realize that their first goal is to encourage their students to begin writing and to become comfortable with writing. If a student chooses to write a story instead of a poem, we encourage him or her to explore this avenue. If a student switches back and forth between two languages or linguistic forms, we welcome his or her ideas. Acceptance of alternative ways of expressing written language has its own rewards. For example, after completing his draft of a peace poem (see Chapter 8), Tian-an spontaneously rewrote his peace poem in Chinese, as shown in Figure 5.2.

Drafting

During this stage of writing, students focus on transforming their thoughts into written form. According to Humes (1983), drafting makes huge demands on writers' cognitive processes. Writers must simultaneously record their ideas and thoughts while dealing with conventions of writing—structure, spelling, handwriting, typing, punctuation, and grammar. To alleviate these cognitive demands, teachers need to help students realize that what they write is temporary. They need to reassure their students that information and content are more important than the correct spellings of words, for example. As students have more experiences with writing in this supportive environment that allows them to use their temporary or invented spellings, they can devote fuller attention to topic information and content. Over time,

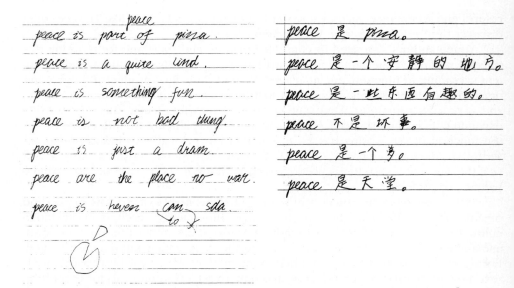

FIGURE 5.2   Tian-an's peace poem in English and Chinese.

students learn the conventions of spellings, which become more automatic. As Graves (1983) and Clark (1987) explain, students who take control of their information soon acquire the mechanical conventions through practice.

By approaching writing as a series of drafts, young authors realize they can modify their earlier decisions about their writing piece in order to communicate more effectively. Strategies that enable students to consider their writing temporary include: skipping lines as they write drafts, placing arrows to rearrange text, using cross-outs to delete sections, cutting and pasting text to insert new information, and stamping papers with a ROUGH DRAFT stamp. In classrooms where word processors are available, this shifting and deletion of text becomes even quicker and easier.

Through experimentation and manipulation of language during the drafting stage, therefore, young writers gain valuable knowledge about written text and mechanical conventions. Rescued from their concerns about the conventions of written language, students are able to discover the words to express their ideas more readily. They soon find that writing becomes an outlet for venting their feelings and sharing their experiences. Expressing their emotions and feelings through writing enables them to understand themselves better and to discover solutions to problems in their daily lives. Once their thoughts and feelings become more fluid in their writing, the voice—the imprint of the writer—emerges more naturally. Later, during editing, mechanical errors can be corrected.

Revising

The subprocess of revising is characterized by backward movements to read and determine "whether or not the words on the page capture the original sense intended" (Perl, 1979, p. 331). Revision is more than polishing writing; revision is rereading, reexamining, deleting, shaping, and correcting the written message to meet the needs of readers. The ability to revise or "see again" emerges as students view words as temporary and information as manipulatable (Calkins, 1979; Graves, 1983).

Some revisions occur naturally during drafting as students make changes in word choices, cross out words or phrases, or insert new words or phrases. After completing a first draft, writers need to distance themselves from the draft for a few days and then reread the piece from a fresh perspective—the viewpoint of a reader. While rereading, they make more changes by adding, substituting, deleting, and rearranging text.

To help students view their writing from the reader's perspective, they meet in writing response groups—small writing groups consisting of three to five writers— to share their compositions. As students read their drafts aloud, they often spontaneously insert, delete, or substitute words to clarify their ideas. This is the beginning of revising. These response groups further support writers by offering them choices, giving them feedback and praise, and showing them plans and strategies for expressing their ideas. As authors share their writing with their writing response group, the listeners follow the **PQP (Praise, Question, Polish) Formula:** The listeners **praise** the author's writing and ask **questions;** the authors then share their plans for **polishing** the writing piece.

Specifically, students meet in their writing response groups to share their composition by following these sequential activities:

- The author reads the writing piece aloud to the group.
- Listeners respond with specific praise about the piece.

FIGURE 5.3 Demetrius and his writing response group reread his story, thinking of ways to clarify its meaning and make his story more interesting.

- The author enlists the help of the listeners for trouble spots.
- Listeners ask questions to help clarify meaning and offer suggestions and comments for improving the writing.
- The author shares two or three revisions he or she will use to improve the composition.
- Each writer in the group repeats the process.

Throughout this stage of the writing process, all authors are acknowledged, respect for each is emphasized, and each author's successes are celebrated. Consequently, motivation increases; reading and writing become intertwined naturally.

When writers first meet with their writing response groups, however, they often feel awkward and uncomfortable; they are not sure what comments they should make about their peers' writing and they are not used to asking questions. We find that brainstorming lists of acceptable responses to writing and examples of questions facilitates this process. The responses to writing (see Figure 5.4) usually focus on word choice, descriptive words, dialogue, interesting leads to stories, or organizational strategies such as a surprise ending. Questions (see Figure 5.5) listeners ask usually focus on additional information about the characters, the setting, or the events in a story or information about the topic, the details, or the clarity of the ideas expressed (adapted from Clark, 1987; Tompkins, 1990). By taking time to model praise and questions and to discuss possible responses to questions about an author's writing, teachers provide students with strategies to use in their response groups. Gradually, students overcome their feelings of awkwardness and discomfort. In fact, they begin to look forward to writing response groups. (See "Using Multicultural

FIGURE 5.4   Examples of Responses to Students' Writings.

Responses to Writing

I love the words you used to describe. . .
I love the words you used to explain. . .
I love your use of colorful words. . . I could picture the events in my mind.
I love your leading sentence. It. . .
I like your use of dialogue. . . I could hear the people talking.
I like the part where you . . . it made me laugh.
I like the part where you. . . I could just imagine it.
I especially like your title because. . .
Your ending was great. It. . .
Your story made me feel. . .
Your writing reminds me of. . .
You told the story just like it happened. . .
Tell me more about. . .
What happened next. . .
What is your pet's name. . . What does he eat. . . What kinds of things does he like to do. . .
How did you feel when. . . happened. . .

Questions Listeners Ask

Introductory Comments and Questions:

- Tell me about your writing.
- Why did you choose this topic?
- Why is this topic important to you?
- Who is your audience?
- What form will you use?
- How will you start your draft?
- How will you plan to organize your writing?
- What is the setting for your story? Who are the characters?
- What part do you like the most so far?
- Do you know what I like best about your writing?
- What will you plan to write about next?
- Are you having any problems?
- Do you have any questions you want to ask me?

Questions that Deal With Meaning:

- Do you have more than one story in your draft?
- Can you point to the part that tells me what your draft is about?
- What is the most important thing you are trying to say here?
- Can you tell me more about. . .?
- How did you feel when this happened?
- How did you show us. . .?
- How do you feel about your descriptions?
- What words can you use to describe. . .?
- Where did your story take place?
- What part doesn't make sense?
- Does your writing answer the questions: Who? What? When? Where? Why?

Questions that Deal With Voice:

- How does your draft sound when you read it out loud?
- Underline the part that is most exciting to you.
- Can you show me a place where we hear you speaking?
- Can you show me a place where we hear the characters speaking?

Design Questions:

- What do you like about your introduction?
- Does your leading sentence grab the reader's attention?
- What do you like about your ending?
- Does the middle tie the beginning and ending together?
- Do you need to add any details?
- Do you need to add more to this part?
- Do you need this part?

Clarity Questions:

- Can you tell me more about. . .?
- What words can you use to describe. . .?
- What are your action words? Can you add others?
- Can you say this in a different way?
- What is the best word to use here?

Questions That Help Writers Continue:

- What do you want to do next?
- What can you do to make your draft better?
- What works well in your writing? Can you develop this in another part of your writing?
- Can you add more to this part?
- Do you need a closing for your writing?
- Can you combine some sentences to say the same thing?

Questions That Help Writers See Their Growth as Authors:

- What is your favorite part? Why?
- Can you think of something new you tried in this draft?
- How did you make your writing clearer?
- What changes did you make in your writing?
- How does this piece compare to your other writing?
- Do you see ways you are improving your writing?
- If you were writing this again, what changes would you make?
- How did you use the writing process in your writing?
- What did your audience like about your writing?

FIGURE 5.5 Examples of questions listeners might ask writers.

Literature Stories as a Model for Writing: Revising the Story" p. 157 for more specific details about this process.)

According to Graves (1983), students must learn that revising means "messing up the page" (p. 87) and must acquire the viewpoint that writing is temporary if they are to become effective writers. Inexperienced writers, however, are reluctant to mar a page of writing. To soften these feelings of discomfort, we encourage students to skip lines on their first drafts, and we praise students who are revising their writing. We also model strategies for inserting new words with carets, deleting information with line-outs, and rearranging information with arrows through communal writing pieces—pieces written together as a class. While composing a poem, myth, or legend as a class on the overhead transparency, for example, we can model the strategies we naturally use as we write. Using line-outs, carets, or arrows demonstrates how a messy draft can help clarify ideas for readers.

Throughout this process, teachers provide guidance and direction about composing and revising. As students share and discuss their writing in response groups, culturally and linguistically diverse students further have numerous opportunities for oral discussion and supportive interactions about their writing. Over time, they learn strategies to elaborate and clarify their written expressions in an environment that appreciates and accepts their ideas (Peregoy & Boyle, 1993).

Editing

During this stage of the writing process, the focus shifts from content to mechanics. Writers polish their writing by correcting spelling, punctuation, capitalization, grammar, and word usage. Young authors learn that mechanics—commonly accepted conventions of written standard English—make their writing readable to others. By interweaving the conventions of language in a purposeful, meaningful context, we notice students acquire these skills more readily.

We find that students are more effective editors when they work in pairs (usually of differing ability levels) and after they have set the writing piece aside for a few days. We use editing checklists that arrange specific errors in order of priority so that students can proofread particular categories of error without becoming overwhelmed. These checklists range from two to six items, depending on the grade level and the number of proofreading experiences students have had. A primary-grade checklist or a first experience with proofreading, for example, might include two items—one for capitals at the beginning of sentences and one for punctuation at the end of sentences. Similarly linguistically diverse students need more time and support during this stage of writing. Focusing on one or two items, therefore, enables them to learn and talk about the features of the English language without feeling discouraged. As the year progresses, checklists (see Figure 5.6) are extended to emphasize mechanics they have learned or are learning.

At the bottom of the checklist is a place for students to sign their names. This strategy underscores the importance of proofreading carefully and emphasizes responsibility for proofreading. Pairs of students who complete the checklist without checking for errors are asked to review their work once again, trying to find their mechanical errors. If a group needs additional cues to find their errors, we place a dot by a line that needs to be proofread more carefully, or we ask students to proofread

Primary Editing Checklist

— I spelled my words correctly.
— I ended each sentence with a period, question mark, or exclamation mark.
— I began each sentence with a capital.
— I began all the words in my title with a capital letter.
— I used a capital for the word *I*.

Editing Checklists for Elementary Students

— I spelled my words correctly.
— I used correct punctuation (periods, question marks, exclamation marks, commas, quotation marks).
— I began each sentence with a capital.
— I began all the words in my title with a capital letter.
— I used capital letters for names of places, things, or people.
— I used a capital for the word *I*.
— I used complete sentences.
— I indented each paragraph.
— Each paragraph has a topic sentence and detail sentences.

FIGURE 5.6 Examples of Items for Editing Checklists for Young Writers

the beginning, the middle, or the end of the writing piece more closely to find an error. In this way, students are actively involved in the editing process under our guidance.

Because the teams are of mixed ability levels, we find the need to use cues becomes less necessary over time. We also find that all students are more willing to use the dictionary, the thesaurus, or grammar books to locate information and correct mechanical errors. Working with a partner to use these tools makes the task less overwhelming.

As all students become familiar with the conventions of language in the meaningful context of peer editing, they soon begin to apply these strategies in their own work. To facilitate this transfer of learning, we follow Clark's (1987, p. 137) model of teaching grammar, usage, and mechanics "as tools not rules"; we preteach the tools students should apply in their writing. For example, if students are going to write a paragraph about Native American beliefs after reading several Native American myths and legends, we review topic sentences, the importance of detail sentences about the topic, and indentation of paragraphs. Having students use these conventions in their writing and proofread for correct usage of the conventions in this way makes the learning more meaningful and purposeful. Working in editing teams with supervision further enables them to gain the reader's perspective and solve problems in their writing so that a reader can understand their message.

Sharing

Sharing, a critical element of the writing process that should occur during all stages of the process, is the time to celebrate students' compositions. Whether sharing the lists of words from a word web during the prewriting stage, the opening sentences of a new story, the revised ending of a poem, or the published writing piece, sharing becomes a catalyst for more writing to evolve. By simply allowing students to share their reading with their peers, teachers can change students' viewpoints about themselves as writers. The spontaneous laughter, the natural comments of praise, the murmurs of excitement in anticipation of events to come, or the spontaneous applause encourages young authors. These feelings grow when authors read their writing while seated in the author's chair—a special chair, frequently placed in a carpeted area so that the class can gather around the author, where students read or tell about their writing pieces. Students further develop sensitivity to an audience and confidence in themselves as writers through this social activity of sharing.

Multicultural awareness and appreciation further evolve naturally during this stage of writing. As young authors sit in the author's chair, sharing their writings about multicultural themes and books while their peers listen to their ideas, students gain new insights about diverse cultures, traditions, and heritages. Using the author's chair in these ways parallels the custom of storytelling, an important feature of many groups of people.

To guide appropriate peer responses to the writing, as cultural organizers we teachers continuously model how to respond to writing. We express our joy in their choice of picturesque descriptive words, their use of lively verbs, their captivating lead, or their surprise ending. As our students hear our specific praise about their writing and what makes it interesting, they begin to echo these words of praise within their writing response groups.

Other examples of formally sharing include published books of class poems, myths, legends, or folk tales that mirror diverse cultures; stories that are bound and placed in the library; shape books; big books; bulletin board and hall displays; posters; letters; a class newspaper; mobiles; and published plays, reader's theater, choral readings, filmstrips, videotapes, or puppet theaters. Ways of informally sharing include reading their writing aloud to their writing response groups or their classes, their parents or siblings, another class, the principal, or other teachers. Of importance, all students benefit from multiple opportunities to share their writing in both formal and informal ways. Through casual exchanges, students learn from each other; through formal exchanges, listeners gain new insights about the diverse experiences and histories of their peers. Simultaneously, young writers acquire a better perspective of audience.

HELPING YOUNG AUTHORS DISCOVER WRITING

Cultural organizers and mediators realize that young writers need to be introduced to the writing process, whether they are in first or eighth grade, they come from different cultures or linguistic backgrounds, or they have differing ability levels. Helping students discover how the writing process can help them express ideas is equally important. According to Clark (1987), writers depend on the process to generate their ideas for writing. They learn which steps will lead to a desired result, even when they are unhappy, lazy, insecure, or troubled. He further asserts that the process gives writers confidence as they realize that writing is an act of self-knowledge and self-discovery.

As we continue to work with students of diverse cultures and linguistic backgrounds, we realize that these goals—self-knowledge and self-discovery—are essential. When students uncover ways to express their ideas and thoughts, they legitimize their cultural experiences, ideas, and histories. They further begin to understand themselves and the world around them more clearly; solutions to problems surface. In the following sections, we provide some strategies that we discovered to help students become successful writers who love composing. We hope they will all share Adelle's feelings about writing; she said, "I love to write in my spare time; I love to write long stories, songs, and stuff like that."

Helping Students Understand and Appreciate the Writing Process

To help our young writers begin to think about and remember the writing process and its stages, we display its recursive stages on classroom charts and bulletin boards. Over time, we have found that the process becomes more automatic, reliable, and versatile, yet somewhat predictable, for our students.

Even though these stages of writing are described in a linear fashion, they are recursive in nature. Students easily move back and forth among them, generating ideas from their inner speech. While composing, they develop, refine, and polish these ideas to create meaningful texts.

Not all writing, however, needs to move through each stage formally. A journal entry, for example, might be abandoned after drafting, or a Predict-O-Gram story about *The Hallowed Horse* (see Chapter 4) might be scrapped after it is shared orally with the class. We recognize that publishing all writing formally can become overwhelming to both students and teachers. Students and teachers who are burned out from publishing their writing formally will no longer want to write. This would defeat our goal to help students communicate effectively.

Reading and Writing: Similar Processes of Constructing Meaning

Our teachers also realize that writing, which is considered to be an integral component of literacy, is an important element of the multicultural literacy curriculum. As explained in Chapter 1, background knowledge and prior experiences influence both reading and writing development, which are similar processes of constructing meaning. Specifically, students use their prior experiences and knowledge to *generate* meaning while they write; they use their prior experiences and knowledge to *create* meaning while they read.

Language, the medium for transforming thought into symbols, is the foundation of the reading/writing process. According to Vygotsky (1978), young children are at first dependent on others for expressing their thoughts. During infancy, when they are unable to generate elaborate ideas about things and execute or plan complex tasks, they rely on the external speech of those around them. Simultaneously, they learn to speak, themselves, by experimenting with and exploring language. Having good language models enables young children to enrich their own language and thinking. Opportunities to talk and express their ideas in a risk-free environment further brings this knowledge to a conscious level.

If students are to become readers and writers, they, too, need multiple opportunities to talk and express their ideas; they need a comfortable, safe environment where they can experiment and explore language in varied grouping configurations. Creating a print-rich, socioculturally sensitive environment that is shaped by positive student-teacher interactions, is a primary component of our multicultural program. (See Figure 1.1 in Chapter 1.) Teachers are cultural mediators and organizers as they guide, monitor, support, observe, evaluate, and revise instructional techniques to support literacy, which develops from the personal and cultural experiences of their learners. Students are actively involved in their own learning—observing, using, and transacting with print in meaningful, functional contexts that are compatible with their cultural backgrounds.

By integrating reading and writing, we strive to support and strengthen the reading and writing processes. Multicultural literature, combined with whole language and multicultural perspectives (see Figure 1.1), is one way to promote this integration naturally. Following whole language principles, we help students become readers who think about writers and writers who think about readers. Moreover, when reading and writing are integrated in meaningful, purposeful ways (Bromley, 1989; Graves & Stuart, 1987; Langer, 1986; Moore, 1991; Shanahan, 1988; Tierney & Pearson, 1983), research indicates significant gains in reading and writing performance occur. Furthermore if reading and writing experiences become compatible with students' cultural and linguistic backgrounds, our research demonstrates that there can be significant gains in reading and writing performance (Moore & Diamond, 1992).

Creating a Risk-Free Environment for Writers

Teachers who acknowledge this relationship between reading and writing realize they need to provide more time for writing activities within their curriculum. But many teachers are not yet comfortable with teaching writing because they perceive a reluctance among their students to write. Such reluctance is sometimes characteristic of culturally diverse students who express their thoughts in their dialect or informal language styles. Similarly, bilingual students are sometimes hesitant writers because they have not yet gained fluency in the second language; many times their written expressions are a blend of their native language and English. Other students have not had positive experiences with writing because no one has allowed them to develop as readers and writers. In fact, many times their writing bleeds from the red ink pen of teachers who are trying to help them acquire the mechanics of written language. Too often these concerned teachers have overemphasized the product rather than the process. They have not recognized that many of these students have valuable ideas but are more proficient in expressing their ideas through oral language; they do not realize that all students can learn to express these ideas successfully through written language, with nurturing and support.

To overcome students' feelings of discomfort, we urge teachers to begin with students' strengths, whatever they might be. Rejecting the language and culture of our students jeopardizes future academic performance. Recognizing the cultural and linguistic strengths of students enhances academic performance (Cummins, 1986;

Florez, Cousin, & Diaz, 1991; Quintero & Huerta-Macias, 1990; Reyhner & Garcia, 1989). Once we acknowledge and affirm their ideas—whether expressed in oral or written language—we can use the writing process to help them record their message in conventional language. First attempts to transform some students' oral language into written language may be facilitated by teachers or their peers as we record their ideas on paper for them. When students see their ideas in print and hear themselves read the printed message, they soon realize they are authors. They learn that the message is far more important than correctly spelled words or properly punctuated sentences.

To further bring out ideas, our program's teachers give students an opportunity to write each day in a warm, accepting atmosphere where they are free to take risks and experiment with language. Once students believe we are pleased with their writing—even if it is a single line of temporary or invented spellings, a mixture of Spanish and English symbols and sounds, or scribbling—they gradually become more comfortable with written language and begin to express their ideas and thoughts in print.

The mechanics of writing emerge later in the meaningful context of the revising and editing stages, when students are ready to acquire these skills. Writing is a highly complex process. During the beginning stages of writing, students cannot simultaneously monitor their ideas and the conventions of writing. Forcing conventions of language too early stifles expression. Many students, in fact, will leave their pages

FIGURE 5.7 Through writing, Dominique discovers she is an author.

blank or compromise their ideas for something that is easy to spell because of their fear of the red ink pen. Therefore, we help our students first become comfortable with writing, encouraging them to share their writing orally with their peers. Revising and editing begins as students express an interest in publishing their writing formally for others to see and read.

As teachers who are sensitive to all students, therefore, we:

- Give students many opportunities to make choices in their writing.
- Provide an atmosphere rich with environmental print.
- Provide a positive role model for reading and writing.
- Provide an environment that emphasizes learning to read and write naturally.
- Focus on the writing process, not the writing product.
- Eliminate criticism and minimize emphasis on mistakes.
- Avoid premature emphasis on mechanical skills.
- Model respect for differences.

As students learn to use the writing process in this caring environment, which includes readily accessible materials for writing, they begin to look forward to writing. Some important suggestions include:

- Use words of encouragement and specific praise.
- Help writers feel "I'm O.K.," even when they make errors.
- Give students a variety of writing tools and materials readily available.
- Create opportunities for collaborative writing.
- Surround students with multicultural literature, drama, art, music, dance, and play.
- Use multicultural books that include a variety of language patterns and dialects.
- Emphasize meaning.
- Avoid punitive writing interactions.

Once this nurturing context is established, our teachers are fascinated with how quickly their students generate their own excitement about reading and writing. They are also impressed with their students' renewed understanding of themselves and their world. They see students asking questions, making observations, and recording their ideas on paper. Culturally and linguistically diverse students simultaneously acquire the conventions of language and grow in oral and written expression.

The remainder of this chapter describes how students learn to take charge of their own learning through writing. To help others understand the process more fully, we will use vignettes to describe how the activities were implemented. We also include samples of students' writing during the various stages of writing.

LEARNING TO EXPRESS IDEAS THROUGH INFORMAL WRITING ACTIVITIES

Personal Journals

Clark (1987) emphasizes that real-life writing enables students to learn about themselves, about others in their community, and about issues that influence their lives. Personal journals, informal journals that are used for writing about topics of choice, are wonderful tools for helping beginning writers discover themselves and ways to communicate their ideas and feelings to others. Because the writing usually emerges from their own lives and experiences, students are able to express their ideas more easily and freely. These early encounters with written language become positive experiences, which are critical for students from diverse cultures and linguistic backgrounds, as well as for at-risk students. Kindergarten and first- and second-grade teachers usually construct personal journals by stapling several sheets of paper together with colored construction paper covers. Teachers in the upper elementary grades and middle school prefer to use colored folders with pockets, or spiral notebooks.

By having students record their ideas in their personal journals on a daily basis, Miss Bortz finds that her students become more comfortable with writing. And the more her students write, the better they write. She observes that journal writing becomes a safe place for her students to express themselves and discover their ideas. To help her students find topics for writing, she begins each week with a five-minute brainstorming session of possible ideas to write about in their journals. As she records their ideas on large chart paper, her students write the ideas down on their own sheets of paper. These ideas are then clipped to the front of their journal. Whenever writers are not able to come up with a topic on a given day, they refer to these sheets for possible ideas. In this way, they become authors who are no longer dependent on their teacher for writing topics.

The following entries illustrate the variety of topics Miss Bortz's writers choose:

Black history means a lot to me. Like what my great untis done for me. Like Harrit tubman done she freed the black slaves. now Put yourshelf in their shatawation [situation] it would be hard. Now liten to what some people went throw . . . My teacher told us a story about a black woman who was try to get away she had a baby the baby would cry she held it to her chest and when thay got across the border her baby died. Now put your shelf in that shitwaytion [situation]. What would you do? Think of what they went throw. Think of what I told you even thow I am a 11 year old child I still understand.

Erica, Grade 5

I live a pretty exciting and a different life from some of the kids still I live a normal life. When I was age two was one of my exciting years and a war was going on. I would have a feeling that my family and me would never be free cause my family and me were kept by the thai soldiers and there would be a river near the village where my family were kept on. One day my family was saying they were going fishing to one of the guards, but really they were trying to get across from the river. Cause that river leads to freedom and there would be my dad's brother across the other side of the river. My parents would give me a sleeping pill so I wouldn't make any noise cause there was guards and soldiers on ships. This is the time and they have to do it. They would swim underwater and manage to escape. But I wish I could go back in the pass and see how it felt like. being kept in thai and don't have freedom but I kind of know how it felt. I call that river freedom river. I really miss loas. I had never seen most of my relatives cause they live in loas. Someday I would go back to my country. But most of all I want to learn about loas history, how they felt like in the way and learn their culture and see my relatives.

Vangchai, Grade 5

As one can see, these students are learning about themselves, their past, and their culture through writing. Vangchai continued to write his story about his family's escape to freedom. Later he revised his journal entries and submitted the story to a Young Authors Conference in his school district. (See Appendix.) As students choose their writing topics, their voice emerges and the message flows.

Miss Bortz further says her students become more motivated to complete their journal entries each day if she invites a few students to share their journal entries with a friend or the class at the end of the writing session. Other teachers prefer to have students share a favorite journal entry with a friend or the class each Friday. Having an audience for his journal entry, for example, helped Vangchai realize that his story was interesting to others. This experience seemed to spark his enthusiasm to write more about his experience and eventually publish the story for the Young Authors Conference. As Vangchai and Erica spontaneously share their knowledge and experiences through their journal entries, new opportunities for cultural understanding and sensitivity also emerge. As students listen, they ask questions and discuss their feelings and thoughts about their peers' experiences.

Dialogue Journals

Mrs. Reaume, a first-grade teacher who uses personal journals, periodically includes her comments about their journal entries. These dialogue journals are very similar to personal journals, except that Mrs. Reaume responds to her students' entries by asking questions, sharing additional information about a topic, or adding information about her own personal experiences that relate to the topic. While responding to her students' writing, she models effective conventions of language. Through her responses, her students begin to realize what a sentence and words look like, how to express their ideas more clearly, and how to use the mechanics of language. Even though she never critiques their written responses or points out misspelled words or missing capital letters, her students quickly begin to imitate her model of spelling, punctuation, and capitalization in future journal entries.

Mrs. Reaume reports that her students become more motivated to write, and they begin to write longer, more elaborate responses once she begins using the dialogue journals. She also observes that the journals help her learn more about the personal experiences of her students and perceive their growth and development in writing. Figure 5.8 shows an example of a child's journal entry.

Mr. Flynn, a special education teacher, likes to keep his own dialogue journal for a few minutes each day. Each day one student responds to his journal entry. The following is an example of his journal entry with the accompanying student response:

9/17/92

   I am really excited today. I am going bowling tonight. I bowl every Thursday night with my friends. It's really the only night that I really get to see my friends.

9/17/92

   It sounds like fun to go bowling. So who are your friends? Hope you have good time.

One can see that Mr. Flynn's students are reflecting his model of responding to their writing. They react to his ideas and the content of his message. They also enjoy asking him questions, just as he asks them questions.

Consistent with Peregoy and Boyle (1993), many teachers find that dialogue

FIGURE 5.8 An example of first-grade journal entry.

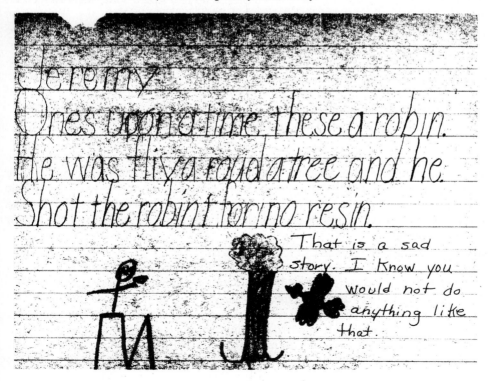

journals are particularly effective with students from diverse linguistic backgrounds. Students acquire the conventions of book language naturally from their teacher's model, which includes elaboration and expansion of English. The dialogue journal provides teachers with regular opportunities to guide and assist written language development as they question, model, and elaborate on written language patterns within the natural flow of interpersonal communication.

Literature Response Journals

Mrs. Streeter enjoys using literature response journals, in which students write their thoughts about and reactions to a novel they are reading. Using booklets of paper stapled together with construction paper covers, Mrs. Streeter encourages her students to reflect on information about the setting, characters, problem, events or actions, and resolution of the problem.

Using the book *Search for Delicious,* by Natalie Babbitt, for example, she has her students keep a list of each character in the story, descriptions about the character, and their definition of the word *delicious.* To help her students listen more carefully to character descriptions while she reads the novel, she has them illustrate the characters. These illustrations become more elaborate as the story unfolds.

Other days, Mrs. Streeter asks her students to respond to a favorite part of the story, an interesting character, or a perplexing problem in their journals. When reading *Sounder,* by William Armstrong, with her class, Casey shares her feelings about the judge's penalty for the boy's father, who had stolen some meat to feed his family.

I think that it was a harsh decision to give him a severe penalty. I think he sould have a penalty but not a severe penalty. I don't like that Judge. He would be stupid to do that because he stole some {meat}. And if a white person would have stole the meat they would of said nothing and let him take the meat that to me is not fiar because every(body) is the same nobody is or has more athoraty than anybody.

When reading *The Sign of the Beaver,* by Elizabeth Speare, Mrs. Streeter's students learn about Native American traditions and points of view as they use their journal as a diary, pretending they are Matt, who must try to survive on his own while his father returns to their cabin in Maine to get his mother and sister. One of Marissa's diary entries describes how Matt learns to survive through the help of his Native-American friend, Attean.

Today I put the seventh notch on my last stick. My family would be back soon. Attean took me out to the woods and taught me about the sign of the beaver on the tree and that when Indians go through the woods they leave secret signs like broken twigs and rocks standing certain ways. These things wore very interesting to me because my father had always put blaze marks in the trees with his knife and made it very easy to spot.

In one of his diary entries, Jeremy describes Matt's encounter with a bear.

> All of a sudden I heard a thing in the bush and I am scared to death. I want to run but I didn't I just stood their. The Bear came out and it saw me. I hit the bear with my rabbit so I would disstaced (distract) him. Atten took his bow and arrow and shot him.

Throughout, Mrs. Streeter provides her students with many choices to write in their journals. After the students respond in writing, they share their reactions and reflections with the total group, presenting new opportunities to discuss the book and the story parts in more depth.

Sometimes Mrs. Manchester uses the Literature Response Journal in another way, called Reader Response Reaction. Reader Response Reaction is an activity that stimulates more focused reflections about a story. After reading an exciting part of the story *Sadako and the Thousand Paper Cranes,* by Eleanor Coerr, for example, she asks her students to record their thoughts and feelings about this incident in their journals. Places she stops include: (1) when Sadako found out that she had leukemia; (2) when Chizuko made Sadako a golden crane, reminding her of the old story about the crane that grants one's wish; (3) after she learned that her friend, Kenji, died; and (4) after her visit home with her parents. Examples of students' entries follow.

> I would feel very sad and down that I didn't teel anyone that I was feel week and dizzy And now I found out I cought a disease from the atom bomb and for ten years and never knew about it. I would feel very poorly how would you feel if you had leukemia for ten years a just found out and you mit die?
>
> And I would feel very lonely and miserable just like she is and if I wnated to do something before I dies I would put something throo the window and climb down and go hang some cranes on the big statgue that is just like me and build the best statgue of all call the golden grane
>
> Daniel

> But I gust wont her to live. I fell so sad because she is kind of a pen-pal to me. I also fell she is kind of like a siether. But she died. I think it is very importo to have dreams because if you didn't have dreams you wode have no hope that you would get beder. And you would be like Kenji. You would gust wast away in a snape of your fegers. And I didn't want that to happin.
>
> Katie

Electronic Dialogues

Mrs. Streeter further uses computer communications in which a computer network, similar to a telephone exchange, is created by linking a modem and telephone system to a computer (Moore, 1991). By teaming each fifth-grader in her class with an undergraduate student taking a reading course called Teaching Reading in the Elementary School, she provides opportunities for her students to dialogue about the book *Search for Delicious.* After each student and undergraduate student pair introduce themselves, they begin a general discussion of *Search for Delicious,* exchanging general reactions to the story. (See Chapter 9 for more details about this experience and samples of dialogue exchanges.)

Simulated Journals

Mrs. Andrews enjoys using simulated journals with her students periodically. When reading biographies or studying a historical period, she encourages her students to assume the role of a historical character. While reading Jean Fritz's *Where Do You Think You're Going Christopher Columbus,* for example, she has them assume the role of Christopher Columbus through a series of log entries. Through these entries, her students gain new insights into the lives of the crew and the Native Americans during this time. By weaving information about Columbus with the historical events, which are arranged in chronological order, her students come to understand this historical period more completely and change many of their views about the explorers and their relationships with the Native Americans.

Similarly, Mrs. Streeter has her students assume the role of a pilgrim child aboard the Mayflower. Students choose their pilgrim name from the list of all the pilgrim children on the Mayflower. (See Chapter 6 for more information about this activity.) These are examples of students' entries:

September 1, 1620—In just 5 days we will be leaving for religious freedom. I'll miss my friends but I'll be back in one or two years. The ship that my mother, sister, and I are going on is the Mayflower. My father and brother are on the Speedwell. My mother is going to have a baby in one month.

Damaris Hopkins

September 10, 1620
Life is meserable! The food is hard and cold. People are very sick already. There are one hundred and two people on the boat. My mom is sick! I hardly get to see her. My dad is always taking care of her so I don't get to see him either! I sleep by my new friend Meg. She's a real good friend. I know I'm going to miss her when we get to the land because she said her father won't let her live by me because he doesn't like living by other people. So I know we will loose each other.

Elizabeth Tilley

LEARNING TO EXPRESS IDEAS THROUGH COLLABORATIVE WRITING

Many of our students are reluctant writers at the beginning of the year because they have had their writing scrutinized with red ink pens for errors in spelling, punctuation, capitalization, and grammar. Over time, their writing dwindles to one or two sentences at the most, consisting of safe words they know how to spell and simple, short statements.

To help overcome early anxieties about writing, Mrs. Raglin plans short writing activities that guarantee positive experiences with writing at the beginning of the year. She frequently uses paired writing activities with her students.

According to Mrs. Raglin, patterned writing is a perfect way to begin the year. A patterned activity her students especially enjoy in September is the following bio-poem. Working in pairs, students interview one another, asking for words to describe themselves, their loves, fears, and needs. They record the responses on their bio-poem sheets. Once the interviewer has completed the biopoem, partners switch roles and the interviewee becomes the interviewer, following the same format. After completing their interviews, students quickly realize they have created poems that describe one another.

BIOPOEM

Name
Son of
Lover of (3 things)
Who feels (3 things)
Who needs (3 things)
Who fears (3 things)
Who gives (3 things)
Who would like to see (3 things)
Resident of
Last Name

On the next day, partners revise their biopoem in writing response groups by combining their team with another team. In their groups, students share their poems, praise one another for their ideas, and help one another consider alternative word choices or additional words to complete the lines of the poem. Then each partner in the writing response group pairs off with a partner on the other team to edit their poems. Their checklists require that they check for spelling errors, placement of commas, and capital letters at the beginning of each new line. Once the teams have edited their poems, they sign their names at the bottom of the checklist. Mrs. Raglin then has her students publish the biopoems on the word processor. She mounts the printed-out biopoems on colored paper with accompanying photographs and displays them on the bulletin board. Everyone becomes a successful writer; everyone's self-esteem is heightened. Students also begin to realize that people are similar and different. Roger's biopoem illustrates what the poem looks like when completed:

Roger
Son of Roger and Linda Johnson
Lover of Nintendo, mom and dad, sister
Who fells energetic, happy, sad
Who needs Nintendo, family, G.I. Joe's bike
Who fears drugs, early death, and wild animals
Who gives friendship, happiness, and partnership
Who would like to see no homework, Holleywood and a perfect world
Resident of Planet Earth. Ferris St.
Johnson

USING MULTICULTURAL LITERATURE
STORIES AS A MODEL FOR WRITING

After students have had several positive informal and formal experiences with writing, they are ready to take a writing piece through all the stages. Many multicultural stories provide both a stimulus for writing ideas and a model of language expression. *Knots on a Counting Rope,* by Bill Martin, Jr. and John Archambault, a story that students love to hear over and over again, is an example of such literature. To help others understand how to plan a variety of activities that lead young authors through the stages of writing, the following five sections give a description of the activities we followed with the Native American story *Knots on a Counting Rope.*

Prewriting Strategies

Heeding the advice of Murray (1985), Mrs. Caldwell spent 70 percent of her time in the prewriting stage, beginning by reading the story aloud. Before that, to build background and heighten interest, Mrs. Caldwell discussed Native American customs of storytelling with her students. Explaining that Native Americans did not record their ideas in books, she asked them how Native American stories and legends were preserved. Students shared that paintings on their tepees or clothing frequently told stories about their life and that of their ancestors; others contributed that many Native Americans told their stories over and over so that children would be able to tell the stories to their children. Mrs. Caldwell affirmed these understandings and further explained that many of their stories and legends also explain the Native Americans' traditions and value systems; others explained the relationship between nature and human or natural phenomena. To help listeners remember these stories, Mrs. Caldwell explained, some Native Americans tied a knot in their rope after each retelling to symbolize the recording of the story.

Mrs. Caldwell then said that the story she would be reading was a recounting of a grandson's life. She began to read the story aloud interactively to her class, pausing to ask questions and elaborate on the meaning of the story. After reading the story aloud, she had her students practice and perform the dramatic interpretation of *Knots on a Counting Rope* on the following day. (See Chapter 4.) These experiences enabled the students to internalize the author's use of dialogue to tell a story and use of figurative language to express ideas.

On day three, we visited Mrs. Caldwell's class, asking students to review the story with us. After they retold parts of the story, we explained how our own children loved to hear stories about themselves when they were smaller. One of their favorite stories, we shared, was our trip to a fast-food restaurant one Friday afternoon. We explained that we wrote the story for them using Bill Martin's dialogue format. As we read our story aloud, students smiled and giggled, remembering similar stories about their own childhood. We felt a closeness and rapport to the students as they learned a little bit more about ourselves and our family. Next, we asked them if they could remember any family stories they liked to hear over and over again. Hands popped up as many students recounted favorite family stories with us.

Tell me the story again, mom. Tell me about the time we went to McDonald's for dinner.

I've told you the story many times, Chris. You know the story by heart.
But it sounds better when you tell it, Mom.

It was a Friday evening. I was very tired when I got home from work. Cooking dinner was not something I wanted to do.
Then what happened, Mom?

Chad and Tiffany saw that I was tired and began to plead, "Let's go to McDonald's! Please, mom, please."
Then we drove to McDonald's. What did I say?

Just as the golden arches came into view you said, "McDonald's! McDonald's! Let's go!"
And you drove up to the stand.

Yes and I ordered three cheeseburgers, three large fries, three medium cokes.
And a chicken sandwich and diet coke for you, right?

Right. Then we drove up to the window. I handed the man the money. Then he gave me the change.
Then you drove off, didn't you mom?

Yes, I was so tired, I just drove off. Tiffany and Chad began to shout, "Mom, mom you forgot the food!" "Great!" I moaned.
Then you saw the policeman's car, didn't you mom?

Yes, as I looked through my rear view mirror I noticed a policeman's car was behind me. Chad and Tiffany were mortified.
Then what happened, mom?

I parked the car and went up to the window to ask the man for our food.
Then the policeman waved, didn't he?

Yes, the policeman waved and said, "I did the same thing last Saturday. Have a nice dinner!"

After giving several students a chance to share their family stories, we modeled how we wrote the first draft of the story, using the sequence boxes in the overhead transparency displayed in Figure 5.9 below. We asked students to volunteer what we might have written in the first box. One student, Scott, quickly responded, "Tell me the story again, Mom." We recorded these words in the first box. A second student, Tamika, continued, "Tell me about the time we went to McDonalds for dinner." Again, we recorded these words in the second box and asked what would we write in the next box. Guy replied, "I've told you the story many times, Chris. You know the story by heart." After brainstorming what would be written in successive boxes, we asked different students to share what they might write in their first box, second box, and so forth.

Drafting the Story

Students were now ready to begin writing their own stories in the sequence boxes. Using the sequence boxes helped students to distinguish the dialogue between the

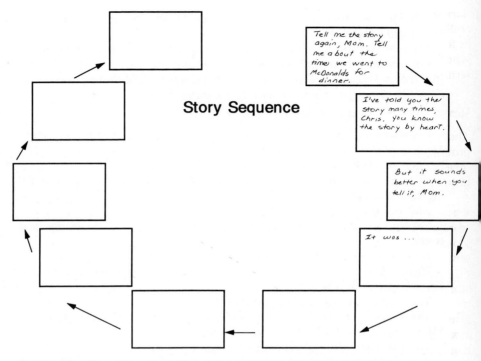

Figure 5.9 Story Sequence Chart of story about going to McDonald's.

storyteller and the listener as they drafted their stories. If they left out a part of the dialogue, they were able to insert the information easily between the boxes.

After students had been writing for a few minutes, we asked those who were successfully recording their ideas to share what they had written so far with their peers. Students who were not yet sure about how to begin their stories became more confident and began to write. After three or four shared their stories, everyone began to write again. We circulated among the students, praising them for their ideas and their choices of words. If they were having difficulty, we asked them questions about their experience; these questions seemed to help them organize and retrieve their ideas. As we moved on to help others, we noticed that they began to write.

Once again, after about seven minutes, we asked students to stop writing for a few minutes so that more of their friends might read their stories to the class. We encouraged all students to listen carefully to their friends—they might get some ideas to use in their own stories. As the students listened to their peers share their stories, they spontaneously laughed or applauded. They also commented about the words an author used or the actions described, following the model we had provided as they had shared the first time.

Students then continued writing their own stories. Before long many had completed all the sequence squares; others had continued their stories on the back, tracing new sequence squares for the dialogue. By the end of the 45-minute lesson, all students had completed their stories. Several new students read their stories aloud during the last five minutes, while some students finished theirs. All drafts were collected and placed in a folder for the next lesson. We always place the rough drafts in folders for safekeeping. We have found that, too often, students lose their drafts when they are placed in their desks and thus become reluctant to continue the writing activity.

Revising the Story

About a week later, we returned to Mrs. Caldwell's class to begin writing response groups. To help students understand the revising process, we asked Mrs. Caldwell to divide her class into groups of four students of mixed ability levels and to select one group to model the PQP Formula for the rest of the class.

We began the lesson by writing the letters *PQP* on the board for all to see. Then we asked the students how authors like Bill Martin were able to write such beautiful stories. We discussed how authors write and rewrite their stories—deleting certain words; substituting more colorful, descriptive words for dull, boring ones; inserting new information to make the story clearer to the reader; or rearranging information to follow the correct sequence. We also explained how many authors share their stories with others, who suggest changes to make the story more interesting.

When authors share their stories, however, we emphasized that listeners usually give the author *praise* and ask *questions.* As we stated these words, we placed them next to the corresponding letters. Then I asked students to share some *praise* they might give Bill Martin about his *Knots on a Counting Rope.* Andy responded that she liked the boy's name, Boy-Strength-of-Blue-Horses. Mina explained that she liked the way he described the boy's blindness as a "dark curtain before his eyes." Jared commented that he liked the title of the story because it told about the Native American tradition of tying a knot in the rope each time a story is retold. After several students gave examples of *praise* they might give the author, we asked them to think of *questions* they might ask the author. Nadia wanted to know how Martin came up with the name for the grandson. Mike wanted to know how the boy learned to memorize the trail in his mind. Arif inquired how Mr. Martin got his idea for the title. Akiba questioned what the colors, red, or orange might be for the boy.

As we discussed our words of praise and our questions, Mrs. Caldwell recorded them on the board, so that we could remember them as we revised our own stories. To help her students continue to consider ideas for words of praise and questions, Mrs. Caldwell also decided to list those ideas on large chart paper for display.

Finally, we explained that if Mr. Martin were here with us, he would listen to our ideas and then tell us a few that he might use to *polish* or revise his draft. As he wasn't present, we let them share some possible ideas. LaToya suggested that he might want to explain more carefully how the boy learned to memorize the trail. Tony commented he might tell what another color was, just as he had explained what blue is.

Just as we followed the PQP Formula with Mr. Martin's story, we explained that we could use the formula with our own stories. We asked one student from the group selected by Mrs. Caldwell to volunteer to read his or her story aloud to the group. Aaisha volunteered. While she read the story, we instructed the other group members to listen for *praise* they might give Aaisha and for *questions* they might ask. After they had shared their praise and questions, we explained that Aaisha would share how she would use this information to *polish* her story. We further emphasized that the rest of the class was to write down any words of praise and any questions they heard on their papers. After the group members shared their notes, we told them they could give additional words of praise to Aaisha and ask her any additional questions they might have.

Before Aaisha began reading, we reminded her to read in a very loud voice so everyone could hear her story. In her best voice, she began, "Tell me a story, mother . . ." When Aaisha finished reading her story, everyone clapped. Then her group began to share their words of praise. Paul said he liked the way she began the story. Shelly agreed and commented that she like the way Aaisha ended the story.

After providing words of praise, each group member began to ask questions. Jessica asked Aaisha where her aunt got her ideas for acting like Superman. John wanted to know what the wall next to the bed was made of. Paul wanted to know if her aunt was O.K. and what happened to her at the hospital. Aaisha explained that she had cut her head and had to have stitches, but she was O.K.

Once the group had shared their praise and their questions, the rest of the class reviewed what words of praise and questions the group members had used. Additional questions included: "How did she crash through the wall?" "How much was she bleeding?" "How did they stop the bleeding?" "How did she get to the hospital?"

After listening to the praise and questions, Aaisha shared how she would polish her story: She planned to insert information about the wall, which was made of plasterboard, and about her aunt getting her ideas for playacting from watching TV. To help students understand how to insert this information, we held up Aaisha's paper and pointed to the box that told about the wall, showing them how Aaisha could easily insert the information about the plasterboard wall next to that sequence box and then draw an arrow to the exact place the sentence would be inserted in the final draft. Then we asked Aaisha where she would insert information about her aunt getting ideas from TV. She pointed to the correct box as we illustrated how to insert this new information on her draft. Again, we emphasized that this was a draft; authors were not to be concerned about neatness at the moment.

On the following day, all students began to share their stories with their writing response groups, following the PQP Formula. After all group members had an opportunity to share their writing, students returned to their desks to insert, delete, or rearrange information in their drafts. All drafts were then collected and placed in a folder for the next day, when they would complete their final drafts and illustrations.

Editing

Students recopied their drafts with revisions on the following day, after which they edited their stories, working in pairs. Mrs. Caldwell used a checklist that required that they search for two or three misspelled words and proper use of beginning and ending marks. After each editing team had edited their stories, they signed their checklists and began their illustrations. Mrs. Caldwell circulated, checking to see that each pair had edited their writing carefully. If partners had not found errors, she gave them cues by asking them to look at the beginning, middle, or end of the story for errors. With this additional prompting, all partners successfully completed their editing. In some cases, students were interested in learning how to use quotation marks and accompanying punctuation. These students worked on that together with Mrs. Caldwell at a table located at the front of the room.

Sharing

Mrs. Caldwell published her students' dialogue stories by displaying them and their accompanying illustrations on the bulletin board. The following are Aaisha's story, as well as another story written by Travis.

Tell me a story mother
What story would you like to hear
The one about Auntie Pat and Superman
I've already told you that story
So tell me agin I like the way you tell it.
Okay, One day your Auntie Pat who was 10 had on a cape and was acting like Superman.
Were did she get her ideas from, Mom?
From watching tv. Any way she was jumping from bed to bed. There was a wall next to the bed. it was a plaster board wall.
Then what happened, Mom.
She jumped to hard and far and then her head went through the wall. At first I thought it was funny but then she was bledding.
Then what happend Mom.
Then we took her to the hospital.
Then she was ok right.
Right now you can tell the story to your class.

Aaisha

"Tell me a story grandfather."
"What story do you want to hear today, Paul."
"I want to hear about the strange Halloween you once had."
"Okay. One dark HALLOWEEN night My friends and I went trick or tre—"
"No! Not that part! Start from the exiting part."
"You mean the part about the strange house?"
"Yea, that part."
My friends and I got up to a strange house. we rang the door bell and waited.
"After a few minnits we decided to go inside the spooky house!"
"We looked around for a little bit, and my friend found some slimy stuff (it was only year old dog food) and got so scared that he ran out of the house, he triped over a stick and ended up with his face in a Jack-o-lantern.
"Was he alright?"
"Yes but it was so funny he even laughed."

Travis

PREDICTING NEW ENDINGS TO A STORY

Students love to make predictions as we read stories aloud. They especially enjoy predicting endings. By following a process approach as they create these new endings for stories, we can model how authors discover their endings.

First-Graders Predict Tiblo's and Tanksi's Dream

Mrs. Addy, a first-grade teacher, follows the writing process approach as she has her first-graders illustrate and write about Tiblo's and Tanksi's dreams for the book *Dream Wolf,* by Paul Goble. Before sharing the story with her students, Mrs. Addy asks them to predict what the story might be about, just by looking at the pictures. Mark predicts the story will be about Native Americans; Kristin says the story is going to be about two Native American children and a wolf; and Steven adds that he thinks two Native American children and a wolf will go for a walk in the country.

Reinforcing their observations, Mrs. Addy explains that *Dream Wolf* is going to be about two Native American children from the Plains, Tiblo and Tanksi. Then she extends their prior knowledge about the Native Americans by asking a few questions about their homes, their clothing, the animals, and examples of food they eat, while slowly turning a few pages of the book. As she continues to turn pages, she explains that the author of the story, Paul Goble, illustrated and wrote this story about the Native Americans from the Plains.

"Today," she adds, "we are also going to illustrate and write part of the story." Using chart paper she models how authors sometimes use "temporary" spelling when they are writing. By using temporary spelling, she explains, authors don't have to worry about correct spelling; they can just write down their ideas and create a beautiful story. Then she asks them to tell her how they might write the word *Plains.* Bryan replies that he would write a *p* and a *n* and a *s.* Similarly, Mrs. Addy asks how they might write the word *tepee.* Keisha says she would write a *t* and a *p.* As the students share how they will write these words and others, Mrs. Addy records their temporary spelling on chart paper, thus affirming their temporary spelling as an acceptable form of written language.

Next, Mrs. Addy begins to share the story with her students, asking her students questions to reinforce understanding of the story. When she comes to the part where Tiblo and Tanksi, who are lost, find "a small cave among the rocks," she stops and asks her students what they think Tiblo and Tanksi might dream about in the small cave that night. Terrence suggest they might dream about their mother and father finding them the next day; Danielle says they might dream about a bear whose fur would keep them warm during the night; Sean adds that they might dream about an old Native American man who would help them find their way home; Ryan thinks they might dream about a wolf that would help them find the way home.

Once various students have a chance to share their predictions, Mrs. Addy asks them to return to their seats, where they will find drawing paper. She then reminds them that they are both illustrators and authors today. First, they are to draw what they think Tiblo and Tanksi might dream about, and then they will write about the dream. "Before you begin," she explains, "I would like you to close your eyes and pretend you are either Tiblo or Tanksi in the small cave. As your eyes are closed, what are you dreaming as you fall asleep in the cave among the rocks?" Pausing for a few moments while her students reflect, she then asks her students to open their eyes and begin drawing their dream. After they have been drawing for about six minutes, Mrs. Addy asks her students to stop and listen while some students show their illustrations and tell about Tiblo's or Tanksi's dreams. As her first-graders share their drawings, Mrs. Addy praises them for their colorful drawings and ideas about the Native American children's dream. Sharing in this way gives others ideas for their pictures or dreams. All are eager to continue their drawings. In about 10 minutes, almost all have completed their drawings and are beginning to write. To help her students make this transition, Mrs. Addy asks each student to show his or her drawing with a neighbor, telling the neighbor about the dream. Having all students verbalize their ideas with a neighbor enables them to record the ideas more easily on paper.

As we walk around, we notice that everyone is using beginning and ending sounds of words to record their ideas. Some students are also finding words such as *boy, find,* or *the* on charts or bulletin boards displayed in the room. Mrs. Addy is particularly excited that Chris, who has only been able to write the word *I* on previous stories, is writing a whole sentence at the bottom of his page. Certainly, all students are successful. An example of one student's writing is found in Figure 5.10.

Fourth-Graders Predict an Ending for *Song of Trees*

Similarly, Mrs. Manchester, a fourth-grade teacher, uses a process approach with her students as they create their own ending to Mildred Taylor's *Song of Trees,* which takes place during the depression. This enthralling story is about an African American family struggling to keep their land and the forest behind their home, which was being cut down by white lumbermen. After reading the part where Stacey rides off into the night in search of his father, who is working for the railroad in another state, Mrs. Manchester stops and asks the students to predict what might happen as Stacey rides off and whether he will reach his father in time to save the forest.

After her students brainstorm various possibilities, Mrs. Manchester reviews how authors develop plot structure by introducing a problem, inserting various roadblocks in the path of characters, creating a high point or climax in the conflict situation, and finally devising a solution to the problem. Using an overhead of the Diagram of Plot Development, adapted from Hoskisson and Tompkins (1991), Mrs. Manchester encourages her students to think of a movie or a television show that introduces a problem, the roadblocks that complicate the problem, the climax, and finally the resolution of the problem.

After they share various examples, Mrs. Manchester explains that they are going to develop their own plot diagrams for Stacey as he rides off into the night. After reviewing the problem—finding Stacey's father in time to save the trees—she asks students to share some possible roadblocks Stacey might encounter. Marvin decides Stacey might get lost because it is dark; Antone suggests that a storm might have caused a tree to crash to the ground, blocking the trail. Mrs. Manchester then encourages them to begin their diagrams. Just as she allows authors to share their writing after a short time, she asks her students to stop and share their plot diagrams.

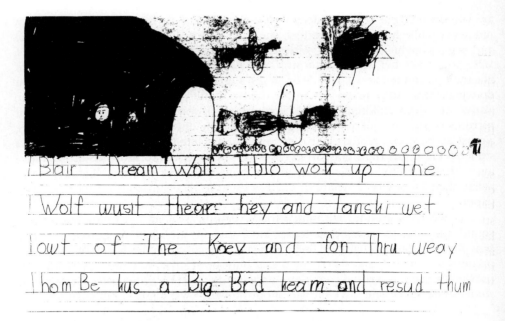

FIGURE 5.10 Example of first-grader's story and illustration.

Students who are not yet sure how to begin listen to their friends' ideas; suddenly the task seems easier, and they, too, begin to plot roadblocks on their diagram. By the end of the class period, in fact, everyone has completed a diagram. (See Figure 5.11.) All diagrams are collected and placed in a folder until the next class session.

The next day, Mrs. Manchester reviews plot structure. She reemphasizes that the climax is the highest point of dramatic action. What happens at this point determines if the character will achieve the goal or solve the problem. Then she asks her students to share their diagrams with a partner, deciding if the roadblocks are reasonable and whether the climax is the highest point of dramatic action, leading to Stacey's achievement of his goal—to find his father—or to the destruction of the family's trees. She further encourages students to consider revising their diagrams to make the story more interesting or realistic. After sharing with partners, some students read their diagrams aloud to the class.

Next, Mrs. Manchester explains that they are going to transfer their ideas to the sequence chart. (See Figure 5.12.) The first box, she explains, will include a sentence about Stacey riding off into the night; each sequential box will include details about his journey, roadblocks he encounters, and finally how the problem is solved. Before having them begin, however, she asks students to brainstorm a lead sentence, which she explains is usually a statement that entices a reader to read the story. Jeremy reads, "One stormy, dark evening, Stacey rode off into the night to find his father."

Shelly shares, "Holding his bundle tightly, Stacey trotted off into the night." After listening to these ideas, her students are ready to begin writing. Using their diagrams, they are eager to write.

Mrs. Manchester follows her routine of pausing periodically so students might share their writing. By the end of class, many students have completed their stories. Mrs. Manchester is impressed that several of her students have revised their stories, integrating more realistic roadblocks that lead to the climax and resolution of the problem. Using alternative forms during the prewriting stage appears to encourage students to revise their stories so that they are clearer and more meaningful.

On day three, Mrs. Manchester explains that they are going to publish their stories in a book format with illustrations. First she asks them to look at their sequence chart and decide where each page will begin and end. After marking page beginnings and endings on their charts, students are ready to begin their books. Most students decide to write the text at the top of the page and illustrate on the bottom half. They rewrite their stories carefully, checking again for clarity of ideas. Once again, many students revise their roadblocks, integrate more details to make the story more interesting, or improve their ending of the story by using more descriptive words. Students work on their books for two or three days, adding text and illustra-

FIGURE 5.11   Diagram of plot development.

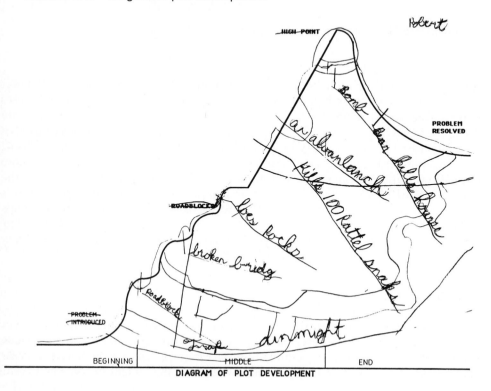

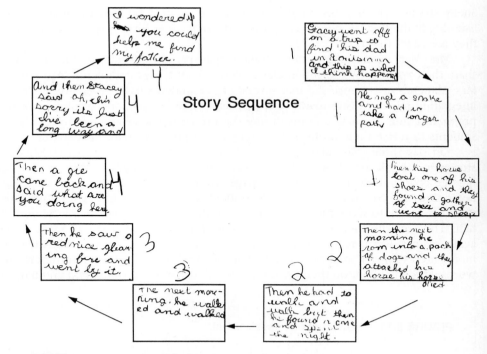

FIGURE 5.12   Marci transfers her ideas to story sequence chart.

tions and a cover for their book. As they complete their stories, Mrs. Manchester confers with her students, helping them with simple editing procedures. She also uses gummed tags to give them editing clues if they forget to place periods or capitals within the text or if a word is misspelled. Mrs. Manchester and her students are very proud of their published books. Figure 5.13 includes sample pages from one student's book.

This powerful experience enables Mrs. Manchester's students to become more engaged with this gripping story and the social issues that are the foundation for the story. They are eager to finish the story and to determine how similar the author's ending is to theirs. Integrating multicultural literature with writing further helps students understand themselves and others and discover solutions to problems. Students further discover alternative ways of thinking and knowing as they share their writings with one another.

SUMMARY

In this chapter we described ways to integrate writing with a multicultural literacy program, beginning with a description of the writing process and its recursive stages: prewriting, drafting, revising, editing, and sharing. As each of the stages was described, we shared ways to support young writers so they might become successful authors. We further emphasized ways in which the process can become compatible with the interactional patterns and language learning styles of students from diverse

Stacy rode off in the night deep in the woods. Stacy was very scared to be alone, but he was brave and he went on. When he got real deep in the woods he came to a cave. In the cave there was a wolf and her pups. But Stacy didn't know that wolves were in there . . .

Stacy went in for shelter, because it was about to rain. Stacy went in, it was dark and damp it was hard to see. When Stacy walked in he tumbled on one of the pups. Stacy ran out before the mother could come out. It was too dark for the wolf to see so she didn't see out but stayed in and soothed her babies. And Stacy rode on.

Stacy found a path that led him to a little more trouble, but Stacy knew that the path led to something so Stacy went on. He came to two men with a rifle. They said, "Get off the horse boy." So he got off, the men searched him, but they found nothing. They said, "Go on you little boy."

He saw his dad. Stacy was so happy that he jumped in his dad's arms. Stacy told him all about his adventures in the woods. David said, "we better get home, before they cut down all the trees." When David got home they told him that Mr. Anderson is trying to buy the trees from Big Mama. David was very mad. So David went right up in Mr. Anderson's face and said . . .

Then Stacy came to a log house in the woods. He went up to the house for food. Stacy knocked on the door two times, the door open, a very tall man looked down at Stacy and said, "what do you want?" He said with a kind voice. Stacy said, "I am very hungry could I have some food?" "Come on in," said the fellow. When he got inside he saw something . . .

"Mr. Anderson get out of here." "O.K. David I'll give you 50% of the money that will come from the trees. David said, "No! I don't want the money." Mr. Anderson said, "what do you want?" "I want my trees!" David said. "Get out of here before I kill you and your whole crew!" "I'm going, I'm going," said. "O.K." "Good job dad!"

FIGURE 5.13 Darrell's published book about *Song of the Trees.*

cultural and linguistic backgrounds, as well as reluctant writers. Throughout, we emphasized that teachers who follow a writing process approach will eventually see all their students blossom into young authors who use their knowledge and experiences to generate ideas for writing and to create meaningful, coherent texts.

After describing each of the subprocesses of composing, we highlighted strategies that help young learners begin to write. We further described specific techniques for designing a risk-free classroom environment that nurtures the development of enthusiastic young writers. Once students are able to transform their ideas, thoughts, and feelings into written language freely, without concerns about the conventions of language, they are able to express their ideas more easily. Through writing, revising, editing, and sharing their writing, they simultaneously renew their understanding of themselves, their histories, and their world.

Finally, we charted how to manage and organize a process-oriented classroom that follows whole language and multicultural perspectives. To help others understand the process more fully, we used vignettes and samples of students' writing during the various stages of writing. The vignettes further illustrate how teachers who use a process approach to learning enhance the growth and development of young readers and writers of all ability levels.

We demonstrated how multicultural literature enables students to acquire varied models of language for their writing. As students discover linkages between their own cultural and personal experiences and what they are reading, they develop a richer source of ideas for written expression. Multicultural literature also provides a natural way to integrate the reading and writing processes. When multicultural literature is combined with opportunities to write frequently, when strategies are offered to solve problems in writing, and when writing is shared, all students become readers who read like writers, and writers who write like readers. Simultaneously, all students grow and develop in oral and written language expression.

REFERENCES

Bromley, K. (1989). Buddy journals make the reading-writing connection. *The Reading Teacher, 43,* 122–129.

Calkins, L. (1979). Andrea learns to make writing hard. *Language Arts, 56,* 569–576.

Calkins, L. (1986). *The art of teaching writing.* Portsmouth, NH: Heinemann.

Clark, R. (1987). *Free to write.* Portsmouth, NH: Heinemann.

Cummins, J. (1986). Empowering minority students. *Harvard Education Review, 56,* 866–898.

Daiute, C. (1985). *Writing and computers.* Reading, MA: Addison-Wesley Publishing Company.

Emig, J. (1971). *The composing processes of twelfth graders* (Research Report No. 13). Urbana, IL: National Council of Teachers of English.

Florez, B., Cousin, P., & Diaz, E. (1991). Transforming deficit myths about learning, language, and culture. *Language Arts, 68,* 369–377.

Flower, L., & Hayes, J. (1981). A cognitive process theory of writing. *College Compositions and Communication, 32,* 21–32.

Graves, D. (1978a). *Children's writing: Research directions and hypotheses based upon an examination of the writing processes of seven-year-old children.* Ann Arbor, MI: University Microfilms.

Graves, D. (1978b). *Balance the basics: Let them write.* New York: Ford Foundation.

Graves, D. (1983). *Writing: Teachers and children at work.* Portsmouth, NH: Heinemann.

Graves, D., & Stuart, V. (1987). *Write from the start.* Portsmouth, NH: Heinemann.

Hoskisson, K., & Tompkins, G. (1991). *Language arts: Content and teaching strategies.* Columbus, OH: Merrill Publishing Company.

Humes, A. (1983). Research on the composing process. *Review of Educational Research, 53,* 201–216.

Langer, J. (1986). *Children reading and writing.* Norwood, NJ: Ablex.

Moffett, J. (1982). Writing, inner speech, and meditation. *College English, 44,* 231–246.

Moore, M. (1991). Electronic dialoguing: An avenue to literacy. *The Reading Teacher, 45,* 280–286.

Moore, M., & Diamond, B. (1991). *A staff developmental model for promoting literacy and cultural awareness: A multicultural literature-based approach.* Paper presented at the annual meeting of the American Educational Research Association. Chicago, IL.

Moore, M., & Diamond, B. (1992). *Promoting teacher empowerment in a multicultural literature program.* Paper presented at the annual meeting of the American Educational Research Association. San Francisco, CA.

Murray, D. (1978). Internal revision: A process of discovery. In C. R. Cooper & L. Odell (Eds.), *Research on composing: Points of departure.* Urbana, IL: National Council of Teachers of English.

Murray, D. (1985). *A writer teaches writing.* Boston, MA: Houghton Mifflin.

Perl, S. (1979). The composing process of unskilled college writers. *Research in the Teaching of English, 13,* 317–336.

Peregoy, S., & Boyle, O. (1993). *Reading, writing, and learning in ESL.* New York: Longman.

Quintero, E., & Huetera-Macias, A. (1990). All in the family: Bilingualism and biliteracy. *The Reading Teacher, 44,* 306–312.

Reyhner, J., & Garcia, R. (1989). Helping minorities read better: Problems and promises. *Reading Research and Instruction, 28,* 84–91.

Rosen, N., Hoffman, J., & Farest, C. (1990). Language, literacy, and at-risk children. *The Reading Teacher, 43,* 554–559.

Shanahan, T. (1988). The reading-writing relationship: Seven instructional principles. *The Reading Teacher, 41,* 636–646.

Tierney, R., & Pearson, P. (1983). Toward a composing model of reading. *Language Arts, 60,* 568–580.

Tompkins, G. (1990). *Teaching writing: Balancing process and product.* Columbus, OH: Merrill Publishing Company.

Vygotsky, L. S. (1978). *Mind in society.* Cambridge, MA: Harvard University Press.

chapter 6

Using a Thematic Approach to Learning with Multicultural Literature

OVERVIEW

In this chapter we present strategies to forge more effective links among reading, writing, social studies, science, mathematics, art, and music. We first discuss theoretical issues related to thematic learning, which is learning that integrates themes or topics across the content areas. We then share ways to make connections between the core subjects and students' cultural background and experiences. Using multicultural literature as the foundation for learning puts literacy development in a context that is more meaningful and purposeful for all students. We use examples of classroom activities to illustrate this multidisciplinary, holistic approach to learning. We further demonstrate how to plan and organize thematic units and how to develop interconnections between cultural experiences and new knowledge.

THEORETICAL PERSPECTIVES

> From the standpoint of the child, the great waste in school comes from his inability to utilize the experiences he gets outside of school in any complete and free way; while, on the other hand, he is unable to apply in daily life what he is learning in school.

Even though this quotation, written by John Dewey (1956, p. 75) at the beginning of this century, may continue to characterize learning in some of our nation's schools, it does not reflect the learning that occurs within classrooms in our multicultural program. No longer believing in simply delivering information to students in a traditional, fragmented style, teachers in our program prefer to approach learning in a thematic, holistic way. They focus on hands-on, whole language experiences in which all students are active learners and critical thinkers. Meaningful and purposeful activities keyed to multicultural themes offer students multiple opportunities to read, create, share, discuss, imagine, listen, and write in a personalized social environment. Cooperative learning experiences with people from varied backgrounds help students to bond. Moreover, teachers no longer feel the need to use workbooks and commercial materials that emphasize pencil and paper drills, isolated skills, and rote memorization of facts.

Consistent with Goodman's whole language theory, we believe that the foundation of literacy is language across all content areas. Specifically, he says, "If language is learned best and easiest when it is whole and in natural context, then integration is a key principle for language development and learning through language. In fact, language development and content become a dual curriculum" (1986, p. 30).

Through language, therefore, our students engage in a variety of investigations to explore places, characters, events, and information using multicultural literature, the thread that unifies learning for *all* students. Specifically, we define *thematic learning as a holistic approach to learning that applies methodology and language from more than one discipline to examine a central theme, issue, problem, topic, or experience.*

Using a Whole Language Approach to Literacy Learning

As explained in Chapter 1, multicultural literature, a whole language perspective, and a multicultural perspective are three components of our multicultural program, which is grounded in a socioculturally sensitive environment. We believe that a whole language approach to literacy creates natural opportunities for purposeful intertwining of the core subjects—reading, language arts, social studies, math, and science—to achieve multiple goals. Language becomes the foundation for this guided, purposeful intertwining of the core subjects. Multicultural literature becomes the thread for unifying learning across the core subjects.

Through a multidisciplinary, integrated process, students are able to group concepts into categories and see the relationships among the categories rather than study isolated bits of information. When students further cluster concepts into categories, they understand and remember information more easily. Similar to Bennett (1986), our teachers find that overlapping of subject matter is eliminated and learning time is increased when they interconnect the elementary curriculum.

Specifically, how do students learn about content through language in a holistic, thematic curriculum? In our multicultural program, language development and content are a dual curriculum. We agree with Goodman (1986, p. 26) that "Language learning is easy when it's whole, real, and relevant; when it makes sense and is functional; when it's encountered in the context of its use; when the learner chooses to use it."

To mold this dual curriculum, teachers need to consider certain guidelines. First, if language learning is whole, real, and relevant, they need to incorporate the four language modes—reading, writing, listening, and speaking—with instruction across all content areas. Connections between subject areas evolve more easily as students participate in meaningful, purposeful literacy activities that use these four language modes.

Second, for students to view the core subjects as meaningful, functional, and relevant, teachers, as cultural organizers, need to help them understand how the subjects relate to their daily lives. Integration builds on this need to make sense of the world and to relate learning to the daily lives of students (Farris and Kaczmarski, 1988; Pappas, Kiefer, & Levstik, 1990). Effective integration further evolves from using themes that are relevant to the curriculum and students' personal and cultural experiences.

Third, language learning flourishes in a socioculturally sensitive, print-rich environment that values creating and sharing. As already discussed, students need to feel comfortable expressing their ideas, strategies, and imaginings. This means that knowledge is constructed through a social process as teachers and students publish and share their knowledge and experiences with others in an environment that respects and affirms all learners. Forming cooperative learning groups to include mixed ability levels provides social support systems (Cohen, 1987; Slavin, 1983) for diverse students or reluctant readers and writers.

Fourth, language learning grows and develops in a meaningful context—one that emerges from the students' cultural backgrounds and experiences and reinforces academic performance across all content areas. As demonstrated in the earlier chapters, multicultural reading and writing experiences create natural links between the cultural backgrounds and experiences of students and the core subjects. Combined with thematic instruction, multicultural literature provides a scaffolding to connect students' personal and cultural experiences with the other subjects they are studying (Howe, 1988). As they relate their personal experiences and cultural background with new knowledge (Cummins, 1983, 1986; LeSourd, 1988), they are able to construct their own knowledge more easily and develop interconnections among concepts and facts. To perceive these interconnections, students need to use content area instructional materials and books that are part of their cultural context so that they might understand, remember, and enjoy reading and learning (LeSourd, 1988; Lipson, 1983; Machet, 1992; Rosier & Holm, 1980). Using quality literature provides intrinsically interesting learning experiences for students and makes learning events memorable (Cullinan, 1992).

Fifth, the academic performance of culturally and linguistically diverse and underachieving students increases when visual, holistic, kinesthetic instructional techniques are followed (Jordan, 1985; LeSourd, 1988; Peregoy & Boyle, 1993; Tharp, 1989). Teachers create a student-centered curriculum that provides manipulative materials, hands-on activities, field trips, videos and filmstrips, collaborative activities, and authentic reading and writing experiences stemming from students' cultural and personal experiences.

Finally, Au (1992) and Heath (1983) highlight the importance of capitalizing on the oral traditions of many cultures. Providing students more opportunities to talk and verbally express their ideas aligns the curriculum more fully with their cultural backgrounds and home environment (Au, 1992; Heath, 1983; Cummins, 1983, 1986; Marzano, 1991). Peregoy and Boyle (1993) similarly stress that second-language learners need multiple opportunities to talk and share their ideas in order to develop proficiency in a second language.

Organizing Thematic Learning Events

How does one organize this holistic, thematic approach to learning? Applying our definition of thematic learning as an interdisciplinary, holistic approach to learning that examines a central theme, we provide opportunities for organizing content-area learning. To help learners see and understand connections between the subject areas, teachers talk about these connections and illustrate ones that exist among the content areas.

In the early stages, teachers organize thematic units by independently selecting topics that match the interests and needs of their students. Using webbing techniques, teachers explore materials and activities related to the theme, which is broad enough to incorporate a variety of books, resources, and activities across several disciplines, yet not so broad that students lose sight of the connections among the content areas. (See examples in Figures 6.1a and 6.1b.) Resources are compiled and organized to answer initiating questions and stimulate new interests and directions. Content and strategy lessons are then designed for investigating the topic.

Selecting Themes.   Along with Routman (1991), we follow specific procedures when selecting themes to ensure meaningful, purposeful learning. First, we determine the educational aims and goals of the theme by addressing the following questions:

1. **What concepts can be identified and learned?** We brainstorm the major ideas and concepts first, then the language arts concepts, and finally the concepts in the content areas that relate to the theme. These major

FIGURE 6.1a   An example of goals and objectives for a thematic unit on Native Americans.

Goals and Objectives
Content Area Goals

Students will:
1. understand and appreciate the customs, culture, language, relationship with nature, beliefs, etc. of Native American tribes.
2. realize that it is inappropriate to generalize about or stereotype Native Americans as there were (and are) many variations in their customs, ways of life, etc., depending on the region in which they live and the tribe.
3. know that the differences between Native Americans and European settlers do not equal deficiencies. Their lifestyles are different, but one is not better or worse than the other.
4. begin to understand some of the problems Native Americans face today.

Study Skills/Language Arts Goals

Students will:
1. be introduced to the process of collecting research.
2. be introduced to the process of note-taking.
3. move through the writing process in order to write a research paper.
4. keep a literature log of their thoughts and questions.
5. keep a learning log.
6. write a bibliography.

Thematic Web on Native Americans

Social Studies
*Look for articles in newspapers/
magazines about current N.A.
issues.
*Research a N.A. topic.
*Learn about N.A. in relation to
Columbus and European
settlers.
*Study the geography of N.A.
land.
*Learn N.A. names (still used
today) for places and objects.
*Research famous N.A. and their
contributions.
*Study laws related to N.A.
*Learn about N.A. religions and
beliefs.
*Develop map skills while locat-
ing N.A. tribal lands.
*Look at the causes and effects
of numerous N.A. wars and
battles.
*Choose a N.A. name for self.

Science
*Study the foods grown by N.A.
and the plants they ate and
used for medicine.
*Study N.A. hunting and tracking
techniques.
*Make arrows and study how
aerodynamics affects how well
and how far they fly.
*Research how N.A. respected
and cared for the environment.
*Pretend to dissect an animal
(such as a buffalo) and learn
how N.A. used every part of it
for some purpose.
*Dye yarn using different plants.

Reading
*Read a work of historical fiction
or a biography.
*Read parts of several nonfiction
books in order to collect
information.
*Read many folk tales.

Music
*Create N.A. instruments (rasp,
rattles, drums) and have a
performance.
*Listen to N.A. music and com-
pare it to other forms.
*Write a chant.

Theater
*Conduct an interview with a pre
tend N.A.
*Perform a skit about the daily
life, beliefs, and customs of a
N.A. child.
*Use a Reader's Theatre format
to present some folk tales.

Movement
*Learn a N.A. rain dance.
*Have a pow wow.
*Learn N.A. sign language.
*Create and play N.A. games like
the crab race, bear race, kick
stick race, and toss ball game.

NATIVE AMERICANS

Art
*Weave a small blanket.
*Create paper beads to make jewelry.
*Prepare and eat N.A. food (like fry bread). Collect
the recipes in a class cookbook.
*Create a 3D village.
*Make a tissue paper scene.
*Create masks and totem poles from papier-mâché.
*Create N.A. homes (teepee, longhouse, hogan,
etc.)
*Weave a model blanket.

Writing
*Create class books on graphs, N.A. stereotypes,
folk tales, and other topics.
*Write a story using symbols and put it on a pre-
tend cave wall and/or animal skin.
*Create a pourquoi myth explaining an event in
nature.
*Write a business letter to a N.A. agency, the gov-
ernment, or a tribe requesting information.
*Write a research paper.
*Add to a class "Did you know?" chart.
*Write poetry with N.A. themes.
*Keep a literature and a learning log.
*Create a story pyramid and a character web.

Listening/Speaking
*Present research to the class.
*Actively listen to peers' presentations and teach-
er's mini-lessons
*Debate how N.A. history would have been differ-
ent if you could change one event.

Math
*Participate in a trading activity to learn about the
equivalent value of goods.
*Estimate and compare the percent of N.A. alive to
day to the total U.S. population using a pie graph.
*Collect statistical data about N.A., graph the re-
sults, and summarize the information on the
graph.

FIGURE 6.1b An example of a thematic web.

concepts, which become the root of thematic planning, are related to the goals and objectives of the curriculum and to what the students need to learn.

2. **What concepts are relevant to students' personal and cultural experiences and lives?** We extend our list of concepts to match the needs and interests of our students, the school, and the community. We further consider what strategies we need to follow to link the concepts to students' personal and cultural experiences and their daily lives.

3. **What meaningful, purposeful learning will result from this experience?** After we determine the theme's major concepts and ideas, we consider ways to create natural, meaningful relationships among the content areas. We begin to brainstorm and plan learning experiences that foster the development of the major concepts and learning outcomes within the content areas. Using the four language modes—reading, writing, listening, and speaking—to promote meaningful learning across the content areas, we design activities that reinforce the acquisition, organization, evaluation, and application of knowledge (Routman, 1991).

4. **Do included subject areas extend learning for students?** We move beyond merely creative, entertaining activities. Once the important concepts have been identified, we plan significant, relevant learning activities. These activities (a) foster critical and creative thinking, (b) develop conceptual understandings, (c) develop skills and strategies within content areas, (d) develop positive attitudes towards reading, writing, and other cultures, (e) promote inquiry, choice, and active student involvement, (f) heighten transfer of knowledge and experiences across the content areas, and (g) demonstrate the relationships among the content areas. Throughout the planning process, we follow the principles of a holistic approach to literacy learning.

Reflecting on the Process. Determining the theme's major aims and goals and brainstorming learning activities are only the initial steps in the process of developing thematic learning experiences. We then reflect on the process, asking ourselves the following questions: (1) How is this theme relevant to students' cultural experiences and backgrounds? (2) How is the theme relevant to the curriculum and its goals and objectives? (3) Will the experiences enhance learning across the curriculum? (4) Do students have choices to accommodate their interests and needs and to promote responsibility for their own learning? and (5) Are the principles of literacy respected and adopted? These questions enable us to verify that the thematic learning experience is meaningful, relevant to the curriculum and students' personal and cultural experiences, consistent with holistic literacy learning principles, and authentic in its interdisciplinary, language processes (Routman, 1991). Different from correlated units that cluster interesting, creative activities around a theme without regard to developing major concepts, thematic learning fosters the development of major concepts, skills, and learning. Thematic learning further demonstrates the relationships between content areas to ensure that information is remembered and retained.

Involving Students in the Process.   Even though teachers might begin the year by brainstorming and listing the major concepts themselves, they quickly discover that the theme expands and develops more powerfully when they involve their students in this process. By sharing the theme with their students, using webbing, KWL, or similar procedures, teachers begin a collaborative effort to learning. Together, teachers and students set the direction for the theme, determine problems and questions they wish to pursue, find resources related to the theme, and organize learning that is significant and related to students' lives. As they brainstorm, free associate, and list ideas that come to mind, categories and connections emerge naturally. Teachers, however, always guide and facilitate this interactive process; they further help their students learn to make wise decisions so that learning is consistent with the goals and objectives of the curriculum.

Once the ideas are collaboratively webbed, resource materials are selected by the teacher and students. Well-known books and resources surface through the help of librarians, curriculum supervisors, teachers, parents, students, and people within the community. These people are also helpful in obtaining manipulative materials and resources: artifacts, props, equipment, and resources within the community such as people, animals, videos, slides, filmstrips, or places to visit. A balance of fiction and nonfiction literature, including a variety of genres, is compiled. Other sources of printed information—newspapers, magazines, diaries, letters, or other primary sources—are located as well. Encouraging student participation in the process fosters student ownership of their learning experiences. Students further learn how to access and retrieve information.

In these ways, we recontextualize learning. (See Chapter 2.) Classrooms become supportive, multicultural communities where students participate in making choices for topics and pursue learning under the guidance of cultural mediators. Together, teachers and students extend and broaden their understanding and appreciation of information, while interacting with people from diverse backgrounds, interests, and cultures. Students simultaneously construct their own knowledge and explore language.

Creating an Environment for Holistic Learning

How does one support this holistic, thematic approach to learning? The approach requires a socioculturally sensitive environment that nurtures learning. As orchestrators of social contexts, we use movable tables and chairs that can be arranged in clusters, pairs, or hexagonal or u-shape formations. We recognize that literacy across the curriculum evolves more smoothly when classrooms are organized to foster partnerships and collaborations among diverse students as they talk, listen, read, think, and write (Hansen, 1987, 1992; Marzano, 1991; Pappas et al., 1990; Peregoy & Boyle, 1993; Tierney, Soter, & O'Flahavan, 1989). These arrangements further support higher levels of cognitive or thoughtful learning as students offer one another support, suggest new possibilities or solutions to problems, and evaluate ideas.

Just as student-to-student exchanges enhance learning, teacher-to-student exchanges mediate learning as they help learners clarify their ideas (Au, 1992). By arranging the classroom in hexagonal or horseshoe formations, teachers can maneuver easily among learners to provide just the right degree of "scaffolding." They can easily ask questions, comment, extend, elaborate, and validate ideas during discussions. While supporting and shaping critical thinking and learning, teachers model respect for all learners and affirm multiple ways of viewing and learning.

Creating a print-rich environment that stimulates and appeals to students also helps students see core subjects as meaningful and relevant. Colorful bulletin boards, wall hangings, charts, semantic maps, and exhibits enable students to perceive the relationship between core subjects and their daily lives more easily. Attractively displayed multicultural books and materials, for example, encourages students to read and reread the books during SSR or their free time. Similarly, when bookshelves and tables feature a collection of dioramas, group projects, or "big books," students are drawn to these areas of the room to read and explore the materials again and again. Because information is visually available to all students, these words and ideas become part of their thinking and writing. Concept development and language learning are enhanced for diverse students who need visual, spatial, and other paralinguistic cues (Peregoy & Boyle, 1993).

LITERACY LEARNING IN THE CONTENT AREAS THROUGH MULTICULTURAL LITERATURE

When students advance to higher grade levels, they shift emphasis from learning how to read to reading to learn. Many students experience their first difficulties with reading as they make the transition to content-area texts (Alverman & Ridgeway, 1990; Vacca, Vacca, & Gove, 1991). Expository writing, which includes description, classification, explanation, and persuasion, is often dry and uninteresting to readers. Brozo and Tomlinson (1986) describe this encounter with content-area texts as a "journey into the uncharted sea of exposition" (p. 289).

Using a thematic approach to learning, however, can provide learners with opportunities to read informational texts at an earlier age so that these difficulties may be avoided. Transitions to expository texts, which are frequently difficult for learners of all ages (Alverman & Ridgeway, 1990; Alverman & Swafford, 1989), can be eased by using literature-based programs that include a variety of sources — biographies, informational books, picture books, realistic and historical fiction, manuals, magazines, pamphlets, and reference books. Literature (Brozo & Tomlinson, 1986; Vacca et al., 1991), and in particular multicultural literature, extends and enriches thematic learning so that content-area learning becomes stimulating and interesting. Providing a balance of reading selections (Rosenblatt, 1978, 1985) opens multiple avenues to learning. These selections include efferent literature (literature used for acquiring skills or information) and aesthetic literature (literature used for its emotional appeal of colorful, descriptive words, images, lyrical language, or emotions).

Multicultural literature provides opportunities to connect learning across the content areas with the cultural and personal experiences of students through these components:

1. **Illustrations.** As Aliki explains in her book *How a Book Is Made,* modern printing capabilities produce illustrations that have sharper images and bolder hues and colors and can produce a wider variety of illustrative forms in literature. Pictures transport readers to another culture (e.g., *Bringing the Rain to Kapiti Plain,* by Verna Aardema)

or another period of history (*The King's Day,* by Aliki); they visually chart information to increase understanding of text (*Corn Is Maize,* by Aliki, or *Linnea's Windowsill,* by Christina Bjork); or they provide graphic reminders of issues relating to war (*The Journey,* by Sheila Hamanaka), nuclear destruction (*My Hiroshima,* by Junk Morimoto), and environmental issues (*The People Who Hugged the Trees,* by Deborah Lee Rose). In our visually oriented society, young people are already accustomed to using visual clues to increase their understanding of information through television, movies, computers, and videos. Picture books that include drawings (*A Medieval Feast,* by Aliki), graphics (*Pyramid,* by David Macaulay), or photographs (*Volcanoes,* by Seymour Simon) provide comfort to these visual learners. Because picture books have a limited amount of text and illustrations, this medium is not overwhelming to learners. In particular, second-language learners benefit from picture books; they support the visual-verbal connection necessary for literacy development.

2. **Text.** By its nature, the picture book text is brief, yet it must follow high literary standards. This factor makes picture books particularly attractive for instructional planning. Through the colorful illustrations and rich language, students of all ages are able to grasp new ideas and concepts more quickly; then they can move on to application of the information through creative activities. Concise, illustrative formats enable students to extend their knowledge about a topic without becoming bogged down in the content. For example, *The Popcorn Book,* by Tomie dePaola, introduces students to the history of popcorn, which originated with Native Americans, as well as the scientific principles of how popcorn pops. Presented in an interesting, colorful, humorous format, the content stimulates new interests and questions for students to pursue in other sources. Other examples of informational books with interesting formats are Aliki's *A Medieval Feast,* Seymour Simon's *Animal Fact/Animal Fable,* and Michael Chinery's *Rainforest Animals.*

3. **Building Background Knowledge.** Through multicultural literature, teachers generate background knowledge and vicarious experiences related to the personal lives and experiences of their students. For example, reading *The Black Snowman,* by Phil Mendez, would be an interesting way to begin studying Africa, after which teachers can provide more background knowledge about African clans, beliefs, and varied lifestyles by having students read *Ashanti to Zulu,* by Margaret Musgrove, or *Skaka-King of the Zulus,* by Diane Stanley and Peter Vennema. Once this bridge between the known and unknown is formed, students can more easily grasp concepts about Africa in their social studies textbook.

4. **Intense Involvement with Core Subject Areas.** Typically, elementary-level textbooks compress information to present important ideas, events, and concepts rather than develop them fully (Brozo & Tomlinson, 1986). Greenlaw (1988) argues that informational books

that appeal to the students' interests are an alternative to bland textbooks. While reading *Chasing the Moon to China* or *Kenya, Jambo!* by Virginia McLean, for example, students are introduced to a country—its people, culture, history, language, and traditions—through the eyes of students who are traveling through the country with their parents.

5. **Multicultural Understanding and Appreciation.** Multicultural literature provides a natural way of extending knowledge and understanding of diverse cultures and countries. As students read *How My Family Lives in America,* by Susan Kuklin; *People,* by Peter Spier; *Talking Walls,* by Margy Burns Knight; or *This is My House,* by Arthur Dorros, they begin to perceive differences and similarities among other cultures and their own culture. Rather than laugh or giggle at the differences, they learn to identify and discuss different beliefs and how values affect actions and lifestyles among people from other countries. The colorful, detailed pictures and descriptive texts of these stories highlight the significant aspects of the groups so that students become involved and eager to learn more about diverse people. As students read and discuss other related books and stories, they increase their cultural knowledge. In the process of working together and exchanging ideas, they build a sense of community in their classroom and school. While developing more positive attitudes about themselves and others, students become more understanding of their own problems and the problems of others (Bishop, 1992).

6. **Multicultural Appreciation of the Arts.** Appreciation and understanding is further enhanced as students have opportunities to experience the music and art of various cultures. Jeanette and Jonah Winter's use of bilingual text and primitive art fosters an appreciation of the life and art of the Mexican artist Diego Rivera in their book *Diego.* Similarly, Christina Bjork's book *Linnea in Monet's Garden* kindles appreciation of the French Impressionist artists and Monet's art, specifically, in its exquisitely illustrated text. Through the narration of a young girl, students learn about Monet's life and how he captured impressions through his art. Lulu Delacre's *Arroz Con Leche: Popular Songs & Rhymes from Latin America* acquaints students with Latin American music and songs. As they hear and sing the songs and rhymes, they acquire a greater appreciation of lyrical language, while developing fluency and automaticity in their reading. Similarly, students experience African American rhythm and folk songs as they read and sing rhymes and chants framed with the kente cloth in *Shake It to the One That You Love the Best,* by Cheryl Mattox.

7. **Social Issues.** Picture books can introduce young readers to social issues of our nation and the world (Bishop, 1987, 1992; Norton, 1991). Mildred Taylor's *Mississippi Burning* and *The Gold Cadillac;* Eleanor Coerr's *Sadako and The Thousand Paper Cranes,* or Yukio Tsuchiya's *Faithful Elephants* provide opportunities for focused and carefully planned discussions about the issues of prejudice and war. These discussions need to emerge in a culturally sensitive context. All

students need to be able to express their feelings and thoughts freely so that they can perceive the impact of these issues on their own and others' lives. As teachers and learners become engaged in such discussions, learners will begin to think critically, develop problem-solving skills, and make better decisions to guide their own lives and act against social injustices.

8. **Accommodating Various Ability Levels and Interests.** Providing students with a variety of multicultural books enables them to select books that match their ability level and interest. As teachers model reading *A Medieval Feast* or *Mummies Made In Egypt,* by Aliki, which provide information about European and Egyptian life styles within a historical context, all students will become more comfortable reading picture books in their spare time. Similarly, the captivating illustrations and lyrical language of *The Legend of El Dorado,* by Beatriz Vidal, or *The Great Kapok Tree,* by Lynne Cherry, charm readers of all ages and ability levels, who feel as if they are traveling through Mexico and South America. Frequent encounters with these engaging multicultural stories transform students' perceptions of picture books. They see them as resources for their inquiries or their interests rather than as books for younger students or low-ability readers.

USING WRITING AS A TOOL FOR LEARNING IN A HOLISTIC CURRICULUM

Writing, which is a process of discovery and new understandings (Emig, 1977), is an effective tool for learning across the curriculum and for meaningful integration of the core subjects. Completing work sheets and end-of-chapter questions are often boring writing activities that fail to engage students in learning. Following whole language principles, we prefer to design authentic writing activities that emerge from students' cultural experiences. Writing as a tool for thematic learning accomplishes the following:

1. As students express their thoughts, feelings, and ideas about what they read, **their writing extends their knowledge and understanding about content and informational texts** (Harste, Short, & Burke, 1988; Herrmann, 1990; Langer & Applebee, 1987). For example, when students keep journals, recording their thoughts and feelings about *The Journey,* by Sheila Hamanaka, they can better relate to the fears of immigrants and the horrors of war and relocation centers. Similarly, as they write their feelings about Diego Rivera's artwork or Monet's paintings, they begin to see how artists use color, form, shape, and line to recreate life.

2. Writing helps **students learn to organize their thoughts, refining and clarifying their understandings.** As they participate in note-taking activities while reading *Count Your Way through the Arab World,* by Jim Haskins; *One Mesquite Tree,* by Gizela Jernigan; *Jambo Means Hello,* by Muriel Feelings; or *From A to Zen,* by Ruth Wells, they can use their notes

to create their own number or ABC book about the Arab, Japanese, or other cultures. As they create their own books, students acquire new information while learning how writers organize information to improve readers' comprehension of what they are trying to say. They then apply these new understandings about exposition as they read new informational books.

3. Writing helps **students improve their comprehension of stories and information as they integrate their ideas with the story, make decisions, and discover their knowledge** (Langer & Applebee, 1987; Clark, 1987; Hoffman, 1992; McGinley & Madigan, 1990). After reading *The Sign of the Beaver,* by Elizabeth Speare, for example, they can devise their own way of teaching Attean how to read. After coming up with words for each letter of the alphabet from his environment and writing these in their literature journal, they can describe (in their journals) how they would help him learn to read.

4. Through observing and note-taking activities, **students collect, organize, and synthesize information so that they can achieve a better understanding of their world.** After reading *Corn Is Maize,* by Aliki, for example, students can collect information and learn how corn grows, its history, and its uses. Using these notes, students can then organize and synthesize information to write about their new knowledge and understandings—in this case, blending social studies, science, and history concepts.

In sum, while communicating what they know and imagine to others in ways linked to their personal and cultural backgrounds, students come to view learning across all content areas as relevant and meaningful (Kleiman & Kleiman, 1992). Writing simultaneously enables students to understand themselves and their world better (Clark, 1987). The following vignette details strategies to follow when introducing the powerful tool of note taking to young learners.

Using Note Taking as a Tool for Learning

Recognizing that students need information, quotations, anecdotes, and details to record their ideas on paper, Mrs. Harkama uses note taking as a way to help her students become efficient collectors of information. According to Clark (1987, p. 80), "notetaking is a lifelong educational skill, a way of collecting, organizing, and synthesizing information." Note taking has become an integral component of Mrs. Harkama's social studies curriculum; it easily accesses information for discussion, cultural comparisons, and ultimately greater knowledge about cultures. Her students are no longer passive receivers who absorb information, wring it out for exams, and forget it, but are active listeners who write about what they are learning while taking notes and generate new writing from their notes.

Mrs. Harkama is beginning a thematic unit on China. To help build her students' background knowledge about China, she reads *Chasing the Moon to China,* by Virginia McLean, to her students. Before reading the story, however, she asks her students to brainstorm what they know about China, following the semantic webbing technique. (See Chapter Four.) All ideas are always accepted, because she knows that any misconceptions will be clarified as they learn more about China through an assortment of activities she has planned to follow throughout the month. When students contribute words unfamiliar to many students—for example, *the Great Wall* or *calligraphy*—Mrs. Harkama asks them to explain more about the word, concept, or person, which helps students increase their vocabulary and background knowledge about China.

After pooling their knowledge, her students are ready to listen as she reads the book *Chasing the Moon to China.* The story, which is narrated by a girl who is traveling to China with her parents, contains many interesting facts and information about China. After reading the story interactively, she explains that she will read the story a second time and they should take notes in order to remember this information.

Because this is the first time her students have taken notes, she first demonstrates how to organize notes. While modeling, she asks her students to fold their paper into four sections and label each section of the paper. Demonstrating on the chalkboard, she labels the first section People; the second, History; the third, Beliefs; and the fourth, Country. Then she reminds her students that they need not worry about their handwriting, for neatness is not important when they are taking notes. She further explains that they may use either cursive or manuscript writing—whichever is easier for them. Finally, she tells them that spelling does not matter when they are taking notes. In fact, she says she often abbreviates words when taking notes. She emphasizes that they must write fast to keep up with her pace of reading.

To further help them decide which facts to include in their notes, Mrs. Harkama prepares note cards with important facts about China included in the story. To prepare these cards, she records at least one important fact about China on each note card. (There is at least one note card for each student in her class.) For example, one note card reads, "The capital city is Beijing"; a second note card reads, "In the past, emperors, called 'Sons of Heaven,' governed China." Before beginning the note taking activity, she distributes these note cards to her students, asking them to read the cards silently. To ensure that all her students know all the words on their note card, she asks them to read the card aloud to a partner once all cards have been distributed.

After all students have practiced reading their cards, she asks volunteers to share their card with the rest of the class. As they read the card aloud, she asks the others to listen so they can decide where the information on the card will be placed in their notes. When Audrie reads her card, "Chinese people ride bicycles to work or shopping or wherever they're going," aloud, the class decides that this information would be placed in the section labeled People. Mrs. Harkama asks her students to think about the important words in the sentence. The class decides on "people," "ride," "bicycles," and "everywhere."

After working through two more examples, Mrs. Harkama begins reading the story aloud to her class. When students hear her read the information on their card, they raise their hand, holding up their card. This immediately signals the class to record this information in their notes. As they listen to the reader reread the information, they have time to decide where to place their notes and to select which words are the important words to be recorded. Having readers verbalize where they place the information and which words are important enables all students to learn how to classify the information and how to choose the important words for their notes.

Not one paper remains blank. All students are successful in this supportive atmosphere. Higher-level thinking skills are involved, but students are given time to record their notes and assistance in how to monitor their thinking. All students are engaged in the process; their faces beam as they see their papers quickly fill up with more and more information about China—its people, culture, history, and geography. As Mrs. Harkama continues reading the story, she finds that her students are able to write down the ideas quickly with less and less cuing from her.

Not wishing to overwhelm her students, she stops about halfway through the story on the first day. Then, on the next day, she asks her students to work with a partner, sharing their notes with one another, inserting any information they do not have in their notes. After briefly reviewing note taking strategies, she continues reading as students add to their notes. When Mrs. Harkama glances around the room, she sees that everyone has at least one page of notes; many have two pages by the end of the class period. Students are now ready to use their notes to write paragraphs about China.

To ensure that all students have adequate notes for this activity, she has them work with a new partner, pooling their notes. After regrouping as a class, she reviews paragraph writing, highlighting: (1) Paragraphs include a sentence that provides the main idea for the paragraph, and (2) paragraphs have additional sentences that provide details about the topic sentence. As her students review their notes, she asks them what the main ideas and the details might be. Her students readily see that each of the categories represents the main ideas and the notes under each category represent the details about the topic. Next she asks them to brainstorm possible topic sentences for each category. Brittany shares, "China's history is a vast history that covers over thousands of years." Demetrius reads, "In China there are 100 billion people."

Once students have brainstormed possible topic sentences for the categories, Mrs. Harkama asks her students to select one of the categories and write a paragraph about this topic. Enthusiasm springs from what is apparently a strong sense of ownership and an abundance of information to write about. Students quickly begin writing their paragraphs. Many students, in fact, write more than one paragraph. The selections below demonstrate the knowledge and information they have gained from this experience:

In China there are 100 billion people. There are so many because 1 out of every 4 people are born in China. They do not have vicals [vehicles] like we have but they do have bikes. The bikes are black and look alike. There is almost complet silence on the streets. They eat mostly rice, noodles or pasta, and vegetables. The bowls they eat out of are called commeal bowls. Adults drink either red or green tea, beer, and rice wine. The kids drink mostly orange pop. They don't have machines so they work with their hands. Many medicines can be found in China. When a baby is born it is 1 year old. Babys have two names, a family name and a given name. Instead of wearing dipers have slits in the back of their pants. In school they have to learn thousands of symbols instead of our 26 letters. They have to use ink and brush to write. When they do art they use their chop which here in the United States is called a stamp.

Bryan, Grade 5

China—The History

China's history is a vast history that covers over thousands of years. There is a big wall there. It was the biggest wall of all. It was the Great Wall of China. The Great Wall protected the people of China long ago. Now it is a special feature in the country. Long ago, Emperors ruled China. The Emperors color was yellow. Anyone who wore yellow besides the emperor would be in trouble. Also, the youngest Emperor ever was 2 years old. Aduts in China wore dark clothing. Children wore bright clothing. The Chinese calendar is and was round and based on the moon. The calendar is divided into 12 years. Each year is an animal. I was born in 1980, for example, and I am a monkey. Every 12 years the cycle of the calendar repeats. In the Chinese writing there is 1 symbol for 1 syllable or sound. Well, I could go on forever writing about the Chinese history.

Brittany, Grade 5

As Mrs. Harkama's class continues to read many other folk tales, poetry, and informational books about China and Chinese Americans during the month, their knowledge base expands. They keep track of this information on large chart paper, which is divided into the same four sections—people, country, history, and beliefs. When students discover new and interesting facts about China while reading independently, they add these ideas to the chart, using the marker lying near the semantic map. Through this process, students are able to see the cultural connections between the beliefs, values, and lifestyles of the Chinese and Chinese Americans.

Let us now turn to how teachers follow a thematic approach to learning through the use of multicultural literature and reading/writing activities. These vignettes are merely one way to approach thematic learning. Certainly, teachers must design the learning experiences according to the context of their classrooms, their schools, and their communities.

THEMATIC LEARNING: NATIVE AMERICANS

The following vignette describes how one teacher, Mrs. Streeter, creates a context for thematic learning. Throughout her thematic unit on Native Americans, Mrs. Streeter builds and extends understanding of the Native American culture, linking this knowledge to concepts in her fifth-grade social studies curriculum, which centers on early American history. By beginning the school year with a focus on the Native Americans, believed to be the original inhabitants of America, she feels her students will gain a better perspective on the Native Americans and their central role in America's history. By integrating the learning experience unit across the curriculum through reading, writing, speaking, and listening experiences, she believes that her students will perceive more meaningful, natural relationships between subjects areas. Native American literature provides the thread that links learning across the content areas.

Because this is her students' first experience with thematic learning, Mrs. Streeter begins this unit by brainstorming the major ideas and concepts she would like her students to gain from the experience. She then links these ideas and concepts to the goals and objectives of her social studies curriculum and to what her students need to learn in other content areas. To determine if the thematic learning experience will be meaningful, she further reflects on the process, asking herself the five questions proposed by Routman (1991) (see section on Organizing Thematic Learning Events) and making refinements as needed.

Building Background Experience and Interest in the Native Americans through KWL

Stimulating an Interest in Learning about Native Americans. Wanting to relate learning about the Native American culture to students' personal experiences, Mrs. Streeter begins her thematic unit with Tomie de Poala's *The Popcorn Book*. The story provides a natural connection to the Native American culture through the familiar topic of popcorn, which was discovered by Native American people thousands of years ago. Following the KWL (what we know, what we want to know, and what we learned) process (Ogle, 1986) (see Chapter 2), an effective strategy for helping students learn how to collect information, she first has them brainstorm everything they know about popcorn and lists this on chart paper in the first column (see Figure 6.2). Second, she encourages them to brainstorm questions they might

FIGURE 6.2 K-W-L strategy sheet.

K-W-L STRATEGY SHEET		
WHAT WE KNOW	WHAT WE NEED TO FIND OUT	WHAT WE LEARNED

have about popcorn. When students mention words or facts that are not familiar to their peers, she invites her students to "Tell us more about . . ." or asks, "Can you explain . . .?" Students pool their knowledge, explaining concepts in their own words, which broadens others' knowledge and understanding. Frequently, Mrs. Streeter also extends and develops certain concepts, clarifying information as needed. Now that everyone's interest is piqued and learning has become personalized, they are ready to listen as Mrs. Streeter reads *The Popcorn Book.*

After she interactively reads the book aloud, the class returns to the KWL chart. As students recall information from the story that responds to their questions, Mrs. Streeter records the ideas in the last column—what they have learned about popcorn. She places a star by questions that are not discussed in the story, asking them how they could find answers. Of course, students reply, by finding other books about popcorn and corn in the library, their classroom, or at home.

While responding to their questions, students discuss additional information they have learned about corn and popcorn, in particular the information about Native Americans. Mrs. Streeter records this information in the last column of the chart. Reading about the different ways Native Americans used popcorn—how the Iroquois people popped popcorn, how the Algonkians brought popcorn to the Pilgrims in a deerskin pouch, and how Native Americans used corn in their daily lives—motivates them to investigate Native Americans in more depth.

After discussing the story, therefore, Mrs. Streeter encourages her students to brainstorm new questions they have about the Native Americans. Students want to know the names of other tribes, where they live, how they dress, what their beliefs and customs are like, what their daily life is like, and what other foods they eat. She records these questions on a new chart, using webbing techniques. Students are now ready and eager to learn more about the Native Americans. They have become actively involved in the process, making choices about their learning with the guidance of their teacher.

Creating an Environment for Learning about Native Americans. Mrs. Streeter gathers a number of books about Native Americans for her class to read. These include informational books, biographies, folk tales and legends, and poems, as well as their social studies textbook (see Figure 6.3a and 6.3b) and displays these throughout the classroom. By providing a balance of efferent and aesthetic selections, she invites all readers to investigate Native American culture, traditions, and history.

To help her students understand how climate and location might influence Native American living styles, she also posts a large map of the United States, which is marked into sections, on the bulletin board. (See Figure 6.4). As the class reads about the different Native American nations through varied sources, she places the names of the tribes on the map according to their region. Information about each nation's cultural features is also recorded on small semantic maps strategically placed on the large map according to location. (See Figure 6.5).

By using a variety of sources, Mrs. Streeter helps her students acquire rich, detailed information about various Native American tribes, the differences among the lifestyles of the tribes, and the influence of climate and geography on their way of living. Simultaneously, students gain more insight into the Native American dreams,

FIGURE 6.3a Partial list of teacher reference materials.

Bibliography

Teacher Reference Materials

Name of Book	Author
Indians: An Activity Book	Artman, John
Americans, Too!	Aten, Jerry
The Native Americans: An Illustrated History	Ballantine, B. & Ballantine, I. (Eds.)
Don't Know Much About History	Davis, Kenneth C.
Indian Chiefs: A Teaching Guide	Hoven, Leigh
A People's History of the United States	Zinn, Howard

FIGURE 6.3b Partial list of Native American books for Native American thematic unit.

Children's Books on Native Americans

Name of Book	Author
Land of Sky Blue Waters W/Guide	
Corn is Maize	Aliki
Baby Rattlesnake	Ata, Te
Rising Fawn and the Fire Mystery	Awiakta, Marilou
Crickets & Corn	Back, Peg
And Me, Coyote	Baker, Betty
Where the Buffaloes Begin	Baker, Olaf
Earth Mother Lullabies From Around the World	Ballingham, Pamela
Before Columbus	Batherman, Muriel
Desert is Theirs, The	Baylor, Byrd
Everybody Needs a Rock	Baylor, Byrd
Hawk, I'm Your Brother	Baylor, Byrd
I'm in Charge of Celebrations	Baylor, Byrd
The Other Way to Listen	Baylor, Byrd
They Put on Masks	Baylor, Byrd
When Clay Sings	Baylor, Byrd
Our Fathers Had Powerful Songs	Belting, Natalia
Cry From the Earth: Music of the N. Am. Indian, A	Bierhorst, John
Naked Bear, The	Bierhorst, John
Goat in the Rug, The	Blood, C. L. & Link, M.
When the Legends Die	Borland, Hal
Keepers of the Earth	Caduto & Bruchac
How Raven Freed the Moon	Cameron, Anne
Orca's Song	Cameron, Anne
Raven Returns the Water	Cameron, Anne
Spider Woman	Cameron, Anne
Enchanted Caribou, The	Cleaver, Elizabeth

(continued)

FIGURE 6.3b (*continued*)

Adventures of Nanabush: Ojibway Indian Stories, The	*Coatsworth, David*
Mud Pony, The	*Cohen, Caron Lee*
Girl Who Married a Ghost, The	*Curtis, Edward S.*
I Once Knew an Indian Woman	*Cutler, Ebbitt*
Time Before Dreams	*Czernecki & Rhodes*
Land of the Sky Blue Waters	*Dailey, Sheila*
Popcorn Book, The	*de Paola, Tomie*
Legend of the Bluebonnet, The	*dePaola, Tomie*
Legend of the Indian Paintbrush, The	*dePaola, Tomie*
Star Maiden	*Esbensen, Barbara*
Double Life of Pocahontas	*Fritz, Jean*
Talking Earth, The	*George, Jean*
Julie of the Wolves	*George, Jean Craighead*
Art of the Woodland Indians, The	*Glubock, Shirley*
Lone Bull's Horse Raid	*Goble, Paul*
Beyond the Ridge	*Goble, Paul*
Buffalo Woman	*Goble, Paul*
Death of the Iron Horse	*Goble, Paul*
Dream Wolf	*Goble, Paul*
Gift of the Sacred Dog, The	*Goble, Paul*
Girl Who Loved Wild Horses, The	*Goble, Paul*
Great Race of the Birds and the Animals, The	*Goble, Paul*
Her Seven Brothers	*Goble, Paul*
Iktomi and the Berries	*Goble, Paul*
Star Boy	*Goble, Paul*
Legends of the Sun and Moon	*Hadley, Eric and Tessa*
Mouse Woman and the Mischief-Makers	*Harris, Christie*
Native American Cookbook	*Henry, Edna*
Ceremony of Innocence: Part Two of the Ghost Horse Cycle	*Highwater, Jamake*
I Wear the Morning Star	*Highwater, Jamake*
Moonsong Lullaby	*Highwater, Jamake*
Paddle to the Sea	*Holling, Clanay*
One Green Mesquite Tree	*Jernigan, Gisela*
Trees Stand Shining, The	*Jones, Heltie*
Legends of the Animal World	*Kervin, Rosalind*
Ishi, Last of His Tribe	*Kroeber, Theodora*
Squaw Man's Son	*Lampman, Evelyn*
Legend of the Milky Way	*Lee, Jeanne M.*
Choctaw	*Lepthien, Emilie M.*
All of You Was Singing	*Lewis, Richard*
Hiawatha's Childhood	*Longfellow, Henry*
Crow and Weasel	*Lopez, Barry*
Knots on a Counting Rope	*Martin, Bill Jr. and Archambault, John*
Arrow to the Sun	*McDermott, Gerald*
Defenders, The	*McGovern, Ann*
Linda's Indian Home	*McKeown, Martha Ferguson*
Indian Way, The	*McLain, Gary*

(*continued*)

FIGURE 6.3b (*continued*)

Annie and the Old One	*Miles, Miska*
Legend of Tarik, The	*Myers, Walter*
Who-Paddled-Backward-With-Trout	*Norman, Howard*
Island of the Blue Dolphins	*O'Dell, Scott*
Streams to the River, River to the Sea	*O'Dell, Scott*
People Shall Continue, The	*Ortiz, Simon*
Dogsong	*Paulsen, Gary*
Bring Back the Deer	*Prusski, Jeffrey*
Fire Came to the Earth People	*Roth, Susan*
Story of Light, The	*Roth, Susan*
Kanahena: a Cherokee Story	*Roth, Susan L.*
Legend of Scarface, The	*San Souci, Robert*
Whale in the Sky	*Siberell, Anne*
Dancing Teepees: Poems of American Indian Youth	*Sneve, Virginia Driving Hawk*
Sign of the Beaver, The	*Speare, Elizabeth*
Fire Stealer	*Toye, William*
Mountain Goats of Temlaham, The	*Toye, William*
How Rabbit Stole the Fire	*Troughton, Joanna*
Old Father Story Teller	*Velarde, Pabliita*
In the Shadow of the Wind	*Wallin, Luke*
Wampanoags, The	*Weinstein-Farson, Laurie*
New England Indians, The	*Wilbur, Keith C.*
Girl Who Loved the Wind, The	*Yolen, Jane*

beliefs, values, and lifestyles. These experiences provide a context for understanding the Native Americans' existence in this country, their history, and their perspective— a perspective that is frequently overlooked or inaccurately represented in the curriculum and social studies textbooks. Native American literature further provides them with a frame of reference for evaluating and examining how geography, history, and climate affected the lives of Native Americans. As students develop an understanding of these concepts, they are able to generalize the influence of these factors on other cultures.

Creating Connections with Mathematics

The Popcorn Book and the KWL chart on popcorn become resources for future activities in other content areas. For example, knowing that her students would want to have popcorn after studying the story, Mrs. Streeter popped popcorn for her class the night before. Before eating the popcorn, which she placed in paper cups, students estimate how many pieces of popcorn are in their cup and record this information on a sheet of paper. Then they count their popcorn and record this number on their paper and compare the two figures.

Everyone then eagerly begins to eat their popcorn while they brainstorm how they can graph the amount of popcorn in each cup for the class. The students decide

FIGURE 6.4. Map illustrating location of Native American tribes.

that one large piece of paper popcorn on the graph would represent 10 pieces of popcorn in their cup. Students then cut out pieces of paper popcorn to represent the amount of popcorn in their cup and glue the paper popcorn to the graph just above their name. The completed graph is then displayed in the hallway for others to view.

Mrs. Streeter prepares problems about the popcorn graph for them to solve the next day. After discussing the Native Americans' belief in working cooperatively to accomplish tasks, she arranges them in small groups to solve the problems cooperatively. As soon as they determine the solutions, groups prepare two problems for other groups to solve. Groups then exchange problems and work together a second time, finding solutions.

What a fun, meaningful way to learn about graphs! By working together, her students are discovering the benefits of collaborating to solve problems. As they help one another understand the concepts, they move beyond getting "right answers" to internalizing information. They are also able to relate this concept of cooperation to the Native Americans' way of living, learning, and caring as they read more stories.

Creating Connections with Science

Focusing on the popcorn seed and how plants grow, Mrs. Streeter also creates connections between science, language arts, social studies, and math. To reinforce understanding of how plants germinate and grow, Mrs. Streeter reads Aliki's book, *Corn Is Maize.* Not only do students learn new scientific facts about corn and how it grows, they also build on their new knowledge about its history and uses by the Native Americans. They learn how Native American tribes began to discover new ways to cultivate corn so that the plants became stronger and larger; how corn could be eaten fresh or ground for bread, tortillas, candy, popcorn, or mush; and how the husks became stuffing for mattresses, burned cobs became fuel, or woven dolls and toys for children.

To extend students' concepts about the Native Americans' close relationship with nature, Mrs. Streeter also reads the Cherokee legend, "The Coming of Corn," found in the book *Keepers of the Earth,* by Michael Caduto and Joseph Bruchac. This symbolic legend helps her students see that the Native Americans helped the corn to grow by clearing the land and preparing it for the "seeds." They learn that soil, which

FIGURE 6.5

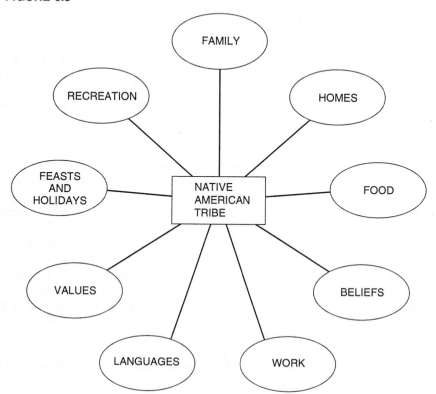

is the fertile bed from which new life springs, is a key component of the giving and receiving cycle of the planter, the crop, and the soil.

Just as the grandson helps the corn to grow in the legend, Mrs. Streeter's students help their own corn seeds to grow. She gives each student three seeds, a damp paper towel, and a resealable baggie. After carefully placing their seeds on the damp paper towel, students insert the towel in their baggies and seal the baggie. While caring for their seeds, they learn more about the scientific principles of plant growth. They write down these observations in their Seed Journal, which includes the date, pictures of their seeds, labels of the individual parts of the plant (following Aliki's model), and written records of the daily changes they observe in their seeds.

Mrs. Streeter's students enjoy reading their journal entries with their peers during the last five minutes of class. Sharing their entries provides an audience for their writing, which, in turn, encourages students to expand and develop their observations on subsequent days. She also encourages them to add to their journal entries while listening to their peers, inserting information they might have overlooked. Through these journaling experiences, her students explore their environment, learning to investigate and explain physical phenomena. By relating this experience to the Cherokees' traditions and beliefs, Mrs. Streeter helps her students develop an awareness of how Native Americans see themselves as part of nature and how their stories teach about the relationships between people and the Earth.

Creating Connections with Language Arts

Having developed background knowledge through these interdisciplinary activities, Mrs. Streeter continues her thematic unit by reading more Native American stories, which have been passed down through the generations by storytellers. Her students discover the Native American's imaginative and magical ways of explaining the mysteries of life, and the stories, which center on the relationship between man and nature, further become springboards for student learning about science, social studies, math, and the arts. To recreate the beauty and magic of these stories, Mrs. Streeter plans many aesthetic responses to literature.

Choral Readings and Dramatic Interpretations.   Choral readings (e.g., *When Clay Sings* or *I'm in Charge of Celebrations*) and dramatic interpretations (e.g., *Knots on a Counting Rope*) are two strategies she uses to draw aesthetic responses to literature with her Native American unit. (See Chapter 4.) These activities help her students *experience* the spirit of Native American storytelling. As they read the stories aloud, using the lyrical language in their choral readings or dramatic interpretations, they perceive the images and emotions created by the language and rhythm of the stories. Hearing and saying "hands that shape the earth this way have time to know the cool touch of the sand" in the story *When Clay Sings* enables students to understand the Native Americans' reverence for the land. Similarly, the Native Americans' respect for wisdom gained through age and experience is highlighted when they hear and recite, "They say that every piece of clay is a piece of someone's life"; or the importance of patience in one's life is understood as they chorally read, "They know the molding of clay has always been a slow and gentle world. No Hurrying. No rushing."

Invitations to Read. To further develop independence and student ownership in learning, Mrs. Streeter has each student choose a book from the reading table display of Native American folk tales and legends. All students choose a book to take home and read to their parents, a grandparent, sister, or brother. After reading the story aloud to a family member, students complete a story frame (see Chapter 4). These story frames are used to help them retell their story and share enjoyable parts of their story with a partner and, the following day, with their cooperative learning group. Through this experience, her students learn about storytelling and how Native American storytellers used words to formulate meaning about the human experience (Caduto & Bruchac, *Keepers of the Earth,* p. xvii).

Mrs. Streeter's students also enjoy illustrating their book by folding paper accordion style into eight sections. The first section is used for the title of the story; the next three for the categories of setting, characters, and problem or goal; the following three sections for the actions; and the final section for the resolution of the problem. Following the format of the story frames, students draw pictures to represent each category and record the important information about the categories beneath the drawing. Mrs. Streeter finds that displaying these illustrated books encourages class members to read and reread the books shared by their peers during SSR or their free time. The activities quickly become incentives for others to read the books.

Literature Logs. To help her students reflect on their reading about Native Americans, Mrs. Streeter has them keep a literature log. She varies how the log is used in order to maintain interest in the activity. For example, after silently reading *Ishi, Last of His Tribe,* by Theodora Kroeber, her students stop and respond to their readings. Chris, usually a reluctant reader and writer, wrote:

I youst to think indians werent a big deal. But ever since we started to do stuff on them and reserch I like indians now. Because like reading Ishi they say such preety words and they do neet stuff. I like how they made there home. When we fist started reading Ishi and the book tolled us how they made there homes me Ken, Kiven, and a couple other friends started to make a fort like Ishi's home. And after a whale it it turend out good. But I think that this book was fasanating becaus it told us there storys and how they lived and what Ishi's dream was and how it came true and what acturuely happed in some of Ishi's life and how he was the last Indian.

Although most log entries follow this free response format, she might have them respond to questions listed on the board. Examples might include: How have your feelings changed about the Native Americans or the white men? What new things have you learned about Native Americans or the white men? What suggestions do you have on how things could have been done differently? Why don't the good Saldu stop the evil Saldu? Marsha wrote the following response. This response reflects how Marsha's viewpoints on Native Americans are changing:

Reading About ISHI made me think about . . .

How we treated the Indians how we made them so scard that they ended up hiding.

How we are *so* proujudce about everyone who aren't like us.

It hasn't been resolved over *all* these years, mabe gotten a littel better but . . . mabe it never will be.

On alternate days, Mrs. Streeter asks them to draw the images they are picturing in their mind as she reads and to list interesting words around the drawings. Other days, she has them record metaphors, similes, or onomatopoeia in their logs.

Throughout, Mrs. Streeter encourages her students to take pride in their entries. Having them share their responses in small groups is one way she accomplishes this goal. As students read their logs in small groups, they have new opportunities to talk about their feelings and thoughts about these stories and their meanings with their peers. She also provides time for two or three students to share with the whole class. Through these expanded class discussions, Mrs. Streeter reinforces their awareness of the differences and similarities among the various nations, the influence of climate and geography on various nations, the vital link between the earth and Native American beliefs, their lifestyles, and the difficulties they experienced when new people came to their country.

Creating Connections with Art

As Mrs. Streeter's students continue to read about the Native Americans, they also enjoy learning about the crafts of several Native American nations. She begins by sharing that Native Americans tried to imitate the natural beauty of their environment through their art. She further explains their aspirations to beautify their world through art. To help her students experience this respect and admiration for nature and art, she plans a variety of art activities connected to stories they are reading. After reading *Annie and the Old One,* by Miska Miles, for example, she likes to introduce paper weaving. Just as the Navajos wove a piece of their life into rugs and tapestries, students choose two colors that represent their own cultural heritage and weave the paper together to form a placemat. The finished placemats are then displayed.

After experimenting with paper weaving, Mrs. Streeter's students learn more about the art of weaving as they weave an "Ojos Dios" (Eye of God), using twigs and colored yarn. Some parents help prepare the materials for the activity prior to class; other parents come to class to help students complete their Ojos Dios in small groups. (Mrs. Streeter has parents sign up to do various class activities at the beginning of the year; parents who cannot come to class help by cutting, folding, or organizing materials for various activities.) As her students participate in these activities, Mrs. Streeter reinforces the concept that many Native American weavings, which are intricate, with multicolored yarns, tell stories about the life of their nation.

To give her students experience with other art media, Mrs. Streeter also has them complete sand paintings, which are stories about the relationships between man and nature. Students first design a piece of their life with pencil and paper, filling in their rough drafts with colored markers and crayons. After experimenting with their designs, they transfer their final design to precut cardboard strips. This time the drawings are completed with the colored sand. (Mrs. Streeter discovered that sprinkling powdered tempera paints into jars of sand and rapidly shaking the jars to color the sand is the most economical way of completing this project.) In this way, students learn they can revise their drawings and designs to tell a story, just as they revise their writing.

Creating Connections with Music

Music is also a natural vehicle for experiencing and appreciating other cultures. Mrs. Streeter helps her students understand that all Native American songs had a purpose. Many songs and dances were directed toward objects in nature; others were prayers to the gods. As her students listen to the tape *For My People,* by Brooke Medicine Eagle, for example, they see more clearly the Native Americans' respect for nature and its influence on their lives. They enjoy singing some of the songs together as a class, especially "Dawn Star." When they go outside for recess, many are still humming, "The dawn star has risen, the new day has come."

Mrs. Streeter also creates opportunities for self-expression for her students as they integrate Native American music with their choral reading of *Brother Eagle, Sister Sky.* As students listen to the music of *Authentic Indian Dances and Folklore,* by Kimbo Records, and *Myth, Music, and Dance of the American Indian,* by Alfred Publishing—keeping time to the music with drums, tom-toms, rattles, and flutes—they become more familiar with the rhythms and melodies of Native American music. They apply this understanding as they create a musical introduction and conclusion to their choral reading, using the authentic Native American instruments. To create the setting of their choral reading, students also work in small groups to illustrate the Native Americans' ways of living during this period of history. Pleased with their production, they videotape the choral reading and take turns bringing the tape home to share with their parents. Just as we publish students' writing, we need to publish their reading.

Extending Connections with Social Studies

Throughout this thematic unit, which lasts for three months, Mrs. Streeter persistently builds and extends understanding of the Native Americans—their diversity, their contributions, their hardships, and their wisdom—and links this knowledge to concepts in her social studies curriculum, which emphasizes American history. One portion of her social studies curriculum, for example, is the journey of the Pilgrims to America. By beginning the school year with a focus on the Native Americans, she helps her students initially view and evaluate this journey from the perspective of the Native Americans, rather than the settlers. As they learn about the historical accounts of Wampanoags, from whom the Native Americans of this region descended, they begin to consider the hardships and difficulties the Wampanoags and other native nations experienced when the settlers arrived. Through extensive discussions, they reflect on how they would feel if someone new came to their land; how they would feel when they spotted the first European; or how they would act toward someone who looked different from them.

Students then change their point of view. They become Pilgrims journeying across the ocean in the Mayflower. By keeping a diary about the journey, students now more easily view the journey from the Pilgrims' eyes and become more in tune with their thoughts and feelings. Each student chooses a Pilgrim name from a list of children who were actually on the Mayflower. As they write in their diary, assuming an authentic name, they are able to become the young Pilgrim, viewing the events from his or her perspective.

As always, Mrs. Streeter builds background information for the diary through a variety of prewriting activities. To build understanding of the events leading to the voyage, the journey aboard the Mayflower, and the establishment of a new community, the Plymouth Plantation, Mrs. Streeter draws on a variety of resources, including books, videos, brochures, and films. She begins the activities by giving her students a list of questions that will be answered through the activities and resources she has developed and organized. As they read the questions aloud, she encourages them to brainstorm their prior knowledge and information about the pilgrims. Once she arouses their interest and motivates them to seek answers to the questions, she reads *The First Thanksgiving Feast,* by Joan Anderson. While reading the story, which includes photographs of people from the Plymouth Plantation and Native Americans dressed in authentic clothing, she highlights additional information about Pilgrims and Native Americans, making connections to students' prior knowledge. As she reads the story and shares the illustrations, her students realize that their Pilgrim names correspond to the name of the Pilgrims in the illustrations. The students naturally want to find a picture of their Pilgrim parents!

Mrs. Streeter then reads *A Pilgrim's First Thanksgiving* and *If You Sailed on the Mayflower,* by Ann McGovern, which provide additional information about the events. After sharing and discussing the stories, she revisits the list of questions. In these ways, her students begin to gain authentic knowledge that is critical to their understanding of historical events.

Following these prewriting activities, students begin their Pilgrim diaries, which include five entries: (1) before the departure, (2) during the voyage, (3) during their landing at Plymouth, (4) during the first winter, and (5) in the fall at the Thanksgiving feast with the Native Americans. As students complete their entries during the next three days, Mrs. Streeter circulates among them, asking if students are unsure of what to write next, such questions as: How do you feel? What is happening? What was it like on the Mayflower? What did you find when you landed? How did everyone feel? What is the mood of your family and your friends? Who came to the feast? These questions enable students to elaborate their ideas. Periodically having the students stop to share their entries helps other students gain ideas and new directions for their own journal entries.

When the rough drafts are revised and edited, students publish their diaries using the word processor. By recording the diary entries at the bottom or the top of the page, students can also add their own illustrations to their texts. The following are examples of students' entries:

September 3, 1620
Dear Diary,
We are leaving in three days for the big trip. I am excited to see the new land, but I am worried about my mother. It will be hard for her to manage

because she is going to have a baby in a few months. My sister Constance and I are going to have to help our mother as much as we can. Constance and I get along great. We tell each other many secrets. It will be great to have my sister along. We will have to stick together all the way.

Sincerely,

Demaris Hopkins

Oct. 1621

Good day! We are having our Thanksgiving celebration. Chief Massoit brought about 90 Indians and Samosett and Squanto came. I had to stand up through the whole thing and eat with my fingers. I even had to put my hat on. We played hide-and go-seek and we played with our knickers. I had a lot to eat, actualy I got stuffed.

Sincerely,

Giles Hopkins

This simulated experience, combined with the new perspective on the Native American people, enables students to view and evaluate historical events with a critical eye and sensitivity. As students recreate the events surrounding the arrival of the Pilgrims from two perspectives, they see alternative viewpoints, while identifying basic desires and needs that are common to both groups. Students are further able to comprehend these concepts better because they have linked this information with their own personal experiences.

MAINSTREAMING: A THEMATIC LEARNING EXPERIENCE ON THE ASIAN CULTURE

Mrs. Streeter believes that multicultural understanding and sensitivity move beyond cultural and linguistic similarities and differences to include physical similarities and differences as well. To help her students experience this firsthand, she uses group mainstreaming with Mrs. Kathy Micallef, who teaches a self-contained class of physically or otherwise health impaired (POHI) students. Specifically, Mrs. Micallef's students have disabilities such as cerebral palsy, attention deficit problems, physical disabilities, severe hearing impairment, and cognitive problems. She explains that her students' reading abilities range from the first-grade level to the fourth/fifth-grade level, "with everything in between and a lot of spotty learning."

Both teachers believe that modeling positive attitudes and high expectations is an important way for our youth to learn about these values in their own lives. They further believe that inclusion gives all students opportunities to work together and share their experiences. New opportunities for literacy development emerge for POHI students as they engage in a variety of social interactions with adults and peers of different strengths and abilities. Mrs. Micallef, for example, says her students are acquiring the language associated with plot analysis, story analysis, story maps, story grammar, and the writing process as a result of these cooperative learning activities.

She expects that as they begin to use the language, POHI students' understanding of the stories and the writing process will increase.

Working together, Mrs. Micallef and Mrs. Streeter plan modified thematic units centered around a specific culture for the school year. In 1993, for example, they integrated a thematic unit on the Asian culture with their reading/writing curriculum. Because there were no Asian students in their classes, they wanted to develop their students' understanding and appreciation of the Chinese, Japanese, and Korean cultures. Even though they had combined their classes to share various activities on numerous occasions, this was their first experience with organizing an interdisciplinary thematic unit for the combined classes. As a result, they selected this theme and the initiating questions for the unit. To help their students relate to Asian cultures and lifestyles, they created links between this new cultural information and their students' personal experiences. For example, by comparing the familiar Cinderella folk tale by Charles Perrault with the Chinese and Korean versions, students might see links between their prior knowledge and personal experiences and the Asian cultures. As the classes continued the thematic unit, Mrs. Streeter and Mrs. Micallef focused on the daily activities of Japanese, Chinese, and Korean children, providing additional connections between their personal experiences and those of Asians. The following vignette illustrates the steps they followed as they collaboratively planned thematic units for the fifth-graders and the POHI students.

After determining the goals and objectives and global scope and sequence of the unit, they used webbing techniques to identify materials and activities that would ensure meaningful, purposeful learning for their students. Next, they began collecting a variety of books, videos, resource materials, and artifacts from these cultures and contacted a number of resource people in the community to share additional information about the cultures, as well as their personal experiences in these countries. Throughout this process, Mrs. Streeter and Mrs. Micallef consistently checked to see that the thematic unit was relevant to the curriculum and to their students' needs, interests, and personal experiences, following the guidelines established by Routman (1991).

As the two worked together, for example, they realized a need to plan a variety of activities that would also foster hand-eye coordination and fine and large motor skills development for the POHI learners. They decided that the fifth-graders could participate in the learning process of their peers by modeling and guiding their participation in these activities through cooperative learning activities. To help her students learn this process, Mrs. Streeter discussed and modeled appropriate behaviors for her students to follow. She modeled how to show the POHI students how to cut paper; how to be patient when others need more time to complete a task; how to praise and encourage students who complete a task; how to ask questions when someone doesn't know what to write about; and how to ignore certain physical behaviors that students cannot control. As her students applied these behaviors with the POHI students, Mrs. Streeter and Mrs. Micallef supported them through praise, encouragement, and constructive feedback. Over time, the fifth-graders became more adept and sensitive to the needs of their POHI peers, supporting their learning.

Building Background Knowledge about and Interest in China

Mrs. Streeter and Mrs. Micallef began their thematic unit by having the two classes complete a semantic map on what they knew about China. (See Chapter 4.) As Mrs. Streeter guided the brainstorming activity, Mrs. Micallef recorded the information on large chart paper. Having a bulletin board and centers that display many books, pictures, and artifacts from China, Japan, and Korea helps students access their prior knowledge about the cultures.

Mrs. Streeter and Mrs. Micallef then followed Norton's (1991) sequence for introducing literature from a particular culture by beginning with folk tales. Specifically, they began with the Cinderella story. The teachers divided the classes into three heterogeneous groups to listen to three versions of Cinderella: Mrs. Streeter read *Korean Cinderella,* by Shirley Climo to her group; Mrs. Micallef read *Yeh Shen,* by Ai-Ling Louie; and Ms. Strong, a preservice teacher, read *Cinderella,* by Perrault. After interactively sharing the folk tales, highlighting the cultural features, each teacher guided discussion of the story elements within these small groups. Ideas were recorded on a large Cultural Story Map, while the students simultaneously recorded the ideas on their own maps. (See Figure 6.6.) During the next two days, students moved from one group to the next to hear the other folk tales, completing individual maps for each one. This process enabled them to compare the cultural settings, characters' actions and appearance, characters' dreams and values, and the themes.

On day four, the class came together to discuss their inferences about the similarities and differences among the three versions of Cinderella. Using the large chart paper with the completed Cultural Story Map on it, students reviewed these elements and added new information to the categories. They also discussed and completed the last categories, Similarities and Differences. The POHI learners actively participated in these discussions, easily using the vocabulary about the elements and sharing many inferences and insights about the folk tales. After completing the Cultural Story Map, students worked in heterogeneous groups of three or four and wrote their own version of Cinderella. The story below is an example from one group story.

Cinderella

Once upon a time, there was a girl named Cindy. Cindy was very beautiful, kid, and smart. cindy always got straight A's. Cindy was 6, she had a brother who was 2, and a sister that was 10.

One day when Cindy came home from her friends house, her sister (Jane) was crying. Cidy asked what's wrong, her sister told her that their mother died in a horrible car accident.

Then her father got remarried to a fat, ugly, dumb, and selfish lady. Her stepmother had a daughter named Lori. Lori was 7.

About a year after her father got remarried, he died. Everybody was sad. Now her Stepmother showed her true color. She never treated Cindy nicely. She made Cindy, Jane, and Mark (her brother) do all the chores. Their stepsister was also mean.

Cindy got nicknamed "Cinderella", Jane nicknamed "Sloppy Joe" and

Cultural Comparison
Group 3 — Jamie

	Title	Title	Title	Similarities	Differences
Setting	Korean cinderella — Small village in Southern Korea	cinderella home — town	Yeh-shen — In the Dim Past		
Characters	black cow road Kongjee stepmod stepsister gourna father, weaving Maid	cinderella god mother Stepsisters Prince Stepmother	Yea-shen King fish Stepmother Stepsister Old man		
Problem	mean Stepmother	Cinderella wanted to go to the ball and to meet the Prince	She lost her slipper fish got killed stepmother and stepsisters		
Magic	cow toad weaving maid birds talked helped her human cha	She turned them into outher things	the fish is magis old man Slipper magic stepmother		
Events	mother died father marri Kongjee back lots of work roses, Shoe	going to the ball two times			
Ending/ Solution	governor falls in love and marries Kongjee	leting her stepsisters live with her.	gets ma		

FIGURE 6.6 Cultural comparison of Cinderella folk tale.

Mark was was nicknamed "Cinderfella". The wicked stepmother was always jealous of Cindy's beauty. Life was full of chores.

Then one day, the prince's messajer said there will be a ball next week. The wicked stepmother and stepsister were so happy.

Finally it was the day of the ball. The stepmother (Lisa) didn't let Cindy, Mark, or Jane got to the ball. Lisa loaded them with work. After the step-mother and stepsister left, they all started crying. All of a sudden a magic limousine honked it's horn. Cindy, Jane, and Mark went outside to the limo. Then the limo said, "don't cry, I can help you get to the ball, just sit down in the car, when you buckel-up you all will be wearing fancy clothe."

When they got to the ball, they looked the best. The prince danced with Cindy all night long.

A week later Cindy and the prince got married, Jane and the messenger got married and Mark and the princess got married. After that, the stepsister and stepmother got run over by a fire-engine. Everyone else lived happily ever after.

Extending Understanding of the Chinese Culture Across the Curriculum

Mrs. Streeter and Mrs. Micallef realized the importance of also using informational texts to increase students' understanding of the Chinese culture. Using the same format of reading books in small groups, they read: *Lion Dancer,* by Kate Waters and Madeline Slovenz-Low; *Chinese New Year,* by Tricia Brown; and *Chin Chiang and the Dragon Dance,* by Ian Wallace. The teachers observed that reading in small groups improved listening habits and allowed them to develop the cultural information presented in these colorfully illustrated stories through discussion. Small groups also helped students connect the insights gained from the folk tales with knowledge gained from the informational texts and provided more opportunities for all students, particularly those reluctant to talk in large groups, to ask questions and to participate in these discussions.

After learning about the Chinese New Year celebrations—such as the way Chinese dress in new clothes to keep away evil spirits; give tangerines, sweets, and red envelopes to their relatives; and celebrate the Lantern Festival—the two classes made their own lanterns. Students cooperatively designed lanterns shaped like fish, vegetables, fruit, or other objects—just as the Chinese children do—and decorated them with glitter, sequins, and colorful buttons, which also reinforced eye-hand coordination for the POHI students.

Students also used the Chinese calendar, which is based on the cycles of the moon, to determine their birth dates. They not only enjoyed learning about their teachers' and peers' birth dates, but also became motivated to learn more about the significance of the animals on the calendar.

After building background knowledge about China in these ways, each teacher read *In the Year of the Boar and Jackie Robinson,* by Bette Lord, within their individual classes, while students followed along in their own books. They could more easily understand some of the difficulties Shirley Temple Wong, a young girl who left her home in China to come to Brooklyn, New York, encountered as she adjusted to a new country and culture. The confusion over Shirley's age, her placement in the wrong grade level, and her way of counting, using the Chinese calendar, were incidents the students could now regard with insight and sensitivity. Participating in the cultural activities prior to reading the story gave them the knowledge and understanding they needed to relate to Shirley's adjustments.

Most important, however, were the discussions about Shirley, her culture, and her adjustments to a new school; the different ways teachers and students interacted in school; and the different ways the school day was organized in this new culture. As more and more people come to America from countries around the world, students need opportunities to consider how they might help students from diverse cultures adjust to a different language, unfamiliar customs, and lifestyles that may seem peculiar to them. Jennifer, one of Mrs. Micallef's POHI students, further made a connection between the adjustments Shirley must make within a different culture and the adjustments she makes as she uses her wheelchair. Others similarly shared their inner thoughts and feelings about using walkers or hearing devices. As her students discussed their thoughts and feelings about being different, they begin to see the different ways their peers dealt with these feelings.

Students also took turns reading and talking about the story with a partner. While reading aloud, sometimes Mrs. Streeter and Mrs. Micallef paused, allowing students to read words, sentences, paragraphs or parts of pages as a total group. They saw that varying the way the story was read aloud helped maintain interest and attention.

Building Background Knowledge about and Interest in Japan

To further help students perceive ways they are similar and different from people of another culture, Mrs. Micallef and Mrs. Streeter showed them a video about Japan. As the children watched, they took notes on differences and similarities between Japanese children and themselves. (See Figure 6.7.) After viewing the video, students shared their notes with the whole class while Mrs. Micallef recorded their ideas on large chart paper. Even though the children began the task thinking they would see more differences than similarities as they compared their culture to that of the Japanese, they discovered that there are far more similarities than differences. They saw Japanese children riding bikes, skateboarding, playing in a band, and skiing; they saw children wearing shorts, T-shirts, and sneakers just as they do. Students need to see the similarities and differences among cultures, the features which validate each.

Extending Understanding of the Japanese Culture Across the Curriculum

Following this experience, teachers interactively read aloud *Count Your Way through Japan,* by Jim Haskins. As they took turns reading each page of the informational text, Mrs. Micallef and Mrs. Streeter alternately displayed the Japanese numerals, using Japanese characters, and English pronunciations, written phonetically on the overhead projector. Students learned about the history of Japan, sights of the country, and its geography as they listened. Having students take notes as they listened to the

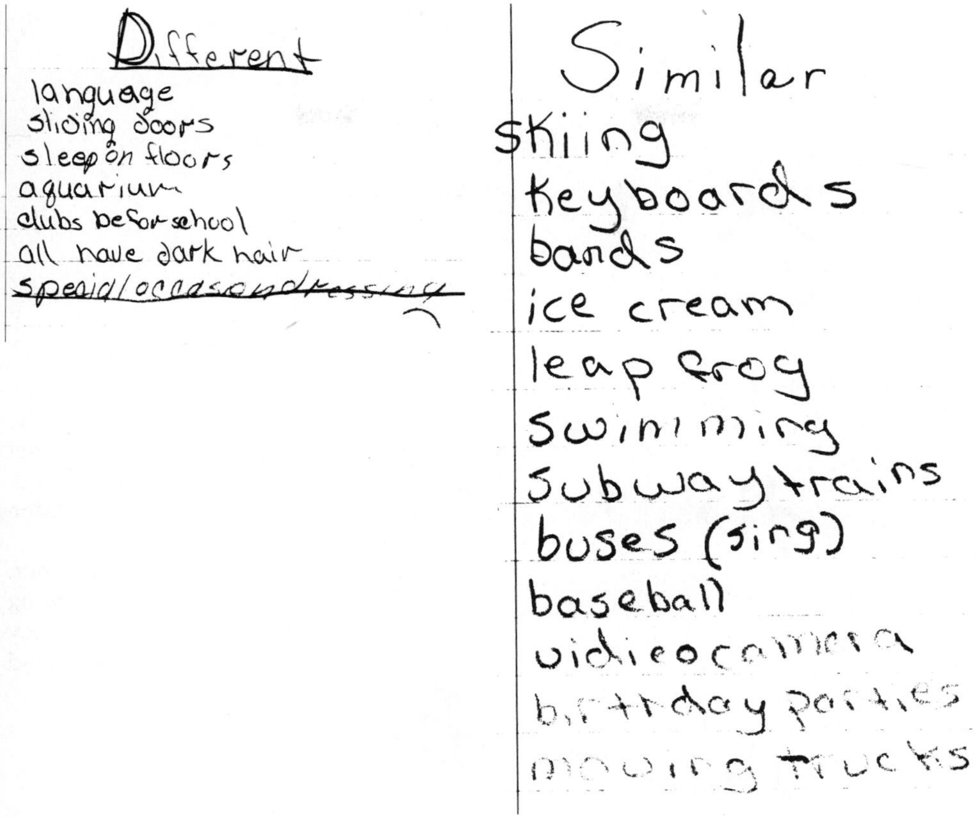

Different
language
sliding doors
sleep on floors
aquarium
clubs before school
all have dark hair
special occasion dressing

Similar
skiing
keyboards
bands
ice cream
leap frog
swimming
subway trains
buses (sing)
baseball
video camera
birthday parties
moving trucks

FIGURE 6.7 Students list ways they are similar to and different from Japanese children.

story the second time helped them remember the information and discuss ideas more fully. After the class discussion about Japan, students worked in small groups, generating additional questions.

Students especially enjoyed counting to 10 in Japanese and writing the Japanese numbers—using the Japanese characters—after the story was read. The real challenge, however, was completing the addition and subtraction work sheets using Japanese characters. (See Figure 6.8.) Students who finished the worksheets early created their own addition and subtractions problems for their friends to solve.

Learning about Japan became even more exciting when a guest speaker who lived in Japan for several years, Mrs. Hueur, visited the classroom. To help the students understand more about the lifestyles and customs of the Japanese, she centered her presentation around a child's day in Japan from morning until night. Using a large chart paper with various greetings displayed in English and Japanese (including Japanese characters), she began with "Good Morning," a greeting children might give their mothers or fathers upon rising in the morning to show their respect for their elders. Using pictures and artifacts, Mrs. Hueur continued her story, interspersing

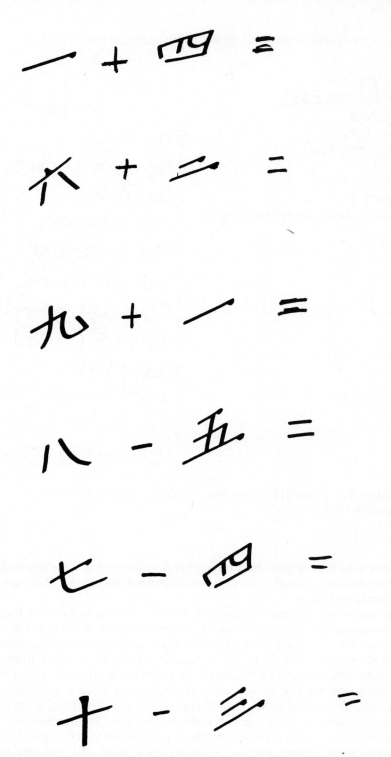

FIGURE 6.8 Examples of addition and subtraction problems using Japanese characters.

various greetings from her chart as the day progressed. After sharing her story, she let the children try on Japanese clothing—a kimona, a jacket, a wedding dress, and a monk's robe.

Mrs. Hueur visited the class on two additional occasions to help them learn more about the Japanese culture and language, which is rich in symbolism because each sound can refer to several characters and have several meanings. One day, she brought a chart of the Japanese symbol-sound relationships. After students learned that each character stands for certain sounds and how to pronounce them, they referred to the chart to identify the sounds of their names. They verified the sounds of their name by looking at a second chart, which included everyone's name written in Japanese characters. Before long, all discovered their names on the chart and delighted in saying one another's names over and over in Japanese. On the third visit, Mrs. Hueur brought paintbrushes and paint so that students could paint their names and practice forming various Japanese characters, using the Katakana Alphabet. (See Figure 6.9.)

Students learned more about the Japanese language when Mrs. Long, a parent in the school who had a Japanese exchange student staying with her family, visited the classroom and taught them the song "Mary Had a Little Lamb" in Japanese.

The Japanese culture was even evident in their physical education classes, where both classes learned a Japanese dance, Tanko Bushi, and two Japanese games, Group Line Hoop and Human Obstacle Course, which emphasize cooperation. They faced new challenges as they discovered cooperative ways to hold hands, move rhythmically to music, and go over various obstacles with walkers and wheelchairs. While all students improved their problem-solving skills, the POHI students advanced their large motor skills development.

The students' knowledge and understanding of the Japanese culture grew and developed as the teachers read *The Painter and the Wild Swans,* by Claude Clément; *The Stone-Cutter,* by Gerald McDermott; and *The Magic Fan,* by Keith Baker, in small groups, using the format developed for the Cinderella stories. Through the charming illustrations of these books, many of Mrs. Streeter's students discovered that the Japanese, like the Native Americans, respect nature and their surroundings.

After listening to these stories and discussing elements of the Japanese culture that relate to the stories, Mrs. Streeter and Mrs. Micallef shared two forms of Japanese poetry—Haiku and Lantern poems. As students read various Japanese poems, they discovered how figurative language symbolically conveys the beauty of life and nature. Using this knowledge to create and illustrate their own poems enhanced their understanding of this theme. They also learned more about the value of cooperation as they revised one another's poems, checking to see if the correct number of syllables were used in their poems. Choices about which words to eliminate or substitute became challenging because the meaning of the poem must always remain in tact. Here are examples of poetry by the students:

        Clouds of morning mist,
        Float over the summer hills,
        Like a painted dream.
                Nicole

KATAKANA

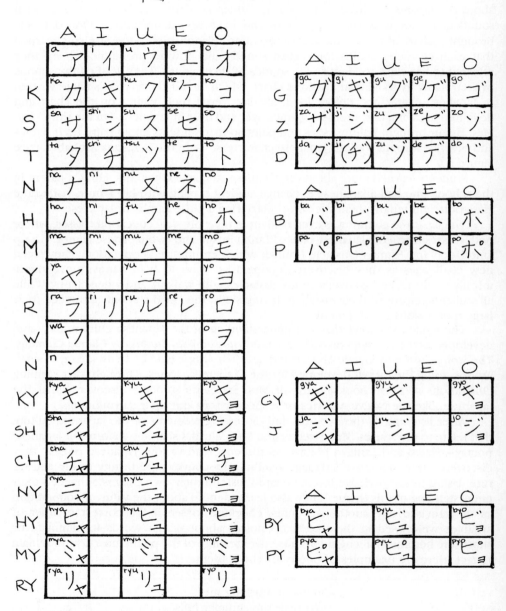

FIGURE 6.9. Chart of Katakana alphabet.

Clouds are beautiful
Nice, soft, fluffy, humongous
Clouds different sizes.

Angela

Water falls
Wispy wet, cool rocky, beautiful
Real rainbows within

Alison

As a culminating activity, students brought art and poetry together by making a hanging scroll, called a *kakemono*. After learning how the Japanese value beauty in the simple things and that the decor of their homes is restful, never gaudy or heavy, students used this knowledge to create their own scrolls from wallpaper that had a restful, simple design. With crayons and paint, they decorated their scrolls to represent one of the four seasons. The finished *kakemono* was then placed in their own beauty spot, the *tokonoma,* in their rooms at home. Eye-hand coordination, spatial awareness, following directions, measurement, and aesthetic awareness were further enhanced for the POHI learners as they worked cooperatively with the fifth-graders.

Extending Understanding of the Korean Culture Across the Curriculum

To review students' prior knowledge about Korea, Mrs. Streeter and Mrs. Micallef used semantic webbing techniques again. Students quickly saw that they had learned some things about Korea from the Korean Cinderella story. Reading *Count Your Way Through Korea,* by Jim Haskins, provided a natural way to extend students' knowledge of the Korean culture. Following the same format they developed for reading *Count Your Way Through Japan,* Mrs. Streeter and Mrs. Micallef alternately read the story aloud to their students. Students learned about Korea's history, geography, and lifestyles and compared and contrasted this information with what they had learned about Japan and China. They also used the Korean number characters to create multiplication and division work sheets for small groups to solve.

After participating in these activities, students wrote down their questions about Korea for their guest speaker, Mrs. Micallef's sister-in-law, Mrs. Langman, and her two adopted Korean children. Similar to Mrs. Hueur, Mrs. Langman shared information about Korean lifestyles and customs by focusing her presentation on a child's day, using her two children, who came with her dressed in traditional Korean attire. The POHI learners and fifth-graders thus learned about greetings in Korean, the ways Koreans dress, what they eat, what they do in school, and what games they play. Students especially enjoyed seeing the Korean clothing and the Korean flag. After sharing her story, Mrs. Langman gave all the students a paper bag decorated with the Korean words they had learned, containing treats, such as Korean chips and Korean bubblegum.

To reinforce students' understanding of the adjustments Korean children must make when their family moves to the United States, Mrs. Streeter and Mrs. Micallef also read *Aekyung's Dream,* by Min Paek, aloud to their individual classes. After listening to the story and discussing how Aekyung struggles to understand herself in a different culture where people speak a foreign language, dress in strange clothes, and behave in ways unfamiliar to her, they wrote letters to Aekyung, sharing how they might help her adjust more easily to her surroundings. Kenya's and Marvin's letters follow:

Dear Aekyung—don't feel left out. We dont bite. Ignore the people who call you names. They don't know you'r not Chineise so maybe if you tell them they won't tease about your eyes. I like your language better than ours. everyone's impressed by you talents. They don't show it.

Marvin

Dear Aekyung,

Here's some timps how to fit in: If possible find a tutor to help you with your English, Maybe you could teach the class the Korean language then we could all talk in the same language, Maybe tell the class about Korean holidays or something.

Here's some tips for how to deal with kids who tease you: If kids start to tease you walk away or get some back up (some kids (like me) to help you go against bullies) You can't try to impress bullies. If all else fails get a teacher or princapal.

Here's some tips for feeling accepted: I can try to get my friends to like you, or you could show us some things from Korea.

-I hope I gave you some ideas.

Your friend,
Kenya

The two teachers thought that writing letters to Aekyung would help their students become more sensitive to the needs of students who come to their school from countries around the world. As students shared their letters, they decided on the most sensitive ways to interact with students from a different culture or country.

Finally, opportunities emerged to integrate what they had learned about the three Asian cultures as students worked cooperatively in small groups to make their own Count Your Way books. Using the varied resource materials and books in their classes, plus their notes, students planned, wrote, illustrated, and published their own books about one of the three cultures, following the pattern of the Count Your Way books they read together as a class.

THEMATIC LEARNING: MULTIPLE DIMENSIONS

Although Mrs. Streeter and Mrs. Micallef initially organized their multicultural, thematic unit around a specific culture, they are currently implementing a new thematic unit, Ethnic Pride. Realizing there is a need for developing pride in one's ethnic heritage, they are celebrating the unique contributions we all bring to our nation by first focusing on each person's heritage and origins. They believe that their students will develop more sensitivity towards others as they become proud of their own heritage. Beginning with an investigation of their names, all students discover information about their heritage from their family members. In this way learning first evolves from students' personal and cultural experiences. Appreciation of others begins with an appreciation of self.

Like Norton (1991), Mrs. Streeter and Mrs. Micallef then read a variety of folk tales from the diverse cultures found within their classrooms, making comparisons and contrasts between the stories. As the year progresses, they explore other themes such as celebrations, geography, calendars, immigration, or food, following these concepts cross-culturally. Similarly, other teachers are exploring such themes as grandfathers, celebrations, folk arts, famous people, historical places, and names.

When planning and organizing multicultural units, teachers and students can pursue many different avenues for integrating the curriculum. Many of our teachers initially organize their thematic units around a specific culture, as Mrs. Streeter and Mrs. Micallef did. As they become more comfortable with this learning approach, they discover new themes to pursue. We must, however, be sure to move beyond merely creative, entertaining themes and activities so that relevant, purposeful learning happens. Learning experiences should be related to the goals and objectives of the curriculum and the needs of students as they participate in the process of planning thematic units. Simultaneously, we need to create natural, meaningful relationships among the content areas, using the four language modes of reading, writing, listening, and speaking.

SUMMARY

We have presented ways to create effective links between reading and writing and the content areas. Using a multicultural thematic approach to learning tied together by the threads of multicultural literature offers students opportunities to perceive connections between the core subjects and their cultural backgrounds and experiences.

We began with a definition of thematic learning, followed by a discussion of the theoretical perspectives on this approach to learning. After establishing a rationale for multicultural thematic learning, we shared specific strategies teachers can follow to organize thematic learning events and create an environment for holistic learning.

After providing a context for thematic learning, we described how multicultural literature links learning across the content areas through fictional and informational texts on a variety of multicultural topics. Many of these provocative texts also introduce young readers to social issues through characters from diverse cultures. Similarly, we illustrated how writing, which is a process of discovery and new understanding, can be used as a tool for learning across the curriculum.

Finally, we provided examples of how teachers use a multicultural thematic approach to learning in their classrooms. We emphasized that these vignettes are merely one way to approach thematic learning. Teachers must plan learning experiences according to the context of their classrooms, their schools, and their communities. Involving students in the process provides the most powerful approach to thematic learning events, for students share ownership in their learning. Through this process, learning becomes a living example of our multicultural nation.

REFERENCES

Alvermann, D., & Ridgeway, V. (1990). Implementing content area reading with limited finances. In G. Duffy (Ed.), *Reading in the elementary school.* (pp. 200–208). Newark, DE: International Reading Association.

Alvermann, D., & Swafford, J. (1989). Do content area strategies have a research base? *Journal of Reading, 32,* 388–394.

Alvermann, D., Dillon, D., & O'Brien, D. (1987). *Using discussion to promote reading comprehension.* Newark, DE: International Reading Association.

Au, K. (1992). Constructing the theme of a story. *Language Arts, 69,* 106–111.

Au, K., & Jordan, C. (1980). Teaching reading to Hawaiian children. Finding a culturally appropriate solution. In H. Trueba, G. P. Guthrie, & K. H. Au (Eds.), *Culture and the bilingual classroom: Studies in classroom ethnography.* (pp. 139–152) Rowley, MA: Newbury House.

Bennett, W. (1986). *What works: Research about teaching and learning.* Washington, DC: Department of Education, Report ED 26399.

Bishop, R. (1987). Extending multicultural understanding through children's books. In B. Cullinan (Ed.), *Children's literature in the reading program.* Newark, DE: International Reading Association.

Bishop, R. (1992). Extending multicultural understanding. In B. Cullinan (Ed.), *Invitation to read: More children's literature in the reading program.* Newark, DE: International Reading Association.

Brozo, W., & Tomlinson, C. (1986). Literature: The key to lively content courses. *The Reading Teacher, 40,* 288–293.

Caduto, M., & Bruchac, J. (1988). *Keepers of the earth. Native American stories and environmental activities for children.* Golden, CO: Fulcrum, Inc.

Clark, R. (1987). *Free to write.* Portsmouth, NH: Heinemann.

Cohen, E. (1987). *Designing group work: Strategies for the heterogeneous classroom.* New York: Teachers College Press.

Cullinan, B. (1992). *Invitation to read: More children's literature in the reading program.* Newark, DE: International Reading Association.

Cummins, J. (1983). *Heritage language education: A literature review.* Toronto: Ministry of Education.

Cummins, J. (1986). Empowering minority students: A framework for intervention. *Harvard Educational Review, 56,* 28–46.

Dewey, J. (1956). *The child and the curriculum and the school and society.* Chicago: University of Chicago Press.

Emig, J. (1971). The composing processes of twelfth graders (Research Report No. 13). Urbana, IL: National Council of Teachers of English.

Farris, P., & Kaczmarski, D. (1988). Whole language: A closer look. *Contemporary Education, 59,* 77–81.

Goodman, K. (1986). *What's whole in whole language.* Portsmouth, NH: Heinemann.

Greenlaw, M. (1988). Using informational books to extend the curriculum. *The Reading Teacher, 42,* 18.

Hansen, J. (1987). *When writers read.* Portsmouth, NH: Heinemann.

Hansen, J. (1992). The language of challenge: Readers and writers speak their minds. *Language Arts, 69,* 100-105.

Harste, J., Short, K., & Burke, C. (1988). *Creating classrooms for authors: The reading-writing connection.* Portsmouth, NH: Heinemann.

Heath, S. (1983). *Ways with words: Language, life, and work in communities and class-rooms.* Cambridge: Cambridge University Press.

Herrmann, B. (1990). Cognitive and metacognitive goals in reading and writing. In G. Duffy (Ed.), *Reading in the elementary school.* (pp. 81-96). Newark, DE: International Reading Association.

Hoffman, J. (1992). Critical reading/thinking across the curriculum: Using I-Charts to support learning. *Language Arts, 69,* 121-127.

Howe, G. (1988). Expecting miracles—How to develop a learning consciousness in high school classrooms. *The Social Studies, 79,* 228-231.

Jordan, C. (1985). Translating culture: From ethnographic information to educational program. *Anthropology & Education Quarterly, 16,* 105-123.

Kleiman, M., & Kleiman, G. (1992). Life among the giants: Writing, mathematics, and exploring Gulliver's world. *Language Arts, 69,* 128-136.

Langer, J., & Applebee, A. (1987). *How writing shapes thinking: A study of teaching and learning.* Urbana, IL: National Council of Teachers of English.

LeSourd, S. (1988). Using an advanced organizer to set the schema for a multi-cultural lesson. *Journal of Reading, 32,* 12-18.

Lipson, M. (1983). The influence of religious affiliation on children's memory for test administration. *Reading Research Quarterly, 18,* 448-457.

Machet, M. (1992). The effect of sociocultural values on adolescents' response to literature. *Journal of Reading, 35,* 356-362.

Marzano, R. (1991). Language, the language arts, and thinking. In J. Food, J. Jensen, D. Lap, & J. Squire (Eds.), *Handbook of research on teaching the English language arts.* (pp. 559-586). New York: Macmillan.

McGinley, W., & Madigan, D. (1990). The research "story": A forum for integrating reading, writing, and learning. *Language Arts, 67,* 474-483.

Norton, D. (1991). *Through the eyes of a child: An introduction to children's literature.* New York: Macmillan.

Ogle, D. (1986). K-W-L: A teaching model that develops active reading of expository text. *The Reading Teacher, 39,* 564-570.

Pappas, C., Kiefer, B., & Levstik, L. (1990). *An integrated language perspective in the elementary school: Theory into action.* New York: Longman.

Peregoy, S., & Boyle, O. (1993). *Reading, writing, and learning in ESL.* New York: London.

Rosenblatt, L. M. (1978). *The reader, the text, the poem: The transactional theory of the literary work.* Carbondale: Southern Illinois University.

Rosenblatt, L. (1985). The transactional theory of the literary work: Implications for research. In C. R. Cooper (Ed.), *Researching response to literature and the teaching of literature.* Norwood, NJ: Ablex.

Rosier, P., & Holm, W. (1980). *The rock point experience: A longitudinal study of a Navajo school.* (pp. 33-53). Washington, DC: Center for Applied Linguistics.

Routman, R. (1991). *Invitations: Changing as teachers and learners K-12.* Portsmouth, NH: Heinemann.

Tharp, R. (1989). Psychological variables and constants: Effects on teaching and learning in schools. *American Psychologist, 2,* 349-359.

Tierney, R., Soter, A., & O'Flahavan, J. (1989). The effects of reading and writing upon thinking critically. *Reading Research Quarterly, XXIV,* 136-173.

Slavin, R. (1983). *Cooperative learning.* New York: Longman.

Vacca, J., Vacca, R., & Gove, M. (1991). *Reading and learning to read.* New York: HarperCollins.

chapter 7

Promoting Cultural Appreciation and Understanding

OVERVIEW

We now return to the concept of teacher as cultural mediator to discuss the importance of teachers' personal reflections on their assumptions, biases, and interactions with their students. We offer ways that teachers might become knowledgeable about the cultures of their students in order to help them learn about themselves. After discussing methods of helping students understand their cultural backgrounds, we suggest ways that teachers can connect literacy development to students' families and communities. We further present specific ways of using literature to help students understand traditional cultural beliefs and values. Next, we share techniques to promote critical examination and understanding of diverse cultures, including: role play, cross-cultural comparisons and contrasts, and participation in cultural experiences through poetry, music, and art. Finally, we examine barriers to cultural understanding, providing specific ways that teachers might help students recognize stereotyping, racism, and discrimination when it exists, and thereby act as advocates for justice and equality.

INTRODUCTION

The possibilities for good or evil within the continental United States are precisely the possibilities for good or evil in the vexed postwar world. No other nation on earth has had the opportunity the United States has had to bring so many peoples and cultures together into one society, to learn from all of them, to grow by the contributions that all have made. It follows that no other nation, despite the tragic failures of our principles in many instances, has come so close to promoting a real brotherhood of man. Without our minority groups and the diverse strains of our culture, American society is a pale imitation of Europe. With them, it is something newer and stronger.

(Stegner, 1945, p. 15)

Although these words were written almost a half century ago, they ring true today. The promise of the "brotherhood of man" is still unfulfilled; whether we are closer now than 50 years ago is certainly open to debate. The hope lies, however, in the fact that we are still trying. The hope lies in those who have not formed prejudices, narrow perspectives, and intractable positions. The hope lies in the students that teachers see each day, and in teachers' abilities to promote cultural knowledge, sensitivity, and understanding.

THE TEACHER AND CULTURAL MEDIATION

How does a teacher begin to promote cultural understanding and appreciation? What is the secret to accomplishing this goal? It is helpful to return to the notion of teacher as cultural mediator discussed in Chapter 2. We have stated that teachers as cultural mediators are learners among learners, who engage in critical reflection about themselves and their interactions with others. In a recent conversation with us a respected colleague stated that teachers generally do not want to hear that they need to engage in critical reflection and self-examination. Rather, she said, they want to know what they can do to teach their students to learn about themselves and other cultures. She further suggested that teachers do not want to be confronted with uncomfortable truths, but with workable ideas that they can immediately implement with their students.

While there may be some teachers who feel this way, we believe that most educators can be moved to look inward if they know that their students will ultimately benefit. Fuerstein, Yaacov, and Rynders (1988) support the belief that all change must begin with self. They suggest that if teachers are to grow professionally, they will need to continually invest in reflection and self-modification. They emphasize that professional complacency is harmful to the educational intervention process because it glosses over differences among children—their capacities and conditions —as well as many other sociocultural factors that are pertinent to successful education. Teachers who do not engage in self-examination often place excessive demands on students without making adaptations in themselves to correspond to their students' needs (Fuerstein et al., 1988). Learning and reflection challenge teachers to look inward and to try to understand their own assumptions and actions related to culture, as well as the incidents in their life stories that fueled these assumptions and actions. Through this self-examination process, teachers can begin to change.

Teacher Learning through Reflection

Recently, in a university class on multicultural literacy, several teachers began the reflection process as they read about diverse cultures and engaged in discussion with others who held perspectives different from their own. They were asked to reflect, over several weeks, on their experiences and how these experiences might affect their own teaching—and to think about why it is critical to understand how past incidents can affect future behaviors. These are examples of reflections that were generated when teachers began to learn about themselves:

> I think back to my own childhood, growing up in a Jewish neighborhood. In our school that was somewhere around 60% Jewish. We had a Christmas show each year in which no songs other than Christmas songs were included. The amazing thing to me now is that none of us thought there was anything strange about this. It makes me realize how strong the dominant culture is and how children who are raised with no access to multiculturalism feel that they must conform. It seems so obvious to me now, yet not so long ago, I didn't even consider it.—Julie

> It has been an adjustment learning to deal with families from a different culture. The Indian families we receive appear to value education much more than the families we are used to. We were told by one Indian family that in India, education is a means to eat. If you don't do well in school, you may starve . . . I love most of what I've learned from the experiences I've had so far. My concern with multicultural education is that I want to know enough so that while presenting multicultural curriculum, I am not offensive to anyone due to my ignorance.—Sandy

> I need to broaden my perspective; my point of view. For so many years I have been conditioned to think in one way.—Sue

> My eyes have been opened considerably. Every year at Thanksgiving time I have taught my students about the Indians, usually teaching about their history from the time white men came to live here. Being politically correct, I always tried to give the fair story about how they had been wronged. Now I have begun to learn that there is a great culture of history, art and music and literature to share . . .—Shelly

The biggest change that teachers in this university class talk about is a *new awareness.* As they think about themselves and how their beliefs were formed, they discover that they have always viewed the world from the perspective of the dominant culture. They are now aware of the need to think about and plan instruction that incorporates the diverse population of students they are teaching and the need to use materials and practices that are sensitive to the students' background. These teachers also realize they will not gain all the knowledge they need immediately and that they might make mistakes. Nevertheless, as one teacher said, the "light has been turned on" and teachers can continue to learn and grow. Vivian Paley (1979) similarly offered her reflections about her approach to teaching in a multicultural environment:

> Each year I greet thirty new children with a clear picture in mind of who shall be called "bright" and who shall be called "well-behaved." Ask me where these "facts" come from and I will probably refer to my professional background. Yet I doubt that the image I carry of the intelligent, capable

child has changed much since my own elementary school days. It has been intellectualized and rationalized, but I suspect it is much the same, and that image was never black. The few adult blacks I knew were uneducated laborers and I never played with a black child. . . . In the beginning it was more comfortable to pretend the black child was white. Having perceived this, I then saw that it was my inclination to avoid talking about other differences as well. (p. 11)

A significant aspect of these comments is the tendency that Paley had to make the children fit a mold, to be like her, to pretend they were "white" or without differences in color—or speech or weight or family structure. She makes the assumption that if children do not fit this mold, they cannot be intelligent. There is a lesson in these comments for teachers of all colors, classes, and cultures. If teachers begin to understand themselves and how they interact with their students, based on their assumptions, they can take on a new role. This role is not one of judge and jury, but of friend and facilitator.

Change in habitual ways of interacting does not occur instantly, for we are laden with assumptions, fears, and conditioned ways of behaving. As evident in the reflections above, teachers can begin to rethink traditional modes of behavior. Beginning with self is an initial step in mediating a cultural environment so that it becomes a positive learning community for all children.

Gaining Cultural Knowledge about Students

During the past three years, we have watched teachers develop an awareness of their own assumptions and biases, confront them, and work to develop and mediate a positive environment. However, when they begin to realize the need to be knowledgeable about the cultures and backgrounds of their students, some question their ability to learn about the different cultures within the time constraints of teaching. Other teachers question how they can learn about so many cultures, especially given the lack of available resources. As teachers discover that culture is universal and that they already have some knowledge that can be applied to all cultures, their task may not seem so overwhelming.

What Is Culture?   Even though there are many definitions of the word *culture,* there are common themes among the definitions (Banks, 1991; Bullivant, 1984; Goodenough, 1981; Saville-Troike, 1978). First, culture is a socially constructed phenomenon; that is, it is created by human beings in interaction with one another. Second, culture often carries with it the idea of nurturing all members of a group. In this sense, culture refers to developing and supporting knowledge of music, dance, literature, and the visual arts. This implies that the arts are taught to the young as a means of nurturing them so that eventually they grow to appreciate and be a part of their social group.

In addition to these two themes are the distinctions made by Triandis (1972). He identifies objective and subjective components of culture, describing the objective components as the tangible, visible aspects, including the artifacts people make, the clothes they wear, and the names they are given. On the other hand, the subjective components are intangible aspects such as attitudes, values, norms of behavior, and social roles. This notion of objective and subjective culture is consistent with Phillips' (1983) description of the visible, or physical, aspects of a culture and the invisible, or mental and behavioral, aspects. The subjective/invisible aspects of a culture are the most difficult to distinguish in students and indeed, all people of diverse backgrounds.

By examining these concepts of culture, it becomes apparent that many teachers already have some knowledge about the cultures that might exist in their classrooms. They might know some objective aspects of the culture of their Puerto Rican students, for example, some types of food they eat, the types of music they enjoy, or some holidays they celebrate. The need, then, is for teachers to build on this knowledge and learn about the subjective/invisible aspects of the culture. They can also learn about the differences within different cultural groups, and thus begin to dispel some of their common stereotypical viewpoints.

Learning about Specific Cultures.   By beginning with only one or two cultural groups, the task does not appear as formidable for teachers. These cultural groups can be those that have particular interest to teachers and their students. In a monocultural classroom, teachers may decide to build on their students' interests.

Mrs. Thomas, whose class was 98 percent African American, decided that she would take an African American history class sponsored by a local bookstore. Her students raised many questions about contemporary Africa after they read *Jambo Means Hello,* by Tom Feelings, and *Rehema's Journey,* by Barbara Margolies. Significantly, the more she learned, the more she wanted to learn. As an African American, she was surprised as she realized how much she still needed to learn about her own culture.

After reading children's books about the Mayan and Aztec civilizations as she prepared for the Multicultural Fair in her school district, Mrs. Jones decided to read in more depth about the Mexican American and Puerto Rican American cultures. As background for the students' study, she was able to find reference books, as well as narrative and informational texts for her students to read.

Similarly, in her preparation for the fair, Ms. Clark, who had relatives from Jamaica, wanted her students to learn about the island cultures. She and her students decided to learn about Jamaica and display their reports and artifacts at the Multicultural Fair. Ms. Clark used her uncle and aunt as contacts. She was fortunate because she was able to go to expert resources, people who actually lived the culture, who were able to supply her with books from the island. Those books, coupled with books from the library and local bookstores, provided Ms. Clark with more of the cultural knowledge that she needed. This was only a beginning. Ms. Clark and her students continued to gain information together.

Other teachers learn about cultures through personal contacts with people of the culture. Mrs. Paldan, a student in the multicultural literacy course mentioned earlier, relates through her journal how she learned more about the Native American culture.

Last November, we had a Native American visit our room and teach us some sign language, dancing, and customs. I was impressed with what she taught us, but I was more impressed by her desire for us to understand her people. . . . I found so much information on Native Americans that tie in with our school district's curriculum that next year I plan on devoting a special unit to Native American culture (I am hoping my friend can return). My visitor's desire for us to understand her people has driven me to understand more about more people.

As teachers acquire knowledge, they are able to capitalize on the diversity existing in the classroom. As demonstrated in these examples, teachers use whatever resources are available—experts, books, resource materials, relatives, parents of students, and formal classes to become informed about cultures.

HELPING STUDENTS DEVELOP AN UNDERSTANDING OF SELF

As children grow and learn academically, they also are striving to understand themselves and how they fit into their classrooms, their community, and their world. Several scholars and researchers discuss the importance of students' positive self-image and the correlation between positive self-image and student success in school (Edelman, 1992; Phelps, Hilliard, & Christmas, 1989). One way students can develop a positive self-image is through knowledge of their culture and their history. According to Cushner, McClelland, and Safford, "Culture is a secret." They state that learning about culture is made more difficult because most people generally know very little about themselves. Few people receive formal training about how to be a member of a culture; they learn through experience, through observing others, through trial and error, and through continuous reinforcement. For teachers, then, the task of making the students' culture visible becomes a challenge.

Making Differences Visible

Mrs. Livisay, conscious of her role as cultural mediator, takes note early on of the diversity within her classroom. She knows that her class is comprised of students of different abilities, varied academic strengths and weaknesses, and different cultures (European Americans, African Americans, Korean Americans, and Mexican Americans). On the first day of class, rather than list arbitrary rules of behavior, she and her students talk about the need to listen to others, to respect differences among students, and to acknowledge students' rights to have different viewpoints and ideas. She encourages students to talk about themselves and express their likes and dislikes.

Early in the year, after creating this positive climate for learning, she reads books to the class that affirm differences. She helps her students realize that people are unique in appearance, in likes and dislikes, and in what they believe and value. To help her students understand these concepts, Mrs. Livisay groups her students in pairs. After folding a paper in half and labeling one side similarities and one side differences, the two brainstorm ways that people are alike and different. As the students talk, they make interesting discoveries about the characteristics of people. This conversation is an example:

JUSTIN: Let's see [*pauses for a minute, as if to think*]. Here's an idea . . . we all go to school, and we all have families.

GERARD: Yeah, and we can all read and write.

JUSTIN: Do you think that's what she means [*referring to Mrs. Livisay's directions*]?

GERARD: She said how we're alike and these are ways that we're alike.

JUSTIN: OK. Let's see. We all have eyes and noses.

GERARD: Yeah, and skin and hair.

As their list grew, the boys decided to flip to the other side of the paper. They continued:

GERARD: Ummm. Let's see, differences. We have different houses and we like to do different things.

JUSTIN: We look different, too. Different color hair, different eyes. But we said these were the same.

GERARD: Yeah, some of the differences are opposites of the way we're the same. It's like we're the same . . . but we're different.

While the students continue, Mrs. Livisay moves around the room. Some students share their lists with her, and she asks a few students to read their ideas orally. Justin offers his observation that some of the similarities are also differences in an "opposite sort of way." Mrs. Livisay praises him for his insight; other students agree. She plans to build on this concept while reading the book *People,* by Peter Spier. Through intricate pictures and text, Spier illustrates that there are billions of people in our world; no two people are exactly alike.

As Mrs. Livisay reads this book to her students, they realize that physical differences—hair, noses, and eyes; cultural differences—food, shelter, games, religion, language; and social differences make people unique and special. While reading the book interactively, questioning students and encouraging them to offer their own ideas and feelings, she reinforces these concepts. Through this collaborative experience, students learn to appreciate Spier's concept: "Now, isn't it wonderful that each and every one of us is unlike any other?"

When the book is completed, Mrs. Livisay asks the students to write down additional similarities and differences among people. As the students talk about these differences and similarities, one student, Delvin, explains that the part about the different religions makes him think about how some students talk about him because his religion doesn't allow him to celebrate Halloween. When another student laughs, Mrs. Livisay quickly reminds the class that they must always be respectful of one another's ideas and feelings and offer supportive comments to each another. Mrs. Livisay further uses this opportunity to revisit Justin's point that similarities are also differences. While many people have religious beliefs, she explains, the ways we affirm those religious beliefs are different. During this process, Mrs. Livisay helps her students understand how they are different and unique and how to establish their identity. In the process, she continually mediates the environment so that students feel safe, share their ideas, and work together.

These discussions lead to her next activity, the I Am poems. (See Chapter 4.) She asks students to first brainstorm ideas about themselves—their likes and dislikes, their physical features, and what things are important to them. After brainstorming their ideas, Mrs. Livisay asks students to share their thoughts with a partner. Several students, while listening to others, add new words to their lists. The students then begin writing their I Am poems, using words and ideas from their brainstorming sheet.

After completing the first draft, the students share them in small groups. After revising and editing their poems, Mrs. Livisay publishes them in a class book, entitled, "We Are the Greatest."

To extend their concepts about diversity of colors, dress, and other physical and cultural differences, she discusses how this diversity is an integral part of our nation. To illustrate this idea, students use magazine pictures to make a collage of faces within a map of the United States. The completed collage is displayed on a bulletin board near the door to symbolize the diversity of our nation. (See Figure 7.1.)

Some teachers find other ways of helping students develop a sense of their uniqueness. Mrs. Bree and Mrs. Thiesen work together in motivating students to identify aspects of themselves that are important and special through the use of poetry. Mrs. Bree reads several books of poetry, which include poems written by children or by adults about children. As she reads the poems, she helps the students see how poetry is filled with unique images and ways of viewing the world. After listening to the poems and keeping a list of words and images from them, students begin writing their own poems. (See Figure 7.2.)

FIGURE 7.1   After creating their cultural map of the United States, all students begin to understand our nation's diversity.

FIGURE 7.2   Poem from Mrs. Theisen's class.

As students write and share their poems, they realize they are learning new things about themselves that they were not aware of until they made a conscious effort to turn inward. Those who listen marvel at the insights they are gaining about their peers.

Expanding the Circle of Understanding: The Family

Once students discover information about themselves, their dreams and their beliefs, a natural step is to explore their connections to their families and communities. Because the concept of family is central to many cultures, many students find this transition to be very natural. The majority of Hispanics living in this country, for example, find family to be the "first priority in life" (Cintron de Esteves & Spicola, 1982, p. 5). Thus, students' understanding of themselves and the development of a strong self-concept can be effectively established by learning about their family connections.

Mrs. Nolen, like Mrs. Theisen and Mrs. Livisay, is striving to help her students, who are Mexican American and African American, learn more about themselves and their families. To enable her students to personalize their experiences around family events, she reads *Family Pictures,* by Carmen Garza, which describes, in bilingual text and illustrations, the author's experiences growing up in a Mexican American community in Texas. Mrs. Nolen selects this book because it authentically portrays contemporary Mexican American social life and customs. As she reads the book interactively, she encourages her students to look for specific ways that the family engaged in activities together, how the children and adults appeared to feel about what they were doing, and why they think the activities were important to the family members. For example, one scene from the story describes the parents' kitchen. In it, the entire family is involved in making tamales, including the two sisters who are helping to soak dried leaves from the corn, the mother who is spreading the corn-meal dough on the leaves, and an aunt and uncle who are spreading meat on the dough. Grandmother completes the process by lining up the rolled and folded tamales so that they are ready for cooking. This scene evokes several comments from the students. Rosina notes that "even the men were helping with the cooking"; Jennifer likes the "way the children and adults were all in the kitchen together." Mrs. Nolen asks the following questions to stimulate discussion about the family and the values that the scenes in the book might suggest.

- Why do you think everyone is involved in helping make the tamales?
- How do the children, parents, and grandparents seem to feel about what they are doing?
- What is the value of working together like the family is doing?
- Does this event remind you of any activities that your family does? How is it different? How is it similar?

Through such questions, Mrs. Nolen stimulates and leads the students in the discovery of underlying concepts about the family—their beliefs and values.

After completing the book, Mrs. Nolen lists on the board, with the help of her students, many of the "understandings" about this Mexican American family. The students realize:

- Children are accepted and given responsibility
- Aunts and uncles and grandparents are a part of the family
- Everyone works together for a goal
- Families do a lot of things together

Following this discussion about the book, she reminds the students that family pictures often trigger special memories and help us learn about ourselves and our families. During the next few days, students bring in photographs of special family events to share with the class. Because of variations in socioeconomic situations and differing interests in photography, Mrs. Nolen reassures students that they can draw pictures about important family events even if they don't have photographs. She is aware of and sensitive to her students' needs and family circumstances. She further emphasizes the importance of the students' presence in the photographs or pictures so that they can share their experiences as an actual participant.

Students bring in pictures of weddings and graduations of siblings, birthday parties, picnics, or holiday celebrations. Realizing that discussion can stimulate writing, Mrs. Nolen gives the students an opportunity to share their pictures informally in small groups. She asks questions to help them highlight important information, encouraging them to tell who is in the picture, what they are doing, whether this is a tradition, how the family feels about the event, and why it is important to them. Within their groups, students take turns talking about the family events as Mrs. Nolen circulates.

By sharing and discussing events, students begin to see and appreciate differences in the way families live and behave, what they like to do, and how they choose to do it. They are given opportunities to see that these different ways are fun to hear about and that one way is not better than another. Finally, they begin to see how they are connected to their families, that most children tend to like what their families like, and that their families' views and values, in large part, reflect who they are. In this way, they receive personal validation for their own lives.

Following these activities, Mrs. Nolen asks students to write a paragraph describing one of the pictures. Because students have had time to talk about their photographs or pictures, the writing is more detailed. Sharonda describes a picture of her uncle's wedding:

My mother, daddy, and brother are at Uncle Will's reception. We are having dinner served. It is roast beef and potatoes, broccoli. The dessert was a delicious chocolate pie. I liked that the best! At the wedding the music was kind of classical with harps. After dinner at the reception Uncle Will and Caryn watched African dancers in costumes dance to drum music. Two children introduced the dances. One was very shy and nervous. It was lots of fun.

Other opportunities for students to learn about families are provided by interviewing relatives and friends. Zimmerman's (1992) *Instant Oral Biographies* was an excellent resource for Mrs. Gilkey's class. This book provides a method to help students become instant biographers or reporters so that they can tell stories about their families and friends. They discover that the oral biographies:

- Provide a means by which a family can be drawn together in a more meaningful way to record and listen to the stories of grandparents, parents, aunts, uncles, and children.
- Enhance the joy and excitement of get-togethers, especially such family occasions as a parent's birthday, anniversary, religious holidays, and vacations.
- Make the storytellers feel better about themselves.
- Preserve the special voices of loved ones when the world is rapidly changing and families are becoming scattered around it.
- Help elderly people break their silences and loneliness by making them feel it is important to be heard.

As students discover more and more about their families, the teacher encourages them to think about how they come together in ways that they do, how they come to believe and value what they do. By connecting these ideas to students' personal lives and experiences, teachers are able to facilitate interest in further exploring diverse cultures.

UNDERSTANDING TRADITIONAL CULTURAL VALUES

Consistent with Norton (1991), we recommend using folklore to help students gain an understanding of the origin of traditional cultural values and beliefs, discover a rich literary heritage, and gain respect for the creativity that exists in people of their culture. Because of the large number of folk tales and legends about all cultures, teachers are able to select a variety that mirror and convey the values and traditions of a culture.

The Oral Tradition

The words of a Swahili poet-novelist Shaaban Robert (Holt, Rinehart and Winston, 1992) remind us of our common connections through the oral tradition. He says:

> In the saying which goes, "What there is in Pemba is in Zanzibar as well," take away Pemba and Zanzibar and say, "What is in Europe is in Africa as well"; take away Europe and say, "What is in Africa is in Asia as well"; take away Africa and say, "What is in Asia is in America as well"; take away Asia and say, "What is in America is in Australia as well." The created word repeats itself within the nations of human beings in order to show their common origin and their great unity. (p. 91)

We have referred to the value of oral tradition in transmitting the beliefs and values of people. It is important that we share this knowledge with students so that they realize that storytelling, the heart of the oral tradition, is a natural part of every culture. It may surprise students to know that tales were handed down for many years before they were written. In some countries, much of the literature remains oral. In fact, Stewig (1988) reminds us that writing is far from universal, citing the fact that of 2,796 languages in the world, all have an oral form, but only about 153 have a written form.

In societies where writing is rare, people are bound by the spoken word. In these societies, in a very real sense, the individual is his word (Holt, Rinehart and Winston, 1992). Writing can store information, but in oral cultures, people *are* information. In oral cultures, the telling of stories has several purposes. Dailey (1988, p. 6) notes that on one occasion, an Ojibway elder was performing stories for non-Native Americans. A woman spoke to the elder after the telling and said, "Oh, those were wonderful stories; have you ever thought about writing them down?" The elder smiled and said, "If I write my stories down, you will go away and you will read them—but we can't be together. I have time and, if you have time, I'll tell you my stories."

The opportunity to come together is indeed a valuable part of the oral tradition. Another function is that storytelling is a convenient way of passing down cultural history to the next generation, as children hear stories and repeat them to their children. Finally, these stories serve to inculcate a culture's current mores, informing the young of the accepted behaviors of the group (Stewig, 1988).

In some cultures storytellers went from village to village carrying a "storyvine." Even though the stories were in the head of the storyteller, the storyvine, which is a group of intertwined circular branches from which objects are suspended, symbolized the stories that the storyteller could tell. According to Kingsley (1964), story minstrels carried nets that resembled fishing nets, containing objects such as pieces of china and bones. After the audience chose an object, the minstrel would tell a story about it. Similarly, the Iroquois storytellers kept their props in storyteller bags. These were decorated with designs of feathers, dolls, and beads that replicated the culture.

Sharing the Tradition—Bringing Stories to Life

Mrs. Gilkey, a fourth-grade teacher, loves to share this storytelling tradition with her African American students. She has created her own storyvine so that the students can see how the tradition works. She tells them that storytellers often take a box or a bag to keep their stories in; others carry something to hang them on, following traditions of long ago. She then shows them her storyvine, which has: a toy spider (for Anansi); a picture of a mosquito (for Verna Aardema's *Why Mosquitoes Buzz in People's Ears*); a picture of a caterpillar (for Aardema's *Who's in Rabbit's House?*); a small box containing stories (for Gail Haley's *A Story, A Story*); and a garden snake (for John Steptoe's *Mufaro's Beautiful Daughters*). (See Figure 7.3.) As the students come closer, Mrs. Gilkey asks Monica, who enjoys hearing stories, to select an object (or a card) from her storyvine. Monica carefully chooses the picture of the mosquito. Before Mrs. Gilkey tells the story, she asks the students to guess what the story might be about and how the mosquito fits into the story. After stimulating interest, she begins her interpretation of *Why Mosquitoes Buzz in People's Ears,* which has a strong oral language pattern and varied animal characterizations, lending itself to the traditional African storytelling style. Using her arms, Mrs. Gilkey mimics the iguana as "he happened to pass by a python"; using variations in her voice, she imitates the rabbit's "krik, krik, krik" and the slithering python's "wasawusu, wasawusu."

When the story is complete, the students ask her to tell the story again. She tells them that in many African countries, storytellers encourage audience participation. She offers to retell the story only if the students join in. As she retells the story, the students mimic the body movements, the animal sounds, and the repeated patterns.

Realizing that storytelling is something students should experience, she has each student complete a story web with the details that they remember from her telling of the story. When their webs are finished, the students tell the story to a partner, using their web as a guide. Mrs. Gilkey circulates among the partners, providing assistance and feedback. She reminds them that they will get better as they practice. To enhance their knowledge about storytelling styles, Mrs. Gilkey has the students listen to Ashley Bryan's tape, *The Dancing Granny and Other African Stories (1985).*

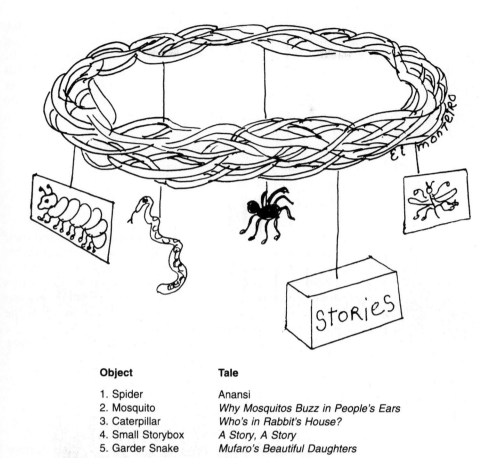

Object	Tale
1. Spider	Anansi
2. Mosquito	*Why Mosquitos Buzz in People's Ears*
3. Caterpillar	*Who's in Rabbit's House?*
4. Small Storybox	*A Story, A Story*
5. Garder Snake	*Mufaro's Beautiful Daughters*

FIGURE 7.3   Storyvine with objects.

As the week progresses, Mrs. Gilkey makes other African American folk tales available for the students to read. After reading these tales, she encourages the students to repeat the storytelling process with partners. She further suggests that they make props to go with their tale, which she puts on her storyvines.

Developing Themes to Understand Values and Beliefs

After introducing the oral tradition, teachers will find it useful to encourage students to read folk tales to identify the values and beliefs found in them. Although we know that folk tales convey or mirror the values of a culture, students may need assistance in identifying approaches to use to discover how this is done. Norton (1991) suggests that folk tale themes are closely related to the values and beliefs of a culture. By identifying the themes, students will discover many underlying values and beliefs.

Mrs. Thomas, a Chapter 1 teacher who works with fifth-graders, begins her lesson by introducing the concept that, although folk tales are fun and entertaining, they also reveal information about a given culture. She explains that by listening closely and asking strategic questions, they can identify the folk tale's message or the theme. Often, she adds, there may be more than one important message. She reads Demi's *The Empty Pot,* a Chinese folk tale that tells the story of a young boy who, in spite of his love for flowers, is unsuccessful in his repeated efforts to grow a beautiful flower to take to the emperor. As she reads, she tells the students to ask the following questions of themselves:

- What is the story saying that might pertain to me?
- What is the message that it is telling me?
- How do I know it is telling me this?

After hearing the tale, the students share their responses to the story and their reflections on the questions. Most students decide that the primary message is that honesty is important and is rewarded. Mrs. Thomas asks several students who chose this theme to verify their choice with information from the story. Students note that Ping was honored for his honesty by the emperor and the entire kingdom. He was subsequently made emperor of the land. Other students point to the fact that the emperor was displeased with those children who had been dishonest.

Other themes suggested by the students are written on the board. These include:

- Hard work pays off.
- It's important to do your best.
- It's important to never give up.

Mrs. Thomas suggests that these might be important values in the Chinese culture. She then tells the students to look for similar themes or new themes as they read other folk tales from China. Before the lesson ends, she briefly introduces other folk tales she has gathered for them to read, including Demi's *Liang and the Magic Paintbrush,* Ai-Ling Louie's *Yeh Shen: A Cinderella Story from China,* Robert San Souci's *The Enchanted Tapestry,* and Ed Young's *Lon Po Po: A Red Riding Hood Story from China.*

Subsequently, the students meet in groups with students who have read the same folk tale to discuss their folk tales and the themes they have identified. After developing a list of themes, each group shares them with the entire class, and Mrs. Thomas writes these on the board. The students realize that as the lists are presented, several of the themes are repeated. The students are then asked whether the themes are values and beliefs of the Chinese culture. Many of the students speculate, based on their knowledge of the Chinese culture. Mrs. Thomas tells them that they will be learning more about the Chinese culture as they read more books. She realizes that her students, who are beginning to understand how traditional literature can reflect the values and beliefs of a group, will be able to use this knowledge later as they search for values and beliefs found in historical fiction, biographies, poetry, and realistic fiction.

UNDERSTANDING DIVERSE GROUPS
THROUGH HISTORICAL EVENTS

One of the best opportunities within a multicultural literacy program for students to gain knowledge and develop decisionmaking skills is through activities that center around historical events. Learning about important moments in the history of diverse peoples helps students relive the past vicariously. While reading multicultural books, they experience the joys of celebrations as well as the pain of conflict; they learn to comprehend the various perspectives of people who are players in these events.

Mrs. Harkema's students have been studying the Northwest Indian Nations during the period of the 1850s. They have learned about their ceremonies and rituals; their belief in the spirit of the eagle, beaver, and whale; and their reverence for the earth and all living things. She wants the students to go beyond this basic knowledge, however, to perceive how these values and beliefs influenced the Native Americans' actions and reactions to the ordeals and dilemmas of this time period of turbulence and struggle in their homeland. She uses the recording of a speech delivered by Chief Seattle found in the volume *Great American Indian Speeches* by Junaluska as a place to begin discussion and provide background for the lessons. She especially likes the recording because most of the speeches used in the recording can be found in the Congressional Record of the period as well as in the State Records. In some cases the speeches can also be found in the recorded proceedings of the Native American treaty negotiations of the specific historical period.

Before sharing the speech with her class, Mrs. Harkema puts the speech that Chief Seattle delivered in its historical context. She explains that Seattle was Chief of the Dwamish, Suquamish, and other tribes of the area of Washington around Puget Sound. She further reminds the students that during this historical period many chiefs were being pressed to sign treaties which would relinquish their land to the White man. In the speech that they will hear, Seattle will identify fundamental differences between the Whiteman and the Redman. To help students activate their knowledge and to set a purpose for listening, she asks the students to brainstorm ways that they think the two peoples are different. She also encourages students to listen for the eloquence of the Chief's words, as he responds in his speech to a speech by the Governor of the Washington Territory. Chief Seattle begins the speech with an impending sense of doom for his people.

> Yonder sky that has wept many tears of compassion upon my people for centuries untold, and which to us appears changeless and eternal, may change. Today is fair; tomorrow it may be overcast with clouds.

Chief Seattle continues the speech, referring to The Big Chief at Washington whose "people are many". He relates . . .

> They are like the grass that covers vast prairies. My people are few. They resemble the scattering trees of a storm-swept plain.
> . . . Our people are ebbing away like a rapid receding tide that will never return.

Seattle questions whether the two races can ever be brothers because of their separate origins and destinies. He underscores this point by accentuating the differences between his people and the Whiteman.

> To us the ashes of our ancestors are sacred and their resting places are hallowed ground. You wander far from the graves of your ancestors and seemingly without regret. Your religion was written on tablets of stone . . .
> Our religion is the traditions of our ancestors and dreams of our old men given them in the solemn hours of the night by the Great Spirit.

In the final portion of the speech, Seattle appears exhausted and resigned to his "destiny" as he is being pressed to sign a treaty to give up the land in exchange for peace. He states:

> However, your proposition seems fair and I think that my people will accept it and will retire to the reservation you offer them. Then we will dwell in peace.

The students listen intently to the Chief's words. Mrs. Harkema stops to ask questions and discuss several phrases, then continues the recording. Chief Seattle, as he ends his speech, forewarns the Whiteman that his time of decay will come and he will forever be reminded of the spirit of the Native people.

After completing the recording, Mrs. Harkema and the class discuss the figurative language and the power of the words. They consider Chief Seattle's position and the fact that he has to convince his people to sign the treaty.

In subsequent lessons, the class discusses the treaty council and its importance to the Native people. Mrs. Harkema has the students reenact a treaty council meeting. She believes this will increase the students' understanding of the critical issues that must be considered and the decisions that have to be made. She first asks one of her parents, a Native American, to share the tradition of the Talking Stick (a decorated branch that symbolizes the right to speak) used by Native Americans at important meetings. The parent helps the students realize the importance and seriousness of the Talking Stick at important tribal meetings and shares the rules for its use. (See Figure 7.4.)

With the parent's assistance, the students revisit the speech of Chief Seattle, discussing the seemingly unreconcilable differences in the two races that are cited by the Chief. Seated in a circle, students raise their hands when they want to talk. The parent, as chief, models the use of the talking stick by holding on to one end while the speaker, the student, holds the other end.

Understanding Chief Seattle's perspective in greater depth, students are now prepared to have a Native American treaty meeting, just as many chiefs had with their tribes. This time, however, in order to set the context in their home state, Mrs. Harkema will use information from the 1821 treaty involving the Potawatomi tribe and Lewis Cass, the regional governor of Michigan. Mrs. Harkema recreates the setting by reading the treaty. (See Figure 7.5.) She then explains that they will all have a role in this meeting. The class is divided into four groups with three to six students assigned to be chiefs. The designated groups are (1) young warriors, (2)

RULES FOR THE TALKING STICK/NATIVE AMERICAN TREATY MEETING

1. The talking stick symbolizes that one may speak.
2. The (primary) chief is in charge of the talking stick and conducting the meeting.
3. One who wishes to speak raises his/her hand.
4. Those not holding the stick *must listen.* It is a dishonor not to pay attention.
5. The chief keeps the discussion on track.
6. All should participate.
7. Tell whether you agree or disagree and why.
8. After all members have spoken, the chief makes the decision of whether or not to sign the treaty.

FIGURE 7.4   Rules for use of talking stick.

elders, (3) hunters and scouts, (4) Chippewas and Ottawas, and (5) the chiefs. Each group and chief get copies of the treaty and their script sheet or card which describes their roles in the meeting. (See Figure 7.6.) The groups meet for about 15 minutes to discuss their reasons for signing or not signing the treaty, as explained in their script. Students also brainstorm and add their concerns about the environment and what they "see" settlers doing. Students become intensely involved in the role-play because of the amount of time they have spent discussing the issues and becoming sensitive to diverse perspectives.

Mrs. Harkema and the parent reconvene the class in a circle for the treaty meeting, reminding them of the rules for the Talking Stick and that after the discussion, Chief Chebass, the primary chief, will decide what is best for his people, following the Potawatomi custom. The students become involved in a gripping discussion.

One of the Elders says, "We do not want our people to die; our people must continue for our ways to be continued. We should sell the land and live in peace."

FIGURE 7.5   Treaty agreement between Potawatomi and United States.

THE TREATY THAT WILL BE READ TO THE STUDENTS
(NOT THE ORIGINAL)

Treaty Agreement Between the Potawatomi of Southwestern Michigan Territory and the People of the United States of America:

The people of the United States of America agree to give the Potawatomi of Southwestern Michigan territory the following:
 —$5,000 each year for a period of twenty (20) years
 —$1,000 each year to support a blacksmith and a teacher to help the Potawatomi learn the arts of civilized society and preserve peace and order among the tribes

In exchange for this payment the Potawatomi agree to sell to the people of the United States the land bordered on the North by the Grand River, on the East by the 1807 Treaty line, on the South by the St. Joseph River, and on the West by Lake Michigan.

Five reservations within the treaty area, including the sites of most villages, will remain under Indian ownership.

Lewis Cass
Governor - Michigan Territory
Representative of U.S. Government

GROUPS AND CHIEFS FOR THE TREATY MEETING

YOUNG WARRIORS:
You have not yet had the chance to prove your bravery in battle, and are looking forward to war. You are angry with the settlers for taking your lands and treating the Potawatomi like children.

ELDERS:
You are the older men of the tribe and you are sad to see the old ways disappear. You feel that the settlers do not understand the ways of the Native Americans. You feel the younger Native Americans have depended too much on the settler's goods. However, you know that war is a bad thing and many people will die if it comes to that.

HUNTERS AND SCOUTS:
You love the land you live on for it gives you everything you need. You have seen more and more settlers moving into your hunting grounds, making hunting difficult. You know that the Native Americans need the animals and the land.

CHIPPEWAS AND OTTAWAS:
It is not your land that is in question at this treaty. You have come with your friends, the Potawatomi, simply to get the gifts which are given out after a treaty has been signed. If the Potawatomi hesitate to sign the treaty, your tribe will receive no gifts. You become impatient and urge them to sign so your people can get what they came for.

CHIEFS:

CHIEF CHEBASS:
As the primary chief of the Potawatomi you are in control of the Talking Stick, and must make the final decision of this treaty. You are faced with a difficult choice. If you accept this treaty, peace will continue and you will receive money to buy settlers' goods; but the tribe will lose its traditional home and the old way of life will disappear as the Potawatomi become more dependent on the settlers' goods. To turn down the treaty would mean a war your tribe cannot win. The old life would last a little longer and your people would keep their honor, but war would mean death to the men and the end of the Potawatomi as a tribe. You must choose what is best for all of your people.

FIGURE 7.6 Script for participants in the treaty signing.

A Young Warrior takes the Talking Stick and speaks up, "The settlers will not allow us to live in peace. We must fight for what is ours before it is too late!"

"We can't continue to let the settlers move into our hunting grounds. We see more and more settlers each day. They kill our animals. The more settlers that come, the fewer animals we see," explains a Hunter.

Chief Chebass, the primary chief, listens intently to the various views. It appears as if she has been transported back to that time. When the last person speaks, everyone turns in silence to the chief, who, with a look of intense anguish, proclaims softly, "This is a nightmare!" All of the students are moved by the tremendous weight that the decision holds.

For most students, the role-play is the first time that they have taken the perspective of the Native American in any historical event involving European settlers and the native inhabitants of the land. According to studies by Pate (1988), the level of prejudice is reduced considerably by empathic role-playing or other vicarious experiences in teaching activities. This simulated activity enables students to take the point of view of a person of another culture. They are then stimulated to understand the values of that culture and to use their decision-making skills to discover a solution to a complex problem. In assuming the various roles, even though scripted, students have to understand the ways in which their decisions (whether to continue to fight or to sign the treaty) reflect values, purposes, and assumptions of the Native Americans. Students are not passive consumers of knowledge from the teacher; they are critical thinkers using knowledge to act in a way that seems most appropriate.

PROMOTING UNDERSTANDING THROUGH CULTURAL COMPARISONS

Throughout the book we have emphasized the desirability of students' active involvement in literacy development. Rosenblatt (1976, 1978) argues that a literary work only exists in the live circuit that is set up between the reader and the text. Readers infuse their meaning into what they read, based on their experiences. Further, they often bring different meanings to the same text as they read and reread, because time intervenes and new experiences occur. There is a point, however, at which readers may reach a degree of consensus about the meaning of a text. Degroff and Galda (1992) state that this is possible because our experiences overlap to some extent, and we hold common understandings at very basic levels, such as the level of word meanings.

The combination of unique contributions that individuals bring to the text and common consensual meanings that groups discover as they work together becomes important as students clarify and compare what they read. This process can be particularly significant in a multicultural literacy classroom as students strive to gain a deeper understanding of themselves and of other cultures.

Comparisons within a Cultural Group: Understanding Arabs

Mrs. Abboushi, a third-grade teacher, uses three stories about Arabs to help her students improve their understanding of the Arab culture. She discovers that her students hold many misconceptions about the Arab people; thus, her goal is to present them with an accurate and more rounded view of the Arab world. She identifies three books that become the focal point of the lesson: The first book, *The Day of Ahmed's Secret,* by Florence Heide and Judith Gilliland, details the experiences of Ahmed, who helps his father in the busy city, and the secret that he shares at night when his work is finished. A second book, *Ibrahim,* by Frances Sales, recounts the experiences of a young Arab boy who helps his father in the marketplace. He faces a personal dilemma at an early age, however, when presented with an inviting yet difficult choice by his best friend. Finally, in *Nadia, the Willful,* by Sue Alexander, a young girl who was disobedient and arrogant comes to terms with her behavior.

To build background knowledge, Mrs. Abboushi uses the world map to locate the country of Morocco in Africa, the setting for the first story, *Ibrahim.* She points out that although the country is in Africa, the people of Morocco are predominately Arabs. In addition to locating the continent and country, the students find the city of Marrakesh, which is mentioned in the book. A river, a mountain range, and a desert that are discussed in the book are also identified on the map. From the cover of the book, the students are able to determine that the story takes place in the marketplace. She asks the students to brainstorm items that might be found in the marketplace while she has a student list these items on the board. The students are now ready to begin reading the story.

As Mrs. Abboushi reads the first book, she stops to answer questions and clarify concepts that are unfamiliar to her students. For example, she stops on the page in which the term *nomad* appears. She knows that there are enough contextual clues for the students to develop their own definition. After the students have offered their meanings, she gives them additional information. She points out that although Arabs were traditionally nomadic, today most people in the Arab world do not live in the desert. Another page shows men with their faces covered. In response to a student's question, Mrs. Abboushi explains that the men have their faces covered to protect them from the sand. She further explains that the palm trees are date palms, not the coconut or banana palms that may be more familiar to the students.

Mrs. Abboushi similarly reads and discusses the other books. Through interactive discussions, she is developing their understanding of the Arab people and their everyday life experiences. To ensure that students will retain and extend their knowledge, she plans another activity to help them identify similarities and differences within the Arab culture.

The students are divided into six groups of four, with two groups receiving a copy of *Ibrahim,* two a copy of *Nadia, the Willful,* and two a copy of the *Day of Ahmed's Secret.* In addition, Mrs. Abboushi gives each group a Cultural Feature Analysis chart, explaining that the features listed across the top—culture, setting, characters and traits, family relationships, and message—are elements they should consider as they discuss the stories. Moving from group to group, she assists the groups as they discuss, come to consensus, and record their ideas on the Cultural Feature Analysis Chart.

After completing each element on the chart for their book, each group shares their information with the whole class, while Mrs. Abboushi records the information on a large Cultural Features Analysis Chart. After the chart is completed, she leads the students in a discussion of the elements of the stories, bringing out cultural features that aid the students in understanding the Arab culture. (See Figure 7.7.) They learn that not all Arabs live the same way, dress the same way, or look the same way. They also develop an appreciation for the merging of the traditional and modern worlds; they see variability in living conditions, customs and values, architecture, clothing, and modes of transportation. The students, many of whom knew little about the Arab culture before reading the books, come away with a new sensitivity and appreciation of the Arab people.

After completing their Cultural Feature Analysis chart, the students draw scenes highlighting similarities and differences among the three books, such as the drawing shown in Figure 7.8. The process and the Cultural Feature Analysis Chart can be used to make cross-cultural comparisons, as well.

Comparison of Characters: Malcolm and Martin.   Another type of comparison that helps students gain new perspectives on a specific culture is the examination of the beliefs, thoughts, and actions of two people of the same culture. This type of instructional activity is most appropriate for students in fifth grade and above. It first

CULTURAL FEATURE ANALYSIS

TITLE	CULTURE	SETTING	CHAR. & TRAITS	FAMILY REL.	MESSAGE
Ibrahim	Arab	City Marketplace	Ibrahim - happy, thoughtful, sad Father - kind, helpful	Caring Loving	Personal decisions are difficult. Family support is important.
The Day of Ahmed's Secret	Arab	Large city- Cairo	Ahmed - hard working quiet, sensitive Family Members -hardworking, kind Father - wise	-Loving, sharing, -Giving, even though poor	Sharing an accomplishment with family is special.
Nadia, The Willful	Arab	Desert	Nadia -unkind, -lonely at times -likes to have her way	Sometimes good; sometimes not good	Self reflection is important. Bad judgement often means trouble

FIGURE 7.7 Mrs. Abboushi completes a large Cultural Feature Analysis of the three books with the class.

requires teacher knowledge about the characters or figures to be discussed. It also requires that students view the classroom as a learning community in which different perspectives and voices are respected.

In Chapter 1, we said multicultural literacy activates silent voices, opens closed minds, promotes academic achievement, and empowers students to think and act critically. Although this may seem like a lofty goal, we are discovering that if teachers create an atmosphere of acceptance, and if multicultural literature is integrated as a standard part of the curriculum, students can achieve this goal. In a classroom of European American, African American, and Mexican American students, for example, the teacher found a clear example of student motivation, interest, academic learning, and critical thinking.

"Why isn't Malcolm X remembered like Martin Luther King?" This question was posed by Jeff and Reginald, after their fifth-grade class had completed a choral reading of *Cornrows*. It was directed at Mrs. Birdyshaw, a teacher/consultant in our multicultural literacy program who previously conducted several lessons with this fifth-grade class. Resisting the temptation to respond to their question with her own viewpoints, she suggested that the next time she came, they might read about the two men and answer the question for themselves. When Mrs. Birdyshaw returned to the class, she began with the question, "What do you know about Malcolm X?" The students responded:

FIGURE 7.8   Student drawing comparing three books.

- His father was killed by white people.
- The Ku Klux Klan burned their house when he was young.
- He had to stay with foster parents.
- He went to jail.
- He changed to become a Muslim in jail.

Mrs. Birdyshaw noted that most of their knowledge about Malcolm X came from the movie *X,* by Spike Lee, based on the biography by Alex Haley. One of her goals for the lesson, however, was to help the students get beyond facts and begin to understand the motivations, values, and beliefs of Malcolm X. She felt it was critical that students see the relationships between a person's goals and their beliefs. Another goal for the lesson was to facilitate the students' ability to compare the two men, Malcolm and Martin, critically.

To achieve these goals, Mrs. Birdyshaw began by reading Arnold Adoff's *Malcolm X* to the class. As she read, the students were encouraged to ask questions and use the note taking strategy modeled in Chapter 6. She asked students to organize information into four categories, Family, Major Events, Goals, and Beliefs, and list one category in each section of their papers. They were to record notes in the four categories from the information they heard. While reading, Mrs. Birdyshaw stopped periodically to ask students to share their notes. She saw that the students were completely involved and were taking copious notes with detailed information. Scott, a student who started out by challenging authority, is one of the students who volunteered a great deal of information as Mrs. Birdyshaw continued reading. In fact, as the lessons developed, it was obvious he knew a considerable amount about Malcolm X.

During the next two periods Mrs. Birdyshaw continued this strategy with the class. At the end of the class period, Mrs. Birdyshaw and the students listed Malcolm X's beliefs and goals sequentially on chart paper. They were thus able to see how Malcolm's goals and beliefs changed over time. For example, one of his beliefs initially was that money and clothes were the "good life," and his goal was to do what he had to do for the "good life." Later, however, he held the belief that there was power in thought and language. His goal at this time was to study and read everything that he could. Significantly, the students were able to make connections, as she had hoped, between his beliefs and goals. Further, they began to realize how peoples' beliefs and goals can be modified by the cultural context in which they find themselves.

By the fourth class period, Mrs. Birdyshaw felt that the students had enough information to compare the two men. They completed their discussion of Martin Luther King with the classroom teacher, Mr. Jennings, who was using several books about King to help his students gain information beyond the simple facts. Through these experiences, students learned things about both men. In addition, some of the students were motivated to bring in their own resources about them. Notably, Scott volunteered to read Walter Dean Myers's *Malcolm X,* a book that Mrs. Birdyshaw did not have an opportunity to read and review. He read it at home on a "snow" day.

Mrs. Birdyshaw wrote the two men's names on the board at the top of two columns. The class then brainstormed experiences and bits of information common to both men, even though not identical. For example, King was a preacher, and Malcolm was a minister; King completed college and beyond, and Malcolm was self-taught and only completed eighth grade. Mrs. Birdyshaw knew this process of generating ideas was an excellent opportunity for the students to review, discuss, and share what they knew. It created exchanges that helped critical thinking. Students were comparing information from various sources, adding to points made by their classmates, raising questions about sources, making inferences, and validating their information.

After they listed the information they had, Mrs. Birdyshaw asked students to go down the list and put a plus by experiences and information that were similar and a minus by those that were different. The students found that there were more similarities than differences. As they became aware of this fact, Stephanie posed the question that was raised at the beginning of the lesson: "Why isn't Malcolm X remembered like Martin Luther King?" After students suggested several reasons, one student volunteered that the media played a big part in how the men are viewed. After more discussion and examples, most students supported this thought. Mrs. Birdyshaw returned to the board and listed *media coverage favorable* in King's column and *media coverage unfavorable* in Malcolm's column. They decided they must put a minus by *media* because the media coverage was positive for King and negative for Malcolm. They concluded that the media greatly influences peoples' opinions about public figures.

A final question that Jason asked, "Who do you think contributed the most to society?" was an appropriate question to end the lessons. It was also a good way to assess the students' understanding of the two men. After considerable discussion, there was a consensus that King will be remembered because he caused legislation to change and that Malcolm X will be remembered because he caused people (African Americans) to take pride in themselves and their heritage. The students felt that the contributions of both men were important and that both men should be respected equally.

In this vignette, we see European American, African American, and Hispanic American students gaining valuable knowledge and insight from this experience. Students who seldom participated, and in fact often challenged the teacher, became positively involved. Some of the African American students who were normally silent began speaking out—excitedly—because the discussion was relevant to their lives. Special Education students, who often achieved below their classmates, were taking notes as did the higher-achieving students in the class. Through the discussion, all students in this culturally and academically diverse class became more critically involved with their learning.

It is important to note that although these lessons focused on two notable African Americans, similar comparisons can be made between significant figures of other racial, cultural, and ethnic groups.

APPRECIATION OF CULTURE THROUGH POETRY, MUSIC, AND ART

Earlier in the chapter we discussed the objective and subjective aspects of culture, describing the objective components as the tangible, visible aspects of a culture, including the artifacts people make, the clothes they wear, and the names they are given. The subjective components are described as intangible aspects of a culture such as attitudes, values, norms of behavior, and social roles. The subjective components are much more difficult to understand, particularly for students. Cushner et al. (1992) compare cultural identity to an iceberg, explaining that only a very small part of the whole is seen and that most of the substance and support lie hidden beneath the surface. Through the arts, teachers can provide links with these less visible aspects of culture.

Poetry

Poetry has the capacity to bring to the surface the soul of the culture that is hidden from view. It can form a bridge between what is hidden and what is visible. According to Le Pere (1980), poetry helps children identify with characters and situations; it expresses moods to which they often can relate, helping them better understand themselves while developing their sensitivity to universal feelings and needs. Thus, poetry can have wide appeal to children of all cultural and ethnic backgrounds. For example, in Byrd Baylor's poem about Native Americans, "The Desert Is Theirs," the poet develops the theme of sharing—that Native American children believe the land is to be shared among the smaller creatures and animals, as well as people. In Eloise Greenfield's "Under the Summer Tree," children are treated to the many positive experiences of life on the Bahama Islands. "Father and Son" is another poem that highlights the experiences between parent and child on the islands, while Jo Carson's

Stories I Ain't Told Nobody Yet are poems written by people from the Appalachian region of our country, expressing feelings and needs of children of all cultures.

Prelutsky (1983, p. 18) found that the kinds of poetry children respond to are those that "evoke laughter and delight, poems that cause a palpable ripple of surprise by the unexpected comparisons that they make, poems that paint pictures with words that are as vivid as brush strokes, poems that reawaken pleasure in the sounds and meanings of a language." It is important, then, that students have many opportunities to listen to poetry, hear its sounds, and form images from the words. Sebesta (1983) emphasizes the visual impact of poetry as well, highlighting the importance of the arrangement of the words on the page and the illustrations that can arouse interest and enthusiasm in young readers. Stewig (1988) further reminds us to include selections written by students in the poetry that we share with them. There are a number of anthologies written by children from which to select. These selections may motivate students to begin to believe in themselves as poetry writers.

It is understandable, then, that poetry plays an important role in a multicultural literacy program. It has the power to inform the mind and lift the spirit as students listen and respond to the poems.

Mrs. Ssengoba's sixth-grade class has been studying Japan. Because she enjoys reading haiku, she wants to extend her study of Japan by sharing this poetic form. She realizes, as Tiedt & Tiedt (1990) affirm, that children are more successful with haiku if the thoughts they are expressing are emphasized rather than the number of syllables. She begins her introduction to haiku by writing on the board, "Haiku—A brief interlude of an image, put into descriptive words," explaining that she likes to think of haiku as a part of a larger composition—as in music—or as a closeup of a larger picture. The students seem to like the idea that haiku is an image, a picture in the mind that can be described through words.

Some of the sixth-grade students are reluctant to participate, at first. The boys, especially, are somewhat detached. Mrs. Ssengoba begins by reading haiku poems written by students of the same age, several of them boys. She asks the students to relax, listen, and enjoy, explaining that responses to poetry are a very personal experience. As she shares the haiku with her class, she attempts to convey the importance of the experience and process, and deemphasizes the need to rush to a finished product. Thus, students share their reactions to the poetry, pointing out images that the poems evoke.

Continuing, Mrs. Ssengoba explains to the students that Japanese people express their love for beauty through the arts. Perhaps in no other culture has art been more integrated with daily life than in Japan.

To illustrate this concept, Mrs. Ssengoba shares one of her favorite books, *The Painter and the Wild Swans*, by Claude Clément, with her class. In the book, the author and the illustrator capture the strong passion and emotion that Teiji, the main character, feels for the alluring beauty of the swans. While listening to the story, her students experience the beauty of the Japanese setting in the story and hear the sounds (of the words) that capture this beauty. To help her students focus on these words and thoughts, she asks students to find words and phrases that evoke strong images and record them in their literature response journal. Following this reading, the students share their reactions to the story. They are impressed by Teiji's perseverance and sacrifice in his attempt to capture the beauty of the swans. The students also share their lists of words that convey images of the swans or capture the beauty of the surroundings.

Through these discussions, students make connections between Teiji's pursuit of beauty through art and the Japanese integration of art into their lives through poetry and painting. Mrs. Ssengoba believes the students are now ready to write haiku. She reminds them of the explanation of haiku, telling them that they want to create an interlude of an image, using some of the descriptive words from their logs. She further explains that the poems generally have only 17 syllables, but encourages them to think about their ideas rather than become locked into the number of syllables.

When Mrs. Ssengoba pauses to let students share beginning phrases of their poems, Jesse offers:

Gliding in the breeze

Everyone spontaneously exclaims how much they like his beginning. Mrs. Ssengoba then asks students to think of another line that might continue Jesse's thought. Students refer to their notes. Several hands go up, and Nicole suggests:

Peaceful swans—majestic, free

Michael wonders if he shouldn't add "and free in spirit." The class considers his suggestion, but decides that they prefer to leave the phrase the way it is.

Mrs. Ssengoba says they need a thought to complete the poem. Students are writing on their papers; several students raise their hands. Jessica offers:

---

your beauty captivates us

Kevin thinks that "we are captivated by your beauty" might be better. Jessica agrees. Mrs. Ssengoba writes this line, praising the students for their ideas. At this point, she suggests that they might want to revisit the structure of haiku poetry and count the number of syllables. Together the students count the syllables:

Gliding in the breeze
Peaceful swans—majestic, free
We are captivated by your beauty.

They discover that there are too many syllables for the poem to be a true haiku. Stephanie suggests changing the last line to:

A joy to behold.

Everyone agrees. The haiku is complete:

Gliding in the breeze
Peaceful swans—majestic, free
A joy to behold.

Through this experience, students realize how they can collaboratively compose and listen to one anothers' ideas.

Everyone is now ready to begin writing individual haiku poems, motivated by these prewriting experiences and their knowledge that poetry can express the simplicity and beauty of nature. They are also learning that even though the haiku form appears quite simple, its message often conveys strong emotions and ideas. They discover that sometimes words must be rearranged to meet the poetic form. The meaning, however, is paramount; requirements for form and method are secondary. The students appear to have a heightened awareness of the beauty of nature and the importance of pausing to appreciate it.

As a culminating activity, Mrs. Ssengoba introduces the students to a modification of *sumi-e* (*soo-me-a*), the Japanese art of painting with ink. First, food coloring is applied in drops near the bottom of the paper. The wet food coloring is then blown gently with a straw to move it in the desired direction. Blowing across the ink causes it to branch attractively, allowing students to achieve a variety of designs. The students use the designs as a scroll or frame for their poems. (See Figure 7.9.)

According to studies by Terry (1974), Kutiper (1985), and Fisher and Natarella (1982), haiku is one of the least popular poetic forms among students that they surveyed. Our experiences, as supported here, indicate that students enjoy haiku if the *process* is highlighted.

Music

"If you can walk, you can dance; if you can talk, you can sing" are the words (from Zimbabwe) written on the sign that Mrs. Sauer, a Multicultural Literacy Project staff member, carries with her when she conducts workshops and visits classrooms. She readily admits that even though she is a music teacher, she initially lacked confidence in her singing ability. An instrumental music major in college, she always dreaded the short intervals in which she had to sing. These feelings changed, however, when she became the music teacher for an elementary school. She learned that you do not need a beautiful voice to sing. She discovered that practice, with support from an audiotape, could build her self-confidence and help fellow teachers bring music to their classrooms. She also learned that there are many ways to integrate music into the curriculum and into a multicultural literacy program.

We believe students should understand that music, which is a universal language known around the world, bridges languages, cultures, and ethnicity. We continue to find that music can be effectively incorporated into a multicultural literacy program.

Through Books and Tapes.   There are many books that have music as a part of their narration. *Abiyoyo*, Pete Seeger's Storysong, is a favorite book for students of all ages. Although the book is a delightful tale about a horrible but appealing giant,

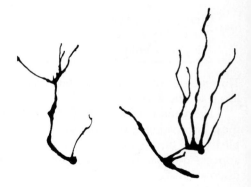

FIGURE 7.9   An example of haiku and *sumi-e.*

Tiny drops falling

Rhythmically 'cross rooftops

Lullaby for sleep

Brandy

Abiyoyo, what lingers with the students is the song about the giant. So that students could actively participate in the retelling of the story, Mrs. Sauer composed a Reader's Theater for the class. As the music was incorporated into the Reader's Theater, the story became even more engaging. Although some students were reluctant to join in at first, their self-consciousness soon disappeared because of the inviting melody. Music, thus, can enhance a story and invite full student participation

Another example, *Shake It to the One that You Love the Best,* by Cheryl Maddox, is an audiotape of play songs and lullabies from black musical traditions. Many of the songs and chants are reminiscent of the lilting, rhythmical language of folk tales. Interestingly, some of the teachers remember playing these games as children. The songs invite students to engage in actions and movements and provide an acceptable way for more energetic students to participate in a constructive, entertaining activity. Teachers of all cultures find these play songs fun to share with their students.

Similarly, *Arroz Con Leche: Popular Songs and Rhymes from Latin America,* by Lulu Delacre, includes examples of children's songs and rhymes from the Spanish-speaking world. The book is beautifully illustrated with scenes from Mexico, Puerto Rico, and Latin America. One of the songs, "Aserrin, Asserran," a lullaby, is a favorite among the younger students. Lullabies have traditionally been shared in families of all cultures. This lullaby might provide an opportunity for students to ask their parents to share lullabies that they remember their parents singing to them when they were younger. The Spanish text further allows teachers to incorporate Spanish into the language arts curriculum.

In the story *Follow the Drinking Gourd,* by Jeannette Winter, the author incorporates the song "Follow the Drinking Gourd" into the text. The song, which is a disguised message to assist slaves in their escape northward, helps students understand how words, through music, can carry a hidden meaning. As students gain insight into the importance of the lyrics and music, their interest and enjoyment are heightened as well.

Holidays are a time to celebrate the similarities and differences among various cultures. At Christmastime, for example, students enjoy *Las Navidades: Popular Christmas Songs from Latin America,* by Lulu Delacre, a beautifully illustrated book of Christmas songs from Spanish-speaking countries. The story includes descriptions of the events of the Christmas holidays arranged in chronological order, with the country of origin included in each scene. The music and illustrations stimulate further exploration into holiday traditions of the Hispanic culture.

Integrating Music with Reading and Writing.   Music can also be used to create a pleasant, quietly stimulating atmosphere as students read and write. Through listening to music as background, we have found that some students acquire an appreciation for music that is unfamiliar to them or that they have not enjoyed previously. Several teachers combine music with poetry writing and reading. Listening to the music of the culture helps students to associate the poem with its cultural theme. Other teachers play Negro spirituals as students write in their response journals after reading Rae Bains's *Harriet Tubman: The Road to Freedom.*

After listening to and developing an appreciation for the music of a culture, students can also compare the music between two cultural groups. One teacher developed an activity to identify similarities and differences between the Navajo and Cheyenne tribes by comparing their legends and music. Her students read Terri Cohlene's *Turquoise Boy—A Navajo Legend* and *Quillworker—A Cheyenne Legend,* comparing the two stories according to the story elements. After listening to selected Navajo and Cheyenne music, students further compared the music of the two nations. These combined activities enabled the students to perceive the differences between the two lifestyles.

Integrating Music through Folk Dancing.   Integrating music and dance with literature is another effective way to help students learn about cultures, as dance is a significant expression of a culture. Students in one class, for example, used the instruments of the Native Americans—drums, flutes, and rattles—as they performed a folk dance, with the assistance of the music teacher, to the choral reading of *Brother Eagle, Sister Sky,* by Susan Jeffers.

Art

Art is a language of understanding. As Schuman (1981) asserts, children who are unaware of the artistic aspects of their heritage might learn and grow from art experiences. If children are already aware of these artistic aspects, they might enjoy sharing this knowledge with their peers. As a result of these experiences, students gain an appreciation of how art is bound to the daily life of a cultural group and the place of importance that it holds. For example, Walters (1989) tells us that there is no word in the hundreds of Native American languages that approximates our definition of art. She explains, "Indians did not set out to create art for its own sake. In traditional Indian thinking, there is no separation between art and life or between what is beautiful and what is functional" (p. 17). Walters's statement reminds us that art should be examined and appreciated in the context of the cultural group being studied. Taken out of this context, the unique perspectives of the group in creating the art are absent, and true understanding is lost.

Art activities can be successfully integrated into a multicultural literacy program, using a thematic approach, as an extension of a cultural topic or after books related to a theme have been read and discussed. When art is used thus, students learn how it enriches the lives of people of all cultures. Students also gain insight into the culture through the actual experience of making or creating something that is special or beautiful. Through multiple experiences with art, students discover that art is an important part of the human spirit to be valued and enjoyed. In order for students to perceive these concepts, however, teachers need to guide students in making connections between art and culture, between art and daily life.

Art Appreciation.   We have discovered that the illustrations in multicultural literature frequently help students develop an appreciation for art and motivate them to experience the story aesthetically. When they attempt to recreate the artistic form in their own drawings, students spontaneously share their positive feelings and thoughts about the illustrations. Through these discussions, they begin to compare the techniques of specific artists and ponder why various artistic techniques convey the message of the story. As teachers become aware of students' interest in the illustrations, they begin to formally include more activities for art appreciation in their curriculum.

Using Art with Thematic Learning.   Several teachers, while studying specific cultures, find they can readily integrate art with other subjects and themes. The following are some art activities teachers have used successfully to help students appreciate Native American cultures:

- **Kachina Dolls**—Students who study the Hopi and Zuni tribes can learn about their belief in supernatural beings called Kachinas. These beings brought gifts of food and other necessary things that saved many lives. The doll is a form of the Kachina. Teachers find that students can be creative in decorating these dolls in the Hopi tradition.

- **Dreamcatcher**—Legend has it that the dreamcatcher was used by the Ojibway to catch all dreams, good and bad. It was hung in the lodge near the bedroom window. The bad dreams which would get caught up in the webbing would be held there until first morning light and then be burned off by the sun's rays. Good dreams, knowing their way to the center of the hole, would filter down into the feathers and be held there, to return another night. After learning about their use, students enjoy making dreamcatchers to capture their personal dreams.

- **Clay Crafts**—Pottery making began as early as 300 B.C. (Schuman, 1981). The early pots had a utilitarian purpose, primarily, as household and ceremonial vessels. Acoma, Zuni, and Hopi continue the tradition today. Different tribes use varied techniques and styles, one of which involves making pots from coils of clay. Students enjoy using this technique to make pottery as part of their study of the Pueblo Indians.

As teachers and students begin to study African countries, they learn that ancient and modern African art is an integral part of the African's life and often reflects religious ideals through abstract symbols. Artists create beautiful objects of wood, clay, beads, and cloth. Like the Native Americans, African art and crafts often serve a utilitarian purpose and sometimes have a religious or spiritual meaning (Corwin, 1990).

While studying several African countries, for example, students learn about the traditions of masks, which are used for many different purposes, and how they are used as a link with the supernatural. Masks are considered only part of a more complete costume (Schuman, 1981). Students enjoy participating in the following activities:

- **Mask Making**—Students enjoy making papier-mâché masks that represent spirits, such as in *Lord of the Dance,* by Veronique Tadjo. When the papier-mâché mask is dry, it is painted with tempera paint and various geometric designs are added. Other decorations, such as hair, seeds, stones, and twine complete the mask. Younger students decorate paper plates with tempera, yarns, grasses, shells, beads, and seeds.
- **Kente Cloth**—Many villagers in Africa still create textiles in the traditional manner, especially in Nigeria, Ghana, and Senegal. The kente is a popular cloth with a colorful design that was once worn by royalty in Ghana and Nigeria. Using strips of muslim about eight inches wide, students create patterns and designs similar to those of the original kente cloth. Crayons or markers in vibrant colors are used to decorate their strips. Teachers and parents then help complete the project by joining all the pieces together and hemming the edges to give the cloth its finished appearance.

During a study of China, teachers and students can learn about several Chinese artwork traditions. Because the Chinese have always revered their past, early skills are not lost but carried on and further developed. Calligraphy, an example of an ancient form of writing, is a challenging art skill for students to explore.

- **Calligraphy**—Calligraphy is a unique combination of art and writing that includes 40,000 characters. Because these consist of pictographs representing animals, plants, people, and objects, they are popular in decorative arts. Using a fine-pointed brush, students dip into paint or ink to make their characters. They practice first before moving to rice or other textured paper. The characters are then mounted on scrolls or colored paper.

Teachers have found one art activity that is common to many cultures: quilt making. Indeed, many European Americans, Native Americans, Appalachians, and African Americans claim quilt making as an important custom. Teachers find quilt making to be an exciting art activity to include in their multicultural literacy curriculum.

- **Quilt Making**—Students can make quilts out of poster board or tag board as well as fabric. When using fabric, each student receives a square of fab-

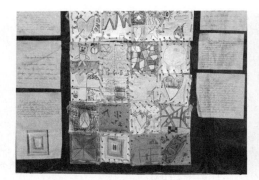

FIGURE 7.10   Students display class quilt and individual kente cloths.

ric to personalize with needlework, fabric crayons, or markers. Some students take the fabric home and work with their parents or grandparents. Teachers frequently have students write about their fabric square, explaining the design they used and why. Parents often assemble the quilt from students' patches. Because it is a class project, some teachers send the quilt home to a different family each night.

Students have been able to experience the art of many cultures through the activities presented here. Figure 7.10 shows examples of two such art experiences.

UNDERSTANDING AND ADDRESSING SOCIAL ISSUES

Thus far we have encouraged students to build personal and group identity by learning about themselves, their families, and their communities so that they might understand who they are and why they are important. We have further suggested that teachers help develop an understanding of diverse cultures by examining cultural values and beliefs and by making cultural comparisons. Through these activities, students may develop positive self-esteem, positive attitudes, and acceptance of diverse cultural groups.

Another important aspect of promoting cultural understanding is to encourage an understanding of social issues, issues of justice and equality. There is a critical need for students to understand their role in helping to bring about justice for people when it is denied. As important members of society, and perhaps our last best hope for true democracy, students can be empowered to act on their knowledge and change inequities and aspects of life that they perceive to be unjust (Pang, 1992; Banks, 1991; Ramsey, 1987).

Beginning with a Sense of Justice

Elementary students—and even younger students—have a powerful sense of justice (Ramsey, 1987). By beginning with experiences of personal fairness that are relevant to students, teachers can help them begin to understand issues of justice involving diverse cultural groups. Children can often be heard wailing, "But that's not fair!" This cry may be directed at the teacher, when one group of students is consistently chosen to be first in line, or at another student, who brings a candy treat for most of the students, but hasn't enough for all in the class. Pang (1992) suggests that students might begin brainstorming synonyms for justice: fairness, being equal, equality, fair play, being a good sport, being just. Students might then identify issues of justice or fairness in books they have read. For example, in *Mufaro's Beautiful Daughters,* by Steptoe, the teacher could have students discuss whether Manyaro was fair when she went ahead to meet the king, leaving Nyasha, her sister, behind. Similarly, they might examine Nyasha's sense of fairness in making Manyara a servant in her household when she married the king.

Babushka's Doll, by Patricia Polacco, a story of a demanding child who becomes the object of a doll's even more demanding behavior, offers another opportunity to discuss fairness. Teachers might ask, "Was it fair for Natasha to treat her Babushka the way she did? Was it fair for Babushka's doll to treat Natasha in such an unkind way? Why or why not?" By forming questions about these issues using familiar books, teachers can sensitize students to the need for fairness in interactions with others. (See Figure 7.11.) Students may also learn that unfair treatment has negative consequences. Through similar student interactions and the use of curricular materials, teachers have daily opportunities to build on the students' perception of justice and develop their sense of fairness.

When Justice Fails

If we lived in a perfect world, justice would always prevail and all people would be treated equitably. However, children and adults sometimes interact in hurtful and negative ways toward those who are different from themselves. These behaviors are often fueled by stereotypes.

It is helpful to clarify these concepts for students. *Stereotyping* is describing an entire group of people as having a certain trait without acknowledging individual differences (Brislin, 1981). People, for example, might describe some groups as violent, artistic, lazy, good musicians, or good cooks. People who are prejudiced frequently point to some example of the stereotype to justify or rationalize their biased behavior.

Pang (1992) suggests that students in second grade and older can understand how stereotypes cloud perceptions and create barriers to just decisions. Derman-Sparks (1991) believes, however, that even 4- and 5-year-old children can begin to engage in critical thinking that is essential for recognizing and resisting the effects of stereotyping. She relates the following incidents:

> Jill arrived this morning with a stereotypic, "Indian Warrior" figure. Sue and Kenji immediately told her, "Don't show that to Suzanne (a Cherokee-Cree staff member); it will hurt her feelings. It isn't the way Indians look."
>
> Malcolm brought Suzanne a copy of National Geographic, and, showing her pictures about Native Americans in the Colonial period, asked, "Are these true?" (p. 73)

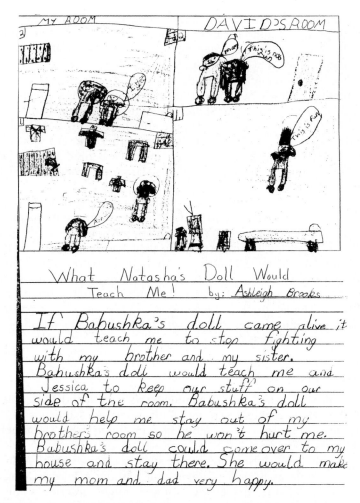

FIGURE 7.11 Second-graders learn to reflect on justice and fairness in their own family life through writing about what Natasha's doll could teach them, as in this example.

Clearly, these examples illustrate that children are aware of stereotypes and are actively involved in learning to challenge inaccuracies.

Even though the concepts of prejudice, discrimination, and racism are not easily defined by young students, the consequences can be felt and understood. Certainly upper elementary and middle school students can recognize and discuss these concepts. The teacher might explain that prejudiced people see the world with a set of blinders and refuse to see people, incidents, and groups that do not reinforce their negative attitudes and stereotypes (Banks, 1991). Helping students distinguish between prejudice and discrimination might be accomplished by explaining that prejudice is a set of *attitudes,* whereas discrimination consists of *different behavior* that is directed toward a cultural or other stigmatized group. Racism is explained by Banks as "not merely a set of beliefs but is practiced when a group has the power to enforce laws, institutions and norms, based on its beliefs, which oppress and dehumanize another group" (p. 75).

Students in the upper elementary and middle school grades might explore some of these practices both in historical and present-day contexts in order to understand how injustices occur. Consistent with Banks (1991), we believe that students who are more aware and knowledgeable about prejudice and who have an opportunity to reason more logically about it are likely to express fewer prejudices than those students who have not explored these issues.

A study of the Japanese Americans' internment in relocation camps, a little-publicized chapter in U.S. history, is an opportunity for an examination of prejudice and discrimination, and even racism. As a result of the bombings of Pearl Harbor by the Japanese on December 7, 1941, hysteria grew on the West Coast, creating and perpetuating myths about Japanese Americans' loyalty to the United States. On February 19, 1942, President Franklin Roosevelt ordered all Japanese Americans into 10 concentration camps, where they were fenced in by barbed wire and guarded by soldiers, an internment that lasted for four years.

The Journey, by Sheila Hamanaka, vividly portrays the experiences of the author's family during these years. She recounts, "I was born after the war in 1949, and grew up unaware that my grandfather had died in a concentration camp, not in Europe or Japan, but in America. His crime—and the crime of 120,000 others: being of Japanese ancestry" (p. 5). This book is the vehicle by which Mrs. Long begins her study of the experiences of discrimination and racism that the Japanese suffered. She believes this book is particularly appropriate because until recently, accounts of the Japanese internment were either omitted from textbooks and tradebooks, or were mentioned only briefly. Mrs. Long views this as an opportunity for students to examine a historical event from the viewpoint of a victimized, nonmainstream writer, thereby gaining unique insight into issues of racism and discrimination.

Before reading the book, Mrs. Long writes *prejudice, discrimination,* and *racism* on the board and asks her class if they know what the words mean. Students often describe what the words mean through examples related to their lives. Mrs. Long writes the following working definitions on the board, summarizing their ideas in more concise and perhaps understandable terms:

- Prejudice is a set of negative attitudes about a group that is not based on fact.
- Discrimination is negative behavior that is directed toward a group that isn't liked, or that is different.
- Racism is practiced when a group enforces laws that oppress (keep people down) and dehumanize another group.

Mrs. Long explains other concepts related to Japanese Americans that are mentioned in the book but that students may not be familiar with. She explains, for example, that *Issee (ee-say)* refers to the first generation of Japanese to arrive in America; that *Nisei (nee-say)* refers to their American-born children; and that the

Sansei (*sahn-say*) are children born after the war. She further tells them that this text and its photographs portray the history of the Japanese people in America.

The class then reads the book in pairs. As they read, they are asked to write down words that describe the group in power—the United States—and the group that is oppressed—the Japanese. After reading three pages, the class regroups to share the words that they have recorded as Mrs. Long writes them on the board. As the pairs share their words, she asks why they chose the words and encourages them to use examples from the book. The students suggest the following words:

Powerful: mean, evil, oppressive, unfair, unjust, awful, unkind, immoral, hateful, hurtful, uncaring

Oppressed: hardworking, fearful, confused, afraid, protesting, suffering, scared, sick, ashamed

The rest of the class either agrees or disagrees with the appropriateness of each term. As the students continue their discussion, they learn that the Japanese Americans met with prejudice and discrimination when they came to this country in the late 1800s. They further learn that they worked hard but were denied access to the advantages of the dominant group. Due to stereotypes, prejudice, and discrimination, the Japanese Americans became the victims of racism. One student is outraged by the following excerpt from the book, written by a columnist for the San Francisco *Examiner:*

Herd 'em up, pack 'em off, and give 'em the inside room in the badlands. Let 'em be hurt, hungry, and dead up against it. . . . Personally, I hate the Japanese. And that goes for all of them.

The student comments that when people hate, it can lead to awful things. Through this type of sharing and discussion, students are able to see the negative consequences of racism at the hands of their government.

Mrs. Long then asks students to pose alternatives to sending the Japanese Americans to concentration camps after the bombing of Pearl Harbor. Students suggest:

• Have people who disagreed with the actions to speak out.
• Have the Japanese fight in the war with other American soldiers.
• Give a trial to those Japanese who were suspected of being against the United States and for Japan.

By the end of the discussion, all of the students are more involved, including those who were initially hesitant to enter the discussion.

Mrs. Long feels it is important to note that the reactions of the Japanese to their internment was not always passive and submissive. She asks the students to find examples in the text of rebellion and protests. Frequently, she notes, oppressed people rebel because of injustices. As the discussion ends, Mrs. Long reminds the students that in 1988 the survivors of the Japanese internment received an apology and $20,000 apiece from the Commission of Wartime Relocation and Internment of

Civilians of the United States. Even though late in coming, the United States finally admitted publicly the mistake of its actions.

Hamanaka ends the book with this explanation of the final panel of *The Journey:*

> As I write, the Japanese American community still works to see that reparations are actually paid: Half of the camp survivors have already died. In the painting's final panel, one man's shirt bears swallows, a symbol of the repayment of debt; a boy's T-shirt, a wave — symbol of power and resilience. And floating before us, a carp, the symbol of renewal. (p. 37)

SUMMARY

We began this chapter by presenting techniques to promote cultural understanding and appreciation, first examining the teacher's role as cultural mediator. We suggested that through self-reflection and self-examination, teachers are more likely to be effective in helping students to understand themselves. We then presented strategies to help students acquire knowledge about cultural aspects of their background and of their families, as well as about the values that they hold. This self-knowledge prepares students to look beyond themselves to other students who have cultures and experiences different from their own.

We suggested specific ways that students might learn about other cultures, their values, and beliefs. Traditional folk literature, for example, can be used as a valuable source of information in transmitting cultural knowledge. Through collaborative problem-solving activities students learn how to extract this knowledge from stories they read. Similarly, we illustrated how discussion and role play of provocative literature about historical events can be used to promote understanding of differing views and perspectives. We further discussed how comparison of fictional characters, customs, or important historical figures across cultures can help students acquire new understanding. We also demonstrated ways that poetry, art and music can enrich students' lives while providing positive cultural experiences.

Finally, we described an approach to addressing social issues and barriers to cultural understanding, including stereotypes, discrimination, and racism. We then showed specifically how literature might be used to promote an examination of these issues.

REFERENCES

Banks, J. (1991). *Teaching strategies for ethnic studies.* Boston: Allyn and Bacon.

Brislin, R. (1981). *Cross-cultural encounters: Face to face interaction.* New York: Pergamon Press.

Bullivant, B. M. (1984). *Pluralism: Cultural maintenance and evolution.* England: Multilingual Matters, Ltd.

Cintron de Esteves, C., & Spicola, R. (1982). *Four Hispanic groups: Oral and social traditions, education and play implications for educators* (Report No. RC 013872). Chicago, IL: International Reading Association. (ERIC Document Reproduction Services ED 226897)

Corwin, J. (1990). *African crafts.* New York: Franklin Watts.

Cushner, K., McClelland, A., & Safford, P. (1992). *Human diversity in education: An integrative approach.* New York: McGraw Hill.

Dailey, S. (1988). *Taking it further: A study guide for "Land of the Sky Blue Waters".* Mt. Pleasant, MI: Rumplestiltskin Productions.

Degroff, L., & Galda, L. (1992). *Responding to literature: Activities for exploring books.* In B. Cullinan (Ed.), *Invitation to read: More children's literature in the reading program.* (pp. 122-137). Newark, DE: IRA.

Derman-Sparks, L. (1991). *Anti-bias curriculum: Tools for empowering young children.* Washington, D.C.: National Association for the Education of Young Children.

Edelman, M. W. (1992). *The measure of our success: A letter to my children and yours.* Boston: Beacon Press.

Fisher, C., & Natarella, M. (1982). Young children's preferences in poetry: A national survey of first, second, and third graders. *Research in the Teaching of English, 16,* 339-354.

Fuerstein, R., Yaacov, R., & Rynders, J. (1988). *Don't accept me as I am: Helping "retarded" people to excel.* New York: Plenum Press.

Goodenough, W. (1981). *Language, culture, and society.* New York: Cambridge University Press.

Hennings, D., & Grant, B. (1981). *Written expression in the language arts: Ideas and skills.* New York: Columbia University, Teachers College Press.

Holt, Rinehart and Winston. (1991). The Oral tradition. In *African American literature: Voices in a tradition.* (pp. 83-94). Austin, TX.

Junaluska, A. (1976). Great American Indian Speeches. Two Records. Vol. 1. New York: Caedmon.

Kingsley, Mary. (1964). *West African studies* (3d ed.) New York: Barnes & Noble.

Kutiper, K. (1985). A survey of the adolescent poetry preferences of seventh, eighth, and ninth graders (Doctoral dissertation, University of Houston). *Dissertation Abstracts International, 47,* 451-452A.

Le Pere, J. (1980). For every occasion: Poetry in the reading program. Albuquerque, NM: Eighth Southwest Regional Conference. International Reading Association.

Moody, L. (1992). Conversations with parents: Talking about literacy and living. In P. Shannon (Ed.), *Becoming political: Readings and writings in the politics of literacy education.* (pp. 224-233). Portsmouth, NH: Heinemann.

Norton, D. (1991). *Through the eyes of a child: An introduction to children's literature.* Columbus, OH: Charles Merrill.

Paley, V. G. (1992). *White teacher.* Cambridge, MA: Harvard University Press.

Pang, V. (1991). Teaching children about social issues. In C. Sleeter (Ed.), *Empowerment through multicultural education.* (pp. 179-197). Albany, N.Y.: State University of New York Press.

Pate, G. (1988). Research on reducing prejudice. *Social Education, 52,* 287-289.

Phelps, S., Hilliard, A., & Christmas, J. (1989). Is there a black identity? In P. Bates & T. Wilson (Eds.), *Effective schools: Critical issues in the education of black children.* (pp. 11-30). Washington, D.C.: National Alliance of Black School Educators.

Phillips (1983). *The invisible culture: Communication in classroom and community on warm springs reservation.* New York: Longman.

Prelutsky, J. (1983). *The Random House book of poetry for children.* New York: Random House.

Ramsey, P. (1987). *Teaching and learning in a diverse world: Multicultural education for young children.* New York: Columbia University, Teachers College Press.

Rosenblatt, L. (1976). *Literature as exploration.* New York: Noble & Noble.

Rosenblatt, L. M. (1978). *The reader, the text, the poem: The transactional theory of the literary work.* Carbondale, IL: Southern Illinois University Press.

Samuels, S. (1977). *Enhancing self-concept in early childhood.* New York: Human Sciences Press.

Saville-Troike, M. (1978). *A guide to culture in the classroom.* Rosslyn, VA: National Clearinghouse for Bilingual Education.

Schuman, J. (1981). *Art from many lands: Multicultural art projects.* Worcester, MA: Davis Publications.

Sebesta, S. (1983). "Choosing Poetry." *Teaching with books children like.* Eds. N. Roser and M. Frith. Newark, DE: International Reading Association, pp. 66–78.

Stegner, W. (1945). *One Nation.* Boston, MA: Houghton Mifflin Co.

Stewig, J. (1988). *Children and literature.* Boston, MA: Houghton Mifflin Company.

Terry, A. (1974). *Children's poetry preferences: A national survey of upper elementary grades.* Urbana, IL: National Council of Teachers of English.

Tiedt, P. & Tiedt, I. (1990). *Multicultural teaching: A handbook of activities, information, and resources.* Boston: Allyn and Bacon.

Triandis, H. (1972). *The analysis of subjective culture.* New York: Wiley Interscience.

Walters, A. (1989). The spirit of Native America: Beauty and mysticism in American Indian art. San Francisco: Chronicle Books.

Zimmerman, W. (1992). *Instant oral biographies: How to tape.* New York: Guarionex Press.

chapter 8

Integrating Technology
with a Multicultural Program

OVERVIEW

We now focus on ways to integrate technology with a multicultural program. Technology, which stimulates reading and writing, offers many new opportunities for adding breadth, depth, meaning, and interest to the multicultural learning environment. First, we present a rationale for integrating technology with a multicultural program. Then we explore possibilities for using technology to support and enhance literacy through narrations of actual classroom activities. Readers will perceive ways that technology—in particular, hypertext, databases, and word processors—can be used to promote higher-level thinking skills as students access, retrieve, organize, analyze, synthesize, and evaluate information.

**RATIONALE FOR INTEGRATING TECHNOLOGY
WITH A MULTICULTURAL PROGRAM**

The following poem, written by Zimbabwe, a second-grader in a Chapter I program, illustrates one possibility for using word processing to facilitate writing. This is not Zimbabwe's first draft of his poem; it is his revised poem. While participating in prewriting activities, he discovered that he did not know a lot about Jerusalem, but he wanted to know more about it and the Jewish culture. With the help of his teacher, Mrs. Taylor, he got books from the library to help him learn more about Jerusalem. As he continued writing his poem, he incorporated what he learned into it and later published the poem using the word processor. Not only did Zimbabwe learn more about his cultural heritage, but he learned how computers can help him write and publish his work.

Jerusalem

A place where
Sharp eyed eagles
glide
Sidewinder rattlesnakes
move quickly
across loose sand
Some people live in thatch
houses
People speak different
languages
Lots of people go to the
Wailingwall
David's tower built 2500
year ago

Zimbabwe

This is only one example of how technology can be used to support and enhance literacy in a multicultural literacy program. Technology offers an exciting, fresh approach to the learning environment in which a user-friendly computer provides opportunities for students to talk and work in pairs as they write. This personalized environment enables students and teachers to share their knowledge about language, learning, and culture naturally. Many researchers also maintain that technology can help increase attention span, motivation, and student attendance (Becker, 1984; Bialo & Sivin, 1989). But according to Bork (1987), the real value of computers lies in their effectiveness as learning devices. Our teachers are finding that technology provides a powerful learning tool for the multicultural literacy program that supports and promotes literacy in ways that parallel learning to speak. Lefevre (1970) emphasizes that language learning in school should "parallel [children's] early childhood method of learning to speak [their] native tongue—playfully, through delighted experiences of discovery—through repeated exposure to language forms and patterns, by creating imitation and manipulation, and by personal trial and error, with kindly and not too much correction from adults" (p. 75).

Students using computers, especially word processors, learn to communicate meanings in authentic, purposeful contexts that involve social interactions and an audience. The computer screen, which provides a way for students to work in pairs and view the text easily, allows students to talk and discuss their ideas as they compose, revise, and edit their text. The fluidity of the word processor also encourages students to take more risks and explore and manipulate written language by deleting, inserting, or rearranging texts. These natural ways of communicating and interpreting meaning parallel the oral language styles of many cultural groups who negotiate, interpret, and adapt information through social interactions (Heath, 1989). When writing builds on students' oral interactions and provides a real audience in a non-threatening environment, second-language students develop fluency in English more quickly and easily, according to Peregoy and Boyle (1993). All students who use

computers in these ways, moreover, develop literacy while combining verbal interpretive skills, keen listening, and observation skills with written language. Discrete
elements of a written text, such as spelling, vocabulary, grammar, and mechanical
skills, are not isolated from the meaning and interpretation of the written text; they
become part of the process of writing. (See chapter 5.) Through these "delighted
experiences of discovery" that naturally integrate reading, writing, speaking, and
listening with computers, students become more confident and motivated to read
and write.

In our multicultural program we primarily use word processors, computer communications, and hypermedia technology. We integrate technology into our program
in order to promote literacy development through genuine communication experiences. Peregoy and Boyle (1993) and Health (1989) advocate finding more ways to
use oral and written language to develop the higher-level thinking and problem-
solving abilities of culturally and linguistically diverse students. While technology is
another tool for carrying out significant literacy tasks and problem-solving/thinking
strategies of all students, it is also a powerful motivator for thinking, reading, researching, discussing, listening, and writing about one's own culture and other
cultures.

Technology's value in our multicultural program, however, is related to the
supportive learning environment it creates and the way it is integrated into the
curriculum. Consistent with our principles outlined in Chapter 1, important features
of this technological learning environment are:

- Structuring the computer environment to encourage risk taking, exploration, and experimentation
- Helping students become familiar and comfortable with the computer and
  keyboarding skills
- Organizing technology experiences to include social interactions with
  teachers and peers
- Creating opportunities for collaboration as students learn about reading,
  writing, and cultures
- Facilitating and guiding learning through frequent teacher-student interactions and constructive feedback
- Using technology in ways that include meaningful, purposeful literacy
  activities
- Planning activities that follow the natural processes of reading and writing

Within this nurturing environment students use technology to develop literacy and
form steppingstones for more complex learning. The ways teachers are integrating
technology with the curriculum are described in the following sections.

ACQUIRING KEYBOARDING SKILLS

Creating a supportive environment requires successful experiences for all students. If
students are unable to use the computer keyboard with ease, they will not be motivated to use the computer as a learning tool. To ensure that students become familiar

and comfortable with the keyboard, we like to spend a couple of weeks at the beginning of the school year showing students how to use it.

Using color-coded simulated keyboards seems to be an effective way to help students become used to the keyboard and the location of the home keys. Following keyboarding techniques, we designed exercises in home-key practice and the movement of fingers on the keyboard. As students begin to stretch their fingers to reach corresponding color-coded keys, they discover they can reach keys much faster than if they use the hunt-and-peck technique. By using the color-coded keyboards to practice their spelling words, students simultaneously improve their scores on their weekly spelling tests. Similarly, practicing sight words on the keyboard enhances word recognition, fluency, and automaticity when they read. This kinesthetic-tactile approach for learning spelling words and sight vocabulary words further provides a meaningful context for acquiring keyboard skills.

When students begin using the computer keyboard for word processing, teachers simply encourage students to place their fingers on the home keys and to use both hands. Emphasizing which finger to use for a particular key is not necessary;

FIGURE 8.1 Sid models how to place his fingers on the home keys so that he can reach other keys easily and quickly as he types.

speed quickly increases as students begin to use two hands. Before long, students automatically place their hands on the home keys (Figure 8.1) whenever they use the keyboard and learn to stretch their fingers up and down to the keys they need.

Teachers also use keyboarding software to help students learn the location of the keys and move their fingers easily across the keyboard. But they observe that practicing these keyboarding skills in the meaningful context of word processing is the best way to increase facility. Early word-processing activities are usually short—for example, writing poems—to ensure a successful experience with computers. Interestingly, we find that students of all ages easily acquire keyboarding skills.

ENHANCING A MULTICULTURAL PROGRAM THROUGH HYPERMEDIA TECHNOLOGY

If our curriculum is to reflect and validate diverse cultures, information about the various cultures must be readily available to students and teachers. Multicultural literature can become an important source for this information. Technology, particularly hypermedia formats, is also an invaluable source for extending knowledge and understanding of other cultures.

Because of its versatility and semantically organized formats, hypermedia technology allows learners of diverse cultural and linguistic backgrounds, varying abilities, and different learning styles to enter a learning environment that matches their individual needs (Ayersman & Reed, 1993; Min Liu, 1993; Minden, 1993). Specifically, hypermedia is a type of technology that integrates text, sound, graphics, and video, giving students multiple ways of viewing subject matter and a multimodal approach to learning. Through its semantic networks that are organized like semantic maps or webs, hypermedia further enables students to approach learning in ways that make sense to them or interest them. They are no longer constrained by the linear presentation of information used in books. Its semantic network system, which parallels schema theory (Min Liu, 1993), further allows learners to explore and perceive relationships among information and concepts and to integrate new knowledge into their preexisting web of knowledge. According to Marsh and Kumar (1992), "Hypertext and hypermedia are seen as having great potential because they offer a convenient way to represent subject matter knowledge and model the structure of knowledge. If learning occurs when new knowledge is integrated into a pre-existing web of knowledge, then it stands to reason that teaching should incorporate this concept in presentation of material" (p. 27).

Consistent with these theoretical perspectives, we designed a hypertext program called Multicultural Links to be used with our multicultural program. Multicultural Links, created by Martha Irwin, is a resource bank of materials, including textual information about people and their cultures throughout the world, maps, pictures, music, and familiar phrases in different languages. Through its semantic-network learning system, students construct their own knowledge about cultures by making meaningful connections among the cultural information and concepts and their own cultures. Establishing ties between new and existing information promotes deeper processing of knowledge and retention of concepts over time. As students navigate through the semantic networks, they also learn to access, organize, retrieve, analyze, synthesize, and evaluate information through the multiple-modal approaches of text, graphics, sound, and videos. Culture, combined with these multiple-modal approaches, becomes a funnel for understanding content information related to geography, history, literature, biographies, and social studies for students, especially underachievers and students of diverse backgrounds. Spatial and visual displays of information assist these students as they interpret, organize, and remember information (Peregoy and Boyle, 1993; Ruddell & Boyle, 1989). The multiple-modal approaches, combined with peer support, further promote language development, comprehension of information, and generation of written text, and increase content learning.

Unlike many other educational software programs Multicultural Links is designed to match the curriculum and the needs and interests of students and teachers. The software, which includes a large array of multicultural materials and resources, correlates with goals and objectives of a multicultural literacy program, supports a thematic approach to learning, and enhances learning for all. While presenting information in ways that correspond to their cultural backgrounds and learning styles, Multicultural Links also makes information readily available and accessible to teachers and students. As books, materials, and resources about other cultures remain limited and many of these sources are frequently no longer current, teachers and students need to have ways to readily access the information that is available.

Description of the Components of Multicultural Links

Multicultural Links has five major sections, as shown on the main menu in Figure 8.2. Students enter the program by rotating the mouse attached to the computer and clicking on any item on the main menu. Through experimentation and exploration,

FIGURE 8.2   Main menu of Multicultural Links.

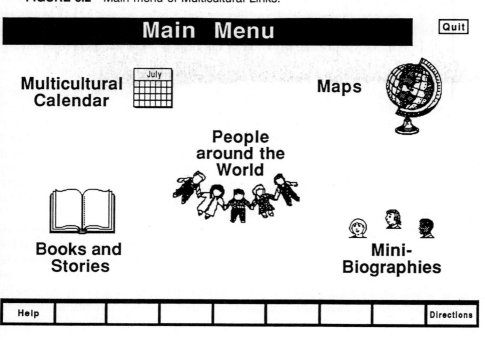

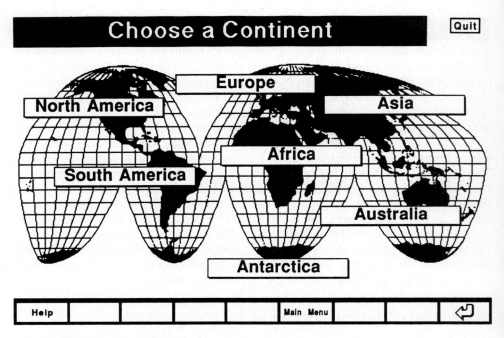

FIGURE 8.3   Map of the world.

they can then link to other parts of the program according to their needs and interests. For example, they can view a map of a country, learn about the language or housing of a people, find informational books and stories related to a country or culture, or learn about historical people or dates associated with a particular culture. Navigating from one part of the program to the next is easy: one just clicks on the major sections shown on the main menu or clicks on the topics one wishes to explore, which are displayed at the bottom of the screen.

If students select "Maps" from the main menu, for example, they initially see a map of the world (Figure 8.3). Consistently viewing the world thus helps them understand the concept that countries are grouped by continents. They also learn locations of countries in relation to the continents. To access a specific map of a country, they type in the name of the country or select a continent and then choose it from a list of countries in that continent. Once they reach the selected country, they see a map of the country on the left side and its location on the continent at the right. To find out the names of cities, mountains, or rivers, students then click on the symbol or the word displayed on the map.

After exploring the map of a particular country or culture, students can learn about the people of that country or culture by clicking on the phrase *More about the country* at the bottom of the screen. Students then see an index of topics about the people of the country or culture displayed on the screen (Figure 8.4). If students choose music, for example, they can listen to the national anthem of any country by clicking on the words, *Play National Anthem,* or they can listen to folksongs of some

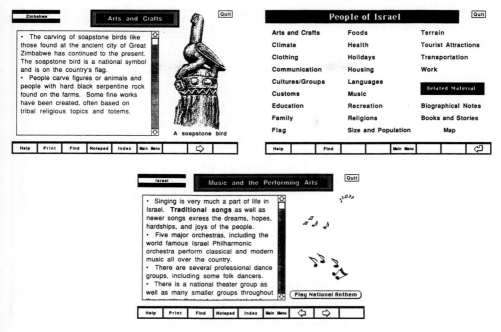

FIGURE 8.4   Index of topics and sample screens for Music and Arts and Crafts.

countries by clicking on the boldfaced words *traditional songs.* Similarly, if students choose Arts and Crafts for the country Zimbabwe, they will see a soapstone bird, the national symbol, displayed on the screen, as well as information about the carvings of the soapstone bird.

While exploring various topics about a particular culture, students can also locate books or stories about the culture by clicking on Books and Stories in the index of topics or by returning to the main menu. Students who are viewing Russia, for example, can click on Books and Stories and see *The Keeping Quilt,* by Patricia Polacco, listed on the screen. By typing the title of the book or its author, students will be able to read an annotation about the book. (See Figure 8.5.)

If students want to read a mini-biography of an author, they can click on the words *Mini-Biographies* and find biographical information about Eloise Greenfield. If they click on the boldfaced word *More,* they will be able to read about Eloise Greenfield's contributions to world society; if they click on the boldfaced words *Related Reading,* they will discover the names of other books she wrote. In this section, students can also read minibiographies about historical figures, inventors, artists, musicians, athletes, authors, or politicians from various cultures. Students can also read about people from their own culture. As students browse among these biographical sketches, they may become inspired by these people and their accomplishments and develop greater appreciation for their contributions to a global society.

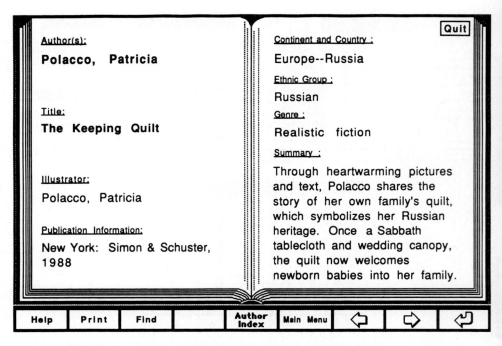

FIGURE 8.5 Annotation of *The Keeping Quilt,* by Patricia Polacco.

Integrating Multicultural Links with the Curriculum

Getting Started. Our teachers like to begin the school year with a demonstration of Multicultural Links using the LC attachment, a device that displays the computer screen on the overhead so all students can see how the program works. After reading and talking about Steptoe's *Mufaro's Beautiful Daughters,* for example, Ms. Bortz takes her class on a journey to Zimbabwe using Multicultural Links. She models how to use the mouse to click on Maps, the continent of Africa, and then the country Zimbabwe from the list of countries, explaining each step as she continues.

After viewing the map and its geographical features, Ms. Bortz demonstrates how to find out more about the country by moving the mouse to the bottom of the screen and clicking on the word *More.* Students enjoy choosing various topics to explore. The flag, language, music, and housing are frequently first choices for young learners.

Similarly, Ms. Bortz shows her students how to navigate among the sections Books and Stories, Mini-Biographies, and Calendar using the story *Mufaro's Beautiful Daughters.* After selecting Books and Stories, for example, they see how they can find annotations of books about Africa; after selecting Mini-Biographies, they can find out more information about John Steptoe by typing in his name; and after selecting Calendar, students can find out what other important events occurred on September 14 by typing in Steptoe's birthdate. (See Figure 8.6.) Students, of course, also enjoy typing in their own birthdates to find out what other important events occurred that day.

The stripes, from top to bottom, are green, yellow, red, black, red, yellow, and green. A white triangle on the left has a yellow Great Zimbabwe soapstone bird on a red star.

| Print | Find | Notepad | Index | Main Menu | ⇩ | ⇧ |

Zimbabwe

Lake Kariba
Kariba
Victoria Falls
Harare
Inyanga Peak
Bulawayo
Masvingo
Limpopo River

| Help | Print | Find | Notepad | More about the country | Main Menu | ⇩ | World Map |

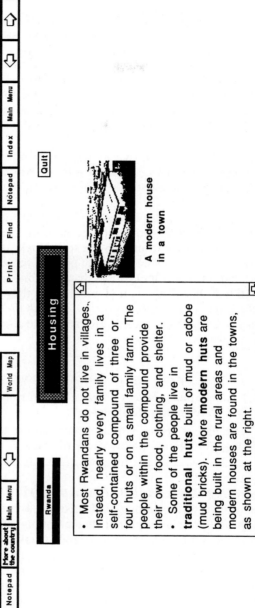

Quit

Rwanda

Housing

A modern house in a town

- Most Rwandans do not live in villages. Instead, nearly every family lives in a self-contained compound of three or four huts or on a small family farm. The people within the compound provide their own food, clothing, and shelter.
- Some of the people live in **traditional huts** built of mud or adobe (mud bricks). More **modern huts** are being built in the rural areas and modern houses are found in the towns, as shown at the right.

| Help | Print | Find | Notepad | Index | Main Menu | ⇩ | ⇧ |

FIGURE 8.6 Map and flag of Zimbabwe and information about housing.

Once students have a chance to see how Multicultural Links works through this interactive presentation, they are ready and eager to investigate the program themselves. Ms. Bortz prefers to have them work on the computer in pairs of mixed ability levels. She has a large class so this helps her move through the class more quickly. As students work cooperatively, moreover, they explore the program and remind one another how to maneuver the mouse, where to click, or what to do next. Students also take turns reading the text displayed on the screen, helping one another pronounce words as needed. After they are finished, they print out a copy of a screen to place in their folder.

Ms. Bortz also trains two students to become the "computer experts" by working with them once or twice for a few minutes before school begins. In this way, all pairs can seek additional assistance as needed from the computer assistants without interrupting her.

Ms. Bortz also displays a schedule that identifies the pairs who are to work together, their scheduled computer time, and the sequence for all students to follow. A smooth transition from one pair to the next occurs as the two students using the computer quietly invite the next pair to report to the computer station. Having scheduled times further ensures that everyone has an opportunity on the computer.

To help her students remember what they have learned on the computer, she has them record three things they learned in their learning logs. (See the learning log entries below.) The printouts of screens are also placed in their log to be used with other activities.

Tokyo is Japan's capital. There is a mountain called Mt. Fugi.

Japanese music is very religion. One intrument is a bamboo flute. This is the way they spell it "Shakuhachi."

The flag of France is blue, white, and red. It is the same as the American flag. The picture below show the French flag.

Integrating Multicultural Links with a Thematic Unit on Cinderella.   After all students investigate Multicultural Links at least twice, Ms. Bortz begins integrating the hypermedia program with her thematic units. She likes to begin the school year by reading different versions of Cinderella from around the world. These include *Cinderella*, by Perrault; *Yeh Shen*, by Ai-Ling Louie; *Korean Cinderella*, by Shirley Climo; *Rough Faced Girl*, by Rolfe Martin; and *The Brocaded Slipper*, by Lynette Dyer Vuong.) Using the Cultural Story Map (see Figure 6.4 in Chapter 6), she helps her students see similarities and differences among the folk tales from these five countries. To help her students see how culture influences setting, characters, events, and themes in the folk tales, she has her students sign up to work in groups of four or five to investigate France, China, Korea, Canada, and Vietnam in more depth, using Multicultural Links. After collecting notes about each culture and putting them in a folder, students compile the information into a booklet about the culture, to be shared with the class.

To begin their research, students first locate their Cinderella country on the map and print out a copy of the map for their folders. Next, they explore the information about their Cinderella country according to their interests, moving among the five sections of the main menu. Ms. Bortz finds that students who have difficulties with reading and writing feel more comfortable with the computer activities because the text is shorter. Many students are also more willing to work at the computer and stay on task because they select the topics they wish to investigate.

After each pair completes a rotation, they return to their seats, placing the map in their logs and recording three things they learned about their culture. Erik, usually a reluctant reader and writer, is more willing to try to pronounce new words while working with his partner on the computer; he also tries his best while recording what he has learned in his journal. All journal entries are gradually getting longer with the inclusion of more facts and examples. Here are samples:

Japan
People eat western style to in Japan. The young kids like pizza and hamburger and they like spaaghetti and fraid chicken. There are many drive there Restaurants to go to. I learned about that Japan is in Aisa.

France
Paris is the capital of France. Nice is a city. Orlans is a huge city. France is in Europe. There is 8 magor citys in France. France is 220,000 square mile and is bigger than texas. Paris is 2,188,918 people that live there. They speak french is France.

They call number one un. They call number two deux. They call number three trois. Thaey call number four quatre.

United States
In 1987, there were 139,000,000 passenger cars and 40,000,000 vehicals in use.

Railroad's go all over the country, they don't use trains that much as did in the earlier days.

There are over 800 airports in the United States.

At the end of each day, Ms. Bortz gives students a chance to share their log entries with the class. Providing opportunities to share this information with the class enables all students to learn more about each culture and to see similarities and differences among the five cultures and their own culture. As students share the information, they also begin to perceive how culture influences setting, characters, and themes of the five folk tales. Displaying the cultural comparison chart on chart paper enables students to see these linkages more clearly.

Once everyone has a chance to investigate the culture, each group meets to decide what topics they will research. Individuals then choose the topic they want to study. When each pair works together this time, they explore additional areas of interest about their culture and then print out the information about their topic. As students continue to record information, their entries become even more detailed. This experience helps students learn how to read informational text and how to write about content-related text by paraphrasing. Since they share this information with the whole class, students become motivated to record specific information by using drawings, labels, lists of actual information, or examples.

As each group compiles information, they are getting ready to begin their sloppy copy for their topics. Ms. Bortz first models how to take information from texts or graphics and rewrite it in one's own words. Beginning with a map of Italy, she has students brainstorm what information they have about Italy from the map. Using clustering techniques, she lists these ideas around the word *Italy*. After the ideas are webbed, she has students brainstorm ways to begin their writing and what sequence they might follow to record additional information. Using their ideas and words, she begins, "Italy is a small country in Europe" on the overhead projector. Similarly, she weaves the additional information about the map into the paragraph, modeling how to form paragraphs. After demonstrating the process, she encourages students to follow the same techniques as they write about their countries. Students are given a chance to share their paragraphs with the class once they finish. For example:

Tokyo is the capital of Japan. Asia is the continent of Japan. Sappora, Hiroshima, and Nagasoki are the cities in Japan. Mount Fiji is called Mount Fujuyana in Japanese. Mount Fuji is a dormant volcano. It last erupted in 1707.

Italy is a peninsula in the continent of Europe and is a small county. Rome is the capital. There are three other cities they are Naples, Pisa, Venice and Milan. The Arno River, Po Rover and Tober River are the rivers in Italy.

On the next day, Ms. Bortz demonstrates how to take information from text, paraphrase the ideas, and record the information. To help her students understand this process, she distributes copies of the information about transportation in Japan to each student. After they read the selection silently, she encourages them to think about the important ideas. Once they decide, as a class, what the important ideas are, they underline these ideas with a colored marker, just as one highlights texts. Then Ms. Bortz asks them to turn the paper over and restate one idea in their own words. After sharing similar ways to paraphrase ideas, she models how to write a paragraph about transportation, using these techniques.

Students are now ready to follow this same process for their individual topics. Once students complete their rough drafts and revise and edit them, they are ready to publish their drafts using the word processor. Ms. Bortz observes that her students are highly motivated and more interested in writing when using the word processor. She says that they are more willing to write and revise on the word processor, adding, "I have yet to come across a student that wasn't extremely interested in using the word processor even though many had very little keyboarding skills."

Throughout this word-processing experience, students are involved, motivated, and enthusiastic. They realize they can make a mistake and not have to start over again. After each group member completes typing his or her information for the book, they create illustrations to accompany their text. The group then decides on a title for their book and prepares an author's page where everyone shares something about their Cinderella country and describes how he or she felt while learning about it. The books are then bound and published to share with the class. The culture-based projects heighten students' knowledge and understanding of new cultures as they question, inform, problem-solve, negotiate, and interact with their peers.

Integrating Multicultural Links with a Thematic Unit on Japan and China.
Mrs. Manchester, a fourth-grade teacher, similarly uses Multicultural Links with her
class. When reading *Sadako and the Thousand Paper Cranes,* for example, they use
Multicultural Links to learn more about Japan. Looking at the maps, students recognize the cities of Hiroshima and Nagasaki from their books. They gain background
knowledge about housing, arts and crafts, and religion, which helps them understand
Japanese people's lifestyles and enhances their comprehension of the story. They
encounter words associated with the Japanese culture, such as bed quilts, tatami
mats, and the celebration of Peace Day. Students are motivated to learn more about
Japan. Examples from their learning logs follow:

Japan
In Japan thae like baseball and thae like basketball gymnastics and soccer
and volleyball and Karate and Judo. Thae like rise. The languages in Japan is
the most comin languages to the peopel in Japan and children.

Japan
Most people wear jeans and "T" shirts in Japan now. They wear the same
kind of shoes—leather shoes, lafers, sneakes, and high-heels. The rickshaw
or jin-rickshaw was invented by the Japanese. The cart that is pulled by a
man is no longer used for transportation.
    September 1st is Kanto Earthquake Memorial Day. This is in re-
membrance of the 57,000 people who died in the great earthquake in 1923.

She also has her students create their own informational books about Japan,
following the process described previously. In her class, students choose three topics
about Japan to investigate and write about in their books. These are examples:

Japanese Books and Stories
I have read many books about Japan. My favorite novel is Sadako and the
"*Thousand Paper Cranes*". This story is historical fiction because its about
World War II and the atomic bomb. It was a sad story because Sadako died
from leukemia from the atom bomb. "*The Stone Cutter*" and *The Perfect
Crane* are folk tales. I also read a nonfiction book *Counting your way to
Japan* I learned how to say and write #'s one trow [through] ten in
Japanese.

Japanese Languages
In Japan the main languages is Japanese. You can go right to left and top to
bottom to read in Japanese. The cover of a Japanese book is at the back.
Nihon is the Japanese word for Japan. The top character means "sun" and
the bottom character means "origin." Japan is sometimes called "The land of
the Rising sun." Sometimes Japanese can also be written with the letters
that are used in English. In Japanese writing they use symbols and characters instead of the alphabet.

Since this is their first time to use a word processor and their texts are quite long,
they only type their author's page. Nicole's author's page is found below:

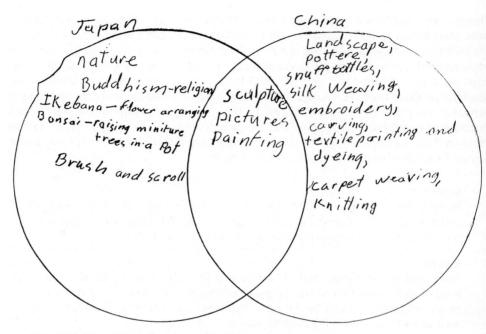

FIGURE 8.7 Example of one student's Venn Diagram.

From reading and studying about Japan, I have learned a lot. I have chosen to write about geography, languages and arts and crafts. I hope you enjoy my book.

As Mrs. Manchester's class continues to read multicultural novels, the fourth-graders use Multicultural Links to learn more about new countries and cultures. To help her students compare Japan and China, she uses the Venn Diagram. First, all students choose a topic to investigate within the two cultures; for example, Doug chooses transportation. After printing out the information related to transportation in China and Japan, Doug reads the text to compare the various forms of transportation used by the Chinese and Japanese. He then places the different forms of transportation in the outer circles and the similar forms in the inner circle. Completing these diagrams helps students learn that there are differences and similarities among Asian cultures. An example of a student's Venn Diagram on arts and crafts is displayed in Figure 8.7.

USING WORD PROCESSING TO PROMOTE READING AND WRITING

Word processing, a highly efficient way to address the needs of a literacy curriculum (Moore, 1989), is the most popular use of technology in our program. Teachers soon discover that word processing complements the writing process. Students easily move back and forth between its stages as they compose, delete, insert, or rearrange text to communicate their message. The collaborative, cooperative nature of the computer screen promotes continuous and recurring transactions between readers and writers as they work in pairs, experimenting with new ways to express their ideas and clarify meaning. Students are no longer constrained by texts that are messy or difficult to read and reread because of poorly formed handwriting; the screen or the printed copy neatly displays the text. Students, especially second-language learners, can more easily talk about ideas and learn clearer ways to express their thoughts with their partner's support.

The verbal and interpretive abilities of African Americans (Heath, 1983, 1989), Hispanics, and Native Americans (Au, 1993) thrive in natural social situations. As students from diverse cultural and linguistic backgrounds have opportunities to use and explore language through social interactions, they discover ways to communicate their written messages. By creating a context for shared learning—which includes collaboration and negotiation—the computer environment provides opportunities for all learners to extend and develop their oral and written language.

Importantly, the screen depersonalizes the text so that students feel more comfortable experimenting with new arrangements of their written language. The word processor's powerful editing tools provide a natural way for students to explore grammatical tools in an environment free of the red ink pen or the need to recopy their writing. Consistent with the language needs of diverse students (Heath, 1989; Perogoy & Boyle, 1993), the word-processing environment provides occasions for extended practice experimentation, and exploration with oral and written language. To maximize these possibilities, however, teachers need to consider pairing students of mixed ability levels.

Using Word Processing to Publish Writing

Mrs. Benns, a Chapter I consultant, enjoys using the computer to publish her second-grader's writing. After reading *Imagine,* by Alison Lester—a charming book whose captivating illustrations allow one to imagine taking voyages through the jungles of South America, the grasslands of Africa, or the Aboriginal regions of Australia—Mrs. Benns encourages her students to brainstorm places they would like to visit on their imaginary trips. Nneka chooses Hawaii, Ben suggests the sea, and Media says she would like to go to Greece. Following the writing process, Mrs. Benns demonstrates how to write the place they would like to visit in the center of their paper, drawing a circle around it. Next, she shows her students how to record things they might see on their imaginary trip, using temporary spelling to write their words. Before long, the second-graders web all the things they might see on their voyages. Nneka's web includes palm trees, Hawaiian dancers, clams, flowers, and the sea; Marcus's web includes sharks, eels, and the hammerhead shark.

Next, she asks her students to place an action word next to the people or animals and a describing word next to other things they see on their webs. To help her students understand this concept, she has them brainstorm a few examples for sharks first. They think of the words *dive* and *swim* for action words and *silver* and *scary* for describing words.

The following day, Mrs. Benns models how to use the pattern of the Imagine poems in the story to create their own poems. After showing how she uses her own web to write a poem about visiting her grandfather's ranch in Texas, she distributes paper with the beginning lines of the pattern, "Imagine if we were in. . . ." Within a few moments all similarly use their webs to create their poems.

A few days later, she pairs her second-grade Chapter I students with fifth-grade Chapter I students to help them learn about editing and revising. The second-graders read their poems to their partners, who help them add or change words as they revise their poems.

Students are now ready to publish the poems on the computer. Because this is their first time to use the computer, Mrs. Benns assists each student as they type. After students type the first two lines of their poems, she finishes the poems for them as they read them aloud. The collaborative nature of the computer screen encourages the second-graders to consider new ideas and words for their poems as Mrs. Benns types them. These revisions are easily inserted as teacher and students work together, typing the poems. As one can see in the following examples, the second-graders can write beautiful poems, using interesting details and colorful words. Through this process, they learn that text is temporary and that writing becomes clearer and more descriptive through revisions. After the poems are bound into a booklet, the second-graders share their published poems with other classes. Then teachers place them in the school library for students to check out and read. Here are three examples of final drafts:

Imagine
by Nneka

Imagine
if we were
in Hawaii
where the palm trees sway
where people stay
where the Hawaiian dancers dance
where the clams stay
where flowers grow
and where the sea sways.

Imagine
by Media

Imagine
if we were
in Greece
where trees blow and boats sail
where sharks and fish swim
where my whole family and baby brother lives
where dogs eat and sleep and scratch
and cats scratch too.

Imagine
by Dennis

Imagine
if we were
in the sea
where divers dive and
where treasures make shiny colors and
where eels shock fish.

As the year continues, Nneka, Media, and Dennis learn to type their poems and stories independently. The more they use the computer, the more fluent they become. Figure 8.8 shows three other students writing on a computer.

Using Word Processing to Publish Writing in a Fourth-Grade Class

Mrs. Theisen, a fourth-grade teacher, also uses computers to publish her students' writing. Composing always begins with many prewriting activities, including brainstorming sessions, webbing, note taking, interviewing, listening, and observing. (See

FIGURE 8.8 Alishia, Randon, and Katherine eagerly learn how to write on the computer.

Chapter 5.) Students then organize and synthesize their ideas in pairs, small groups, or individually as they draft their ideas on paper.

Just after the bombing of Iraq, Mrs. Theisen's class decided to write poems about peace. Their motivation increased after they received the following letter from Guy, a former classmate who moved to Israel just before the bombing began:

Dear Mrs. Theisen,

We came to Israel. And we got a gas mask, We hope coming back to America in seven years it depends on my Fathers work. We are all right for now. Iraq didn't even throw the gas yet, And We hope we won't have a war, We got a lot of toys in the airplane and good food. We learn English in 4th grade.

Mrs. Theisen helped her students gather ideas for their poems by sharing some poems about peace composed by children from Israel and Palestine. As they listened, they took notes on "sparkle" words—words they especially liked. Students then made a web of words from their notes for their own peace poem. Following these prewriting activities, they began drafting their sloppy copy of the peace poem. As students shared their poems, their anxieties and fears about the crisis seemed to lighten. Writing seemed to help them understand their feelings about war and their concerns about relatives and friends who were fighting in Operation Desert Storm. Through this experience, they gained new insights into the negative effects of war and began to consider alternative solutions and new possibilities for world peace.

Once they completed their first draft, students began entering their poems on the computer. Posted schedules helped them know when it would be their turn and guaranteed everyone a chance to work on one of the three computers Mrs. Theisen had arranged to have in her classroom during this stage.

Students then used the printed copies to improve their pieces in revising groups or editing teams. (See Chapter 5.) The neat, legible copies enabled students to recognize the strengths of their writing, identify problems, consider revisions, and proof their final versions. Mrs. Theisen said her students were more willing to consider revisions and changes during this stage of the process because the recopying penalty had been eliminated. Danielle confirmed her teacher's observation when she announced, "It is a lot easier to read, edit, and type our stories. We can't lose our paper, and we can erase without any mess." Similarly, Shavone stated, "The computers have made our work easier to edit, easier to read, and they have even helped us to do our work faster." Using the computer further alleviated the concerns of students who had poor handwriting or who had difficulty with eye-hand coordination. Ruqayyah explained, "Using the computer I can read what I type better than what I write." Braiden similarly reported, "It has made things a lot easier for me. I don't have to worry about having messy handwriting."

After students revised and edited their poems, Mrs. Theisen made three copies of each so that students could have a copy of their poem to take home, a copy to be sent to Guy, and a third to be laminated and bound in a booklet for the class. The following are examples of the published poems:

Peace

Peace—is clouds in the sky
Peace—is a dove flying
Peace—is the snow on the ground
Peace—is a warmth in hearts
Peace—is a child smiling

So say, say the words of peace
it'll come to us and never cease.
Its not just a word

Peace—is Peace for everyone
Peace—is a kite flying
Peace—is a land with no borders
Peace—is laughter from a child
Peace—is a picnic under the sky

So say, say the words of peace
it'll come to us and never cease
Its not just a word.

Peace—is a joyful song
Peace—is a ballon sailing through the air
Peace—is a bird chirping joyfully
Peace—is a sun with its rays pointing up and down
Peace—is a home with happiness

So say, say the words of peace
it'll come to us and never cease
Its not just a word.

Mark

The Wrong Colors of the Gulf

Red—is for spilt blood.
Yellow—is for deathly sand.
Tan—is the color soldiers wear.
Black—is the guns.
Grey—is the color of warships.
White—is the color of sailors.

Jordan

How I Express Peace with Something Else that Has Color

My peace poem is made up of white hard rock candy, beautiful romances,
kisses and hugs, loveliness, kindness, a drug free word, everlasting skies,
suns, doves, positive actions, no negative, pain and soldiers coming home.
But Wait this batter has to have colors. It can't be black and white.

I'll have orchid for candy and I'll have carnation pink, thistle, yellow orange, wild strawberry and blue green for romances. I'll have red violet for loveliness and kindness and I'll have cornflower for a drug free environment. I'll have periwinkle for everlasting skies, golden yellow for the suns and silver for the doves and the positive and no negative actions. I'll mix forest green, green and black and all the colors for paint.

Melissa

After receiving their poems and letters, Guy wrote back:

Hello Mrs. Theisen,

I was very glad to receive the students letters and poems. It is nice of you all not to forget me already. I was happy to come back to Israel, but we had really a hard time during the war. A few missiles fell in the city of Haifa and this is where we live. We were all afraid and every time the alarm went on we entered into a sealed room and put on a gas mask. Which made it very hard to breath. I can tell you it is realy no fun but at least it is over now and I hope for ever. We saw the American soldiers which opporated the patriots, and they were very welcomed here. Now we are back at school after a long "vacation" because of the war. At the beginning it was difficult for me because I forget my Hebrew, but now step by step I am making progress. I really miss you all, my regards to all of you and hope we'll see each other again soon.
Yours,

Guy

Through this moving, expressive experience students understood their fears and anxieties about war, while being supportive to their former classmate, who was living in sealed rooms and breathing through a gas mask. They realized the importance of respecting others' viewpoints and the value of compromising so that the words of peace would "come to us and never cease."

USING COMPUTER COMMUNICATION IN A MULTICULTURAL PROGRAM

Computer communications enables students to communicate their thoughts and feelings to a real audience by using a computer network like a telephone exchange. Rather than transmitting information by voice, it transmits information in the form of text by means of a computer linked to a modem and telephone system. Three components are necessary for this form of communication between computers: (1) A modem for each computer, which allows one computer to communicate with a second computer either directly or via the telephone system; (2) software that controls the connection, transmission, and reception of messages through the modems; and (3) the telephone line, which connects the two modems.

Using computer communications provides a real-life experience with literacy, as students share ideas, personal experiences, and information with one another without the limitations of mail. The capability of storing and transmitting information quickly and easily to other locations at any time opens new avenues for global learning. Students can dialogue with other students around the nation and world and gain new knowledge about other cultures as they research and share information with their "computer pals" worldwide. While expanding their knowledge and experiences, they are developing communication competence and improving their attitudes toward reading and writing.

Electronic Dialogues

Mrs. Streeter and Mrs. Raglin use computers for electronic dialogues. Their fifth-graders are paired with graduate or undergraduate students at Eastern Michigan University. Each student in Mrs. Raglin's class is paired with an inservice teacher in the Reading-Writing Connection course; each student in Mrs. Streeter's class is paired with a preservice teacher in a course called Teaching Reading in the Elementary School. Each teacher-student pair is provided with an interactive conference connection used to conduct dialogues about multicultural books they are reading. These dialogues include (1) an introductory dialogue between the computer pals; (2) a general discussion about the book being read in the fifth-grade class; (3) a discussion of the characters in the book; and (4) a discussion about the book's plot or setting.

This system is very similar to dialogue journal writing, in which students comment about their reading and their teachers reply. Using this approach develops fluency because students are free to concentrate on what they are saying rather than on how they are saying it. The electronic "journals," however, provide each student with an audience for their thoughts, speculations, questions, and understanding through the highly motivating medium of the computer (Moore, 1991). This becomes a valuable activity for second-language learners because it involves functional and purposeful writing in a nonthreatening environment. At the same time, students learn about correct language patterns and forms through the model of their "computer pal."

Getting Started. Initial interactions on the conferencing system began with the teachers sharing some information about themselves and then sharing a biopoem that describes each person's interests, hobbies, and activities.

Aishia
Caring, musical, smart, understanding.
Relative of Cecelia Powell
Lover of skating, shopping, swiming.
Who feels loving, joy, peaceful.
Who needs clothing, money, and music instrument

> Who fears death loved ones dying, and being kidnaped
> Who gives love friendship, kindness.
> Who would like to see world peace, no drugs, kids roll the world.
> Resident of Ypsilanti.
> POWELL

The poem created many possibilities for future personal dialogues between the computer pals. For example, in response to Aishia's poem, her teacher wrote back:

AISHIA,
I REALLY LOVE YOUR POEM! What kind of musical instrument do you play? I always wanted to be able to play the piano. I can play a little bit but not well enough. You certainly sound like a lovely person. I'm happy to see that you would like to see world peace and an end to the drug problem. That really would make our world a better place to live wouldn't it? I'd better be going now. I'm looking forward to hearing from you again soon. Take care.

Certainly, Aishia's self-esteem was enhanced when she read, "You sound like a lovely person." As the dialogue continued, there were new opportunities for her self-esteem to develop. Discovering that someone valued what she said increased her motivation and interest in sharing her ideas clearly.

Discussing Books through Electronic Dialoguing.   After the teachers and fifth-graders became acquainted through the poems, the teachers shared with their computer pal what they enjoyed about the book *Search for Delicious,* by Natalie Babbitt—a story that takes place in the Middle Ages as the king searches for a definition of the word *delicious* in his dictionary. To initiate her dialogue, one teacher, Kim, wrote about her favorite part of the book:

Mary,
So how do you like the book that we are both reading? I really like it so far. My favorite part is when Gaylen bites into the apple and finds the walnut that Hemlock put there. That was a mean thing for him to do. I wonder if the mermaid is still trying to get back to her doll? What was your favorite part of the story?
I will talk to you soon!

At first many students made surface comments about the book, such as, "I like the book because it is funny." Teachers responded by agreeing the book was funny but going on to model effective communication by sharing what parts of the book were funny to them, referring to specific details or sections of the book. When students received their new messages affirming their ideas, they began to expand their responses, reflecting their teacher pal's use of specific details or examples from the book. This elaboration was illustrated in Luke's response:

I have changed my favorite character to Hemlock because he's the bad guy. Bad guys make the story not the good guys. You could have two bad guys and still have a story unlike good guys (unless they became partially bad.) This is my last message because I am moving out to the country.

Luke's response shows that he was thinking about characters and how authors engage the reader's interest in the story through characters and problems. When he writes his own stories, Luke might begin to experiment with the use of "bad guys" to make the story more interesting.

As the dialogue continued teachers modeled effective communication while asking students such questions as, "Who is your favorite character? Tell me why you like him" or "Does Gaylen remind you of someone you know?" or "I am surprised that Gaylen does not seem afraid to be traveling through the kingdom by himself. Do you think that the King should have someone ride with Gaylen? How would you feel traveling through the kingdom by yourself?" or "Did you like the setting or would you have the story take place somewhere else?"

When responding to their computer pals, teachers also sprinkled words of praise throughout the dialogue. For example, Lissa, a preservice teacher, began her entry to Greta, her fifth-grade pal, with, "I liked your poem very much. It would seem that we have a few things in common, for I also love the Lord and need him in my everyday life." Beverly shared, "I can see that you are a caring person. I pray for peace and especially for the innocent children and animals caught in the oil spill." Similarly, Rita built up Tony's self-esteem when she commented, "You are very wise and smart."

Students Take Control of Their Own Learning. Before long, students began to take control of their own learning as they asked their own questions and changed the direction of the conversation. For example, Greta asked her teacher, "What would you choose for delicious?" She further modeled her choice for delicious by commenting, "I would say my choice was hot chocolate with whipped cream after I have been outside sledding on a cold, cold winter's day." Students also began to initiate the direction of the dialogue, as illustrated by Matt:

Hi. We have finished The Search for Delicious. I didn't think their final choice was a good one. I mean come on, a lousy drink of water? I guies it makes a difference whether or not you're thirsty. The next book we're going to read is called the Whipping Boy. I've read that book Have you? Well, I gotta go. Bye!

Janicton began to feel so comfortable with her computer pal that she spontaneously commented,

Did you know that I was African are you any other culture? My fater is african I don't know what my fater looks like because he left because it didn't work out with them Do you know what your father looks like? Time to go! Au Revoir,

Relating Stories to One's Own Life and Experiences.   Throughout the experience, teachers and students explored the meaning of stories by relating the story to their personal experiences. Students began to see connections naturally between their own lives and the lives of the characters they were reading about. In her dialogue about another book, *Superfudge,* by Judy Blume, Bura explained:

> I like tha part when Fudge learns how to ride his bike do you like that part? I like that part because fuge gets all messed up when he fell off his bike. When I learned how to ride my bike I didn't fall off and get holes in my pants. When your learned how to ride a bike did you fall off? My old babysitter taught me how to ride my bike my mother didn't.

Or, in response to her teacher's question about a character in *Superfudge* called Peter, Latoya replied:

> If I was Peter I would not treat my brother or sister like that. I would spend more time with them. I would help them understand things.

Not only did students' comprehension of the stories improve through this experience, but so did their interest in reading and writing. As they realized learning had purpose and meaning, they were more willing to elaborate on their ideas, thoughts, and feelings. Students' responses expanded from one sentence to several sentences or a paragraph very quickly. As they perceived that someone valued what they had to say, their motivation and interest in sharing their ideas in clear, explicit ways increased. The elaboration of student responses over time is illustrated by Chih Ping's responses:

> 11/7
>
> I am enjoying Superfudge. My favorite character is Fudge. I like him because he is so funny.
>
> 11/21
>
> I think Peter's new house is real good because in Pine Grove the aprtments aren't as good. I have moved before. I just moved her and lived here like about two years. This is my second year in Chapelle. It also seemed hard for me at School. After I met Robert (one of my best friends) it became easy at school. He plays in band and I play in orchestra. I am good at playing in orchestra. I play a violin. Sometimes the teacher tells me to teach the violinist how to play a song (Violinist=people who way to play violin) while she taught other people how to play the guitar and a person how to play the viola.

Benefits to Students.   Both Mrs. Streeter and Mrs. Raglin commented that their students gradually wrote longer responses and used more examples and details to explain their ideas. Having the teachers' model of effective communication further contributed to the growth and refinement of students' communication skills. Students were never told that their responses were too general, that their responses lacked examples to support their ideas, that words were misspelled, that capitals were missing, or that they had run-on sentences. They began to acquire these writing techniques, however, by seeing the model of correct language used. Spontaneously, students began to imitate the teachers' language forms and patterns. They elaborated on their responses, including the use of examples and details or referring to teachers' spellings and sentence formations to express their ideas.

Having to learn keyboarding skills and computer communication systems, moreover, did not interfere with their ability to communicate. As students began to apply these techniques while communicating with their computer pals, their speed increased daily.

Perhaps Janicton's spontaneous response reflects the importance of providing computer communication experiences to all learners: "You seem very nice I can't wait until we meet in April. The thing I like about you is the way you talk and they way you tell about things that happen in the book." Janicton did get to meet her computer pal in April at a pizza party prepared by the undergraduate and graduate teachers. This culminating event finally provided teachers and students with an opportunity to talk to one another in person. Both teachers and students explained that the "mystery" of the partner's identity was a thrilling part of the experience.

Extending Computer Communications around the World. Mrs. Streeter and a fourth-grade teacher, Mrs. Kamoi, extended their students' experiences with computer communications by having them talk with students in England. Through computer communications, they corresponded with their computer pals, sharing information about their communities, their schools, their interests, and their hobbies. Mrs. Kamoi's students also learned about the geography and climate of England in connection with their geography unit. Mrs. Streeter's students learned about castles as they read *Search for Delicious.*

SUMMARY

We have described how students learn through playful, "delighted experiences," which include the use of technology. We demonstrated how technology can be used as a tool to: (1) support and enhance literacy and (2) broaden and extend cultural knowledge for all learners. We began with a rationale for integrating technology with a multicultural program, followed by specific strategies for helping students acquire keyboarding skills as they interact with computers.

After building a context for incorporating technology in our program, we described specific ways to integrate technology into the curriculum. First, we described how Multicultural Links, a hypermedia software program developed for our multicultural literacy program, can be used to extend students' and teachers' knowledge and understanding of diverse cultures, and we described how two teachers integrated

Multicultural Links with their curriculum. Then we discussed how word processing reinforces literacy development, especially of students from diverse cultures and linguistic backgrounds. Through vignettes, we further demonstrated ways to integrate word processing with the multicultural literacy program. Finally, we described how computer communication can be used to enhance students' comprehension of multicultural books they are reading and their writing performance as they explore written language with a real audience for their writing.

Through these examples, we illustrated how our students are learning to communicate—through trial and error and repeated exposure to language forms and patterns, without much correction from adults.

REFERENCES

Au, K. (1993). *Literacy instruction in multicultural settings.* Fort Worth, TX: Harcourt Brace Jovanovich College Publishers.

Ayersman, D., & Reed, W. (1993). *A theoretical and historical overview of learning styles and hypermedia environment.* Paper presented at a meeting of the Eastern Educational Research Association. Tampa, Florida.

Becker, H. (1984). *School uses of microcomputers: Reports from a national survey.* Unpublished manuscript, Johns Hopkins University Center for Social Organization of School, Baltimore.

Bialo, E., & Sivin, J. (1989). Computers for at-risk youth: A partial solution to a complex problem. *Classroom Computer Learning, 9,* 34–39.

Bork, A. (1987). Nonintelligent computer-based learning. *Contemporary Educational Psychology, 12,* 269–277.

Heath, S. B. (1983). *Ways with words.* Cambridge: Cambridge University Press.

Heath, S. B. (1989). Oral and literate traditions among black Americans living in poverty. *American Psychologist, 14,* 367–373.

Lefevre, C. A. (1970). *Linguistics, English, and the language arts.* Boston: Allyn & Bacon.

Marsh, E., & Kumar, D. (1992). Hypermedia: A conceptual framework for science education and review of recent findings. *The Journal of Educational Multimedia and Hypermedia, 1,* 25–37.

Min Liu (1993). *The effect of hypermedia assisted instruction on second language learning through a semantic-network-based approach.* Paper presented at a meeting of the American Educational Research Association. Atlanta, Georgia.

Minden, A. (1993). *A theoretical and historical overview of learning styles.* Paper presented at a meeting of the Eastern Educational Research Association. Tampa, Florida.

Moore, M. A. (1989). Computers can enhance transactions between readers and writers. *The Reading Teacher, 42,* 608–611.

Moore, M. A. (1991). Electronic dialoguing: An avenue to literacy. *The Reading Teacher, 45,* 280–287.

Moore, M., & Diamond, B. (1991). *A staff developmental model for promoting literacy and cultural awareness: A multicultural literature-based approach.* Paper presented at a meeting of the American Educational Research Association. Chicago, IL.

Peregoy, S., & Boyle, O. (1993). *Reading, writing, and learning in ESL.* New York: Longman.

Rudell, R., & Boyle, O. (1989). A study of cognitive mapping as a means to improve summarization and comprehension of expository text. *Reading Research and Instruction, 29,* 12–22.

chapter 9

Implementing a Multicultural Literacy Program: A Staff Development Model

OVERVIEW

Our major emphasis in this chapter is on the implementation of a multicultural literacy program in a school district. In-depth descriptions of our extensive staff development program, including detailed discussion of the content and organization of the inservices and visitation schedules, are provided so that other school districts can successfully begin similar programs.

The teachers in the program are from three school districts in southeastern Michigan, each with a unique population. One school district has a predominantly African American, economically disadvantaged population whose academic performance is ranked below average, with a small number of students performing above average. The second school district is a racially balanced, economically varied population whose academic performance is mixed, with a large number of below-average students. The third school district is a predominantly European American, economically advantaged population whose academic performance is ranked as above average, with a small number of below-average students. One of the important aspects of the program was to empower teachers in each of the three school districts to integrate multicultural literature with their reading/language arts program through an inquiry oriented decision-making approach. Therefore, the program began with staff development, rather than curriculum improvement.

We describe the teachers' professional growth, which, in time, resulted in the improved academic achievement of their students. Each of the teachers from the three districts brought to the program their own degree and depth of understanding about diverse cultures, teaching, and reading/writing instruction. Although most of the teachers volunteered to participate, several had been the victims of "friendly persuasion" by their administrators, who were supportive of the program. The needs and concerns of these teachers through all stages of implementation will be reported so that school district personnel can perceive the need for guidance and support during the implementation process. Quotations and comments from teachers and students are also provided to give the model credibility.

KEY COMPONENTS OF STAFF DEVELOPMENT PROGRAMS

> I have not observed a program with more potential than the Multicultural Literature Reading Program. It is having a long-lasting impact on the way people teach in our elementary schools.

> The response by the teachers has been tremendous. They have been excited and frequently shared their experiences informally with other teachers and through presentations to building staffs and at conferences.

These are direct quotations from administrators whose teachers are in our multicultural program. Their statements demonstrate the enthusiasm and interest of participating teachers. Their comments also reveal that teachers are not only modifying their teaching practice, but sharing the new strategies and techniques with other teachers in their schools or at conferences. Teachers participating in our program are asking questions, reflecting, and shifting the way they think about and practice teaching.

What is happening in the three school districts participating in our program, however, contrasts with what is happening in many other school districts. Researchers (Allington, 1990; Alverman & Ridgeway, 1990; Herrmann, 1990; Routman, 1991; Sparks & Simmons, 1989) report that changes in reading/writing practice remain minimal despite the dramatic increase in our knowledge of effective reading/writing instruction and learning. Similarly, in his investigation of programs designed to reverse the pattern of school failure among minority students, Cummins (1986) points out that compensatory programs remain unsuccessful. He reports that additional financial and professional support systems, compensatory preschool programs, myriad forms of bilingual programs, the hiring of additional aides and remedial personnel, and the institutionalization of safeguards against discriminatory assessment programs do not consistently demonstrate patterns of success for minority students.

School districts continue to plan staff development programs to improve the reading/writing instruction of students. The findings, however, indicate inadequate student improvement and persistent failure of the schools to meet the educational needs of culturally and linguistically diverse students and at-risk students. In their review of the research on staff development programs, Newman, Onosko, and Stevenson (1990) emphasize that making deliberate, fundamental changes in teaching strategies and techniques is extremely difficult. They further assert that supplying teachers with new curricula developed by national experts or offering periodic inservice workshops seldom leads to substantial long-term improvement. In fact, research frequently indicates that instructional programs have not been faithfully implemented or have been so modified that they hardly resemble the original (Alverman & Ridgeway, 1990; Conley & Tripp-Opple, 1990; Hall, 1979; Routman, 1991).

As these researchers emphasize, helping students become fluent, willing readers and writers remains one of the greatest challenges schools face. If we are to reverse these situations, there is a need to redefine our educational systems and the roles of educators, especially with respect to culturally and linguistically diverse students and communities (Au, 1993; Cummins, 1986). While working with teachers, administrators, parents, and teachers during the past three years, we have discovered several important components of staff development programs that promote change and professional development. These components, when utilized, might enable educators to implement similar multicultural literacy programs in their school districts. Through these efforts, all students, especially diverse students, improved their reading and writing performance, as well as their vocabulary development (Moore & Diamond, 1994).

Consistent with relatively recent research studies (Fullan, 1985; Hall, 1979; Saxl, Miles, & Liberman, 1988; Routman, 1991; Showers, Joyce and Bennett, 1987; Stevenson, 1987), we designed a staff development model that provides long-term technical assistance for teachers. We determined that we did not want to be prescriptive; we wanted to design a staff development model that was flexible and tailored to the context of the classrooms, the schools, and the community. We worked with teachers, administrators, parents, and students in their school districts to develop a multicultural literacy program. Using research to further design our staff development model (Diamond, 1991; Moore, 1988; Pisano & Tallerico, 1990), we incorporated the following components into our program.

1. **District Commitment.** For staff development programs to become successful, there is a need for district commitment from the program's inception. After this initial commitment, district administrators should demonstrate their support through funding sources within the district. Support for the program might include funding for (a) substitute teachers for inservice workshops conducted throughout the school year; (b) a teacher consultant to spearhead the planning and delivery of instruction for the staff; (c) staff to attend local, state, and national reading/writing conferences; (d) nationally known reading/writing experts to visit the district; and (e) credit toward advancement on the salary schedule or toward the purchase of educational materials and equipment for teachers who attend inservice workshops. Long-term commitment of time and resources over several years is critical if the district expects to achieve the desired outcomes. When teachers are confronted with tasks and expectations that differ from current practice, change will be slow (Crandall, 1983; Hall, 1979; Hord, Rutherford, Austin, & Hall, 1987).

2. **Voluntary Participation.** District-sponsored training in multicultural literacy instruction should be open to all staff members on a voluntary rather than mandatory basis. Beginning with a small group of teachers in one or two pilot schools enables district personnel to tailor the program to their teachers' needs and concerns. Following the implementation of the pilot program, project directors can make modifications and adjustments to maximize implementation of the program in new schools and classrooms. During subsequent years, more and more teachers will become interested in participating in the program as they perceive grassroots acceptance and

praise for the program by pilot teachers. According to Pisano and Tallerico (1990), a ripple effect will occur, and more teachers will voluntarily choose to become involved when a staff development program is truly of value.

3. **Inservice Workshops.** Inservice workshops should be scattered throughout the school year so that workshop content and organization can meet the changing needs and concerns of the teachers as they begin implementing the new program (Hall, 1979; Hord et al., 1987; Moore, 1988). Following the suggestions of Showers, Joyce, and Bennett (1987), the content of the inservice sessions should provide: (a) basic levels of knowledge or skills related to the new approaches; (b) opportunities for teachers to reflect on as well as perform the motions of teaching; (c) instruction that includes a presentation of theory, demonstrations of new strategies, initial practice sessions within the workshop, and prompt feedback about their efforts; and (d) opportunities to receive coaching from their peers or experts as they try the new ideas in their classrooms. (See Figure 9.1.)

4. **On-site Support and Assistance.** In addition to the inservice sessions, classroom visitations should be scheduled with teachers who are implementing an innovative program (Moore, 1988; Moore & Diamond, 1991). These visitations, which are scheduled twice a month during the implementation process, are arranged with experts or teacher consultants— teachers who have been instructed in coaching techniques by the experts. The experts or teacher consultants serve as peer coaches, who model and demonstrate lessons and provide ongoing support, analysis, feedback, and follow-up information about the program. Opportunities for teachers and support personnel to analyze what has occurred and how the instruction can be improved should be provided on a regular basis. Initially, teachers prefer that the experts or teacher consultants model or demonstrate lessons. After teachers become more comfortable with the program, more opportunities for collaborative teaching emerge. While experimenting and

FIGURE 9.1   Teachers share their ideas at an inservice session.

exploring with these techniques in their classrooms, teachers become more comfortable with the program and begin to adapt it to meet their classroom's needs more fully. Whether the teacher observes or is observed by the support teams should always be left to the teachers' discretion; they should never be required to participate in this follow-up opportunity (Pisano & Tallerico, 1990). Throughout, the experts and teacher consultants are facilitators or catalysts for new approaches and strategies, not supervisors or evaluators. These resource persons, who are always knowledgeable, visible, and accessible, must also be sensitive to the vulnerability of teachers, who fear poor performance with new instructional practices.

5. **Administrators' and Principals' Support.** For any staff development initiative to be successful, the school administrators and building principals must not only understand the program and its impact but must also support and encourage their teachers during the implementation process. To achieve this goal, administrators and principals must be consulted prior to the implementation of the program. They need to understand the program's rationale and the goals so that they can play a supportive role for their teachers, who are experimenting and exploring innovative teaching strategies. Essential to the success of a program is an environment that encourages experimentation and exploration and sustains reflective thinking and decision-making among teachers. Effective principals are collaborators, who share responsibilities and leadership with others in this supportive environment; they are also delegators, who carefully and thoughtfully identify and utilize available human resources to facilitate professional growth and development (Hord, et al., 1987). When principals and administrators demonstrate interest and assistance in the implementation of the program, staff development programs flourish.

6. **Parents' Understanding.** As school districts modify curriculum and instructional practices in the classrooms, parents need to be informed about the rationale for these modifications. They need to understand what these modifications will entail and how they can be a part of them both at home and at school. Parents who are recent immigrants or who speak English as a second language require additional support so they can be informed and involved in their child's education. Two important ways to enlist parental support include arranging parent meetings, where teachers demonstrate these innovative practices and strategies, and scheduling open houses or school programs, where students' work is displayed or performed.

7. **Continuous Follow-up.** Teachers who are considering new and different ways of providing instruction need opportunities to meet and discuss their successes and identify areas needing improvement. As teachers have opportunities to share their ideas and discuss the impact of the program on student performance, they become reflective decision-makers who tailor the program to meet the needs of their students and context of their classrooms. As they help one another discover solutions to problems and ways to modify instruction to improve student performance and attitudes, they become more supportive and committed to the program. And when they realize their abilities and potential to become actively involved in the de-

velopment of the program, they become more avid supporters who help new teachers to implement the program.

8. **Ongoing Monitoring System.** By incorporating an evaluation system, which is an ongoing process, staff development programs can foster academic success for students. After a framework has been constructed for program implementation, evaluation procedures can become tools for change as the program is adjusted and modified to meet the needs of the community, the classroom, and the students. The Concerns-Based Adoption Model (CBAM) represents an effective evaluation tool that defines program components by identifying teachers' concerns and needs and by monitoring program implementation (Hall, 1979; Hord, et al., 1987). Through the use of diagnostic tools, including tools to determine teachers' needs and concerns (Stages of Concerns Questionnaires) and their level of use (Levels of Use Interviews), personnel can decide how to use resources and provide intervention strategies to smooth the implementation process and minimize innovation-related frustrations among teachers.

IMPLEMENTING THE MULTICULTURAL LITERACY PROGRAM: OUR STORY

We applied the CBAM model to our program implementation. To meet the needs of the diverse populations of the three southeastern Michigan school districts, we designed our multicultural literacy program to be integrated with the traditional basal reading program. Using multicultural literature, we guided students through reading and writing activities, creative responses to literature, and cooperative learning groups.

Unlike traditional reading programs, this program incorporated the students' language and culture into the reading/writing curriculum to enable students to use their language and their experiences to generate their own knowledge. Examples of multicultural literature-based activities included: interactive reading and writing experiences, choral reading, reader's theater, mapping and knowledge-generating activities, writing in response to literature, interactive discussions, and creative responses to literature through art, music, or dramatizations. (Specific examples of these activities may be found in Chapters 4–7.) By focusing on multiple cultures, we hoped to bridge the gap between background knowledge and the content of the written texts of our students.

To accomplish our goals, we decided to follow a collaborative model involving the school districts and Eastern Michigan University. By integrating the expertise and knowledge of university personnel, school district administrators, and teachers, we designed a staff development program to be compatible with the sociocultural backgrounds and needs of the community, the school, and the specific classroom. First, we met with the superintendents, assistant superintendents, curriculum supervisors, and language arts coordinators in each of the three school districts. We shared our rationale and our goals for the multicultural literacy program, seeking their ideas and suggestions for ensuring the commitment of their teachers and other administrators.

Without hesitation, all administrators expressed an interest in participating in the program and agreed that participation should be voluntary. They provided the names of several principals they thought might be interested in the program and made several important suggestions, which we incorporated into our presentations to these individual principals.

Following these initial meetings, we arranged to meet with the principals to determine their interest in participating in the program. All the principals were enthusiastic and eager to have their teachers become part of the program. To ensure the success of the program during its first year, however, we decided to limit the number of schools and teachers that would be part of the pilot program in each school district. In an African American school district—which was the smallest district—we confined the program to two schools. One school would be part of the treatment group and the other part of the comparison group. In the larger, racially balanced, and predominantly European American school districts, we confined the program to four schools in each district. Two schools would be part of the treatment group and two part of the comparison group.

Once again, the principals shared additional ideas and suggestions to consider in our presentation to the teachers. They emphasized the need to demonstrate how the program might benefit the teachers personally as well as their teaching practice. We clarified these ideas in our handout, emphasizing the specific benefits to the teachers and students—the acquisition of multicultural books and materials, a teaching manual for their own personal use, and the opportunity to attend several inservice workshops. After conducting several interviews with fourth-grade teachers in these school districts, we identified 22 fourth-grade teachers to commit to the program. Eleven would become part of the treatment group and eleven part of the comparison group. We chose the fourth grade because this is the grade where comprehension difficulties surface as young readers and writers encounter longer and more expository and persuasive texts. Moreover, many culturally diverse students become more overtly disconnected from school and learning at this grade level.

District administrators played a key role in this phase of the program. They openly expressed their support of the program and helped us make contacts with principals and teachers quickly and easily. As we began our plans for the inservice sessions, they offered their building sites, materials, and resources for our use. They also provided funding for the substitute teachers to attend these inservice sessions during the school day. Of great importance, they attended some of the inservice sessions and participated in many of the activities with their teachers.

Year One

First Inservice.   The first inservice was a time to bring all the teachers from each school district together to help them gain ownership of the program. Consistent with the CBAM, we asked all of them to complete the open-ended Stages of Concern Questionnaire after initial introductory activities. This questionnaire, which enabled teachers to voice their concerns and needs about the innovative program, was used to plan the remaining inservice sessions. We selected appropriate materials, information, and procedures to help resolve or change these voiced concerns and needs during each successive inservice. Administering the questionnaire symbolized our sincere desire to design this program to match their needs and the needs of their students, communities, schools, and classrooms.

To help our teachers get better acquainted, we had them interview one another. All teachers paired off with a teacher they did not know and interviewed one another, following the biopoem format. Once the biopoems were complete, we shared them orally. We were all pleased to discover many similarities and differences among us. What a perfect introduction to the multicultural theme of our program!

After these activities, we discussed the philosophy, goals, and theoretical underpinnings of the program. (See Chapter 1.) Then we shared a variety of multicultural books and activities that teachers could use with their students. We wanted teachers to leave the inservice with one or two activities they could successfully try when they returned to their classrooms. Specifically, we modeled several reading and writing activities to be used with Peter Spier's book, *People,* and demonstrated how to conduct a choral reading activity, repeated reading activities, and reading response groups. We were eager to get the teachers "hooked" on the multicultural books and to help them see how these activities could easily be adapted to their classrooms, their teaching styles, and their students.

Throughout the inservice, we encouraged teachers to ask questions. They did! They asked about the African American dialect used in the books *Cornrows* and *Patchwork Quilt.* (Teachers had received 10 books to use with the multicultural program prior to coming to the inservice.) They also expressed concerns that some of their students might feel self-consciousness when books about their culture were discussed. They wanted to learn ways to elaborate on issues of racism and discrimination that might evolve as students read these books. To their surprise, many of the answers came from fellow teachers rather than from us. This became a significant learning experience for those who asked the questions and those who gave answers.

After the first inservice we felt that most of the teachers had accepted the program. The doubters, moreover, seemed more willing to consider the program. The majority of the teachers perceived the program as useful and applicable to their classrooms and one they wanted to implement. Some of the teachers' comments on the inservice evaluations were: "I can't wait to get started!" or "Best inservice I've ever attended."

The most rewarding outcome of the day, however, awaited us when we returned to our offices that evening. We had received notice that the grant we had submitted through the Fund for the Improvement and Reform of Schools and Teachers (FIRST), United States Department of Education, was accepted for funding. We had begun the program in good faith, using our own personal funds to purchase books and materials for the first inservice. Now we had the funds to implement the program successfully.

As an ongoing part of the program, we visited the 11 teachers and their classrooms twice monthly in order to support them in the implementation of the program. Even with the overwhelmingly positive responses to the inservice, we knew that teachers, especially the doubters, still had their own questions and concerns about the program. During these visitations, which were scheduled at times that were convenient to the teacher, we modeled and demonstrated lessons they were interested in seeing firsthand. Many teachers asked us to model the choral reading with their students; others asked us to demonstrate a writing activity with their students. These visitations, in addition to providing support for the teachers, gave us credibility. We demonstrated that we were able to teach students in the elementary grades effectively. The teachers began to see us in a new light, away from the "ivory tower." The doubters were reassured. In fact, many of the doubters became our strongest advocates during Year Two.

Second Inservice.   By the second inservice, which was scheduled in October, all the teachers were using the program in varying degrees and all were willing to share their successes as well as their concerns. During this inservice, teachers learned about reader's theater (*Flossie and the Fox* by McKissack); dramatic interpretations (*Knots on a Counting Rope,* by Bill Martin); how to integrate the KWL reading strategy with multicultural stories that included a historical figure (*A Weed is a Flower,* by Aliki) or a social studies theme (*The Popcorn Book,* by Tomie de Paolo); and ways to highlight cultural understandings and appreciation within their curriculum through cultural comparison activities. (See Cultural Feature Analysis.) There were also opportunities for small-group interaction with peers. During this time, they discussed activities that they were using and began to hypothesize future directions for the multicultural program within their curricula.

Following this inservice, we continued to schedule bimonthly visitations with teachers to assist them in implementing the program and to model and demonstrate lessons according to their expressed interests. We strove to encourage teachers to consider us as facilitators rather than supervisors who were dictating programs and the structure of the curriculum. We believed that teachers should become decision makers in charge of their instruction and curriculum. As we continued to visit the classrooms, we also began to co-teach lessons, while coaching teachers about various classroom management strategies and instructional techniques that optimize learning. Teachers spontaneously remarked: "This is the first time that I have heard Erica read with expression" or "Look at the poem Antone wrote . . . This is the first time he has ever written in class." Teachers quickly became convinced that these strategies were helping their students become readers and writers. These observations fueled their commitment and enthusiasm. (See Figure 9.2.)

Significantly, teachers also began to view students of diverse backgrounds in new ways. They acknowledged the importance of incorporating multicultural books and cultural perspectives in their literacy curriculum. They further realized that reading multicultural books helped these students improve their self-esteem and enabled them to connect their cultural and personal experiences with what they were reading.

Third Inservice.   By the third inservice, which was scheduled in January, teachers were ready to discuss important classroom management and organization techniques for a multicultural literature-based classroom. After teachers shared various multicultural activities they had designed to use with multicultural books acquired through the grant, we laid the theoretical foundation for cooperative learning groups and the role of cooperative learning in multicultural settings. We further modeled and demonstrated various organizational and management strategies to use with coopera-

FIGURE 9.2 Publishing is a wonderful way to build self-esteem, as shown by Antone, who proudly points to his story displayed in the hall for all to see.

tive learning activities. (See Chapter 11.) To help them acquire these new skills, we simulated several cooperative learning group activities related to reading, writing, and cultural themes, providing specific feedback and support. We modeled Predict-O-Grams with Demi's *Hallowed Horse;* story grammar with *Flossie and the Fox,* by McKissack, and *Mufaro's Beautiful Daughters,* by Steptoe; and note taking activities with *The Village of Round and Square Houses,* by Grifalconi. (See Chapter 4.) We also highlighted the writing process and the use of prewriting activities to improve writing performance (see Figure 9.3), and we modeled how to make cultural comparisons between African American and African folk tales.

During subsequent visitations, teachers continued to co-teach lessons with us. Many began to incorporate prereading and prewriting activities in their lessons, so that students worked on various projects over a two- or three-week span. We were excited to see that student interest and motivation persisted after one or two weeks. Teachers also perceived that their students were actively involved in the activities and that discipline problems were disappearing. Interestingly, a few teachers were comfortable teaching a lesson they had designed for us and sought constructive feedback about the lesson. We left the decision of whether we would observe them teaching up to the individual teacher, because we wanted to be considered facilitators and catalysts for change, not evaluators.

Fact Sheet

Descriptions of Old Naka

It was dark and smoke was rising from Old Naka. The days long long ago! The black night was split open like a coconut.

What did Old Naka do?

and one peaceful night Old Naka began to groan and rumble. Rose like the sun. Shout her anger to the sky. As red rivers flown down her sides. She stopped.

What did the villagers do?

lay down and pray, because they thought they did something wrong. They ran out of there houses. They lifted there heads. They trembled with fear. Went back to claim their homes. Rebuild the village.

How did the villagers feel?

They were frightened, they thought they did something wrong. Proud to be alive. They talked and laughed. Talk, laugh and sing.

HERRINGBONE CHART

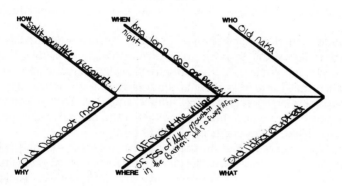

HOW — Split open like a coconut.
WHEN — long long ago one peacefully night.
WHO — Old naka
WHY — Old Naka got mad.
WHERE — In Africa at the village of Tos of Naka Mountain in the Bamton Hills of west Africa
WHAT — Old Naka erupted

OLD NAKA SPEAKS AGAIN

WEST AFRICA—Long long ago in the village of Tos, the women were cooking and the men were out hunting. It was a peaceful night when a big gush of wind came up. Old Naka began to groan and rumble and shouted her anger to the sky. Old Naka split open like a coconut and rose like the sun. Lava started flowing down the sides, looking like melted ruby's.

The villagers layed down and prayed because they thought they did something wrong. They lifted their heads and trembled with fear. Old Naka stopped and the villagers were covered with ashes. They stood up and everybody looked like little ghosts.

When the villagers went back to claim their homes, nothing was left but one round house and one square. The cheif directed that the women live in the round house and the men live in the square. The men planted yams and corn. The women prepared the food and the children cleared the stones out of the field. At the end they all had a feast and the women talked and laughed and the men told tales and stories.

Jason Reinertson

FIGURE 9.3 Fourth-graders use prewriting note taking strategies to record what happened as the volcano, Old Naka, erupted in the story, *The Village of Round and Square Houses,* by Grifalconi. Then students work in groups of three to write a newspaper article about Old Naka.

Fourth Inservice.   During the fourth inservice, in February, we refocused on the project goals. We shared strategies for extending students' cultural knowledge and highlighting cultural themes in the literature. Information about the African American, Native American, Japanese, and Chinese people was presented to help familiarize teachers with the various cultures. We also modeled and demonstrated techniques for relating cultural information to the literature through simulation activities, providing feedback and support as they tried the activities with peers. Finally, we modeled the revision process using the PQP formula (see chapter 5), and additional writing activities that might be incorporated into their multicultural program.

As we continued to visit classrooms, teachers became more willing to teach a lesson and have a shared dialogue about the outcomes. They were also much more involved in the cultural aspects of the program, seeking additional sources about the diverse groups the students were reading about. Many teachers assumed a proactive role as they described what they wanted to see when we demonstrated lessons.

Fifth Inservice.   By the final inservice, in March, teachers listened as we provided information but were eager to bring their own knowledge to the group, to discuss modifications and tell what their students had learned. Significantly, some teachers began to realize that there was more to understanding a culture than some of the more visible artifacts such as clothes, art, homes, and food. They began to express the need to learn more about the values and beliefs of the people, the important aspects of a culture that make people special and different.

To help the teachers reflect on the past year, its successes and potential problems, and to begin thinking about modifications for their program in the fall, we provided time for them to brainstorm in small groups about: (1) their perceptions regarding the successes of the program, (2) any potential problems they noted, and (3) possible modifications to consider for the next year. As teachers met in their groups, they realized that they wanted to ensure that their students would be able to continue the program in fifth grade. They began to brainstorm ways they could encourage other faculty members to become part of the program in the fall. They also saw a need to organize the program more fully. Many considered a thematic approach that would center on the various cultures or genres of literature. As they continued to discuss these ideas in their small groups, teachers saw how the various strategies they had been learning during the year could be adapted to any book or content area. Many expressed a desire to meet during the summer to make these adaptations and to connect the multicultural program to their social studies and science curricula as well. Once the small groups had formulated their ideas, we regrouped to share all our ideas. Enthusiasm and interest heightened as teachers recognized new potentials for the program.

Following these activities, we modeled strategies for using interviews, facilitating storytelling, and responding to poetry. We concluded the inservice with suggested guidelines for selecting multicultural books. In this way, teachers might become familiar with a wider range of books from the various cultures.

Perhaps the true mark of empowerment is the ability to influence others—particularly, in the case of teachers, the ability to empower their students. If this be the case, the teachers achieved that mark of success. They were taking ownership of the program and they were influencing their students' understanding of cultures and their attitudes about reading and writing. Perhaps these student comments reflect this direction:

- "I like these books because they have more to do with culture and the way things are in different lands and in history."
- "I think the multicultural program is fun and it's exciting because you get to learn new things. You get to learn about people you have never heard of and you get to learn about people you have heard of, like Harriet Tubman."
- "I love it because you can just imagine that you're visiting enchanted lands and you can go to any country in the entire world just by reading."
- "I've learned more this year than I have ever before."

Year Two

As we began Year Two, we used evaluation procedures—including formal and informal assessment measures—to guide and direct our staff development program. The results of data analysis of students' performance indicated that students using the multicultural program significantly improved their attitudes toward other cultures and writing. They also significantly improved their writing quality and performance on the California Achievement Tests (CAT) subtests, Total Reading and Vocabulary. The interviews further revealed that teachers and students were very enthusiastic and comfortable with the program. The findings (Moore & Diamond, 1991), therefore, confirmed that the staff development program was successful; changes and modifications would be made, however, to broaden our program to reach more students and teachers.

Getting Started during Year Two.   As we proceeded with our program during the second year, we continued to learn from our teachers and students. At the same time, our teachers and students became self-reflective decision makers as they looked to themselves for solutions and new directions.

Indeed, the fourth-grade pilot teachers did influence the fifth-grade teachers in their schools to become part of the program during the second year. As we visited each school to determine which fifth-grade teachers would become part of the program in the fall, we found that they were all eager and enthusiastic about participating. Significantly, they had fewer initial questions and concerns about the program and wanted to know when the first inservice would be scheduled.

Consistent with Pisano and Tallerico (1990), the ripple effect was taking hold— more and more teachers were interested in participating in the program. Teachers throughout the school districts heard our pilot teachers express their acceptance and praise for the program. Thus, as we interviewed principals and teachers, we found them eager to join. Unable to implement the program in all schools, we first interviewed teachers who had been part of our comparison group. We felt that these teachers had been very helpful to us during the past year, agreeing to let us interrupt their schedules briefly in September and May to administer pre- and posttests. Our pilot teachers' enthusiasm certainly became contagious, for all teachers in the comparison group were eager to begin. We were also able to convince their fifth-grade colleagues to agree to be part of the comparison group during Year Two.

Thus, the fifth-grade teachers in the pilot schools and the fourth-grade teachers in the comparison group during the first year formed our new group of teachers who would receive five inservices spread throughout the school year.

Modifying the Five Inservices for New Teachers.   We followed the same format for the five scheduled inservices during the second year. Modifications, which were minimal, stemmed from the feedback we received from our pilot teachers. We saw a need to emphasize the program's goals more clearly and to highlight the importance of connecting the cultural backgrounds of students with multicultural literature and other aspects of the curriculum. In terms of management, we provided separate inservices for our fourth-grade comparison group teachers and our fifth-grade teachers. This decision was made to accommodate the concerns of our principals — having six teachers from their building attend an inservice could be disruptive.

Additionally, we occasionally altered the order in which strategies were presented in the inservices, and we incorporated additional strategies that we felt corresponded more closely with the curricula. For example, we added String Storytelling activities, modeled by one of our first-year teachers, and strategies to use with multicultural novels. A handout with lists of books and additional teaching ideas was also prepared for them to add to their manuals.

Another significant modification for these inservices was the participation of our pilot teachers. We asked those teachers who were comfortable to attend each inservice to share some of their activities with the new teachers. For example, teachers shared how they created a Cultural Collage Map for their bulletin board or how they reinforced students' knowledge of cultural traditions through storytelling activities with string. Teachers also described how they reorganized their program to introduce a new culture each month or to integrate units across the curriculum, using a thematic approach to learning. Several teachers further explained how they used portfolios to assess their students' growth in reading and writing.

An additional important modification included having some pilot teachers model and demonstrate some of the multicultural activities for the new teachers during inservices. While modeling the activities, they were also able to share examples of their own students' reading and writing or videotapes of their class performing a choral reading or reader's theater. They also provided helpful teaching hints from their experiences, which might ensure a more successful learning format for the new teachers and students. The new teachers caught the visible enthusiasm and interest of the pilot teachers and their students and could not wait to return to their classrooms to try the activities with their own students.

By carefully planning time for these teachers to share and model their ideas and strategies for promoting cultural awareness and improving reading/writing performance, we found that our new teachers became more motivated to try similar activities in their own classrooms. Many of our new teachers were also able to think about organizational themes and plan their program around these themes. Similar to our first-year teachers, however, other new teachers were merely interested in learning the new strategies; they were not ready to organize or structure their programs yet. They needed time to experience teaching these strategies before they were ready to plan their programs around a theme. Nevertheless, each teacher knew that we were there to support and assist them as they began trying the new activities.

Modifying the Visitation Schedules   We continued to schedule bimonthly visitations with each of the new teachers at their convenience. But because the number of teachers increased significantly—we now had 41 teachers who were part of the program—we needed to enlist the help of school district personnel or pilot teachers to conduct these visitations. Not only would this help us to schedule these numerous visitations, it would also help each school district begin institutionalizing the program. In this way, the program could be continued once the grant terminated after Year Three.

By giving each school district a choice in how it would begin institutionalizing the program—by using personnel or pilot teachers who would become teacher consultants to conduct these visitations—we hoped that each district would feel comfortable tailoring the program to match its particular needs. One school district decided to use its language arts supervisor; the other two districts decided to use teacher consultants.

So that the three might become comfortable with their roles, we encouraged them to shadow us during our visitations in September and October. As we modeled lessons for other teachers, they observed our strategies and our culturally responsive discussions and interactions with students. They participated in the coaching activities as students worked in small groups, pairs, or individually. At the beginning and conclusion of each day, we emphasized specific strategies that we followed to develop cultural awareness or to gain the interest and enthusiasm of teachers and students. We also pointed out ways to support teachers who are trying innovative teaching techniques. After modeling various activities, we further discussed possible modifications while working with new classes.

Once the language arts supervisor and teacher consultants had a chance to see various strategies modeled, we encouraged them to try the techniques with new classes while we observed and gave them constructive feedback, following peer coaching techniques. After exchanging roles of demonstrating and observing lessons during these two months, the three became comfortable with the visitation format and began scheduling their own visitations with the new teachers.

Periodically, we teamed up with one another again during the course of the year to share lessons, ideas, and techniques we had each developed. We also provided one another with constructive feedback about techniques that we felt needed more polishing, methods of heightening students' cultural awareness, and ideas for extending and improving student/teacher interactions. Certainly, a collaborative model between the university and the school district was evolving!

Inservices for Pilot Teachers.   We felt the need to continue our contacts with the pilot teachers during Year Two. To help our teachers continue this year successfully, we planned three inservices and visited each classroom once a month, always expressing our willingness to schedule additional visits as needed.

These inservices were organized to give teachers time to share and collaborate with one another as they extended and developed the multicultural program and integrated it with other content areas. Two teachers, for example, shared how they were integrating a Native American thematic unit across the content areas. They brought numerous books to show how they were integrating the theme with their social studies and science curricula, as well as math, reading, and language arts. They also displayed examples of student work across the content areas. All teachers brought samples of their student's writing, artwork, or reading so that their peers might see how to implement similar activities within their own classrooms.

To help teachers see ways to incorporate novels in their program, we also modeled such activities as the Opinion/Proof activity with *Sadako and the Thousand Paper Cranes,* or the story grammar frames with *Song of the Trees.* (See Chapter 4.) We introduced more specific ways to incorporate cultural appreciation and understanding in the program. Using Multicultural Links (see chapter 9), for example, we modeled how computers can be used as tools to enhance cultural knowledge. Teachers were pleased to see how easily they could access maps of areas being studied; pictures of people, locations, or artifacts; recordings of folk songs and familiar phrases in different languages; and information about cultural lifestyles, and customs, natural resources, the earth's natural features, and natural phenomena.

Year Three

Similarly, as we began Year Three, we used evaluation procedures to guide the development of our staff development program. Consistent with the findings for Year One, data analysis indicated that students using the multicultural program significantly improved their reading and writing performance. Interview data similarly revealed that teachers and students were very enthusiastic and comfortable with the program and that teachers were moving to higher levels of using the program (Moore & Diamond, 1992). Because the findings consistently confirmed that the staff development program was successful, changes and modifications were made to broaden and institutionalize the program in the three school districts.

Getting Started during Year Three. As we proceeded with our program during the third year, we found that we were all—project directors, teachers, and students —learning and growing together. Our teachers and students were becoming decision makers in charge of their own learning.

The ripple effect described by Pisano and Tallerico (1990) persisted in all three school districts during Year Three. The rejoined efforts of our pilot teachers and the new teachers influenced sixth-grade teachers to become part of our program. In fact, they began asking when their first inservice would be before we began the interviews! Similarly, our comparison fourth-grade teachers influenced their fifth-grade colleagues to become part of the program. We soon realized we were receiving more requests than we could accommodate.

Again, after interviewing the fifth- and sixth-grade teachers in the schools that were part of our program, we felt that the teachers who were part of the comparison group should be interviewed next. The overwhelmingly positive responses from these three groups of teachers increased the teachers in the program to 73.

Modifying the Five Inservices for New Teachers.   As in Year Two, we followed the same format we had developed during Year One for the five scheduled inservices. Modifications were minimal. We invited more teachers, including the second-year teachers, to attend these inservices in order to share various strategies, ideas, and methods of implementing the program in their classrooms. One teacher explained how to organize the program with a multicultural theme for each month. Other teachers demonstrated how they organized their program to follow a thematic approach, drawing comparisons and parallels among the cultures. These teachers brought samples of their students' artwork, writing, and reading activities to explain how the program integrates so well across the content areas. Two teachers further modeled ways Chapter I teachers and classroom teachers might work together within the classroom setting, using reader's theater, choral readings, and writing.

Our new teachers, seeing how their peers implemented the program, were encouraged to take risks and try these techniques to promote literacy performance and multicultural understandings. Like the teachers in Year Two, many of our new teachers were quick to organize their program around thematic units. Other teachers were merely getting a flavor of the program, experimenting with these new teaching techniques. Again, each teacher knew that we were there to support and assist them at their own levels of implementation.

Modifying the Visitation Schedules.   Following the visitation format from Years One and Two, bimonthly visitations were scheduled for all new teachers at their convenience. They always determined the content of the demonstrated lesson and became co-teachers of lessons as their comfort zones increased. All Year One and Two teachers received visitations once a month, unless there were special requests. As the numbers of teachers grew, we became more dependent on the school districts to provide support for these visitations, using either school district personnel or teacher consultants. One district decided to create a position for a lead teacher, who would work with the language arts supervisor and continue the program full-time after Year Three; the other two districts decided to continue using teacher consultants. By encouraging the school districts to assume part of this role, we felt the program would be continued after Year Three.

Continuing the process developed during Year Two, the new personnel shadowed us during our visitations in September and October and became familiar with the process. Once this was accomplished, they began scheduling their own visitations in November. Throughout, we provided debriefing time to point our specific approaches to literacy learning, responses to students, and strategies to support and assist new teachers in the use of the multicultural program. Possible modifications for lessons to enhance participation of all learners were also discussed.

Inservices for Year One and Two Teachers.   Maintaining our contacts with Year One and Two teachers was a priority during Year Three. We planned three inservices for these teachers, whom we felt would be instrumental in assisting district personnel as they continued the program after Year Three. We continued to share our recent developments of *Multicultural Links* and demonstrate ways *Links* could easily be used to enhance the multicultural program. We also introduced reflection activities, asking our teachers to brainstorm (1) the successes of the program, (2) the problems they perceived or anticipated, and (3) new directions to consider or solutions to problems. These activities guided teachers' decisions to integrate the program more fully with the content areas and to extend it to additional grades and schools within their districts. They also realized the need to gain more cultural knowledge and to discuss ways of facilitating cultural understanding with their classrooms.

To help teachers consider ways to incorporate the program into the curriculum more fully, we provided time for them to work in small groups. During this time they developed thematic units to correspond with their curriculum across all subject areas, using their social studies, science, math, and language arts curriculum guides. They also developed more choral readings and reader's theater (see Chapter 4) to be used with their thematic units. These thematic units were then retyped to be distributed among all teachers.

To extend cultural knowledge and understanding, we invited guest speakers from the community to share their cultural heritage and traditions. Following these presentations, teachers worked together to develop ways to incorporate this new material into their curriculum and to extend their students' cultural knowledge and sensitivity. At the conclusion of each inservice, we also gave teachers time to reflect on their practices and to share activities they had developed in their classrooms.

FACILITATING THE CHANGE PROCESS
WITHIN STAFF DEVELOPMENT PROGRAMS

Historically, educators strive to restructure curricula and modify instruction to optimize literacy. Innovations involved with instructional strategies and curricula, however, frequently fail (Hord, et al., 1987). Determining whether these innovations failed because of faulty concepts and processes or inadequate implementation of the innovative program remains vague. Too often, program directors and administrators assume that once an innovation is introduced and initial inservice instruction is complete, teachers will begin implementing the program as designed. Guesswork and intuition, however, need not be the tools for assessing implementation of the program. Using the CBAM provides opportunities to monitor the implementation effort to ensure that changes can be made to accommodate the teachers and students and their needs and concerns. The following section describes how we incorporated the Concerns-Based Adoption Model (CBAM) into our staff development program to facilitate implementation of our multicultural program.

Addressing the Process of Change through the CBAM

The CBAM, which is client-centered, offers ways to assist teachers as they begin implementing innovative programs as well as ways to evaluate the progress of the implementation effort (Hall, 1979; Hall & Hord, 1987; Hord, et al., 1987). According to Hord et al. (1987), there are a number of assumptions about the process of change that form the basis of the CBAM. These assumptions, which provided the foundation of our staff development program, include:

1. **Change as a process, not an event.** Change is a process that occurs over time, usually a period of several years.
2. **Individuals as the focus of change.** Because change affects people, their role in the process of change is critical. Individuals, therefore, need to be the focus of attention throughout the implementation of the program.
3. **Change as a personal experience.** Individuals react differently to change. Some people assimilate new practices more rapidly than others; some people engage in the process more readily than others. By tailoring responses and interventions to the diagnosed personal needs of individual users, we can smooth the implementation process.
4. **Change as a developmental process.** As individuals have more experiences with the innovation, they demonstrate growth in terms of their feelings and skills. Facilitators can guide and manage this developmental change by designing intervention strategies that correspond to individuals' diagnosed needs and concerns.
5. **Understanding change through operational terms.** Individuals relate to change according to what it means to them personally or how it will affect their current classroom practice. By addressing their questions, needs, and concerns in concrete, practical terms, facilitators can communicate more effectively with their clients and minimize their resistance.
6. **Focusing on individuals, innovations, and the context.** Too often emphasis is placed on new curricula, materials, equipment, or books. Only people, however, can make changes as they alter their behavior. Facilitators who are adaptive and systemic, designing and altering interventions to fit the client, the community, and the school, will shape the implemented change process to foster academic improvement. The important factor is support and assistance to accommodate the change process.

Using the CBAM as a Diagnostic Tool

To eliminate guesswork and intuition in our program, we applied the CBAM as a tool to identify the support and assistance that we needed while introducing change in teaching practices and monitoring implementation of our multicultural program. The tool, which is based on the premise that the people, rather than the innovation, are the most important factors in the change process, helped us identify and describe various concerns and needs our teachers experienced during change efforts. Through a questionnaire, which can be an informal interview; an open-ended statement questionnaire (Newlove & Hall, 1976); or a pencil and paper questionnaire (Hall, George, & Rutherford, 1979), project directors have a resource system that enables them to promote this change process. Figure 9.4 illustrates the open-ended questionnaire that we used in our program.

Stages of Concerns

Through extensive research, Hall (1979) and Hord et al. (1978) have identified seven stages of concerns that users, or potential users, may have as they begin implementing an innovative program. These Stages of Concern (see Figure 9.5), which are

Name (Optional)_____	RESPONSE SHEET
It is very important for continuity in processing this data that we have a unique number that you can remember. Please use: Last 4 digits of your Social Security #	WHEN YOU THINK ABOUT A Multicultural Literacy Program WHAT ARE YOU CONCERNED ABOUT? (Do not write what you think others are concerned about, but only what concerns <u>you</u> now.) Please write in complete sentences and please be frank.
____ ____ ____ ____	
The purpose of the open-ended question on the next page is to determine what people who are using or thinking about using innovations are concerned about at various times during the innovation adoption process.	(1)
Please respond in terms of <u>your present concerns</u>, or how you feel about your involvement or potential involvement with the innovation of a <u>Multicultural Literacy Program</u>. We do not hold to any one definition for this innovation, so please think of it in terms of your own perceptions of what a multicultural literacy program involves. Remember to respond in terms of <u>your present concerns</u> about your involvement or potential involvement with a <u>Multicultural Literacy Program</u>.*	(2)

(3) |
| Thank you for taking time to complete this task. | Please put a check by the statement that concerns you most. |
| *Adapted from: Procedures for Adopting Educational Innovations/CBAM Project R & D Center for Teacher Education, the University of Texas at Austin. | |

FIGURE 9.4 Open-ended questionnaire used in our multicultural literacy program.

developmental in nature, vary as the implementation of a program progresses. The developmental nature of concerns is further reflected in three dimensions—self, task, and impact. During the early stages of implementation, teachers typically have many self-concerns. They want to know more about the innovation, what type of preparation will be involved, or how it is supposed to work. Teachers may also have concerns about their ability to execute the innovative program and about their personal knowledge and information about components of the program.

Once the program is under way, many task concerns also evolve. Teachers wonder about the availability of resources and materials, how to organize and manage their time to acquire new skills and materials, how to find time to integrate this program into an overcrowded curriculum, or how to evaluate and assess the program.

As teachers continue using a new program and become more comfortable with it, they shift to impact-related concerns. They are concerned about the impact of the

---

0 Awareness: Individuals show little concern about the innovation.

1 Informational: Individuals indicate a general awareness of the innovation and an interest in learning more about the innovation.

2 Personal: Individuals indicate an uncertainty about the demands of the innovation, their ability to meet the demands, and their roles regarding the innovation.

3 Management: Individuals focus their attention on the processes and tasks of using the innovation. Issues include efficiency, organizing, managing, scheduling, and time.

4 Consequence: Individuals focus on the impact of the innovation on students. Issues include evaluation of students' performance and attitudes and changes needed to improve performance and attitudes.

5 Collaboration: Individuals focus on ways to coordinate and share the use of the innovation with others.

6 Refocusing: Individuals focus on exploring major changes in the existing innovation.

FIGURE 9.5 Stages of Concern, adapted from *Procedures for Adopting Educational Innovations/CBAM Project,* by S. Loucks, B. Newlove, and G. Hall, 1975. R & D Center for Teacher Education, the University of Texas at Austin.

program on student performance and what can be done to improve the effectiveness of the program. Some teachers express concerns about time to collaborate with others to improve the program; a few teachers might wonder how to modify the program to reach more of their students.

Only a few teachers, however, achieve these highest stages of concern— Consequence, Collaboration, and Refocusing. Teachers advance to new stages as their concerns are reduced and they become comfortable with the program. Even though self- and task concerns have been addressed, new self- and task concerns emerge as teachers become implementers of the program. Movement through these stages of concern, however, cannot be forced; they can merely be facilitated through assistance and support. The more complex the innovation, the more important it becomes to attend to the needs and concerns of teachers by providing help and encouragement. As each individual's pattern of concerns varies, there is a further need to individualize interventions to correspond to each participant's needs and concerns in the setting—the classroom—in which the change occurs.

Adapting the CBAM to our Multicultural Literacy Program

We incorporated the CBAM into our staff development program. Following the advice of Hord et al. (1987), we first identified principals and teachers who might be interested in participating in the program. We emphasized that participation was voluntary for all principals and teachers, because we believed that those teachers who were hesitant to begin the program needed time and space to determine whether they would like to become part of the program. If they wanted to wait until the second or third year before joining the program, we accommodated their wishes.

During our first inservice (see "Implementing the Multicultural Literacy Program: Our Story" section of this chapter for more specific detail), we administered Newlove and Hall's open-ended statement questionnaire. We used this form because we felt that if our teachers were able to express their concerns and needs in writing, they might realize our sincere desire to tailor the program to meet their needs and concerns.

Figure 9.6 reveals teachers' statements, which include many self-concerns and task and management concerns, about the multicultural program at the beginning of the year. Figure 9.7 demonstrates how their needs and concerns shifted. As their self-concerns and task concerns were reduced through our intervention strategies during inservices and classroom visitations, teachers advanced to impact-related concerns at the Consequences stage of concern. Figure 9.8 shows how many teachers' concerns progressed to the Collaboration and Refocusing stages during Year Three. We discovered that our inservices and in particular our classroom visitations provided the support and assistance required for facilitating the change process.

FIGURE 9.6 Examples of pilot teachers' statements about their needs and concerns at the beginning of Year One.

Informational Concerns

- This was not given to me as a choice—I was just told to be here and I don't know much about it.
- My self confidence is low. Please help.
- I would like to see some modelng before I try it myself. I am a "show me" person.
- We are presently bound to a basal reading program.
- Our school board is not too receptive to new approaches if they are not theirs.
- I would like to move to a multicultural literature-based program.

Personal Concerns

- I need to learn more about the background of the various cultures.
- I am concerned about properly answering the children's questions pertaining to unfamiliar cultures.
- I'm completely open as to learning different methods in exposing my students to this approach to reading.
- I feel that this program could only add more to my knowledge and practices in my classroom.
- I am concerned about learning how to implement a good Multicultural Literature Program that includes both the reading and writing involvement.

Management Concerns

- I feel a lack of materials for use in the classroom.
- I am concerned about the resources required to implement and continue such a program.
- Time and materials are a problem.
- I am concerned about the cost of this program.
- A concern of mine is finding the time to do everything I think this project is expecting me to do.
- How should this program be graded for report cards?
- How much time out of the classroom will this program entail?

Consequence Concerns

- I am concerned about helping my students to learn and appreciate the differences between people.
- My concern is helping increase the self-esteem and confidence of my students.
- My concern is promoting my students' knowledge and understanding of other cultures and the differences among these cultures.
- I am concerned about being able to target all of the reading levels and abilities in my classroom.
- I am concerned about leaving out a culture that might be beneficial to my students.
- I am concerned about stereotyping certain aspects of a culture to my students.
- I am hoping that my students will make great gains from using this program.

FIGURE 9.7 Examples of pilot teachers' statements about their needs and concerns during Year Two.

Designing Interventions to Accommodate the Concerns and Needs of Teachers

How did we help our teachers progress through these Stages of Concern? Once we had enlisted teachers' interest in participating in the program, we identified their concerns and needs during our first inservice. Then we designed inservices that responded to these concerns and needs and to the evolving concerns and needs during each subsequent year. Specifically, some interventions we followed to help teachers move through the Stages of Concern included:

FIGURE 9.8 Examples of pilot teachers' statements about their needs and concerns during Year Three.

Collaboration Concerns

- I am concerned that the program will not be continued in the next grade.
- It would be very helpful to categorize the books, per grade level, by the different cultures.
- Another concern is not knowing for sure which activities my students have done the previous year so that I can either skip them or adapt them to be appropriate for this year.
- When I think about the MLP, I am concerned that not enough people are exposed.
- I think this should be a mandatory program for new teachers and teachers already in the system.

Refocusing Concerns

- I am concerned about putting the computer into use with the Multicultural Program more.
- I am concerned about knowing what is going on in other classrooms. Perhaps a newsletter?
- I would like to develop a program for writing—especially editing and revising—that is organized and specifically structured.
- I am concerned about administrative support for inservicing. The inservices are invaluable and important. Administrators need to know and understand this.
- I think this is an excellent program to bridge the reading and social studies curriculum and the reading and writing curriculum, using a whole language approach.

1. **Stage 0—Awareness Concerns**
   a. We met with principals to explain our program and its goals and objectives to determine interest in piloting the program. Two brief handouts were provided to help focus their attention and interest.
   b. We met with teachers to explain our program, its goals and objectives, and our expectations, to determine interest in piloting the program. Once again, we provided teachers with handouts to help focus their attention and interest. We also encouraged teachers to ask any questions they might have about the program.
   c. During the second and third years, we encouraged teachers to talk with other teachers who had participated in the program during the first year.
2. **Stage 1—Informational Concerns**
   a. Through the use of overhead transparencies, we presented a rationale for the program. Following this presentation, we described our program through the use of slides that portrayed teachers and students participating in the various activities that are part of our program.
   b. During Years Two and Three, we invited former teachers to our inservices to share how they are using the multicultural program. These teachers also participated in the inservice, modeling several activities for our new teachers.
3. **Stage 2—Personal Concerns**
   a. Using the information from the open-ended statement questionnaire, we identified each teacher's needs and concerns. We provided encouragement and support to teachers who were not yet comfortable with the program goals and their role in the program.
   b. During classroom visitations, we spent time with each teacher, encouraging teachers to ask questions and discuss their feelings about the program. These miniconferences were usually conducted before school, after school, or during the teacher's free period.
   c. We praised our teachers throughout, focusing on our informal observations about their classrooms, their students, and their teaching styles. We also encouraged our teachers as they began to take risks and try various activities or create their own.
4. **Stage 3—Management Concerns**
   a. During our inservices, we modeled management strategies to follow as they implemented various activities through simulations. After modeling the strategies at the inservices, we demonstrated the activities in their classrooms during our visitations. As we worked with them, we further highlighted our management techniques for maintaining attention and classroom control.
   b. During our classroom visitations, we modified management and organizational strategies to match each classroom situation. Teachers also worked with us, helping us identify strategies that were most effective for their teaching styles and students.
   c. During our inservices, we provided time for our teachers to discuss their problems and derive solutions. We further encouraged them to ask

questions throughout the day and planned time for group reflection and sharing so that they could become supportive of one another.

d. We helped our teachers build classroom libraries of multicultural books with funds from our grant. We also began building a library of additional resources at the university. It included books and materials requested by teachers or recommended through other sources. As teachers began working on activities related to a theme, we brought these sources to inservices for them to check out, or we brought them to their classrooms during scheduled visitations.

e. We assisted teachers in planning and presenting the multicultural program at parent meetings so that parents might become more fully informed and possibly provide additional funds for the purchase of multicultural materials.

f. We worked with teachers to develop a class list of books for each grade level, grades four through six.

5. **Stage 4—Consequences Concerns**

a. We provided opportunities for teachers to share activities they had developed for classroom use. These activities were also put together into a Teacher's Manual.

b. During Years Two and Three, teachers were given time within their inservices to develop activities and organize thematic units to be used with their classes. Teachers were encouraged to further integrate these activities with their social studies and science curriculum wherever possible.

c. Teachers were encouraged to visit one another's classrooms to share their skills with others.

d. Teachers presented the program to other teachers from throughout the state at the Michigan Reading Association Conference and nationally at the International Reading Association Conference. While attending the conference, they were able to go to other sessions related to the multicultural program.

e. Teachers were given praise and support as they took risks, trying innovative strategies.

6. **Stage 5—Collaboration**

a. We assisted teachers who were planning inservices for other teachers in their school buildings. In particular, many teachers at the lower-elementary grade levels were interested in beginning a multicultural program.

b. We made joint presentations with our teachers about our multicultural program at local, state, regional, and national conferences.

c. We worked with teachers as our colleagues, modeling peer coaching techniques to be used when they assumed their roles as teacher consultants. These teachers modeled lessons, co-taught lessons, and discussed ways to organize and manage the program to be consistent with the curricula.

d. We encouraged teachers to present activities or thematic units they had created with new teachers at our inservices.

7. **Stage 6—Refocusing Concerns**
   a. We supported and encouraged teachers who were adapting the program to fit their curricula.
   b. We helped channel their ideas and energies in directions that would be productive.
   c. We encouraged teachers to share their concerns about the program and to act on these concerns.
   d. We helped teachers access resources to refine their ideas and put them into practice.
   e. We encouraged and assisted teachers who were interested in writing grants to receive funding for resources they might need to implement their modifications of the program.

MONITORING IMPLEMENTATION OF INNOVATIVE PROGRAMS WITH THE LEVELS OF USE

Another CBAM diagnostic tool is the Levels of Use (LoU). The LoU is a tool that operationally describes the behaviors of the users of an innovative program during the various stages of implementation. The tool does not focus on attitudinal, motivational, or affective aspects of the user nor does it explain causality; the tool operationally defines what the user is doing. Using the LoU avoids the serious mistake administrators and project directors frequently make of assuming that once an innovation is introduced and initial training has been completed, users will implement the program as designed. In their extensive research, Hord et al. (1987) emphasize that implementation of an innovative program varies among individuals. Some individuals do not use the innovation, even months or years after its introduction; others try to use it, but struggle; still others use it in a disjointed fashion, or in a routine fashion; some use it with efforts toward increasing its effectiveness. Experience, coupled with support and assistance, are needed to ensure that individuals develop high-quality use of an innovation.

Loucks, Newlove, and Hall (1975) identified eight distinct Levels of Use. (See Figure 9.9). Each level, which includes a range of operationally defined behaviors, is limited by a decision point at which actions move an individual to the next level. Determining an individual's LoU is accomplished in a focused interview, conducted by an interviewer trained in the administration of the instrument, and with the help of a chart that is completed with the information from the interview. Combined with observations and informal questioning, the chart and interview give the facilitator information that can be used to guide change.

Using the Levels of Use in Our Multicultural Program

We found the Levels of Use to be invaluable in our multicultural program. By having a consultant conduct the LoU interviews we were able to gain new insights, which guided our actions during Years Two and Three.

The first interviews were conducted at the conclusion of our first year, in May. Our interviewer commented that he was impressed by the teachers' enthusiasm about the program. He further noted that all teachers were very comfortable with the program at Level IVA, a Routine Level of Use. Unlike other innovative programs (Hall,

LEVEL 0:   Users have little knowledge about the innovation. They are not involved with the inno-vation; they are not taking steps toward becoming involved.

LEVEL I: Users have acquired or are acquiring information about the innovation. They are ex-ploring its value and its demands.

LEVEL II: Users are preparing for first use of the innovation.

LEVEL III: Users focus their efforts on short-term, day-to-day use of the innovation with little re-flection. Users are attempting to master the tasks required for using the innovation, frequently resulting in disjointed and superficial use of the innovation.

LEVEL IVA: Users are comfortable with the program, making few changes in the innovation. They do not focus their efforts on improving the innovation and its consequences on stu-dents' performance.

LEVEL IVB: Users vary the innovation to increase its impact on student performance. These varia-tions are based on knowledge of short- and long-term consequences.

LEVEL V: Users coordinate their own use of the innovation with colleagues to provide a collec-tive impact on students' performance. They plan specific actions to increase the im-pact of the innovation on more clients and sharing the innovation with others.

LEVEL VI: Users reevaluate the use of the innovation, seeking major modifications or alterna-tives to the innovation. They plan activities to enhance or replace the innovation.

FIGURE 9.9   Levels of Use, adapted from *Procedures for Adopting Educational Innovations/CBAM Project,* by S. Loucks, B. Newton, and G. Hall, 1975. R & D Center for Teacher Education, the University of Texas at Austin.

1979; Hord et al., 1987), our teachers were using the program and feeling comfort-able with it. For example, Hord et al., reported that 75 percent of the teachers in their project were at Level III or below. They added that 50 percent of the teachers in many other projects were not using the innovation, even after its second year. Our teachers, however, had progressed to this high level of use after one year.

After the second year, our interviewer claimed, "In the 15 years I have been interviewing over 200 teachers across the country who have implemented over a dozen different innovations, I have never encountered the level of enthusiasm, under-standing, and commitment to a project as I have with Drs. Diamond and Moore's project." He continued, "In addition, teachers believe that their students are (1) im-proving their reading speed and comprehension, (2) reading more, (3) enhancing their writing performance, and (4) gaining greater understanding and appreciation of other than Euro-American culture." The results of his interviews during the second year indicated that some teachers were at Level IVA, a Routine Level of Use, and other teachers were at Level IVB, a Refinement Level of Use.

HELPING TEACHERS AS THEY TAKE CHARGE OF LITERACY INSTRUCTION

In general, to facilitate the change process, we attempted to remain flexible and supportive of our teachers as they began implementing the program. We further tried to create opportunities for our teachers to take charge of their learning and to become decision-makers who modify literacy instruction to match the context of their classrooms and the needs of their students. Using the CBAM enabled us to foster the professional growth and development of our teachers. The following comments made by teachers and administrators demonstrate their professional growth and development:

- The strength of the program is learning all different kinds of strategies and being able to use them not only with multicultural books, but any books I open up and read to my class.
- If I didn't do exactly as I was prescribed to do, I thought I might be disciplined for that . . . I don't worry about that anymore.
- They are great facilitators. Many times all teachers need is a structured program and then they can be creative from that point.
- This multicultural program has allowed us to not only be exposed to structured program, but also allowed us to be creative, and also allowed our students to be creative and they really enjoy this program.
- It is a very flexible program which matches the needs of the given class.
- I don't feel like if I decide to do something that they have suggested in the book that I have to follow every little step in there. I can make any changes in this, or do it the way I want. Knowing my own classroom, there are certain ways that they may suggest to do — something that I know is not going to work. Sometimes I can see that something else will work better.
- I've used the activities with any kind of literature and with social studies and science.
- Rather than ordering ditto books or blackline masters to use with stuff, now I spend all my time looking through catalogs and looking for multicultural books I can purchase for my classroom.
- I think that this program is successful because it doesn't matter whether you're in special education, learning centers, or you're a high reader. It doesn't matter where you fall; everyone can do this; everyone can get interested in it. The proof of that is that my learning center kids are reading to first graders from books that they normally had not been reading, over and above the basal.
- I have two students this year who were nonreaders when they entered the class. Now look at them, they both are reading on a fourth grade level. I can't keep these books out of their hands . . . It's like the secret to reading has been unlocked. This program is really working.
- My students were self-conscious when the word *Black* was mentioned. Now they talk openly about their culture and feel proud of their cultural traditions.

Administrators confirmed that teachers were becoming decision-makers who innovated, adapted, and determined teaching lessons to meet the diverse needs of their students. They explained that their teachers were designing multicultural activities and sharing their ideas with others at local, state, regional, and national conferences. As teachers shared these strategies with others, the administrators noted, their understanding and use of these innovative techniques were enhanced. This professional development is illustrated by administrators' comments:

- The program is having a tremendous impact on our students. They are reading and writing more.
- The students appear overwhelmingly positive about the program. The teachers report that the students are actively engaged in reading, they are reading more books, and have a more positive attitude toward reading and writing.
- I have not observed a program with more potential that the Multi-cultural Literacy Reading Program. It is having a long-lasting impact on the way people teach in our elementary schools.
- The response by the teachers has been tremendous. They have been excited and frequently shared their experiences informally with other teachers and through presentations to building staffs and at conferences.

Not only did teachers grow professionally, but, students grew academically as they pursued higher-level thinking and problem-solving skills. Figure 9.10 lists the benefits of the program for students, according to teachers and administrators.

Following this staff development process enables teachers to reflect upon and modify their teaching practices to become more compatible with the diversity of our

FIGURE 9.10 Teachers' observations about their students' behaviors.

- Students were overwhelmingly positive about the program.
- Students were writing longer stories that reflected more clarity and cohesiveness.
- Students' writing began to reflect the language and musical flow of words within the stories they were reading.
- Students were reading more books and enjoyed reading the multicultural books over and over again.
- Students were reading with more expression and fluency.
- Students enjoyed having teachers read aloud.
- Students prefer this program to their basal reading program; they are more motivated and interested in learning.
- Students loved the illustrations in the multicultural books and became more aware of how illustrations relate to the text.
- Students loved creative responses to literature, in particular reader's theater and choral readings.
- Students were ordering more books from books clubs, and parents were buying more books for their children.
- Students ordered more summer reading books than ever before.
- Students learned to appreciate/understand their culture and the cultures of others.
- Students' sensitivity to others increased as they discussed the stories and cultural and social issues related to the stories.
- Students of different cultures were interacting more with their peers as a result of this program.
- Culturally diverse students' self-esteem improved.
- Less able readers and reluctant readers became more comfortable with reading and writing activities.
- Less able readers/writers became more motivated to read/write.

nation and the sociocultural contexts of their classrooms, schools, and communities. Through this ongoing process, students become more motivated and stimulated to extend their literacy and to take charge of their own learning. Evaluation procedures, which guided and directed the staff development process, consistently revealed the effectiveness of the program and its positive impact on the reading and writing performance of students and the professional growth of teachers as they modified and refined the multicultural program to match the needs of their learners and the context of their classrooms.

SUMMARY

In their extensive research, Alvermann and Swafford (1989) observe that teachers who develop expertise in the strategies they learn during staff development workshops spend time adapting these strategies to match the context of their classrooms and the needs of their students. During the past three years, we have seen teachers consistently adapting strategies to match their own settings and the needs of their students. Teachers are further reflecting on their teaching practice in order to develop classroom environments that promote and affirm students of diverse cultural and linguistic backgrounds and to design teaching techniques that optimize learning for their students. This chapter described a staff development model that facilitates this professional development of teachers.

We began the chapter with a description of key components of staff development programs, which provided the foundation of our own staff development model. After explaining these theoretical constructs, we discussed ways to implement a multicultural program in school districts. To help others see the staff development process more clearly, we described the content and organization of our inservices and classroom visitations during the past three years. We further emphasized the need to monitor the staff development process through evaluation procedures, including formal and informal assessment measures. Through narration, we explained how the findings directed the content and organization of our inservices and classroom visitations each successive year.

The final sections of the chapter demonstrated how the CBAM, which is client-centered, was used to guide the change process as teachers began implementing an innovative program. We listed specific interventional strategies we followed to facilitate program implementation, the professional growth of our teachers, and the academic performance of our students.

REFERENCES

Allington, R. (1990). What have we done with the middle? In G. Duffy (Ed.), *Reading in the elementary school.* (pp. 32–40) Newark, DE: International Reading Association.

Alvermann, D., & Ridgeway, V. (1990). Implementing content area reading with limited finances. In G. Duffy (Ed.), *Reading in the elementary school.* (pp. 200–208) Newark, DE: International Reading Association.

Alvermann, D., & Swafford, J. (1989). Do content area strategies have a research base? *Journal of Reading, 32,* 388–394.

Au, K. (1993). *Literacy instruction in multicultural settings.* Fort Worth: Harcourt Brace Jovanovich College Publishers.

Cohen, E. (1987). *Designing group work: Strategies for the heterogeneous classroom.* New York: Teachers College Press.

Conley, M., & Tripp-Opple, K. (1990). Improving staff development through cooperation. In G. Duffy (Ed.), *Reading in the elementary school.* (pp. 209-221) Newark, DE: International Reading Association.

Crandall, D. (1983). The teacher's role in school improvement. *Educational Leadership, 4,* 6-9.

Cummins, J. (1986). Empowering minority students: A framework for intervention. *Harvard Educational Review, 56,* 28-46.

Diamond, B. (1991). A study of higher education-school collaboration. Paper presented at the Eastern Educational Research Association, Boston, MA.

Fullan, M. (1985). Change processes and strategies at the local level. *Elementary School Journal, 85,* 391-423.

Hall, G. (1979). Using the individual and the innovation as the frame of reference for research on change. Paper presented at the annual Association for Research in Education.

Hall, G., George, A., & Rutherford, W. (1979). *Measuring Stages of Concern about the innovation: A manual for the use of the SoC Questionnaire.* Austin: Research and Development Center for Teacher Education, University of Texas at Austin.

Hall, G., & Hord, S. (1987). *Change in Schools: Facilitating the Process.* Albany: State University of New York Press.

Hall, G., & Loucks, S. (1977). A developmental model for determining whether the treatment is actually implemented. *American Educational Research Journal, 13,* 263-276.

Herrmann, B. (1990). Cognitive and metacognitive goals in reading and writing. In G. Duffy (Ed.), *Reading in the elementary school.* Newark, DE: International Reading Association.

Hord, S., Rutherford, W., Austin, L., & Hall, G. (1987). *Taking charge of change.* Alexandria, VA: Association for Supervision and Curriculum Development.

Loucks, S., Newlove, B., & Hall, G. (1975). *Measuring Levels of Use of the innovation: A manual for trainers, interviewers, and raters.* Austin: Research and Development Center for Teacher Education, University of Texas at Austin.

Miller, D., & Pine, G. (1990). Advancing professional inquiry for educational improvement through action research. *Journal of Staff Development, 11,* 56-61.

Moore, M. A. (1988). Effecting change in attitude and classroom practice with word processing technology in the reading and writing curriculum. *Eighth Yearbook of the American Reading Forum,* 55-63.

Moore, M., & Diamond, B. (1991). *A staff developmental model for promoting literacy and cultural awareness: A multicultural literature-based approach.* Paper presented at the annual meeting of the American Educational Research Association. Chicago, IL.

Moore, M., & Diamond, B. (1992). Promoting teacher improvement in a multicultural literature program. Paper presented at the annual meeting of the American Education Research Association, San Francisco, CA.

Moore, M., & Diamond, B. (1994). A staff developmental model for promoting literacy and cultural awareness in a multicultural literacy program: Year Three. Paper presented at the annual meeting of the American Educational Research Association, New Orleans, LA.

Newlove, B., & Hall, G. (1976). *A manual for assessing open-ended statements of concerns about an innovation.* Austin: Research and Development Center for Teacher Education, University of Texas at Austin.

Newman, F., Onosko, J., & Stevenson, R. (1990). Staff development for higher order thinking: A synthesis of practical wisdom. *Journal of Staff Development, 11,* 46-55.

Pisano, A., & Tallerico, M. (1990). Improving writing instruction through staff development. *Journal of Staff Development, 11,* 18-21.

Routman, R. (1991). *Invitations: Changing as teachers and learners K-12.* Portsmouth, NH: Heinemann.

Saxl, E., Miles, M., & Liberman, A. (1988). *Assisting change in education: The ACE training modules.* Arlington, VA: Association for Supervision and Curriculum Development.

Showers, B., Joyce, B., & Bennett, B. (1987). Synthesis of research on staff development: Framework for future study and a state of the art analysis. *Educational Leadership, 45,* 77-87.

Sparks, G., & Simmons, J. (1989). Inquiry-oriented staff development: Using research as a source of tools, not rules. In S. Caldwell (Ed.), *Staff development: A handbook of effective practices.* National Staff Development Council.

Stevenson, R. (1987). Staff development for effective secondary schools: A synthesis of research. *Teaching and Teacher Education, 3,* 233-248.

chapter 10

Involving Parents and Community in a Multicultural Literacy Program

OVERVIEW

We now examine specific ways that parents and members of the community might become involved in the literacy development of their children. Using information from parent interviews and our experiences while working with parents, we begin by suggesting initial considerations for developing positive parental and community relations. We then revisit the goals of the multicultural literacy program and identify ways these goals might be shared with parents, presenting strategies to promote parent/teacher collaboration in meeting the goals. We further identify ways that businesses, churches, and fraternal groups in the community might participate in multicultural literacy events.

INTRODUCTION

> Parents play roles of inestimable importance in laying the foundation for learning to read. A parent is a child's first guide through a vast and unfamiliar world . . . a child's first mentor on what words mean and how to mean things with words . . . a child's first tutor in unraveling the fascinating puzzle of written language. A parent is a child's one enduring source of faith that somehow, sooner or later, he or she will become a good reader.
>
> Anderson, Hiebert, Scott, and Wilkinson (1984, pp. 27–28)

Although the importance of the parent in the child's learning has been well documented (Diamond & Moore, 1992; Teale, 1986; Taylor, 1983; Heath, 1983), the words of Anderson et al. underscore the role of the parent in the child's literacy development. Teale (1986) concludes that the process of becoming literate is inextricably linked with the parents' cultural and social traditions, which define who and what we are. Students will, therefore, bring a variety of literacy experiences and learning patterns to the classroom. When these are closely matched with the way literacy is acquired in the school, the important link between home and school is easy to forge. When there is a marked difference between home and school literacy and culture, however, the school must make a greater effort to bring the two together. Effective teachers will want to reach out to parents in an effort to learn about each child's literacy experiences at home and to involve them in the child's literacy experiences at school, working toward closer home-school compatibility.

UNDERSTANDING AND RESPECTING THE CHILD'S HOME AND FAMILY

Parents are the child's first language teachers. With every event that offers opportunities for meaningful communication, parents model ways of talking and interacting within the family. Through their actions and responses, parents help the child learn the language code, what to say to whom, and how to say it appropriately in a given situation (Hymes, 1967; Saville-Troike, 1978). Getting to know the parents, therefore, provides a deeper knowledge of the child. We have discussed the different contexts for learning that might exist in homes and the diverse ways that the children are socialized in language and literacy processes (Chapter 2). Teachers will want to be aware of these differences and avoid making assumptions that the child is deficient in some way. Neuman and Roskos (1993) found, for example, that black preschoolers from poor homes who displayed limited understanding of verbal routines in a test situation demonstrated language patterns and behaviors consistent with their peers in an office play center. Clearly, although the literacy experiences provided in the home environment may differ from those of the school, teachers must recognize that there are multiple literacies, all of which become experiences on which teachers can build.

As teachers begin interacting with parents, they will need to be aware of the different expectations that parents of diverse cultural and socioeconomic groups may hold for their children. For example, single parents of limited means may place extra responsibility on their children when they have to work and are overwhelmed with dual responsibilities. In these situations, an older sibling may be placed in charge of younger children. Children in charge may be forced to develop sophisticated decision-making and problem-solving skills that extend far beyond those of their peers. Teachers will want to build on these skills and challenge these students. Another less positive consequence of this situation is that the children in charge may not have opportunities to develop literacy skills at home because their parents lack the time for valuable language interactions that are necessary to support learning. In these instances, teachers may have to develop additional literacy activities and support for these students while they are in school.

Teachers will want to be aware that children whose parents do not speak English may have special relationships with their parents as English translators. Trueba (1984) describes how a Mexican American girl translated the teacher's message about the progress of her sister, who had Down's Syndrome, from English to Spanish.

The girl and her sisters also helped their parents fill out documents and other language-related tasks. These students are bilingual, an ability that should be viewed as a strength rather than a liability.

GAINING KNOWLEDGE ABOUT THE COMMUNITY

In acquiring knowledge about the community, teachers must also be sensitive to the fact that the extended family and the community play important roles in some cultures. There are many enclaves of ethnicity in large cities and small towns—Chinatown in New York and San Francisco, Amish communities in Pennsylvania and Ohio, Mexican communities in Texas, and African American neighborhoods in cities, towns, and suburbs. Cushner, McClelland, & Safford (1992) assert that the experiences people share and the experiences through which they learn who they are often develop within these ethnic communities. Teachers can benefit from knowing the established norms of behavior, attitudes, and approaches to literacy that exist in these communities. Frequently, the quality and effectiveness of a multicultural literacy program depend on the degree to which the schools understand, respect, and engage the leaders of these communities. In her efforts to reach the parents of students in the all black rural community of Donaldsonville, Louisiana, for example, Edwards (1994) found that she had to tap into the businesses and the churches of the community. She enlisted the help of restaurant and bar owners, a parish priest, bus drivers, and people sitting on the street corners in order to encourage parents to participate in the school reading program from which they had been alienated for years. By getting to know the relationships, attitudes, and assumptions that existed within the community, she was able to use her insider status to establish home, school, and community cooperation.

To learn as much as possible about the community and the extended context of cultural learning, teachers and administrators may want to define areas that need further study and to develop questions that can guide them in acquiring knowledge about the local community. Figure 10.1 offers suggestions for such questions.

FIGURE 10.1 Questions to assess teachers' and administrators' knowledge of the community.

1. What racial, cultural, and linguistic groups are represented in your class? How many children are in each group?
2. How do these groups fit into the local community? Are they an integral part? Is the community supportive?
3. What are important holidays, foods, and traditions for each of the groups represented? How well can you speak the language of the groups represented in your class?
4. What are the socioeconomic backgrounds of the children in your class? What are the occupations of their parents? How will these occupations affect the parents' ability to help the child?
5. How much contact have the children had with people of other racial, cultural, and socioeconomic groups?
6. How do specific families interact with the community? What have their experiences been with community services, police, welfare workers, and the schools? What informal support systems exist among family members, neighbors, and co-workers?

Once teachers acquire an understanding of the parents and community, they can build clear and open communication about the program. They can then begin to explain and clarify the program's goals and their belief that parents share responsibility for their child's learning. In the following section, we present the methods we used to communicate with parents about the multicultural literacy program.

SHARING THE GOALS OF A MULTICULTURAL LITERACY PROGRAM

Sharing and interpreting the goals of a new program with parents is one of the teacher's most important responsibilities (Kendall, 1983; Ramsey, 1987). Teachers need to realize that reactions to a multicultural program and support for it may vary among parents in a community. Cultural attitudes are very complex and deeply embedded, leading to the possibility that some parents may be highly supportive, whereas others may be negative and resistant (Diamond & Moore, 1992; Kendall, 1983). In relatively homogeneous communities, for example, parents may be surprised that there is a need to implement a multicultural literacy program. They may feel that a focus on working together as one "American culture"—the melting pot theory—is preferable to learning about, recognizing, and appreciating diverse cultures. On the other hand, there may be parents who live and interact with different cultural and racial groups on a daily basis at work and in their communities. Believing that a multicultural literacy program might enrich academic and social learning, these parents may be enthusiastic supporters of the program. They will undoubtedly be eager to receive information about it.

Finally, there may be parents who are relative newcomers to the United States who may have experienced discrimination because of race or nationality. They may be more interested in learning how to assimilate and "be an American" than in learning how to maintain and enhance their cultural identities. These parents may feel that accepting and acknowledging their cultural identities will compromise their opportunity to achieve status as "real" Americans.

The best way to prepare for these varied reactions to the program is to anticipate questions and concerns. This will help teachers feel more confident and less defensive about the need for the program. When teachers are enthusiastic about the program and believe in its strengths, parents will be more supportive of its goals.

Planning the First Parent Meeting in the Multicultural Literacy Program

Teachers in our program find that meetings with parents require a great deal of advance planning. Deciding on time, format, and content are among the most pressing considerations. Teachers also discover that planning parent meetings across grade levels, rather than planning separate meetings for their individual classrooms or grades, enables them to demonstrate to parents how the program is coordinated throughout the school. Significantly, teachers follow the inservice model (see Chapter 9) to organize the content and format of the meetings, and, because they are confident in their decision-making abilities, they generate additional activities for these meetings.

For the first meeting, they decide to explain the program's goals and introduce parents to the type of multicultural literacy learning that occurs as students partici- pate in the program. Realizing that some parents might be apprehensive about attend- ing the meeting, the teachers create a positive and inviting atmosphere by displaying samples of children's art and writing around the room and arranging a variety of books and materials used in the program for the parents to see. Finally, the teachers plan activities that will actively involve the parents in the meeting, rather than have them listen passively.

In one school district, teachers, the parent coordinator, and the Chapter I direc- tor prepare folders for the parents. In the folders are copies of a biopoem frame, a list of program goals and objectives, handouts with suggestions on how parents can support the program goals at home, an article on parent involvement, a bibliography of multicultural literature, note paper, and pens.

The following is a description of this typical first meeting between parents and teachers. The meeting consists of five major components: getting acquainted, over- view of goals, introduction of multicultural literature, participation of students, and closure and looking ahead.

Getting Acquainted

On the morning of the meeting, teachers greet parents informally as they enter the room, introducing themselves, welcoming them to the meeting, and offering them refreshments. Then teachers begin the formal meeting by presenting an overview of the meeting agenda. Following this introduction, the teachers provide an opportunity for the parents to get to know one another and for the teachers and parents to become reacquainted. They begin with the biopoem activity that many teachers use with their students at the beginning of the year. The biopoem provides a format for parents to interview one another (see Figure 10.2), which accomplishes several purposes: (1) parents have an opportunity to interact with other parents in their community; (2) they have a chance to reflect on what makes them unique; and (3) they have the opportunity to participate in an activity that their children use in class, giving them insight into the benefits of this activity for their children. It is im- portant that parents have a chance to see how people are alike and different, because this sets the context for realizing the need for a multicultural literacy program. As teachers participate in this activity, they also get to know their parents better.

After completing their poems, parents and teachers reconvene as a large group, with each person sharing the poem of the person he/she interviewed. This elimi- nates the self-consciousness that individuals often feel when introducing themselves. As the parents share information about one another, what makes them special and what activities they enjoy—holidays, birthdays, Fourth of July, foods—parents begin to see the diversity that exists among families. Typically, parents also find that they have many things in common—concerns about their children, the need for more time and money, love for family, and concerns about world peace. Following this activity, parents are more relaxed and receptive to listening to the program goals.

FIGURE 10.2   Biopoem format used at first parents' meeting.

BIOPOEM

Use this form to make a poem about someone in our parent group. The person you interview for the poem may give more information or less than is called for. Encourage the person to think of words or phrases that would accurately describe her/him. Try several words before you decide which to use.

Line 1 - First Name

Line 2 - Four Words That Tell About the Person

Line 3 - Parent of.....(Name of Child/Children/Teacher's Room)

Line 4 - Lover of...(3 People or Ideas)

Line 5 - Who Needs...(3 Items)

Line 6 - Who Gives...(3 Items)

Line 7 - Who Would Like to See...(3 People or Events)

Line 8 - Residing in (City); (Street)

Line 9 - Last Name

Overview of Goals

Before discussing specific goals, Mrs. Thomas, the chairperson of the meeting, introduces the multicultural literacy program by presenting its rationale. For example, she explains that because we live in a society of many cultures, races, and ethnic groups, students should learn to understand them. She further points out that because students will be faced with many critical decisions in the future, they will need to acquire decision-making and problem-solving skills. She assures the parents that the literacy skills—reading, writing, and oral language—that are a part of the program can help students acquire these important skills. Finally, she emphasizes that the program values all individuals and respects their backgrounds. This approach to learning, she stresses, promotes students' educational growth in a positive, supportive learning environment.

Following the rationale, Mrs. Thomas explains the goals of the program by directing the parents' attention to the goals posted on a chart. She explains each goal, giving examples of how it is implemented in the classroom. For example, in highlighting the first goal—to link the cultural background, language, and experiences of students of diverse cultures, racial groups, and linguistic backgrounds with the written material that they read—she says teachers might read to students the book *Hello, Amigos,* by Tricia Brown, a book about a Hispanic boy and his special day as he prepares for his birthday party. Mrs. Thomas briefly shares excerpts from the book and explains that after reading and discussing the story, students might write about their own birthday experiences. She explains that reading and writing skills are developed as students write about their personal experiences and share them with the class. Through these experiences, she adds, all students have the opportunity to connect their backgrounds and cultural experiences to what they read and write.

As Mrs. Thomas talks about each goal, parents occasionally ask questions. At the first meeting, questions seem to center on the availability of the books and students' opportunities to read individual books. After hearing about the goals, the parents divide into four groups, where each group is given a sheet of chart paper on which

FIGURE 10.3 Complete list of goals generated by parents and teachers.

1. To link the cultural background, language, and experiences of students of diverse cultures, racial groups, and linguistic backgrounds with the written material that they read.

   At Home
   Help teachers look for books of diverse cultures.
   Make a bibliography of books that child might enjoy.
   Help teachers verify cultural authenticity, as a member of a given culture.
   Help to create bilingual texts by translating books into other languages.

   At School
   Share writings and stories from your family with children in the classroom.
   Provide background information about cultures prior to student's reading.
   Read a bilingual text in the English language to help students who are second-language learners.

2. To heighten reading comprehension, writing quality, and vocabulary of elementary students.

   At Home
   Help make book covers and books for students.
   Read stories to child; have him re-tell the story.
   Help child tell what she liked best about the story; the funniest part; the most frightening part.
   Take child to the local library. Schedule a regular time.
   Relate books that are read to everyday activities.
   Keep a continuous family journal in the living room. Have at least one family member write in it each day.
   Make a home dictionary; add words from different cultures and languages.

   At School
   Listen to a student read.
   Help students practice choral readings and reader's theatre.
   Help second-language learners with translations.
   Help students with the computers.
   Help students with the writing process . . . revising, editing, and publishing.

3. To develop understanding and appreciation of one's own cultures and the culture of others.

   At Home
   Share pictures of parents and grandparents with child.
   Help create a family tree.
   Discuss family traditions and how they came to be.
   Share family stories.
   Collect family artifacts, toys, trinkets and share the family history with child.
   Encourage child to interview older relatives.

   At School
   Work with other parents on a family directory; include information about parents' expertise and cultural information that they might share.
   Help students do library research for cultural information.
   Share favorite foods with child's classroom.

4. To develop positive attitudes toward reading and writing.

   At Home
   Have books available that are easy reading.
   Plan "how-to" activities—cooking (following recipes from different cultures), making models (following directions).
   Cut pictures from magazines, newspapers; write or tell stories.
   Praise the child's efforts.
   Model reading and writing at home.

   At School
   Help students with creative extensions of stories.
   Read to the students.
   Help students select books that are interesting and fun to read.

one goal is listed. With the help of the teachers, the parents brainstorm activities they might do at home to help their students achieve that goal. Their ideas are listed on the chart paper, and after about 15 minutes, the parents present them to the entire group. Figure 10.3 is a list of goals that these parents and teachers developed.

INTRODUCING MULTICULTURAL LITERATURE

The teachers invite a local book distributor, who is an excellent presenter, to share with the parents the range of multicultural books that is available. Before the meeting, the distributor sets up an attractive display of books, including books for a range of grade levels, genres, and cultures, so that parents might browse. Although the teachers could have conducted this part of the workshop themselves, they believed that by using a parent from the local community they would show their support for the community and give the parents an opportunity to learn about a valuable resource in their local area.

The distributor gives the parents an overview of the types of books available, noting the beautiful illustrations and the variety of cultures represented. She then reads excerpts from some of the most popular ones, providing pertinent background information about the author, the age range for which the book is appropriate, a brief summary of the story, or samples of the illustrations used in the book. Significantly, throughout the presentation, she relates to the parents as a friend, sharing how she uses the literature with her own children and how much they have benefited from their experiences with them.

Following the presentation, Mrs. Thomas announces a break and invites the parents to meet the distributor, ask questions, and browse while having refreshments. When they come back, she continues, they will have an opportunity to see the program in action, with presentations from some of the students.

Participation of the Students

Parents are most supportive of programs when they can see the benefits for their children. As a final part of the meeting, teachers felt it would be exciting for parents to see the students share some of the highlights of their multicultural literature experiences. Two classes were chosen for the meeting—Mr. Morgan's fifth-grade class and Mr. Humes's second-grade class. The fifth-graders have memorized *Cornrows,* a favorite choral reading. In preparation for the choral reading, the African American girls come to school with their hair braided in cornrows, a popular style in their community. Two students tell how the tradition of cornrows began in Africa as a symbol of pride, often identifying tribes, princesses, and royalty. Then, speaking clearly, mindful of stress and intonation, the students perform the choral reading. The parents give them a standing ovation.

Mr. Humes's class performs next. They completed stories about birthday celebrations after reading *Hello, Amigos!* Four of the students, dressed in their "birthday best," tell of reading the story about the birthday of Frankie Valdez, the main character in the story, and how they compared their birthdays with Frankie's. The students then read the stories they wrote about their birthdays with expression and pride. (Mrs. Thomas explained this activity to parents earlier.)

We find that giving parents a chance to see a live demonstration of their children's achievements is one of the most effective ways to gain support for the program and to build parent-teacher relationships. Sharing choral readings, reader's theater, folk dances, and published stories at parent meetings are a few ways to accomplish these goals.

Closure and Looking Ahead to Future Sessions

After learning about the program's goals and the multicultural literature, as well as seeing the children share multicultural literacy experiences, the parents are enthusiastic and supportive about the program. Following a brief question and answer session, Mrs. Thomas summarizes the morning's activities, and thanks parents for their attendance and participation. She asks teachers to fill out the meeting evaluation form, which includes space for comments and suggestions of topics for future meetings. Finally, she asks for parent volunteers to serve on a committee to plan meetings and handle communication between parents, teachers, and administrators. Six of the 56 parents in attendance volunteer.

Subsequent Meetings

Plans for subsequent meetings are made collaboratively by the teachers, the parent committee, and the coordinator of the program. The topics for the meetings are tailored to parents' concerns and interests and teachers' ideas on what might be important. Parents' and teachers' suggestions for topics are:

- Learning to read aloud to my child
- Developing self-esteem
- Learning about diverse cultures
- Learning about new multicultural literature
- Learning about reading and writing strategies used in the classroom
- Helping second-language learners
- Addressing issues of assessment
- Helping my child at home

The parents and teachers plan to meet bimonthly and discuss the possibility of having a room set aside for family meetings, volunteer activities, and projects and materials.

Keeping Parents Involved

When teachers bring parents in and share the goals of the multicultural literacy program with them, a bond begins to develop between home and school. As parents and teachers meet to plan future meetings, parent participation and presence in the school increases. For example, they help in classrooms, prepare materials, assist with celebrations, and plan activities to raise money to buy more multicultural books for the school.

Teachers are eager to maintain the relationships and support their parent involvement program. Along with Fredericks and Rasinski (1990), we believe that constant efforts to make parents feel welcome, to inform parents, and to concentrate on what they have to offer is a constructive approach to parent involvement. We find that teachers and administrators in the program are able to maintain contacts with parents when very specific needs of their children are defined, when there is a reward or recognition for their efforts, and when their children's classes benefit in some way. Other possible outreach efforts are the following:

1. **Maintain personal contact on a continual basis, calling at times just to share good news.** Because of their busy schedules, teachers might ask parents to help with making phone calls.
2. **Call to find out more about parents who are not involved.** Attempting to address parents' hesitancies and concerns in a positive way seems to open avenues for communication. A friend may offer to serve as an interpreter for a parent who speaks another language, or transportation might be provided for those who want to come to a meeting or volunteer.
3. **Plan projects that involve the entire family.** In cultures where the extended family is important this can have a very positive effect.
4. **Make a special effort to tap the resources of all parents, especially those who might feel they have nothing to contribute.** Through questionnaires, one can find out ways parents might be able to help.
5. **Send home written teasers about upcoming events.** Building up suspense and interest through clever advertising strategies is very effective.
6. **Videotape classroom and school functions.** Circulating these tapes to busy parents who can't attend meetings helps them to feel more involved. Students and parents enjoy rotating published choral readings or reader's theater among the class.
7. **Offer rewards and incentives for both parents and students.** Everyone appreciates recognition and enjoys receiving prizes, particularly books, for their efforts. Parents are especially proud when their children are featured.
8. **Enlist civic and other community groups to support your multicultural literacy program.** Senior citizens can also be a source of support.

THE MULTICULTURAL LITERACY PROGRAM EXTENDS INTO THE COMMUNITY

As parents begin to share their enthusiasm for the multicultural literacy program, word spreads in the community. For example, one of the parents, a member of a local chapter of Delta Sigma Theta, a national public service sorority, and chairperson of its literacy committee, told her group about the program. Several ideas surfaced as the committee brainstormed ways they might help, and throughout the year the sorority was an important source of support for the program and the students.

The "Book and Blanket" Party

One of the most successful parent programs included a "Book and Blanket" party. The evening activity promotes reading, family fun, and togetherness as parents bring their children to school with books in one hand and their favorite blankets in the other. Because of the success of the first party, the sorority's literacy committee decided to sponsor a second one. The members networked with other community groups, eliciting donations and discounts on multicultural books to ensure that each child had a book to read.

On the night of the affair, the sorority members decorated the auditorium with red and white balloons, colorful pictures of children, and lots of stuffed animals of various sizes. As the parents and children entered, sorority members greeted them with bookmarks and balloons. Music added to the atmosphere that something "special" was happening.

After a brief introduction about the Book and Blanket, one of the sorority members, who was a storyteller, shared several stories with the children, beginning in the traditional way of many Navaho storytellers:

In the beginning, when the world was new
At the time when men and animals were all the same and spoke the same
language . . .

She first shared the creation story, *Turtle Dives to the Bottom of the Sea.* Next was an African American story, *The Talking Yam,* in which students become a part of the story as it is told, lining up to attempt to pull the yam out of the ground. Involvement in the story is a part of the African storytelling tradition.

After the excitement of storytelling, students and their families found their blanket spaces and settled in for reading. Parents read to children, children read to parents, and some of the children who were too young to read listened quietly.

The sorority members circulated to make sure every child had a book, a blanket, and a family member. If they found a student who was alone, they took the child, found a blanket from the extras they had brought, and became the child's extended family for the evening. (See Figure 10.4.) After reading several stories, the families, teachers, administrators, and sorority members came together for a dinner prepared by the Deltas.

Sometimes a Book and Blanket party is held overnight, in which case more activities are planned and students bring sleeping bags or bedrolls and pillows. Breakfast marks the end of the event.

Reading in the Mall

Another successful extension of the multicultural literacy program into the community occurred when teachers and parents accepted the invitation of a local shopping mall association to participate in a Read-In in the Mall. The students, in addition to sharing multicultural books, writing, and art with people in the mall, displayed their art, read related stories, and shared the significant relationship of the art object to the storybook characters. A few examples of books and artwork included: kente cloths,

FIGURE 10.4 A family, including an active baby boy, enjoys a favorite book at the sorority-sponsored "Book and Blanket" party.

designed by students after reading *The Black Snowman,* by Mendez; a class quilt, created after reading *The Keeping Quilt,* by Polacco, and *The Patchwork Quilt,* by Flournoy; and wire figures designed by students after reading *Galimoto,* by Williams. Parents took the students to the mall on the day before the Read-in to meet the director of the mall project, find out where they would be situated, and determine how to mount their displays.

On the day of the Read-in, all but three students from the class were present. Many parents of the students dropped by with younger siblings. It was exciting as the students proudly read their well-rehearsed story and shared their art. Although the mall was crowded and several groups participated, the students felt very good about the invitation and their chance to share with the community. Students received certificates of recognition for participating.

After-School Literacy Program

In another district, a local church formed a literacy tutorial program, another example of how community, parents, and teachers can collaborate to benefit students. It is also an excellent model of a church, school, parents, and the local university working together. Concerned about students who were having difficulty in school, parents and teachers, many of whom were members of the church congregation, developed the idea of an after-school tutorial program to be housed in the church. The minister, always receptive to ideas designed to help young people in the community, supported the program enthusiastically. Within a week, the plan was presented to the church trustees and approved, pending submission of a detailed proposal.

The parents and teachers worked on Saturdays to identify the types of learning experiences that might benefit the students. They developed outlines of lessons for the tutors to use and identified sources for books and materials. After establishing guidelines for tutorials, the organizers circulated news about the program, asked teachers to identify students who might benefit, obtained parental approval, solicited volunteers from among local university students, and got businesses to donate materials. Within two months, the program was in place and working very well.

As evidenced in the examples above, we find that parents and the community (1) demonstrate a willingness to work with the schools (if they have a clear sense of what is needed); (2) demonstrate unconditional concern and support for students' education; and (3) view the school as an extended family, a place to turn for help. As one of the single parents that we interviewed confided:

> I'm all on my own. I don't have any help from mother now. Oh, but I get a lot of teacher support. . . . I don't know what I'd do without it. It's like having a family. . . .

A Collaboration between the University and the Public School

The Student Athletes' Program is a pilot program, implemented in the spring of 1993, that provides meaningful volunteer experiences for college students while supporting learning for elementary students. The university students involved in the program were football players from two nearby universities. The public school students were a culturally diverse group of boys and girls in grades three through five who were identified by their teachers as students who might benefit academically and socially from the program, which was housed in the recreation center of a local low-income housing complex.

The student athletes received a half-day training session on interactive reading techniques, using multicultural books prior to the start of the program. They were also trained in effective strategies for leading choral readings. (See Chapter 4.) These literacy activities were a new experience for many of the football players, who were far removed from the elementary classroom. Several were apprehensive about how they would perform during the session and how the younger students might respond to them.

As soon as they began working with the students, they discovered that these apprehensions were unfounded. A typical session included a snack, an interactive reading activity—including the choral reading—for 30 to 45 minutes, and an intermural sports activity for 45 minutes. The elementary students, who were placed in groups of 10 with an athlete, were excited and relaxed from the beginning. On the first day, one student, Marcus, candidly asked one of the athletes, "What are you doing here?" To which Steve, the athlete replied, "Why?" Responding in a matter-of-fact manner, Marcus said, "Because my dad said football players can't read!" Needless to say, Marcus learned that Steve could read; the two ultimately became good friends.

The program had many benefits, and everyone gained something. Coordinator Mrs. Sauer reported that many of the athletes said they felt their experiences in the program were as important as the "booklearning" they experienced in the classroom. The athletes also commented that reading the multicultural books gave them new insights about books and stories. They added that they planned to continue their reading; many even asked if they could take the books home to read to family members.

The experience also challenged some of the players' assumptions. They had had doubts about their ability to work with some of students, whose backgrounds were different from their own. Some athletes recoiled at the idea of teaching girls to play football. By the end of the program, the athletes discovered that they could successfully work with students from diverse backgrounds. In fact, many said it was one of the most rewarding experiences they had ever had.

The elementary students also learned to work together in groups with students that they normally might not choose to work with. They were, of course, thrilled with the athletes, who provided them a role model for literacy. Participating in the program helped them to aspire to achieve academically. Many are beginning to realize that they might also be able to attend college one day if they work hard in school.

A Shared Effort by a Learning Community

Graves and Stuart (1985) describe a good classroom as a place where "the space is shared, responsibilities are shared, reading and writing are shared, experiences are shared, above all learning is shared. The teacher works hard to help the children develop their ability to capitalize on their collective power for the common good" (p. 53). Some of the characteristics of a good classroom are those typical of a good school and community. As we continue to work with students, teachers, parents, and administrators, we see growth toward the realization of a learning community. The Multicultural Fair, which was held during the final year of the literacy project, is one example of how students, teachers, administrators, and community work together.

THE MULTICULTURAL FAIR

Mrs. Long, a sixth-grade teacher, heard rumors that she might be moved to the junior high school the next year because of her district's plans for reorganization. She tells how she promptly went into the principal's office and stated emphatically, "But I don't want to go over there. I can't go over there. I won't be able to do the multicultural project!" This incident shows the extent to which the teachers have taken ownership of the program and supported it. Out of this commitment and support grew the movement for a culminating activity that would make a statement to the community and surrounding areas that something significant had happened in their school district. Although the impetus for the project came from the teachers, the parents and community eventually became involved. The story of the Multicultural Fair is a story of cooperation, collaboration, and empowerment.

A Kernel of an Idea

While we were making a visitation to her school, Mrs. Gilkey shared with us the beginning of an idea—a plan to have a multicultural fair. She related how several teachers were lamenting the fact that the third and final year of federal funding for the multicultural literacy program might mean the end of the project. Thinking that if, indeed, it was the last year, the teachers wanted some way of sharing the impact the program had on the students, teachers, parents, and community. The teachers further discussed the need to make the central administrators and school board members more aware of what the students had learned. Sharing this knowledge with the community might provide the impetus for the administrators to make the program an ongoing part of the curriculum. Asking for our support, Mrs. Gilkey confidently stated, "We're willing to do the work." This was the beginning of the Multicultural Fair.

The First Meetings

Mrs. Gilkey, Mrs. Thomas, and Mrs. Harris set up a series of meetings in late January. First they met with their principal, Mr. Brown, and then with the superintendent of schools and the curriculum director. Mr. Brown was supportive, as always, asking several questions about logistics that the teachers were yet to complete. In their meeting with the two central administrators, the superintendent suggested that the teachers also inform the principals in the other buildings in order that teachers who wanted to be involved in these buildings might also attend the planning meetings.

The three teachers met frequently before school to clarify their ideas and determine a course of action for implementing the project. They wanted all teachers to feel ownership of the project and wanted to involve the parents in the early stages. They set a time and date for the first meeting with the teachers and sent a memo inviting them to the meeting. The teachers were allowed to leave school early to come to the initial meeting.

At the meeting, all teachers were given folders with handouts describing ways a multicultural fair might be set up and summarizing information about diverse cultures that might be included in the fair. When Mrs. Gilkey asked the teachers to give their reactions, most of their concerns focused on the amount of time it would take to prepare and the potential infringement on the other areas of the curriculum. However, they were excited about the idea. When a vote was taken, the teachers decided overwhelmingly to have the fair. Mrs. Gilkey was elected chairperson.

Teachers decided to share information at the fair that was or had been a primary focus of their multicultural curriculum during the year. Ms. Clark's class, for example, was reading fiction and nonfiction stories about Jamaica and the West Indies, and many of their literacy activities focused on the these island cultures. In some instances, teachers had been studying the same culture and thus decided to work together.

The final business items included establishing meeting dates and a date for the fair. After looking at the school calendar, they selected a time in mid May. The teachers planned to meet again in two weeks to establish committees.

Meeting with Parents

The purpose of the meeting with the parents was to seek their assistance and ideas and bring them up to date on the plans. Teachers assured parents that they wanted them to be involved and suggested ways they might help, such as:

- Sharing the news about the fair with other parents
- Identifying community groups that might help with materials
- Identifying resource people who might donate their time
- Helping with invitations and posters to advertise the fair

Mr. Robinson, a local printer, offered his assistance, asserting, "Most parents would be willing to help if they know exactly what you want. Some parents want to help around the school, but feel kind of unsure of themselves." Other parents chimed in. Mrs. Stokes, who loved to cook, offered to help with the food preparation if refreshments were going to be included. Patricia, an older sister of one of the third-grade students, said she was a seamstress and would help Ms. Clark's students with their kente cloths.

The teachers, eager to capitalize on the enthusiasm, asked Mr. Robinson and Mrs. Stokes to cochair the parent group for the fair. They were to be the liaisons between the teachers and parents and would attend the teachers' meetings. Teachers assured parents that there would be much to do as the classes got more involved in their study of specific cultures and prepared for the fair.

Plans Unfold for Students, Teachers, and Parents

The next days and weeks were filled with activity. In their second meeting the teachers made a definite commitment as to which cultural group they would study and present at the fair. They decided that information should be presented through art, music, and dance as well as stories, poems, and reports related to what students had learned about the groups' values and beliefs. The booths should further reflect literacy and cultural understanding.

Some parents became an integral part of the learning activities and, with the help of Mr. Robinson, coordinated schedules and volunteered to assist their students' classes. Ms. Clark's parent from Trinidad-Tobago, for example, visited the class to share calypso and reggae music and tell stories of the island—enrichment that can't be found in books. She told stories about her visits to the marketplace, describing the fresh taste of mangoes, guavas, and coconuts, and about how people gathered there as a meeting place. Students listened attentively, and some took notes so that they could share the information with people who visited their booth at the fair. Other parents helped students design traditional dress for the carnival, a celebration that occurs in August. The students planned to dance at the fair to celebrate the carnival.

In other classrooms, parents helped students with writing, revising, and editing. Some parents gave feedback as students practiced choral readings, assisted with mask making, and helped with Spanish pronunciations for a song. Teachers saw parents in the school who had never been there before, busily helping with invitations and programs. Parents who could not get to school helped at home by making signs or sewing traditional dress that the students would wear. Each visit to the classrooms brought students to the door to greet the parents and show what they were learning and making.

Involving the Community

As teachers continued planning, they learned to be flexible and make modifications. For example, as local citizens and neighboring schools responded positively to invitations, teachers realized that they needed a gymnasium that was larger than any in the school district. Mr. Morgan, the cochair, called the local recreation center, explaining the problem. The director of the center not only waived the usual fee but rearranged the preceding night's schedule so that classes could get in to set up their displays.

Other citizens in the community, as they heard about the fair from their neighbors, church members, and club members, generously contributed their time or financial support. For example, a local lumber store owner provided lumber for the booths. The day before the fair he delivered wood and offered to help build the frames. One of the boutiques in the community sold ethnic fabric at a 50 percent discount, while a local sign maker printed signs for each of the booths in bright letters.

The director of food service for the district was asked to do extra work. She and her staff had to prepare different menus for the day—one for the student participants in the fair, the other for the rest of the school population. She eagerly agreed and even researched recipes from 15 ethnic and cultural groups. On the day of the fair, she and her staff were prepared: The food was attractively presented, with a label on each dish giving its name and cultural/ethnic origin.

The Day of the Fair

The recreation center marquee read:

MULTICULTURAL FAIR—INKSTER PUBLIC SCHOOLS.

The teachers and parents were already setting up in the gymnasium when we arrived. Everything was beginning to take shape. Signs were in place, and many of the poems, stories, reports, and artifacts were already posted. In the corners of the gym, dancers were rehearsing. Ms. Clark's students practiced the limbo in their new traditional dress. The Alternative Education students were rehearsing their presentations about Tanzania. An air of anticipation was everywhere.

As students and teachers arrived around 9:30, they were greeted by two students who asked teachers to sign the guest book for their classes. Students stationed at the booths, which featured various countries, explained what they had learned during the year about the daily lives of the people, both past and present, and about the artifacts and crafts of the country. One student explained the Mankala—an East

FIGURE 10.5 Parent and substitute teacher Ms. Jones stand with students modeling the Mexican attire that another parent made for the fair.

African board game—and demonstrated how to play the game with a classmate. The students at the booths also invited visitors to read their stories, poems, and reports.

The Chinese American display included riddles symbolizing activities the Chinese enjoy during the Lunar New Year and the Lantern Festival. Each visiting teacher was given a copy of the riddles and instructions on how to make a paper lantern.

The guests expressed surprise at the amount of work the students had done. Several commented, "I didn't know it was going to be this big," or "I can't believe how much work went into this," or "The students know so much . . . they really seem confident." It was evident, moreover, that students had gained new knowledge about cultures *and* improved their literacy skills.

After a lunch of ethnic dishes, students prepared for the performance part of the fair, which included songs, dances, choral readings, and stories from the various cultures. Music teachers and parents assisted teachers with the musical part of the performances. When the program came to a close, teachers had tired smiles, parents were proudly beaming, and students were content. (See Figure 10.5.)

SUMMARY

In this chapter we emphasized several important factors to consider in working with parents and the community. These include the need to understand and respect the various ways that literacy is acquired in the home, to view the parent as a valuable resource and partner in the child's learning, and to become knowledgeable about the community.

We then focused on specific ways that teachers can work with parents in a multicultural literacy program. Parental involvement can be gained by clearly explaining the program's goals, maintaining a sensitivity to parents' needs, and engaging parents' strengths and talents. We further emphasized specific ways to sustain parental involvement in their children's learning.

When parents support a multicultural program, their enthusiasm spreads to the community. Specific examples of community involvement include a Book and Blanket party, a Read-In in the Mall, and an after-school literacy program. Parental support benefits students and community.

Finally, planning and implementing a multicultural fair demonstrates how students, teachers, parents, and the community, working together, can be a strong force in achieving the goals of a multicultural literacy program.

REFERENCES

Anderson, R. C., Hiebert, E., Scott, Judith A., & Wilkinson, I. A. G. (1984). *Becoming a nation of readers: The report of the Commission on Reading.* Washington, D.C.: The National Institute of Education.

Au, K. H. (1993). *Literacy instruction in multicultural settings.* Austin, TX: Holt, Rinehart and Winston.

Cushner, K., McClelland, A., Safford, P. (1992). *Human diversity in education: An integrative approach.* New York, NY: McGraw Hill.

Diamond, B., & Moore, M. (1992). Parental attitudes about learning and culture: Implications for African-American students. Paper presented at the annual meeting of the American Educational Research Association, San Francisco, California.

Edwards, P. A. (1992). Involving parents in building reading instruction for African American children. *Theory into Practice, XXXI,* 350–359.

Edwards, P. A. (1994). Connecting African American parents and youth to the school's reading program: Its meaning for school and community literacy. In V. L. Gadsden & D. Wagner (Eds.), *Literacy among African-American: Issues in learning, teaching and schooling.* (pp. 263–281). Creskill, N.J.: Hampton Press.

Fredericks, A., & Rasinaki, T. (1990). Involving the uninvolved: How to. *The Reading Teacher. 43,* 424–425.

Graves, D., & Stuart, V. (1985). *Write from the start: Tapping your child's natural ability.* New York: E. P. Dutton.

Heath, S. B. (1983). *Ways with words: Language, life, and work in communities and classrooms.* Cambridge: Cambridge University Press.

Hymes, D. (1964). Directions in (ethno) linguistic theory. *American Anthropology, 66,* 6–56.

Kendall, F. (1983). *Diversity in the classroom: A multicultural approach to the education of young children.* New York and London: Teachers College Press.

Neuman, S., & Roskos, K. (1993). *Language and literacy learning in the early years: An integrated approach.* Fort Worth, TX: Harcourt, Brace, Jovanovich College Publishers.

Ramsey, P. G. (1987). *Teaching and learning in a diverse world: Multicultural education for young children.* New York and London: Teachers College Press.

Saville-Troike, M. (1978). *A guide to culture in the classroom.* Rosslyn, VA: National Clearinghouse for Bilingual Education.

Taylor, D. (1983). *Family literacy: Young children learning to read and write.* Portsmouth, NH: Heinemann.

Teale, W. (1986). Home background and young children's literacy development. In W. H. Teale & E. Sulzby (Eds.), *Emergent literacy: Writing and reading,* (pp. 173–206). Norwood, NJ: Ablex.

Trueba, H. T. (1984). The forms, functions and values of literacy: Reading for survival in a Barrio as a student. *The Journal for the National Association for Bilingual Education. NABE Journal, 9,* 21–40.

chapter 11

Organizing and Managing a Multicultural Program

OVERVIEW

In this chapter we present the organizational framework for developing a successful multicultural program. After revisiting the assumptions of our program, we highlight ways to organize and manage program content and social context. We describe multiple ways of managing and organizing student learning, including cooperative learning groups, ability groups, paired groups, independent learning, and whole class instruction. We conclude by identifying ways to assess and evaluate student learning on an ongoing basis. Both informal and formal assessment procedures are addressed. Ultimately, we envision that multicultural literacy will not be a separate program but a component of all learning experiences for our students.

MANAGING AND ORGANIZING AN INTEGRATED MULTIDISCIPLINARY CURRICULUM

LITERACY LEARNING FOR ALL CHILDREN

When I was a small child I had a color box.
In it were many bright colors.
The colors were not new, so some of the coats were shabby or missing.
Some of the colors were broken
And some were no longer shiny.
But when it came time to fill in a page, each and every color was important.
It didn't matter whether the colors were long or short,
Whether their coats were new, shabby, or missing.
I needed all the colors to make my picture beautiful.

The best pictures I colored were the ones where someone helped me.
When we put our minds together,
We could make a magical picture.

Now that I am older, I still have a color box,
But it does not hold crayons.
It holds children —
Children of many different colors, shapes, abilities, and backgrounds.
Some of these children don't have new shiny coats either;
Some of their coats are shabby;
Some coats are missing — their parents don't have enough money.

The world has become the picture that I am coloring now.
With all my colors, I can make a beautiful picture.
I need to use all of the children . . .
and educate them all to make the world a more beautiful place.
If I don't give equal chances to all of my students —
No matter their color or social class —
My picture will lose its magical, natural beauty.

My picture also looks better if I can join minds with the people around me.
If I keep the big picture in mind . . .
If I think of all the different colors around me . . .
I can make learning a positive experience for all my children.
But to make my picture the best it can be,
I need everyone's help . . .
Parents, administrators, community members, and politicians.

If we leave children out
Because of their socioeconomic status or their color,
We are not giving our world a chance to be as beautiful as it can be.

My color box has changed from when I was a little girl,
But the idea is still the same.
I need all of my colors;
They all need to be given an equal chance.
Then my picture (our world) will be the best that it can be.

Jana Kaatz

Jana, a second-grade teacher in a nearby school district, spontaneously created this poem in her learning log after reading the book *Risk Makers, Risk Takers, Risk Breakers,* edited by Allen and Mason (1989), for a seminar class: Current Issues in Reading at the university. Jana's poem was prompted by the Taylor and Strickland (1989) chapter, "Learning from Families: Implications for Educators and Policy," in which they note that:

> children benefit when we establish literacy in the social and cultural contexts of their everyday lives. . . . We cannot replace daily life with classroom experiences, but we can recognize the legitimacy of children's social existence and use it as a basis for curriculum and instruction. (p. 275)

Effective teachers like Jana realize that students have cultural and personal experiences outside of school that influence their literacy. As stated previously, when students' family and cultural styles are embraced by the school, school activities become a natural extension of home practices (Au, 1993; Galda, Cullinan, & Strickland, 1993; Neuman & Roskos, 1993).

Like Jana, teachers are learning about their students' cultural and linguistic backgrounds and adjusting their teaching and curriculum to be more compatible with these important aspects of students' lives. As teachers accommodate these varied orientations to literacy through a number of organizational configurations and instructional practices, they embrace and affirm the personal and cultural experiences, needs, interests, and learning potentials of all students. They celebrate the rich diversity within their classrooms and use this diversity to extend and enrich learning for all students. They dwell on students' strengths in order to ensure positive and successful learning experiences.

ORGANIZING STUDENT LEARNING

As teachers read our text, they may say, "These ideas are great, but how do I organize and manage a multicultural literacy program?" Many of our new teachers have the same question at the beginning of the year. We explain that organizing and managing a multicultural program begins with instructional practices grounded in theory.

Our definition of multicultural literacy provides direction and purpose for a program. This definition says that multicultural literacy is "the process of linking the cultural experiences, histories, and language that all children bring to school with the language learning and academic learning that takes place in the school. Multicultural literacy further activates silent voices, opens closed minds, promotes academic achievement, and empowers students to think and act critically in a pluralistic, democratic society." This definition underscores our organizational perspectives, along with the principles that (1) all students can learn, (2) multicultural literacy includes all cultures, and (3) culturally sensitive teaching practices and strategies should permeate all aspects of the curriculum through a thematic approach to learning. Our program is grounded in seven principles, which we review here:

- Multicultural literacy is beneficial and fundamental for all students, not just students of diverse cultural and linguistic backgrounds.
- Schools and teachers must embrace the cultural diversity of their students and affirm the cultural beliefs, views, and personal experiences that they bring to the classroom.
- Teachers' positive attitudes and expectations of how students will perform in school have a marked effect on their ability to achieve success.
- Teachers must empower students as individuals and learners so that they receive validation of who they are.
- Students' learning is heightened when they can connect their personal cultural experiences with what they read and write.

- Students learn best when they take an active role in the acquisition of knowledge and skills.
- Students' learning is enhanced when they are encouraged to cooperate and collaborate, sharing and exchanging ideas, concepts, and understandings with others in the construction of knowledge.

Finally, to organize and manage a multicultural program we must consider its three major components: multicultural literature and resources, a whole language and multicultural perspective on learning, and a socioculturally sensitive learning environment. (See Chapter 1.) Just as whole language theory is a philosophy, multicultural literacy is a philosophy—a way of thinking and acting as informed teachers reflect and refine the literacy process. Teachers continually ask questions and shift the way they think about and practice the art of teaching in a global society. Instruction is dynamic and evolving, based on learning theory and the diverse students within the classroom; understanding of theory is ever-changing as teachers listen, read, and learn with students from diverse cultures; interact with colleagues; and share their knowledge with others.

Becoming a teacher who uses a multicultural literacy approach to learning, therefore, requires risk taking, explorations, decisions, and modifications of one's instructional techniques and styles to become sensitive to the sociocultural factors that influence the lives of the students in their classrooms. There are no blueprints or recipes to follow; there are no shortcuts, and easy or simplistic solutions to problems do not exist. Teachers discover their own paths as they integrate their own prior knowledge and their cultural and personal experiences with theory and practice. Through experimentation and exploration, guided by theory, teachers develop strategies and multicultural learning materials that maximize literacy for all students in their classrooms.

Our personal and cultural experiences, our reading, and our experiences while working with teachers and students from diverse settings provide additional insights about organizing and managing a multicultural program. In the following sections, we will share these insights so that others may adapt this information to their own programs.

ORGANIZING THE PHYSICAL ENVIRONMENT FOR LEARNING IN A MULTICULTURAL LITERACY PROGRAM

Using a multicultural approach to literacy requires an environment that supports its principles and includes a social context for learning. Multicultural classrooms are organized to be a supportive, nurturing learning environment where students are actively involved in the construction of their own learning. Classrooms are arranged to foster partnerships and collaborations as students talk, listen, read, and write. The collaborative nature of these classrooms reflects a community of learners who share their ideas, listen to their peers, and work together. Through these cooperative experiences, students learn to respect and appreciate people who are similar to and different from them.

A sense of community gradually evolves as students begin to look to one another for information, recommendations, encouragement, and affirmation. They acquire literacy strategies and skills with peers who are of varying abilities and talents and who are from diverse cultures and linguistic backgrounds. This caring, accepting atmosphere, which is facilitated and guided by teachers, further enables students to feel free to take the risks necessary for learning.

How do teachers organize the physical environment of the classroom to promote a community of learners who engage in higher-level thinking and problem-solving activities? How do they create a community of learners where all students have the opportunity to be recognized for their knowledge, ideas, and perspectives and to learn from others?

We find that movable desks, chairs, and tables are essential for creating a community of learners. By arranging desks or tables in clusters, pairs, hexagons, or u-shaped formations, we foster a variety of student-to-student exchanges—interactive ways of thinking, acting, and sharing, as well as opportunities for exploring and experimenting with the environment. This arrangement allows students to receive support and feedback from their peers and teachers in ways that correspond to their community and home culture. Importantly, teachers modify these arrangements to serve the various functions and purposes of learning. Whatever the design may be, it creates a sense of invitation and togetherness.

Just as student-to-student exchanges are essential elements of the socioculturally sensitive environment, teacher-to-student exchanges are also important elements. Teachers, as cultural mediators, facilitate and guide learning through meaningful, purposeful literacy activities. They mediate learning, help readers and writers clarify their ideas and thoughts, stimulate critical thinking, and lead students toward self-discipline and self-control. To foster literacy in these ways, teachers need space to maneuver easily among learners. They must be able to move quickly, asking questions, commenting, extending, elaborating, and validating students' ideas and thoughts during discussions, reading activities, writing experiences, and problem-solving activities. Hexagonal or horseshoe-shaped formations and open passages between desks arranged in clusters or pods allow for smooth, flowing movements. Using these alternative arrangements also creates a sense of community within their classrooms.

Creating Open Spaces for Literacy Learning

Having an open, carpeted space where the class can gather in large or small groups is also critical. Younger students, especially, enjoy having teachers read stories aloud in this comfortable environment. Many fifth- and sixth-graders also enjoy coming to this area for reading stories aloud, informal class meetings, small-group work, and sustained silent reading, especially if the area serves as a cozy reading corner as well. Large easels for big books, a rocking chair, or an author's chair are also recommended for this area. If the area is part of a reading center, teachers can arrange large, soft pillows; cushions; bean bags; crates or baskets containing favorite multicultural stories, magazines, newspapers or pamphlets; book racks and bookshelves; and even sofas or benches for reading. Reading centers for younger children can also include feltboards, baskets filled with puppets, feltboard characters, a variety of clothing, and props for retelling favorite stories.

These informal settings are particularly important for young students and second-language learners who need multiple opportunities to use and explore language. If classrooms are not large enough to support these areas, however, teachers can easily create the area by shifting the desks to the side and using carpet squares. With the help of students, this can be done in less than five minutes.

Establishing Other Literacy Centers

Many teachers can also establish additional literacy centers for their learners, which for younger learners frequently include listening, writing, or drama centers. These literacy centers incorporate learners' cultural and personal experiences. Listening centers are often equipped with headphones, listening tapes and a tape recorder for recording favorite multicultural stories, bilingual stories, informational texts, or original stories written or dictated by students. While students follow along, rereading texts or stories that reflect their cultural and linguistic background, they may gain fluency and enhanced comprehension of texts. Writing centers ideally include a table and chairs, assorted writing tools and papers, typewriters, and computers. As young students explore pens, markers, crayons, booklets, envelopes, writing pads, or computers, using their temporary spellings, they discover the variety of tools for writing and the diverse functions and purposes of writing. Composing comes alive as students choose their own topics and experiment with written language that emerges from their experiences.

Drama centers consist of props and articles of clothing from students' homes and community. Puppet theaters, feltboards, assorted puppets, masks, thematic props, articles of clothing, and feltboard or laminated cut-outs are also important features of this center. These literacy centers are designed to stimulate experimentation, invention, and discovery as students talk, listen, read, and write. While students spontaneously interact with one another, they are given new opportunities to explore and try out oral and written language forms in a nonthreatening environment.

Literacy centers for older students, by comparison, function as display stations related to specific curriculum themes. These centers feature informational books, multicultural stories, biographies, magazines and newspapers arranged to invite students to investigate topics in more depth. They also include exhibits of cultural artifacts, relics, language, and clothing from a specific culture; manipulatives and learning tools for math- or science-related themes; pictures of historical figures or monuments from various cultures; pictures of a specific country—its environments, people, lifestyles, animals, and plants; maps; time lines; and current events related to a specific theme or culture. As students visit the display/literacy centers, they can use the cultural materials with various literacy activities related to the culture or theme they are studying.

These centers also include models of written language reflecting diverse cultures and exhibits of students' writing, artwork, or projects. Teachers have found that stringing fishing line or nylon cord provides additional space for students' work, which they attach to the lines with clothespins. Windows, window wells, window shades, and the hallway are also useful for publishing students' work.

Designing a Print-rich Environment

Important features of our multicultural classrooms are colorful bulletin boards, wall hangings, and exhibits that invite students to participate in learning and help them view the core subjects as meaningful and relevant. Labels help young children to learn about how print works (Morrow, 1989); labeling posted information, semantic maps, and charts guide students of all ages to additional information about cultural and content-related themes. By keying materials on bulletin boards or exhibits to the themes being studied, teachers encourage students to read about subjects independently during the day. When related multicultural stories, books, magazines, and pamphlets are easily accessible, we find that students explore and read the materials over and over again. The visual displays also provide the correct spellings of relevant words so that students can use them more confidently in their writings and discussions. According to Peregoy and Boyle (1993), a print-rich environment that includes these visual features further facilitates second-language development.

Having a small, permanent message board promotes class communication, writing fluency, and self-esteem (Routman, 1991). Students write and receive messages from their peers or their teachers during designated times. Teachers also find the message board useful for helping students communicate and work out classroom problems. Common uses include requests for seating arrangements or jobs in the classroom, ways to solve behavior problems, praise of students' or the classroom's behavior, or information related to an upcoming event or daily routines (Harste, Short, & Burke, 1988).

Another small, permanent exhibit within our classrooms features the "Person of the Week," whose biopoem, writing samples, family photographs, artifacts and trinkets, hobbies, and interviews are displayed for all to see. With teacher guidance, students enjoy arranging the exhibits in their own way.

Evolving Classroom Environments

As we design the physical environment of a multicultural literacy classroom, we need to remember that the classroom environment and atmosphere are a way of knowing and coming to know (Van Manen, 1986).* We need to experiment with a variety of arrangements to create classrooms that reflect a community of learners. If the classroom environment and atmosphere invite students to learn and experience life, nurture students in becoming readers and writers, and respect students' cultural and linguistic backgrounds, students will thrive and excel (Au, 1993).

ORGANIZING INSTRUCTIONAL LEARNING IN THE CLASSROOM

In addition to creating a warm, nurturing physical environment to support a community of learners, teachers must organize instructional learning within their classrooms. Teaching in a multicultural classroom requires that teachers think about culture, language, students, learning, and teaching in new ways. They must be flexible in planning their instruction and curriculum to match the learning needs of their students.

---

*The physical aspects of the environment may convey the visible aspects of a culture; the atmosphere, including guided discussions and social interactions, may convey the invisible aspects of a culture.

The role of the teacher has a special significance in the democratic, multicultural classroom. An atmosphere that recognizes and validates all students' cultural and linguistic backgrounds emerges only through modeling. If learning is to be compatible with the diverse backgrounds of the students, they need to understand the cultural traditions and heritages of all students. To mold opportunities for personal and cultural expression and allow all voices to be heard, teachers must guide and facilitate interactive discussions and learning activities.

But how can one remove cultural barriers to learning and still accomplish the goals and objectives of the curriculum? In the following sections we will share strategies and techniques we have learned during the past three years.

Structuring Curriculum and Instruction in a Multicultural Program

To design an effective curriculum, Reutzel and Cooter (1992) suggest it is necessary to pare down the scope and sequence of skills to a few important, nonnegotiable skills that teachers consider to be essential for successful reading and writing. In language arts, for example, teachers and administrators can work together to identify nonnegotiable skills for their grade levels. Through this process, the authors suggest, important writing and decoding skills can be determined so that unnecessary overlap and repetition may be avoided in the reading/writing curriculum.

Michigan is creating core curriculum content standards that includes nonnegotiable lists of skills and strategies all students need to acquire across all content areas. While freeing teachers from needless skill and drill practice, the core curriculum content standards will allow teachers to integrate multicultural interdisciplinary reading and writing activities into the curriculum creatively. Consistent with the research of Harste et al. (1988) and Harste, Woodward and Burke (1984), we feel that the multicultural reading and writing curriculum should not be isolated from the content areas. We regard integration, that is, interdisciplinary thematic learning, as an approach to learning and a way of thinking that reflects the interrelationship of the language processes of reading, writing, speaking, and listening across all content areas.

During the first year, however, many teachers merely integrate multicultural literature with their reading/writing curriculum. What's important is that we *begin* a multicultural program, taking small steps that are comfortable for us. Once teachers become comfortable with multicultural reading/writing strategies, they begin to explore ways to integrate the program across the curriculum. Following a multidisciplinary thematic approach to learning, they begin to design ways to link the cultural experiences, histories, and languages of their students with learning across all content areas. They use multicultural literature as the linking mechanism and reading and writing as the tools for learning across the content areas. Thus the curriculum components become a unified whole, and overlap and repetition are minimized.

How teachers specifically integrate learning varies not only among classes, schools, and communities, but also from year to year. According to Au (1993), the cultural and linguistic backgrounds of the students should influence instruction and curriculum within individual classrooms. Teachers' knowledge and understanding of theory, which grows and develops over time, should also affect instruction and curriculum. Teachers need opportunities to extend their professional development and consider alternative instructional practices so that learning becomes meaningful, purposeful, and relevant to students.

Teachers as Decision Makers in a Flexible Multicultural Program

How does one get started? How does one ensure that all students are learning to construct meaning, share and extend their knowledge, and achieve in all content areas? How does one ensure that all students are performing according to their ability and potential?

There are a wide variety of ways to integrate multicultural literacy with the curriculum. What works best depends on the grade level, the students, the teacher, the school, and the community. Through reflective teaching and thinking and risk taking that is supported and guided by staff development procedures and classroom visitations (see Chapter 9), our teachers organize their curriculum. They begin with strategies and activities that they are comfortable with during the first year, some taking smaller steps than others.

During the second year, they use information about cultures and our seven principles of literacy instruction to design their instruction and curriculum to be compatible with their teaching styles and the needs and interests of their students. What works for one teacher does not necessarily work for another. Here are some ways that our teachers implement the multicultural literacy program.

Integrating the Multicultural Program with the Reading/Writing Curriculum. Many teachers prefer to tailor the program to fit their reading/writing curriculum. For example, Mrs. Mouganis has integrated a multicultural reading/writing curriculum with her basal reading program. She uses the basal reading program three days a week and the multicultural literacy program two days a week. To help her students gain an overview of all cultures and an understanding of similarities and differences among cultures, she begins the year with the book *People,* by Peter Spier. She then introduces a new cultural group each month, reading books and stories about each culture to increase students' awareness of diversity. She designs specific multicultural activities to be used with the stories and invites parents and community members to share information, artifacts, and photographs about their culture with the class.

Other teachers prefer to organize their reading/writing curriculum around broad cross-cultural themes. Mrs. Smith, for example, plans thematic units on such topics as grandparents, holidays, animals, celebrations of light, fairytales and folk tales, or famous people and searches for books from various cultures related to this theme. As students read and discuss the stories, they learn to make comparisons about grandparents, celebrations, or folk tales across various cultures. Mrs. Smith also uses a variety of instructional tools—charts, semantic maps, graphs—to help her students understand these concepts.

Integrating the Multicultural Program with Social Studies and Science. Mr. Osburn and Mrs. Andrews, fifth-grade teachers, prefer to design thematic units to tie in with their social studies curriculum, which is American History. They begin the year by studying Native Americans' lifestyles before the European explorers came to

America and then investigate early European explorers and their voyages to America, supplementing the social studies books with current authentic multicultural materials and activities about Native Americans and early explorers. In this way, their students see American History from two perspectives and form a more accurate, indepth understanding of historical events. As the year continues, they explore such themes as slavery and the African Americans' struggle for freedom and civil rights; various immigrants and their travel westward; the growth and expansion of the Wild West—including African American cowboys and their contributions; or World War II and the plight of the Jewish people.

Similarly, Mrs. Taylor, a second-grade teacher, organizes thematic units around her social studies curriculum, which is centered on the community. After reading *Sing a Song of People,* by Lois Lenski, for example, she plans local field trips. Her students visit different community businesses and institutions and interview various members of the community, learning firsthand about their community, its diverse members, and their varied roles. They also learn how people from different cultures and backgrounds work together to solve problems and improve their community.

Mrs. Holly, a fourth-grade teacher, is exploring ways to integrate the multicultural program with her science program. Using a thematic approach, she organizes her program around broad topics such as shells, trees, or animals. Working with her students, she locates books from various cultures on these topics. After reading *The Great Kupok Tree,* by Lynne Cherry, for example, her students learn about animal and plant life in the rainforest. Students then compare the animal and plant life in the rainforest of South America with those in the desert in the Southwest regions of the United States as they read, *I'm in Charge of Celebrations,* by Bryd Baylor. While reading these stories, they also learn how people from various cultures structure their lifestyles around plant and animal life. Students learn how homes, clothing, and food are also related to one's surroundings. By linking the content areas in these ways, teachers help students appreciate and understand differences and similarities among cultural groups.

Integrating the Multicultural Program with an Interdisciplinary Thematic Curriculum.   Other teachers, like Mrs. Streeter and Mrs. Micallef, follow an interdisciplinary thematic approach to learning (see Chapter 6), integrating the multicultural program across all contents areas. Interestingly, this year they are implementing a thematic unit on ethnic pride in order to enhance their students' self-esteem. As students investigate their heritage, they are learning about their family roots, their cultural heritages and traditions, and their own identity. They begin by exploring the uniqueness of each person's name: the origins of their first names, and the history of their family names. As they investigate the latter, many students begin to realize that they are members of many different cultural groups. To highlight this concept, Mrs. Streeter and Mrs. Micallef draw a graph of students' cultural roots. Students place a small photograph of themselves in the box that represents their cultural background, as shown in Figure 11.1. Once students connect with their cultural roots in this way, they are ready to explore commonalities and differences among other cultural groups.

As the year continues, Mrs. Streeter and Mrs. Micallef look for books that reflect the cultural heritage of their students and portray each group's strengths. They

FIGURE 11.1 Students learn about their cultural heritage and the heritage of their peers through a graph of their countries of origin.

identify poems, folk tales, biographies, and realistic novels from diverse cultures and organize a variety of learning activities across all content areas. Through this process, which emerges from students' family roots, students become more sensitive to the unique contributions we all bring to our nation, honoring and celebrating the differences among us.

Teaching and Learning: An Ongoing Process for Teachers and Students.   In order to accomplish these goals for multicultural teaching and learning, teachers must become reflective decision-makers who plan, implement, evaluate, and modify learning to match the needs and interests of their students. Becoming reflective decision makers further implies that teachers use theory to guide their practice. There is not a "right way" to organize a multicultural literacy program; teachers adapt a plan that corresponds with theory, their teaching style, and their students, schools, and communities. Learning, therefore, becomes an ongoing process for teachers and students alike. This process includes staff development, readings, workshops, classroom research, and university coursework.

MANAGING LITERACY LEARNING
IN A MULTICULTURAL CLASSROOM

When visitors come to our classrooms, they seldom see students working quietly at their desks or teachers delivering lectures. They see teachers who "function more like orchestra conductors than like lecturers, getting things started and keeping them moving along, providing information and pointing to resources, coordinating a diverse but harmonious buzz of activity" (Goodlad and Oakes, 1988, p. 19). Specifically, visitors see teachers who are: (1) **cultural organizers,** facilitating learning that reflects varied ways of knowing, experiencing, thinking, and behaving; (2) **cultural mediators,** who create opportunities for critical dialogue and expression as students construct their own knowledge and generate meaning; and (3) **orchestrators of social contexts,** who coordinate varied learning configurations, including interpersonal and intrapersonal opportunities for seeking, accessing, and evaluating knowledge. (See Chapter 2.) Each classroom is a community of diverse learners that reflects learning experiences that are compatible with their backgrounds.

Managing a Social Context for Learning

To create a match between students' diverse cultural and linguistic backgrounds and instruction, teachers must use a variety of learning configurations—whole class, heterogeneous and homogeneous groups, dyads, individualized learning, and small cooperative learning groups. The implications of the KEEP project (see Chapter 2), for example, reveal the importance of establishing a social context for learning related to the social relationships and interactional styles of the Native Hawaiians' homes. When the learning environment matches the social and cultural context of students' everyday lives, conflicts between home and school dissipate and links between home and school evolve more naturally. Other research studies (Au, 1993; Carbo, Dunn, & Dunn, 1986; Galda et al., 1993; Morrow & Smith, 1990) similarly emphasize the need to vary learning configurations and interactional patterns for students, especially learners with special needs (Peregoy & Boyle, 1993), within the classroom. Their studies indicate that diverse learners require alternative strategies, resources, and environments. To embrace and affirm all learning patterns of all students within our classrooms, therefore, we need to provide multiple social contexts for learning.

Working as a Whole Class.   Working together as a whole class is one organizational pattern commonly used by our teachers. Many teachers prefer to establish classroom organizational and management expectations for their students at the beginning of the year through whole class activities. Teachers who are new to the program need to begin with whole class activities so that they can become comfortable with some of the innovative teaching strategies. After gaining comfort with the strategies in this familiar grouping arrangement, they are ready to begin alternative grouping strategies.

Opportunities to learn within a whole class configuration include: teachers reading multicultural literature aloud, students reading a story or novel together as a class, interactive dialogues, choral readings, reader's theater, dramatic readings, dramatizations, journal writing, responding to literature through writing, or publishing students' reading or writing. As students participate in these whole class activities and discussions, they learn to listen to the diverse voices that comprise their classroom. They further increase their understanding and appreciation of the differences and similarities among people.

Working in Homogeneous and Heterogeneous Groups.   There are also times when students work in homogeneous or heterogeneous groups to receive more guidance and instruction as they read and write. Mrs. Theisen, a fourth-grade teacher, organizes her class into three homogeneous groups to read African American stories, for example, in order to practice decoding and encoding new words, to learn new strategies for comprehending narrative and expository texts, or to increase vocabulary development, reading fluency, and expression. Her first group, which reads at sixth-grade level, reads *Roll of Thunder, Hear My Cry,* by Mildred Taylor; the second group, which reads at fourth-grade level, reads *Freedom Train,* by Dorothy Sterling; and the third group, which reads below fourth-grade level, reads *Song of the Trees,* by Taylor. Students gain new insights into the African American experience as they read, discuss, and respond to the stories in their literature journals, which include free writing, simulated journal entries, character webs, lists of figurative language, illustrations, or personal reflections/reactions to their readings. (See Chapter 5.)

After reading, students work within their group to prepare creative responses, independently and as a group, which they share with the whole class. The first group individually wrote character poems for their favorite character in *Roll of Thunder, Hear My Cry* and worked as a group to create a reader's theater activity from a dramatic chapter in the story. The second group designed choral readings of the spirituals sung by the slaves to capture the spirit of despair and hope as the slaves worked in the cotton fields and created individual raps about Harriet Tubman's Underground Railroad. The third group predicted their own ending to the story when Stacey rode off in the night in search of his father and designed a reader's theater activity, as a group, of what actually happened when Stacey's father returned.

At other times, Mrs. Theisen follows a similar format with her students, who work in heterogeneous groups to read novels of their choice. After displaying three novels in the reading center for a few days, she asks students to sign up to read their favorite book with a group. Once the groups finish it, they also prepare creative responses to be shared with the whole class. Using both homogeneous and heterogeneous grouping is important if we are to meet the needs and interests of all learners.

Similarly, Mrs. Streeter and Mrs. Micallef form three heterogeneous groups, which include fifth-graders and POHI students, to read three picture books related to a theme. In this case, they arrange the groups to include a mixture of ability levels, as well as followers and leaders. They feel that heterogeneous grouping validates and affirms all their learners' unique contributions, abilities, and backgrounds. According to Mrs. Streeter and Mrs. Micallef, having students work in heterogeneous groups further provides more opportunities for students to discuss the stories in detail and to share their ideas.

The groups meet with one of the teachers or Mrs. Kresch, Mrs. Micallef's teaching aide, to read and share the three stories orally for three days. Through these extended discussions, students become more aware of how family, culture, race, gender, education, and work intersect to shape people's choices and experiences. They also improve their problem-solving skills as they discuss possible solutions that arise as a result of these factors.

Mrs. Bortz also forms workshops for students who wish to explore a topic in more depth or who need more practice on a specific strategy. These workshops may be either homogeneous or heterogeneous. She organizes homogeneous workshops, for example, to provide more practice and assistance in decoding strategies, writing paragraphs, reading fluency, or using punctuation and capitalization. She structures heterogeneous workshops that include how to use quotation marks, how to cite references for an independent research study, ways to investigate a topic in more depth, or strategies for designing a play or drama to be shared with the class.

Working in small heterogeneous and homogenous groups promotes both academic achievement and positive attitudes in the classroom. Through extended discussions and guided instruction, students learn subject matter, solve problems, and accomplish tasks. Simultaneously, they learn how to relate to others whose cultural and personal experiences, abilities, interests, or talents are different from their own. Under the guidance and instruction of their teachers, they learn to accept and value individuals. These social skills are transferred to other learning situations with minimal teacher assistance.

Working in Dyads.   Working in dyads, or pairs, is another very powerful learning arrangement that uses minimal teacher assistance. Many teachers prefer to begin the year with activities for students to do in pairs before they begin to work in cooperative learning groups. Reading one's favorite page from a novel or story aloud to a partner, for example, is an easy activity to use at the beginning of the year. Similarly, after students write in their journals or compose a story, they might share their writing with a partner. Once students become comfortable with these activities, they are ready to work in pairs to practice reading a story to be shared with a student in a younger grade or to peer edit their writing. Other activities include journal buddies, who write journal entries to a partner; study buddies, who study their spelling, social studies, or science with a partner; prewriting buddies, who share their ideas for a story, poem, or letter with a partner; computer buddies, who revise and edit one another's writing; or retelling buddies, who retell stories, reexplain the steps to follow when using a specific strategy (spelling, math, decoding unknown words), or share with a partner information related to a topic being discussed in class. Working in pairs enables students to clarify concepts, check their understanding of information, and brainstorm new ideas or information. Teachers find that this configuration is especially effective with culturally diverse students whose language learning is deeply rooted in oral traditions and with bilingual students who need additional practice and assistance in expressing and understanding ideas in a second language. This arrangement provides more opportunities to use and explore language as students express their ideas in the supportive context of peers (Peregoy & Boyle, 1993).

Peer tutoring is another effective dyad confirmation. In peer tutoring, one student who has mastered a concept or strategy helps a second student who has not yet mastered the concept or strategy. Many teachers enjoy pairing students across grade levels—for example fourth-graders tutoring a second-grader. After training older students in how to read or write with younger students, for example, the fourth-grader might give the second-grader support and positive feedback as they read aloud, draft compositions, or revise or edit written work. Similarly, older students can help kindergarten or first-grade students by reading stories aloud and asking questions as they read or record their dictated stories. In addition to improved attitudes toward reading and writing, both the tutor and the student being tutored increase reading and writing performance (Cooledge & Wurster, 1985; Paolitto, 1976; Topping, 1989). Other studies find that the tutoring process also improves social skills (Powell, Wisenbaker, & Connor, 1985).

Working Independently. As students work independently, they learn what is expected of them, how and where to seek help when needed, how to complete tasks, and how to make choices in their learning. They are also free to tap into their personal and cultural experiences. Some choices and opportunities for independent activities include sustained silent reading, journal writing, writing drafts, responding to literature, listening to taped stories or taped excerpts from their social studies or science textbooks, viewing a film, working at the computer on *Multicultural Links* or other computer-based software, writing on the computer, or tape recording a story for others. Teachers find that students learn to work better independently if they can choose from a variety of options. When students choose their own format and the project, they become more engaged with their work, they spend more time on task, and the quality of work is enhanced. Over time, students become more confident in their ability to make choices independently. Working with students to develop time schedules, behavioral expectations, and mutually agreed-upon contracts are important management tools during independent work time (Routman, 1991).

Working in Cooperative Learning Groups. Working in cooperative learning groups is especially popular among young learners. We define cooperative learning as a group of four or five students of heterogeneous ability working toward a common goal. The students may work in small groups to learn material and help others learn the material, or they may work together to acquire academic and social skills, pose and solve problems, and discuss cultural understanding and social issues. Just arranging students in groups of varying abilities will not produce cooperative learning. For cooperative learning to be successful (Johnson, Johnson, & Holubec, 1990) there is a need for (1) positive interdependence among group members as they coordinate their efforts to complete a task; (2) face-to-face interactions that maintain the participation of all group members, who are important, required, and indispensable for the group's success; (3) individual and group accountability measures, which necessitate that all members of the group know who needs more assistance, support, and encouragement in completing tasks and that all members rely on their own performance, rather than the performance of others, when doing the task independently; (4) social skills, as students learn to communicate with others through listening, paraphrasing, checking for understanding, and learning to work with others as they acquire leadership, trust, decision-making, and conflict-management skills; and (5) group processing, as the group accomplishes group goals based on individual accountability.

Students don't automatically have these skills and abilities; they acquire them over time as they participate in more and more cooperative learning groups. To promote these skills, however, we find that the various members of the groups should have designated roles and responsibilities. While these roles may vary, usually one group member is the leader, who guides the group to consensus; another member is the recorder, who writes down the ideas or information; a third member is the informant, who shares the group's ideas or information with the whole class; and a fourth member is the "gofer," who gathers materials for the activity and provides praise and enthusiasm for the various group members as they participate. During a class's first experiences with cooperative learning, teachers find it best to assign these responsibilities and to rotate them during subsequent experiences. After students have more opportunities to work together, they begin to assign the responsibilities themselves, making sure the responsibilities are rotated. By giving them a time frame—usually one or two minutes—we find that the tasks are distributed more quickly and easily.

In addition to having designated responsibilities, students also need to work on their social skills. We find that brainstorming sessions about appropriate social behaviors prior to cooperative learning experiences is helpful. For example, asking students what things they can do to get their group to work together well is important. Through guidance, students decide that praising one another, using words of encouragement for one another, using people's names in their words of praise and encouragement, paraphrasing people's ideas, or asking people to restate their ideas in order to check for understanding fosters positive interactions among group members. Mrs. Andrews likes to display these ideas on chart paper. Seeing these ideas daily reinforces group-processing skills.

To further ensure that the cooperative learning activities will be positive experiences for all students, Mrs. Andrews asks a group of four students to model the process for the class, assigning each member a role as either a leader, recorder, informant, or gofer. Similar to the modeling process for revising groups (see Chapter 5), she then gives the group of four students, who are arranged at a circular table in the center of the classroom, an easy task to complete. The other class members take notes on the group's ability to apply their social skills and perform their assigned responsibilities. An example of an easy task for the modeling group to complete might be to brainstorm a list of ways the members of the group are alike and ways they are different. After brainstorming their ideas for three to five minutes, the group must stop and reach consensus on their best ideas by placing stars beside three ways they are alike and three ways they are different. Once the group successfully models the process, the other class members share their observations of the group's performance and additional strategies or words of praise or encouragement they might use. Mrs. Andrews adds her own observations about the group's performance and offers suggestions.

On the following day, Mrs. Andrews asks the class to apply their understanding of cooperative learning groups. After arranging them in groups and assigning the various roles, she asks each group to complete their own KWL (see Chapter 6) on Native Americans for a thematic unit they are beginning in social studies. (She has modeled the KWL strategy for her class numerous times.) First, she asks each group to brainstorm words related to Native Americans and to place them in the K column. Second, she asks each group to brainstorm questions they might have about Native

Americans and to place them in the W column. After completing the columns, she asks each group to place a star beside three ideas in the K column and three questions in the W column, which will be shared with the group. Because students are learning how to conduct cooperative learning groups, Mrs. Andrews limits individual and group accountability measures to class recognition of each group's ideas and to her recognition of each individual's performance of his/her assigned role, using a checklist as she circulates among the groups. As her students participate in more and more cooperative learning activities, she devises individual and group accountability measures to correspond with the purpose of the learning activity.

Consistent with selected research on cooperative learning groups (Bejarano, 1987; De Avila, Duncan, & Narvarrette, 1987; Slavin, 1983, 1987), students in our program are improving their academic performance, their attitudes toward learning, their self-esteem, their motivation for learning, and social skills. Other research studies (Bejarano, 1987; De Avila, Duncan, & Narvarrette, 1987; Peregoy & Boyle, 1993) find that cooperative learning methods benefit students from diverse linguistic backgrounds. According to these researchers, cooperative learning gives these students more opportunities for face-to-face interactions, which are important for second-language acquisition; improve their intergroup relations and self-esteem; and increase their academic performance. After working in cooperative groups (Bejarano, 1987; Meloth & Deering, 1992), second-language learners are better able to talk about their thinking, communicate more effectively in both their native language and in English, and listen more closely. Importantly, working in heterogeneous cooperative groups motivates students of diverse backgrounds. Homogeneous groups, in contrast, frequently discourage students of diverse backgrounds, who feel that other groups perform consistently better than they do (Au, 1993; Manning & Lucking, 1990; Peregoy & Boyle, 1993).

Coordination. Many students, including a large number of culturally and linguistically diverse students, are frequently removed from the regular classroom to participate in one or more special programs. According to Au (1993) and Routman (1991), isolating these students deprives them of the positive models of language and literacy and the assistance from peers in their classrooms. These students often have lower self-esteem because of this isolation; they do not have the same literacy experiences as their classmates and fail to develop strategies and background experiences that contribute to literacy.

To avoid possible detrimental effects of special programs, the culturally diverse school district in our program is considering an alternative arrangement, coordination, in their Chapter I program. Coordination includes both "pull-out" and "push-in." Chapter I teachers work with their students in their learning centers (pull-out) and in their classroom setting (push-in). Working with classroom teachers, Chapter I teachers plan instructional activities that reinforce literacy for these students. For example, Mrs. Jamieson reads books and stories aloud to her students, discussing the vocabulary and its meaning. After these shared reading experiences, she practices an accompanying choral reading or reader's theater with them. When Mrs. Jamieson and the Chapter I students join the class, Mrs. Jamieson and the classroom teacher collaboratively read the stories aloud. Because the Chapter I students are familiar with the story, the vocabulary, and its meaning, they participate in the classroom discussions about the story with more enthusiasm and interest. As the class practices the choral reading or reader's theater, they often become leaders of their groups, modeling good expression and intonation, because they already know the words and their meanings.

Similarly, Mrs. Weeks and Mrs. Lund plan writing activities, following the writing process, for their Chapter I students. As students participate in the prewriting, drafting, revising, editing, and publishing activities in their learning center, they learn how to take notes, organize their ideas, revise their writing to express their ideas more clearly, and edit their writing in a small setting that includes more guidance and personal attention. When Mrs. Weeks or Mrs. Lund do writing activities with their classroom teachers later in the year, these students are able to use prewriting, revising, and editing strategies successfully—sometimes better than their peers. For example, when her class began writing poems about imaginary creatures found in myths and folklore from various cultures, Thanhphanh created a poem about the Three Headed Elephant of the Thai culture. (See Figure 11.2.) After a choral reading of a poem with her group and listening to her peers do a choral reading of other poems about various mythological and folklore characters found in Eric Carle's *Dragons, Dragons,* she was inspired to write a poem that reflected her own cultural heritage. She made more revisions on her poem than any of her classmates on their poems. Learning about revising and editing in the learning center gave her the tools to create this wonderful poem. Figure 11.3a illustrates her first draft, and Figure 11.3b shows her revised draft of "Three Headed Elephant."

FIGURE 11.2 Thanphanh displays her illustration of her poem, "Three Headed Elephant."

Threes Headed-Elephant

Elephant
Elephant
Elephant
What my name?
I'm so big,
that I could imgination
it.
   I'm strong enough
     to help put,
     stronger then I
      thought.

Three
Three
Three
How many head do
I have?
I have three head,
   and three trunck.

Six
Six
Six
I have six big horn,
   also six sharp hgrn,
   I have six big
    ear, too.

Scarey
Scarey
Scarey
You think I'm scarey,
I can look three way,
but I may look scarey.
I come from Thailand,
   in the jungle.

FIGURE 11.3a Thanphanh's first draft.

THREE HEADED ELEPHANT

Three
Three
Three
I have searched for my favorite
    number in an animal
    that has three things
    but uses the same
        body.
I had searched
    but never found it
Searched all the states
    not any are found
Went to all the countries
    but not one was found.
Went home,
    and heard the parent say,
Our own people had found the bone of the three
        headed elephant.
HAPPY
HAPPY
Went to see how it looked,
What it is like.
Elephant
Elephant
Elephant
You have three heads,
but you use one body,
        you have three big trunks,
    three big faces,
    with three big horns,
You can look three ways
    and are ENORMOUS!
I took your picture
    and got
HAPPY!

by Thanphanh Phommavong

FIGURE 11.3b   Thanphanh's revised draft.

In these ways, classroom teachers and Chapter I teachers are working cooperatively to design instruction that optimizes learning for their students. They are experimenting and exploring several arrangements, reflecting on the process, and making adjustments as needed.

Varying Peer Interactions.   Au (1993) emphasizes a need to be aware of peer dynamics with students of diverse backgrounds. She stresses that the effectiveness of grouping arrangements is strongly affected by cultural differences. What works is frequently dependent on the cultural background of students. For example, she contrasted Native Hawaiian students with Yup'ik Eskimo students. Native Hawaiian students, when seated with peers, speak freely about their work, seeking help as needed. Yup'ik students, in contrast, seldom speak to one another; they do not openly seek or offer assistance. If someone needs help, they make suggestions, as needed through subtle comments.

If learning arrangements are to be compatible with the diverse cultural and linguistic backgrounds of our students, we will need to vary the types of learning configurations and experiment and explore alternative grouping patterns. Au (1993) suggests that we shall discover the most effective learning configurations through observations of students, through conversations with community members or teachers, and through reading professional literature.

Management Tools for Alternative Grouping Configurations

Managing alternative groupings becomes easier when teachers monitor the groups. Circulating from one student to the next or rotating from one group to the next, teachers provide modeling of expected behaviors and give students specific feedback as they approximate expected behaviors. For example, if students are not using praise or asking questions of their peers during revising groups, Mrs. Andrews sits down with the group and models praise or questioning strategies for them. When students use specific praise or ask clarifying questions of peers, she praises them.

Mrs. Andrews shares her observations about the performance of the cooperative learning groups after students practice choral readings, reader's theater, or complete cooperative reading/writing activities. Mrs. Manchester also likes to use specific praise about each group's performance by describing something that each group did well. She might say, "Wasn't it exciting to hear Jeff's group read the words, 'Run for your Lives! Abiyoyo's coming!'? We could feel the fear in their voices." Or "Did you hear how Darlene's group read the words, 'You can tell what's worth a celebration because your heart will POUND . . .'? I could hear the pounding by the way they read the words with forcefulness and vigor." Or "I could feel the stillness and quietness of the night when Trent read the words, '. . . and the night became as quiet as soft falling snow', softly, almost like a whisper."

Likewise, after "revising" groups, Mrs. Coburn might say, "I heard very good examples of specific praise today. Marvin said that the words in Katherine's poem about the Cherokee Indian's Rattlesnake dance formed images in his mind; he could see the shimmering ribbons and the slithering, coiling movements of the dancers. Nnekia shared that Katherine's poem made her feel like she was there because of its rhythm and beat." In order that students might remember these examples, Mrs. Coburn records them on chart paper for all to see.

Teachers also give positive feedback for certain behaviors they see. For example, Mrs. Gilkey states, "I like the way Daphne's group listens as each group shares its Predict-o-grams," or "Thank you for stopping immediately to listen when you heard our signal," or "I'm glad that you are remembering to wait patiently for your friends to finish recording their ideas on their papers."

Whether working in small groups, individually, or as a whole class, students generally want to perform all their activities well and learn to the best of their abilities; many times they are not sure what we expect of them. By discussing our expectations prior to the activity and by brainstorming appropriate behavior, we find that students become self-motivated to meet our expectations. Using cues or signals to gain their attention and readiness for listening are also helpful. Some teachers use short songs or fingerplays; others clap rhythmical patterns that students imitate; others use a bell, a triangle, or a song flute. Finally, when students meet our expectations, we praise them specifically about their performance and behavior. We gradually raise our expectations so that all students can stretch to higher performance levels. Students soon begin to reflect our use of praise, spontaneously offering their observations and evaluations of their own and their peers' performance.

Another effective management tool is self-reflection. At the end of the week, Mrs. Birdyshaw asks her students to write what they learned from an experience or activity, how they might modify their performance the next time, and how they might improve their learning. As students reflect on their behavior and performance, they become aware of their strengths and what they need to improve. Brian, who did not complete his kente cloth, for example, wrote, "Next time I will try an art activity. I know I can't get better at drawing unless I try." Self-reflection helps students gain ownership and develop responsibility for their learning at a young age. Even first-graders can participate in this process. For example, during a student-teacher conference, Shannon reported, "I learned that I can write my story just by putting down the first letters of my words."

Finally, teachers share responsibility and control with their students. If voices are getting too loud, teachers encourage students to think of ways to monitor their voices so they won't disturb neighboring classrooms. In this way, students learn that respect for others is not limited to their classroom walls, but extends to the whole school and the community. These cooperative, respectful skills transfer to new settings and situations.

However, desired behaviors do not emerge magically. They evolve over time. The environment is created one day at a time, one step at a time. Teachers introduce process activities gradually. First, they model expected behaviors; second, they give students many opportunities to learn and practice a new strategy or activity, using praise and more modeling, until they become successful. New process activities and new elements are acquired as students successfully master a strategy or an activity.

EVALUATION AND ASSESSMENT IN A MULTICULTURAL LITERACY PROGRAM

To organize and manage a successful multicultural literacy program, assessment and evaluation must be an integral part of the teaching process. Consistent with Routman (1991), we define assessment as the collection of data and the gathering of evidence. We define evaluation as the process of examining the data carefully through interpretation, analysis, reflection, and decision-making in order to use the findings to guide instruction. Teachers, therefore, continually observe their students, reflect about their instruction and students' performance, and modify instruction to meet the growing and changing needs of their students. The process is slow and evolutionary and includes risk taking and continuous self-examination. Merely using multicultural strategies and techniques will not result in successful literacy.

To maximize literacy performance, evaluation and assessment should incorporate meaningful evaluation techniques. As is true of all students from diverse backgrounds develop literacy at varying rates. Therefore, assessment and evaluation of literacy development in students are best accomplished in a variety of situations across time (Au, 1993; Cummins, 1986; Galda, Cullinan, & Strickland, 1993; Teale, 1988; Teale, Hiebert, & Clittenden, 1987; Valencia, 1990). Consistent with Yetta Goodman (1989), we believe that evaluation and assessment "cannot be divorced from classroom organization, from the relationship between teacher and student, from continuous learning experiences and activities" (p. 4). Assessment and evaluation further lead to action—reflection, decision-making, teaching, and future literacy activities—as we modify and refine our practice to match the evolving needs of our students.

Our assessment and evaluation practices focus on students' strengths. If we are to obtain a fair and accurate picture of how a student performs over time, we need a holistic profile of the student that includes multifactored assessments. Kenneth Goodman (1989) lists five important characteristics of assessment, which guide us. They include:

- Assessment is holistic, using natural language taken from real-life contexts.
- Assessment respects all students and reveals their communication competencies.
- Assessment is consistent with current theory on teaching, learning, and literacy development.
- Assessment is innovative, creative, and dynamic.
- Assessment is open-ended and flexible, allowing for modification and individual, cultural, and linguistic differences.

To this list of characteristics, we add:

- Assessment draws on multiple sources and dimensions and follows formal and informal procedures.

We use a variety of sources to guide our instruction. We need to compare the individual with him- or herself and with others of the same age and grade level. Along with Calfee and Hiebert (1991), we view assessment as the collection and evaluation of evidence about literacy. This includes informal, internally guided classroom assessment through the use of portfolios, and formal, standardized tests of literacy development. All pieces combine to form a profile of our students and their literacy development.

Getting Started

Our teachers frequently ask how to begin using portfolios. Just as instructional practice in a multicultural literacy program is an evolving process that requires risk taking, reflection, and decision-making, assessment and evaluation are also evolving processes requiring these same self-examining behaviors. There are no recipes and no blueprints for assessment and evaluation; the assessment and evaluation that guide and inform our practice are processes that emerge from the diverse students in our classrooms.

Staff development is critical in following informal assessment procedures. Teachers need guidance as they apply these approaches in their classrooms. According to Routman (1991, p. 302), "We need to guard against simply putting procedures into place without understanding the theory behind them." The following section describes our experiences with assessment and evaluation. These experiences evolved from our inservices and classroom visitations with teachers.

Informal Monitoring

First, through our inservice sessions, we stress the importance of collecting the data through informal monitoring. According to Yetta Goodman (1989), we must be excellent observers, or "kidwatchers." Kidwatching includes classroom observations, anecdotal records, conferences, checklists, interviews, oral and written language samples, and interdisciplinary applications. Information from these varied sources provides a picture or "portfolio" (Flood & Lapp, 1989) of students and their learning. Because the literacy patterns of students from diverse backgrounds may not be tapped by formal assessment procedures, the use of a variety of sources becomes an important way of monitoring their literacy (Au, 1993).

Observation.   Observation, a rich source of information for the portfolio, requires focused attention to students as they read, write, listen, and speak. Many teachers naturally use this technique daily as they watch and interact with their students. These observations take only a few minutes; sometimes a glance may provide information about students' progress. We encourage teachers to begin focusing their observations in order to learn more about their students' attitudes, their learning strategies, their interactions with classmates, their use of resources or other students for assistance, their problem-solving skills during group work, and their responses to literacy. These observations provide clues as to the grouping patterns we might use to make these arrangements compatible with students' cultural backgrounds. Using these kidwatching techniques with a class as a whole is not time-consuming. Tompkins and Hoskisson (1991) also emphasize the need to use kidwatching with individual students for short periods. This information, which can be recorded informally, frequently provides the rich data we need to support learning for all students.

Anecdotal Records.   Anecdotal records note students' performance in reading, writing, talking, and listening activities; their asking and responding strategies; and their understanding or confusion about concepts or skills. They include brief, specific comments and provide extended documentation of students' literacy development in a variety of contexts. Organizational schemes for anecdotal notes include files with anecdotes written on small index cards; stick-on notes placed in spiral-bound notebooks that are divided into sections for students; or clipboards with mailing labels that list all students and provide space to record short, running notes about students' performance. Focusing on a specific number of students each day seems to help teachers manage this system without becoming overwhelmed. These notes also facilitate students' placement in resource classrooms as needed.

Conferencing.   Conferences and miniconferences are another important source of information. Conferences are short, informal meetings with students to discuss their reading, writing, talking or listening performance or to help them solve problems related to these areas. Miniconferences, according to Clark (1987), are invaluable sources for data collection about students' performance. As they circulate to monitor students' work, teachers use these miniconferences to gather information, ask guiding questions, provide helpful suggestions, share words of encouragement or praise, and hear students' ideas.

Other types of conferences include: prereading or prewriting conferences, where students and teachers make plans for reading and keeping literature response logs and for organizing and planning their writing; revising or editing conferences, where students and teachers revise or edit their compositions; book discussion conferences, where teachers and students share literature response logs, discuss stories, or make plans for related activities; workshop conferences, where teachers provide enrichment or instructional minilessons on specific skills or strategies; and assessment conferences, where students reflect on their own literacy growth and set goals for future activities (Tompkins & Hoskisson, 1991; Routman, 1991). Combining scaffolded instruction—guided instruction that gradually decreases as students acquire a strategy—with assessment during these conferences increases literacy development for students from diverse backgrounds (Au, 1993).

Checklists.   Using checklists, combined with narrative and observational comments, is another effective way to track students' progress. Some possible checklists might be symbol-sound knowledge, basic concepts about print, basic sight words, reading and writing competencies, reading and writing strategies, types of revisions, or types of editing. Checklists for students are also important assessment techniques, promoting self-reflection and self-evaluation. Students use checklists to take charge of their own learning, checking to be sure they have completed specific skills or assignments before completing an assignment. Accountability is reinforced when students sign their names at the bottom of the sheet, agreeing that they have carefully reviewed and checked their assignments in these specific areas. To be most effective, checklists should be devised by teachers and students together so that they correspond to the purpose and function of the activity. Routman (1991) further cautions teachers to use checklists sparingly, for one can easily overlook the learning that is occurring.

Interviews and Surveys.   Interviews or surveys are an important way of knowing and understanding our students. Although written surveys can be useful, the allotted space often confines students' responses. But with personal interviews, we can probe responses and elicit more information about students' reflections, attitudes, strategies, understanding of concepts, preferences, or levels of confidence. Certainly, teachers can design their own forms corresponding to their class, grade level, and students. Figure 11.4 shows the interview we devised for our multicultural program; Figure 11.5 is the interview we devised for the Multicultural Links software. The interviews note changes in attitudes, in conceptual understanding of information, and in students' preferences. They also provide important suggestions and new directions for instruction the following year.

STUDENT INTERVIEW QUESTIONS

1. How do you feel about the multicultural literature program?
2. What do you enjoy about the program?
3. Why does your teacher read these books to you?
4. What kinds of things are you doing with the books?
5. What are some of the activities you enjoy?
6. What reading activities have you liked?
7. What writing activities have you enjoyed?
8. What are some of your favorite books?
9. How are these books different from the stories in your reading book?
10. How is reading different for you this year?
11. How do you feel about reading? Why?
12. What would someone think about your reading?
13. What does your teacher like best about your reading?
14. How do you feel about writing? Why?
15. What would someone think about your writing?
16. What does your teacher like best about your writing?
17. Who's a good writer? Why do you think so?
18. Who's a good reader you know? Why do you think so?
19. What cultures have you learned about?
20. What have you learned about them?
21. Why do you think it is important to learn about other cultures?
22. Is there anything else you want to say about the multicultural literature program?

FIGURE 11.4 Student interview for multicultural literacy program.

Oral and Written Language Samples. Oral and written language samples are invaluable ways of tracking students' communicative competence over time. Oral language samples might include students' reading, responses to questions, problem-solving abilities, retellings, or discussion during small-group work. Written language samples might include samples of students' journal writing and their writing through all stages: prewriting strategies, rough drafts, revised drafts, edited drafts, and final drafts (Tompkins, 1990). To help determine students' development over time, we like to collect samples at the beginning of the year, midway through the year, and at the end of the year.

FIGURE 11.5 Student interview for computers and multicultural links.

COMPUTER INTERVIEW QUESTIONS

1. How do you feel about using the computer?
2. What did you like best about using the computer?
3. What was most difficult about using the computer?
4. How do you feel about using the computer independently?
5. What part of Multicultural Links do you enjoy most?
6. What culture(s) did you learn about when using Multicultural Links?
7. How did the Multicultural Links Program help you learn about culture?
8. What other culture(s) would you like to learn about?
9. Are there other ways you can use the computer to help you learn?

Across-the-curriculum Applications.　Across-the-curriculum applications are also an important way of collecting data about literacy development. Specifically, teachers gather data on how students apply what they know about listening, talking, reading, and writing across content areas. According to Tompkins and Hoskisson (1991), teachers need to use triangulation—approaching learning from at least three different viewpoints. For example, in addition to teacher-made tests or textbook tests, teachers might use kidwatching, anecdotal records, checklists, interviewing, or oral and written samples of students' work. As students apply their knowledge across content areas, we gain more nearly accurate indicators of their literacy and determine if they are making transfers from one learning activity to the next.

Formal Assessments.　Formal assessments (standardized assessments) provide a quantitative index of reading performance. They include norm-referenced tests, which compare students' performance to a cross section of students in other regions of the country, and criterion-referenced tests, which examine students' reading performance relative to specific instructional objectives at some predetermined proficiency level.

Historically, standardized assessment has dominated the evaluation of reading and writing performance. Such tests frequently serve as measures of educational effectiveness; many school districts, moreover, continue to rely heavily on standardized assessment procedures for evaluating program effectiveness. Nevertheless, there is a need to use the findings cautiously with students of diverse backgrounds because of possible cultural bias.

Portfolios.　To keep representative samples of the data from these informal assessment techniques, teachers store the data in large folders or portfolios. Flood and Lapp (1989) describe the information gained from these approaches as a more complete and personal assessment picture or portfolio of the student. By evaluating the data, which are representative, ongoing, and changing work samples, teachers get to know their students better and can thus interpret their literacy development more accurately.

The portfolio, however, is not just a storage bin of information that serves no purpose; it is part of the learning process. Students and teachers constantly examine the data through interpretation, analysis, reflection, and decision making. Through self-reflection and teacher guidance, students focus on their work samples, noting changes and determining new goals for their learning. This reflection process promotes students' organizational skills, self-reliance, independence, and creativity (Tompkins, 1990) as they: (1) determine which work samples will be placed in the teacher folder, the student folder, and the parent folder; (2) self-assess the quality of their reading or writing; (3) check their work samples to see that they followed the established guidelines, using student checklists; (4) decide what revisions they need to make on their literacy samples; and (5) select and modify their literacy goals.

To expedite this process, many of our teachers keep three folders for data, each arranged alphabetically, with large plastic tabs displaying their names. The teacher folder contains observations, anecdotal notes, interview data, checklists, representative oral and written language samples across the content areas (including the various stages of reading and writing), and results of standardized tests. The selection process for the data for this folder is primarily done by the teacher. The student folder contains student checklists, lists of books read during the year, and specific oral and written language samples across the content areas. With guidance, students participate in the selection, analysis, and evaluation of the data for this folder. The parent folder contains representative oral and written language samples across the content areas. Teachers and students also work together to select, analyze, and evaluate the data for this folder. These folders are also stored in milk crates.

Combining assessment with evaluation in these ways is grounded in theory. Teachers and students examine and reexamine the data, selecting and appraising representative and significant work samples (Routman, 1991). It is important that both teachers and students participate in the process. Sometimes the teachers select and appraise the work samples; sometimes students select and appraise the work samples. For students to learn to verbalize why and how they choose specific pieces for their folder or their parents' folder, they need guided practice. Teachers can facilitate this process more easily by asking questions. Some questions Mrs. Manchester asks include: "Why did you choose this piece? What things do you like about it?" "How did you improve on this piece?" "How could you make this better?" "What are your goals for your next piece?" As the year progresses, her students are able to identify the changes they see in their work, their strengths, their needs, and their goals for future pieces. She finds that self-assessment helps her students take ownership for their learning. She says her students take great joy in seeing their progress as they compare work pieces over time.

Evaluation and Assessment of the Multicultural Literacy Program. During the past four years, we used both formal and informal assessment measures to evaluate the effectiveness of our ongoing multicultural program. Using standardized tests enabled us to assess students at the beginning of the program and then at the conclusion of each successive year to determine growth in reading and writing performance. Using normal curve equivalents, we were also able to compare students across school districts and to compare our students to other students nationally.

Formal assessment procedures, however, provided little usable information for instructional improvement. The findings, moreover, must be used cautiously because of possible cultural bias. Informal assessment procedures, therefore, provided more usable information for planning and modifying curriculum and instruction in our program. These procedures included observations, surveys, interviews, and representative reading and writing samples which are placed in portfolios. These procedures also provided a record of students' progress. Classroom teachers find these sources help them determine areas of strength and how they can assist students to become successful learners.

Applying Informal Monitoring Procedures

Receiving inservice instruction on informal monitoring procedures is only the beginning. Teachers need support and assistance as they apply these procedures within their classrooms through visitations. (See Chapter 9.) We encourage our teachers to begin with the monitoring procedures that feel most comfortable; we do not want them to feel overwhelmed. Many choose observation or miniconferences because these are strategies they often use routinely. Teachers may only adapt these two procedures during the first year of implementing a multicultural program. Focusing on these procedures more closely, however, helps them see how the techniques inform their practice. To provide additional assistance and guidance in the use of these informal monitoring strategies, we dialogue and solve problems together during classroom visitations.

As teachers become more comfortable with the multicultural program, they begin to branch out, experimenting with reading and writing samples, conferencing, anecdotal notes, checklists, and portfolios. Through risk taking and the classroom visitations, teachers find ways to adapt and refine the informal monitoring systems to suit their classes and teaching styles. By having teachers share their strategies for using informal procedures at inservices, more teachers see how they can adapt the techniques to the needs of their own classrooms. By the third or fourth year, teachers are consistently using multifaceted approaches to assess and evaluate literacy.

Using varied approaches enables teachers to assess and evaluate students' literacy more accurately. Combining assessment and evaluation procedures with self-reflection by teachers and students provides a profile that clarifies what students have or have not learned; this process helps to guide instruction. Ultimately, assessment and evaluation will become more balanced, informative, and useful as students, teachers, administrators, educators, and parents work together to uncover the internal and external perspectives of literacy. Students from diverse backgrounds, students with special needs, and students of varying ability levels and talents all have opportunities to display their learning and strengths. All students are successful, and teachers are better informed about their students so they can design instruction to match their changing needs and interests.

SUMMARY

Becoming a teacher who uses a multicultural literacy approach to learning is challenging. Blueprints do not exist. Multicultural literacy is a philosophy—a way of thinking and acting for informed teachers as they reflect about and refine the literacy development of their students. This chapter illustrated ways to organize and manage a multicultural program, which is dynamic and evolving. After revisiting the definition of multicultural literacy and the three components of a multicultural program, we described the physical features of a sociocultural learning environment. As teachers shape their classrooms to become a community of learners, they also design curriculum to affirm and recognize the cultural and linguistic backgrounds of all students. We shared a variety of ways teachers structure their curriculum to integrate multicultural, thematic reading and writing activities across the curriculum.

To facilitate and guide learning for a community of learners, teachers orchestrate learning to include multiple learning configurations, including whole class instruction, homogeneous and heterogeneous groups, paired learning groups, independent learning, and cooperative groups. In addition to demonstrating ways to foster literacy in these alternative grouping arrangements, we described specific management strategies teachers follow as they mediate learning. The final section of the chapter detailed assessment and evaluation as an ongoing part of the teaching process. Monitoring the learning of students with authentic measures, combined with reflection and informed decision making, enables all students to become successful learners.

Importantly, teachers in a multicultural classroom continue to read professionally, ask questions, reflect, collaborate with one another, listen, research, and refine their practice to match the evolving needs of all their learners. Seeking to grow and develop professionally, teachers view theory as ever-changing, leading us down avenues in which all students achieve excellence.

As the nature of our classrooms continues to change, we will be challenged to design instruction and curriculum to mirror the reality of the classroom. To accomplish this goal, assessment and evaluation measures must be ongoing and evolving, grounded in theory and research. Teachers and students further need to engage consistently in self-reflection and self-evaluation of their cultural knowledge and understanding in order to determine avenues that lead to excellence.

REFERENCES

Allen, J., & Mason, J. (Eds.). (1989). *Risk makers, risk takers, risk breakers: Reducing the risks for young literacy learners.* (pp. 125-153). Portsmouth, NH: Heinemann Educational Books.

Au, K. (1993). *Literacy instruction in multicultural settings.* Fort Worth, TX: Harcourt Brace Jovanovich College Publishers.

Au, K., Scheu, J. A., Kawakami, A. J., & Herman, P. A. (1990). Assessment and accountability in a whole literacy curriculum. *The Reading Teacher, 43,* 574-578.

Bejarano, Y. (1987). A cooperative small-group methodology in the language classroom. *TESOL Quarterly, 21,* 483-501.

Calfee, R., & Hiebert, E. (1991). Classroom assessment of reading. In R. Barr, M. Kamil, P. Mosenthal, & D. Pearson (Eds.), *Handbook of reading research: Volume II.* (pp. 281-309). New York: Longman.

Carbo, M., Dunn, R., & Dunn, K. (1986). *Teaching students to read through their individual learning styles.* Englewood Cliffs, NJ: Prentice-Hall.

Clark, R. (1987). *Free to write.* Portsmouth, NH: Heinemann Educational Books.

Cooledge, N., & Wurster, S. (1985). Intergenerational tutoring and student achievement. *The Reading Teacher, 39,* 343-346.

Cummins, J. (1986). Empowering minority students. *Harvard Educational Review, 56,* 866-898.

De Avila, E., Duncan, S., & Navarrette, C. (1987). Cooperative learning: Integrating language and content-area instruction. *Teacher resource guide series.* National Clearinghouse for Bilingual Education.

Flood, J., & Lapp, D. (1989). Reporting reading progress: A comparison portfolio for parents. *The Reading Teacher, 42,* 508-514.

Galda, L., Cullinan, B., & Strickland, D. (1993). *Language, literacy and the child.* Fort Worth, TX: Harcourt Brace Jovanovich College Publishers.

Goodlad, J., & Oakes, J. (1988). We must offer equal access to knowledge. *Educational Leadership, 45,* 16-22.

Goodman, K. (1989). Preface. In K. S. Goodman, Y. M. Goodman & W. J. Hood (Eds.), *The whole language evaluation book.* (pp. 3-14). Portsmouth, NH: Heinemann.

Goodman, Y. (1989). Evaluation of teachers: Teacher of evaluation. In K. S. Goodman, Y. M. Goodman, & W. J. Hood (Eds.), *The whole language evaluation book.* (pp. 3-14). Portsmouth, NH: Heinemann.

Harste, J., Short, K., & Burke, C. (1988). *Creating classrooms for authors: The reading-writing connection.* Portsmouth, NH: Heinemann.

Harste, J., Woodward, V., & Burke, C. (1984). Examining our assumptions: A transactional view of literacy and learning. *Research in the Teaching of English, 18,* 84-108.

Johnson, D., & Johnson, R. (1975). *Learning together and alone.* Englewood Cliffs, NJ: Prentice-Hall, Inc.

Johnson, D., Johnson, R., & Holubec, E. (1990). *Cooperation in the classroom.* Edina, MN: Interaction Book Company.

Manning, M., & Lucking, R. (1990). Ability groups: Realities and alternatives. *Childhood Education, 254-258.*

Meloth, M., & Deering, P. (1992). Effects of two cooperative conditions on peer-group discussions, reading comprehension, and metacognition. *Contemporary Educational Psychology, 17,* 175-193.

Moore, M., & Diamond, B. (1991). *A staff developmental model for promoting literacy and cultural awareness: A multicultural literature-based approach.* Paper presented at the meeting of the American Educational Research Association, Chicago, IL.

Morrow, L. (1989). Designing the classroom to promote literacy development. In D. S. Strickland, & L. M. Morrow (Eds.), *Emerging literacy: Young children learn to read and write.* Newark, DE: International Reading Association.

Morrow, L., & Smith, J. (1990). The effects of group size on interactive storybook reading. *Reading Research Quarterly, 25,* 214-231.

Neuman, S., & Roskos, K. (1993). *Language and literacy learning in the early years: An integrated approach.* Fort Worth, TX: Harcourt Brace Jovanovich College Publishers.

Paolitto, D. (1976). The effect of cross-age tutoring on adolescence: An inquiry into theoretical assumptions. *Review of Educational Research, 46,* 215-237.

Peregoy, S. & Boyle, O. (1993). *Reading, writing, and learning in ESL.* New York: London.

Powell, J., Wisenbaker, J., & Connor, R. (1985). Effects of intergenerational tutoring and related variables on reading and mathematics achievements of low socioeconomic children. *Journal of Experimental Education, 55,* 206-211.

Reutzel, D., & Cooter, R. (1992). *Teaching children to read: From basals to books.* New York: Merrill Publishing Company.

Routman, R. (1988). *Transitions: From Literature to Literacy.* Portsmouth, NH: Heinemann.

Routman, R. (1991). *Invitations: Changing as teachers and learners K-12.* Portsmouth, NH: Heinemann.

Slavin, R. (1983). *Cooperative learning.* New York, NY: Longman.

Slavin, R. (1987). Cooperative learning where behavioral and humanistic approaches to classroom motivation meet. *The Elementary School Journal, 88,* 29-37.

Taylor, & Strickland, D. (1989). Learning from families: Implications for educators and policy. In J. B. Allen, & J. M. Mason (Eds.), *Risk makers, risk takers, risk breakers.* (pp. 251-280). Portsmouth, NH: Heinemann.

Teale, W. (1988). Developmentally appropriate assessment of reading and writing in the early childhood classroom. *The Elementary School Journal, 89,* 173-183.

Teale, W., Hiebert, E., & Clittenden, E. (1987). Assessing young children's literacy development. *The Reading Teacher, 40,* 772-777.

Tompkins, G. (1990). *Teaching writing: Balancing process and product.* Columbus, OH: Merrill Publishing Company.

Tompkins, G., & Hoskisson, K. (1991). *Language Arts: Content and teaching strategies.* Columbus, OH: Merrill Publishing Company.

Topping, K. (1989). Peer tutoring and paired reading: Combining two powerful techniques. *The Reading Teacher, 42,* 488-494.

Valencia, S. (1990). Assessment: A portfolio approach to classroom reading assessment: The whys, whats, and hows. *The Reading Teacher, 43,* 338-340.

Van Manen, M. (1986). *The tone of teaching.* Ontario, Canada: Scholastic.

The Human Spirit

I have lived a pretty exciting life and a different life from some of the other kids. Still I live a normal life. When I was two, it was one of my most exciting years of my life because of a war that was being fought. I had a feeling that my family and I would never be free because we were being kept by the Thai soldiers. There was a river near the village where my family was kept. One day my family told one of the guards that they were going fishing but really they were trying to get across the river, because that river would lead to freedom. My dad's brother was waiting for us on the other side of the river. My parents gave me a sleeping pill, so I would not make any noise because there were guards and soldiers on ships. This was the perfect time and they had to do it. They swam under water and managed to escape. I wish I could go back in time and see how it was to be kept captive in Thai and not have freedom, but I do know how it feels. I now call that river, the Freedom River.

I really miss Laos. I have not seen my friends since I left. Someday, I will go back to my country. But most of all, I want to go back and learn about Laos' history, its culture, and also see my friends. What I have been through, I hope I will never go through again. I feel like I never knew what freedom really meant. I am happy for my parents and they are pleased themselves.

When I was three, I enjoyed my new life in Laos. My parents use to tell me that I was always crying. They took me to many places. I remember once when my dad took me to a temple and some parts of the temple looked like gold. My family was poor and my parents were working hard to earn money. When I was left at home with my aunt, I always felt like I was being trapped because I was not use to freedom. Every time I write about this in my journal, I feel that I am concerned about my past. I had not thought much about it before and now I am concerned. I have learned from writing about my life that the human spirit is stronger than anything and it does not matter how you look, or how healthy, or how strong you are. It is the human spirit that counts. I have learned another thing. It is that dreams can come true if you hope for it and never let go of that dream.

We do not have transportation in Laos, so we would walk and my parents would carry me from place to place. I would normally eat two times a day but mostly I liked eating my grandma's coconuts that grew on her trees along with other tropical fruits. One of my favorite fruits from Laos is a red ball that has spikes around it and the spikes are soft and you cut it open and eat it.

I sometimes dream that I would go back to Laos and visit my relatives. I hope to be a lawyer and save my money to go back to my homeland.

Near my mom's home in Laos, there is a river and the trees are full of fruits. My dad would take me to a place where there are many rocks and strong currents like the Colorado River. However, the Colorado River is stronger. I have a photo of that river where my parents took me. My dad would go fishing and he would come back with big fish. There would be people selling food on their boats for some people live on the rivers. They would sell fruits, rice, soup, fish, and all types of Laos candies.

It has been hard for me to move to another country because I do have a difficult time here. When I first came to America, I thought I would live a happy life but I was wrong. Some people would make fun of me just because I am from a different world and it is hard to live like that. Some people would think that I am Chinese just because I look like them. Just think about it. Would you like living your life in a new country with people from different worlds and going to new places? That place doesn't feel like home to me because of the people. Life here is not like the life I had in the land of my birth and the land of my people.

Vangchai Sayarath
Fifth Grade

Questions Teachers Ask

1. How do I know that the literature book I choose is culturally authentic, that it doesn't contain stereotypes?

In addition to the guidelines (and the references) for selection of culturally authentic literature presented in Chapter 3, teachers will find it helpful to consult with members of the specific culture about which the book is written. Using the guidelines to determine if books are culturally authentic, you will only need to receive verification about those books that are in question. As you read more multicultural books, you will increase your sensitivity to books that are laden with stereotypes or fail to reflect the social and cultural traditions of a group.

2. If I'm expected to use a variety of multicultural literature selections, how do I get enough books for each student?

Some schools will allocate a portion of the budget that they normally use for basal readers to be used for purchasing multicultural literature books. It is important to emphasize that a number of multicultural books can be purchased for the same amount one pays for one basal and its accompanying workbook. Purchasing literature books is cost effective; they never become outdated.

Other teachers use the Book Clubs, such as Scholastic, Troll, or Lucky Books, to order sets of discounted paperback books. Schools and teachers have also been successful in eliciting help from parent groups who want to see students learn about their own culture and other cultural groups. These parent groups sponsor money making activities to ensure that these books become available to students.

3. I'm sort of hooked on my old way of teaching . . . and I find it hard to cover everything I need to cover. Is there a way to incorporate multicultural literacy—which I firmly believe in—into my classroom in a way that allows me to gradually change and feel confident and effective?

Change is never easy. Since you see the value of multicultural literacy, it will be less difficult for you. Importantly, you do not have to change everything that you have done in the past. For example, many teachers continue to use the basal readers and incorporate multi-cultural literature into their curriculum during language arts, social studies, or science. They

363

also find that some stories in the basal readers have multicultural themes which they can build upon and extend across all content areas.

The need to understand, acknowledge, and affirm the diversity in the classroom is created as you model behaviors of tolerance and acceptance. Many of the books also provide opportunities for teachers and students to sensitively discuss classroom social problems. One teacher, for example, used the book, *Molly's Pilgrim,* as a catalyst for a discussion about differences among people and ways to respect these differences.

The manner in which you think about multicultural literacy is also important. If you think of it as an inclusive part of the curriculum rather than an "add-on," you will find that the philosophy and materials will support all the other areas that you have "to cover." Several teachers see this as a strength of the program. A fourth grade teacher noted, "I see how the materials integrate with other curriculum areas . . . they especially tie in with themes from math and social studies."

Once you have begun to change, even in small steps, the changes in the students will encourage you to consider further modifications. Gradually, you will begin adopting a multicultural literacy program in a way that fits your teaching style and the needs of your students.

4. Many of the books have excellent themes and positive messages for the students. However, I'm disturbed by some of the dialect used. How do I continue to promote proper English, if I use books whose main characters speak a dialect?

Because the books are authentic, they mirror the culture in terms of the setting, the actions and events, and the characters—which includes *their language style and grammar.* The non-standard dialect—such as black English, which is how the characters communicate in the story, is often one of the most distinctive features of the culture. The language, therefore, adds to the richness and authenticity of the literature.

Concerns about students' continued use of standard English (SE) dialect—what some teachers refer to as "proper English"—are unfounded. Students who normally use SE will not begin using a non-standard dialect because of the literature. The literature, however, provides excellent opportunities for the teacher to develop understandings about language usage and the variety of dialects in the United States and other countries.

For students who speak a non-standard dialect, the teacher will want to make the students aware of the political and social power of the SE dialect in the United States. It is important, however, that the home language not be eliminated. Rather, the teacher can expand the child's language competencies to include a broad range of cultural speaking styles, including SE. Teachers who would like to assist students in acquiring SE will find useful suggestions in Boseker's (1988) article, *Bidialectalism in the United States.*

5. With several cultures represented in my classroom, how do I learn enough about these different cultures? How am I supposed to know about all the different cultures that are represented in the United States and the world? Where do I go to find expert resources on diverse cultures?

Gradually and *cooperatively.* It is certainly unrealistic to expect that a teacher will know all there is to know about a given culture. We recommend that you begin by focusing on one or two cultures as you begin your quest for more cultural knowledge. There are also many good resource books that will provide information (see Cultural Profiles in Instructor's Manual).

Consulting with people of the culture appears to be another productive method of learning about a culture. Most people are eager to share information about their backgrounds, values, daily activities, and celebrations. Possible contacts who are easily accessible are the parents of students in your class and the students themselves.

Most State Departments of Education and Departments of Social Services offer information and materials on diverse populations within their state specifically and sometimes within the United States. Community resources such as ethnic organizations can also be of assistance. These include such organizations as the Anti-Defamation League of B'nai B'rith, the National Association for the Advancement of Colored People, the Japanese American Citizenship League, and The Puerto Rican Forum.

6. Cultural and racial groups often identify themselves by several names. For example, I have heard the Native Americans referred to as Indians, and Amerinds. How do I know what term to use?

It is true that groups often use different terms for identification. However, in most groups, even though there is not a universally preferred term, we find that there is one term that is most preferred by groups. Therefore, we use terms that we have found (1) in the professional literature and (2) in extended conversations and discussions with colleagues, authors, and members of the specific cultural groups. It is also important to note that preferred names may vary from region to region in the United States. For example, some African Americans in the South prefer to identify themselves as Black or Black Americans rather than African Americans.

7. Is there a danger of reinforcing or encouraging stereotypical behavior on the part of my students when I discuss and identify various stereotypes that are held?

The benefits of discussing and sensitizing students to stereotypes in literature and in the social context of the classroom and everyday experiences far outweigh the possibility that students may hold on to stereotypes that already exist. In fact, educators and scholars (Banks, 1991; Adler, 1993; and Crawford, 1993) recommend that students engage in discussions that identify stereotypes that students hold, discussing how they were formed and the harmful effects that are a result of this behavior.

8. Although I agree with the principles of the Multicultural Literacy Program, I am concerned that it is not an effective approach for all students. Are students of different ability levels—especially lower ability students—accommodated in the program?

The Multicultural Program is effective for *all* students. First, it recognizes that all students have the potential for learning and that they have rich backgrounds that are fertile references for learning. Second, the program focuses on meaning and understanding, using the students' experiences as the basis for learning. Third, the literature and content of the curriculum embraces the history and culture of the members of diverse cultural groups. Fourth, students are able to work in varied grouping patterns that are compatible with their learning styles—cooperative and collaborative learning groups, paired groups, or independently. Finally, the books that are used are at various reading levels so that they can accommodate students who work at lower levels and those who work at higher levels.

Teachers, moreover, have found that the strong emphasis on connecting the writing and reading enhances students' learning across the curriculum. Teachers also report that their students are increasing their ability to decode and recognize words. They share that teaching word recognition skills as students need them and in the context of their reading and writing (i.e., choral readings, reader's theater, predict-o-grams) facilitates learning for *all* their students, but especially those who have difficulty with these skills.

Bibliography of Children's Books

Aardema, V. (1975). *Why mosquitoes buzz in people's ears.* New York: Dial.

Aardema, V. (1977). *Who's in rabbit's house.* New York: Dial.

Aardema, V. (1981). *Bringing the rain to Kapiti plain.* New York: Dial.

Adams, E. (Ed.). (1982). *Korean Cinderella.* Seoul, Korea: Seoul International Publishing House.

Adoff, A. (1973). *Black is brown is tan.* New York: Harper & Row.

Adoff, A. (1982). *All the colors of the race.* New York: Lothrop, Lee, & Shepard.

Adoff, A. (1985). *Malcolm X.* New York: HarperCollins.

Ahenakow, F. (Ed.). (1988). *How the birch tree got its stripes.* Saskatoon, Saskatchewan: Fifth House.

Ahenakow, F. (Ed.). (1988). *How the mouse got brown teeth.* Saskatoon, Saskatchewan: Fifth House.

Alexander, S. (1983). *Nadia, the willful.* New York: Dial.

Aliki. (1979). *Mummies made in Egypt.* New York: Harper & Row.

Aliki. (1983). *A medieval feast.* New York: Harper Trophy.

Aliki. (1986). *How a book is made.* New York: HarperCollins.

Aliki. (1988). *Corn is maize.* New York: Harper & Row.

Aliki. (1988). *A weed is a flower.* New York: Simon & Schuster.

Aliki. (1989). *The King's Day.* New York: Harper Trophy.

Anderson, D. A. (1991). *The origin of life on earth.* Mt. Airy, MD: Sights Productions.

Anderson, J. (1989). *The first Thanksgiving feast.* Boston: Houghton Mifflin.

Armstrong, W. (1969). *Sounder.* New York: Harper & Row.

Artman, J. (1981). *Indians: An activity book.* Carthage, IL: Good Apple.

Ata, T. (1989). *Baby rattlesnake.* San Francisco: Children's Book Press.

Aten, J. (1982). *Americans, too!* Carthage, IL: Good Apple.

Awiakta, M. (1983). *Rising fawn and the fire mystery.* Memphis, TN: St. Luke's Press.

Babbitt, N. (1969). *Search for delicious.* Toronto: Farrar, Straus, & Giroux.

Back, P. (1985). *Crickets and corn.* New York: Friendship Press.

Bains, R. (1982). *Harriet Tubman: The road to freedom*. Mahwah, NJ: Troll.

Baker, B. (1982). *And me coyote*. New York: Macmillan.

Baker, K. (1989). *The magic fan*. San Diego: Harcourt Brace Jovanovich.

Baker, O. (1988). *Where the buffaloes begin*. New York: Puffin.

Ballentine, B. & Ballentine, I. (Eds.). (1993). *The Native Americans: An illustrated history*. Atlanta: Turner Publishing Co.

Ballingham, P. (1984). *Earth mother lullabies from around the world*. Tuscon, AZ: Cross-Cultural Studies Program.

Batherman, M. (1981). *Before Columbus*. Boston: Houghton Mifflin.

Baylor, B. (1972). *When clay sings*. New York: Aladdin Books.

Baylor, B. (1974). *Everybody needs a rock*. New York: Aladdin Books.

Baylor, B. (1974). *They put on masks*. New York: Charles Scribner's Sons.

Baylor, B. (1975). *The desert is theirs*. New York: Macmillan.

Baylor, B. (1976). *Hawk I'm your brother*. New York: Macmillan.

Baylor, B. (1978). *The other way to listen*. New York: Charles Scribner's Sons.

Baylor, B. (1980). *If you are a hunter of fossils*. New York: Macmillan.

Baylor, B. (1986). *I'm in charge of celebrations*. New York: Macmillan.

Baylor, B. (1989). *Amigo*. New York: Macmillan.

Behrens, J. (1986). *Fiesta!* Chicago: Children's Press.

Belpre, P. (1978). *The rainbow-colored horse*. New York: Warne.

Belting, N. (1974). *Our fathers had powerful songs*. New York: Dutton.

Bierhorst, J. (1979). *A cry from the earth: Music of the Native American Indian*. New York: Four Winds Press.

Bierhorst, J. (1987). *The naked bear: Folktales of the Iriquois*. New York: William Morrow.

Bishop, C. H. (1938). *The five Chinese brothers*. New York: Coward-Mcann.

Bjork, C. (1978). *Linnea's windowsill garden*. Stockholm: R & S Books.

Bjork, C. (1989). *Linnea in Monet's garden*. Stockholm: R & S Books.

Blood, C., & Link, M. (1990). *The goat in the rug*. New York: Macmillan.

Blume, J. (1981). *Superfudge*. New York: Dell.

Boholm-Olsson, E. (1988). *Tuan*. New York: R & S Books.

Borland, H. (1963). *When the legends die*. Philadelphia: J. B. Lippincott.

Brown, M. (1982). *Shadow*. New York: Macmillan.

Brown, T. (1986). *Hello, amigos*. New York: Henry Holt.

Brown, T. (1987). *Chinese New Year*. New York: Henry Holt.

Bryan, A. (1987). *Dancing granny and other African stories*. New York: Macmillan.

Bryan, A. (1989). *Turtle knows your name*. New York: Atheneum.

Caduto, M., & Bruchac, J. (1991). *Keepers of the earth*. Golden, CO: Fulcrum.

Caines, J. (1982). *Just us women*. New York: HarperCollins

Cameron, A. (1985). *How raven freed the moon*. B. C., Canada: Harbour.

Cameron, A. (1987). *Orca's song*. B. C., Canada: Harbour.

Cameron, A. (1987). *Raven returns the water*. B. C., Canada: Harbour.

Cameron, A. (1988). *Spider woman*. B. C., Canada: Harbour.

Carle, E. (1991). *Dragons dragons & other creatures that never were*. New York: Putnam Group.

Carson, J. (1989). *Stories I ain't told nobody yet*. New York: Orchard Books.

Cherry, L. (1990). *The great kapok tree*. New York: Gulliver Books.

Chocolate, D. (1992). *My first Kwanzaa book*. New York: Scholastic.

Chow, O., & Widaure, M. (1987). *The invisible hunters*. San Francisco: Children's Book Press.

Clark, M. G. (1980). *Freedom crossing*. New York: Scholastic.

Cleaver, E. (1985). *The enchanted caribou*. New York: Atheneum.

Clement, C. (1986). *The painter and the wild swans*. New York: Dial.

Coatsworth, E., & Coatsworth, D. (1979). *The adventures of Nanabush: Ojibway Indian stories*. Toronto: Doubleday.

Coerr, E. (1977). *Sadako and the thousand paper cranes*. New York: Dell.

Cohen, C. (1988). *The mud pony*. New York: Scholastic.

Cohlene, T. (1990). *Quillworker: A Cheyenne legend*. Mahwah, NJ: Troll.

Cohlene, T. (1990). *Turquoise boy: A Navajo legend*. Mahwah, NJ: Troll.

Corwin, J. (1990). *African crafts*. New York: Franklin Watts.

Cozzens, J. (Ed.). (1992). *Kids explore America's Hispanic heritage*. Santa Fe, NM: John Muir.

Crowder, J. (1986). *Tonibah and the rainbow*. Bernalillo, NM: Upper Strata Ink.

Cruz, M. (1987). *Yaguaa days*. New York: Dial.

Curtis, E. (1978). *The girl who married a ghost*. New York: Four Winds Press.

Czernecki, S., & Rhodes, T. (1989). *Time before dreams*. Winnipeg: Hyperion Press.

Dailey, S. (1988). *Land of the sky blue waters*. Mt. Pleasant, MI: Rumplestiltskin.

Davis, K. (1990). *Don't know much about history*. New York: Crown.

Day, D. (1990). *The sleeper*. Nashville, TN: Ideals.

deCesare, R. (1988). *Myth, music, and dance of the American Indian*. Van Nuys, CA: Alfred Publishing.

Delacre, L. (1990). *Arroz con leche: Popular songs and rhymes from Latin America*. London: A & C Black.

Delacre, L. (1990). *Las navidades: Popular Christmas songs from Latin America*. New York: Scholastic.

Delacre, L. (1993). *Vejigante: Masquerader*. New York: Scholastic.

Demi. (1980). *Liang and the magic paintbrush*. New York: Henry Holt.

Demi. (1987). *The hallowed horse*. New York: Dodd Mead.

Demi. (1990). *The empty pot*. New York: Henry Holt.

dePaola, T. (1978). *The popcorn book*. New York: Holiday House.

dePaola, T. (1983). *The legend of the bluebonnet*. New York: G. P. Putnam's Sons.

dePaola, T. (1988). *The legend of the Indian paintbrush*. New York: G. P. Putnam's Sons.

Dorros, A. (1991). *Abuela*. New York: Dutton Children's Books.

Dorros, A. (1992). *This is my house*. New York: Scholastic.

Eagle, B. M. (1987). *For my people*. Davis, CA: Linda Waite.

Esbensen, B. (1988). *The star maiden: An Ojibway tale*. Boston: Little, Brown, & Co.

Feelings, T. (1974). *Jambo means hello*. New York: Dial.

Feeney, S. (1985). *Hawaii is a rainbow*. Honolulu: University of Hawaii Press.

Flournoy, V. (1985). *The patchwork quilt*. New York: Dial.

Freedman, R. (1987). *Indian chiefs: A teaching guide*. New York: Holiday House.

Fritz, J. (1980). *Where do you think you're going Christopher Columbus?* New York: G. P. Putnam's Sons.

Fritz, J. (1987). *The double life of Pocahontas*. New York: Puffin.

Garza, C. (1990). *Family pictures/ Cuadros de familia*. San Francisco: Children's Book Press.

George, J. (1972). *Julie of the wolves*. New York: Harper & Row.

George, J. (1983). *The talking earth*. New York: Harper Trophy.

Giovanni, N. (1987). *Spin a soft black song*. New York: Farrar, Straus & Giroux.

Girion, B. (1993). *Indian summer*. New York: Scholastic.

Glubock, S. (1976). *The art of the woodland Indians*. New York: Macmillan.

Goble, P. (1978). *The girl who loved wild horses*. New York: Macmillan.

Goble, P. (1983). *Star boy*. New York: Macmillan.

Goble, P. (1984). *Buffalo woman*. New York: Macmillan.

Goble, P. (1985). *The great race of the birds and the animals*. New York: Bradbury.

Goble, P. (1987). *Death of the Iron Horse*. New York: Bradbury.

Goble, P. (1988). *Her seven brothers*. New York: Bradbury.

Goble, P. (1989). *Beyond the ridge*. New York: Bradbury.

Goble, P. (1989). *Iktomi and the berries*. New York: Orchard Books.

Goble, P. (1990). *Dream wolf*. New York: Bradbury.

Goble, P. (1990). *The gift of the sacred dog*. New York: Macmillan.

Goble, P., & Goble, D. (1973). *Lone Bull's horse raid*. New York: Bradbury.

Greenfield, E. (1986). *Honey, I love and other poems*. New York: Harper & Row.

Greenfield, E. (1988). *Nathaniel talking*. New York: Writers & Readers.

Greenfield, E. (1988). *Under the Sunday tree*. New York: HarperCollins.

Grifalconi, A. (1986). *The village of round and square houses*. Boston: Little, Brown & Co.

Grifalconi, A. (1990). *Osa's pride*. Boston: Little, Brown, & Co.

Grinnell, G. (1982). *The whistling skeleton: American Indian tales of the supernatural*. New York: Four Winds Press.

Hadley, E., & Hadley, T. (1983). *Legends of the sun and moon*. New York: Cambridge University Press.

Haley, G. (1970). *A story, a story*. New York: Aladdin Books.

Hamanaka, S. (1990). *The journey: Japanese Americans, racism, and renewal*. New York: Orchard Books.

Hamilton, V. (1986). *The people could fly*. New York: Knopf.

Hamilton, V. (1987). *Zeely*. New York: Macmillan.

Hamilton, V. (1988). *In the beginning: Creation stories from around the world*. San Diego: Harcourt Brace Jovanovich.

Harris, C. (1977). *Mouse woman and the mischief-makers*. New York: Atheneum.

Haskins, J. (1987). *Count your way through Japan*. Minneapolis: Carolrhoda.

Haskins, J. (1989). *Count your way through Korea*. Minneapolis: Carolrhoda.

Haskins, J. (1990). *Count your way through the Arab world*. Minneapolis: Carolrhoda.

Heide, F., & Gilliland, J. (1990). *The day of Ahmed's secret*. New York: Lothrop, Lee, & Shepard.

Helbig, A. & Perkins, A. (1994). *This land is our land: A bibliographic guide to multicultural literature for children and young adults*. Westport, CT: Greenwood Publishing Group.

Highwater, J. (1981). *Moonsong lullaby*. New York: Lothrop, Lee & Shepard.

Highwater, J. (1984). *Legend days*. New York: Harper & Row.

Highwater, J. (1985). *Ceremony of innocence*. New York: Harper & Row.

Highwater, J. (1986). *I wear the morning star*. New York: Harper & Row.

Hoffman, M. (1991). *Amazing Grace*. New York: Dial.

Holling, H. (1969). *Paddle to the sea*. Boston: Houghton Mifflin.

Hopkinson, D. (1993). *Sweet Clara and the freedom quilt*. New York: Knopf.

Hoven, L. (1990). *Native Americans: A thematic unit*. Westminster, CA: Teacher Created Materials.

Howard, C. (1971). *Authentic Indian dances and folklore*. Deal, NJ: Kimbo Educational.

Jagendorf, M., & Boggs, R. (1960). *King of the mountains: A treasury of Latin American folk stories*. New York: Vanguard.

Jernigan, G. (1988). *One green mesquite tree*. Tuscon, AZ: Harbinger House.

Jones, H. (1971). *The trees stand shining*. New York: Dial.

Joseph, L. (1990). *A coconut kind of day*. New York: Penguin.

Kervin, R. (1986). *Legends of the animal world*. New York: Cambridge University Press.

King, S. (1993). *Shannon: An Ojibway dancer.* Minneapolis: Lerner Publications.

Knight, M. B. (1992). *Talking walls.* Gardiner, ME: Tilbury House.

Korty, C. (1975). *Plays from African folktales.* New York: Scribner.

Kroeber, T. (1964). *Ishi, last of his tribe.* Boston: Houghton Mifflin.

Krumgold, J. (1953). *And now Miguel.* New York: Harper Trophy.

Kuklin, S. (1992). *How my family lives in America.* New York: Macmillan.

Lampman, E. (1978). *Squaw man's son.* New York: Atheneum.

Lawson, J. (1993). *The dragon's pearl.* New York: Clarion Books.

Lee, J. (1982). *Legend of the Milky Way.* New York: Henry Holt.

Lee, J. (1987). *Ba-Nam.* New York: Henry Holt.

Lee, J. (1991). *Silent lotus.* New York: Farrar, Straus, & Giroux.

Lenski, L. (1965). *Sing a song of people.* Boston: Little, Brown, & Co.

Lepthien, E. (1987). *Choctaw.* Chicago: Children's Press.

Lester, A. (1990). *Imagine.* Boston: Little, Brown, & Co.

Lewin, T. (1993). *Amazon boy.* New York: Macmillan.

Lewis, R. (1991). *All of you was singing.* New York: Atheneum.

Longfellow, H. (1983). *Hiawatha.* New York: Dial.

Longfellow, H. (1984). *Hiawatha's Childhood.* New York: Puffin.

Lopez, B. (1990). *Crow and weasel.* Berkeley, CA: North Point Press.

Lord, B. (1984). *In the year of the boar and Jackie Robinson.* New York: Harper & Row.

Louie, A. (1982). *Yeh-shen: A Cinderella story from China.* New York: Philomel.

Lovett, S. (1990). *Kidding around the Hawaiian Islands: A guide for young readers.* Santa Fe, NM: John Muir Publications.

Macaulay, D. (1975). *Pyramid.* Boston: Houghton Mifflin.

Macaulay, D. (1977). *Castle.* Boston: Houghton Mifflin.

Margolies, B. (1990). *Rehema's journey: A visit to Tanzania.* New York: Scholastic.

Markun, P. (1993). *The little painter of Sabana Grande.* New York: Bradbury.

Martin, B., Jr., & Archambault, J. (1987). *Knots on a counting rope.* New York: Henry Holt.

Martin, B., Jr., & Archambault, J. (1989). *Chicka chicka boom boom.* New York: Simon & Schuster.

Martin, R. (1992). *The rough-face girl.* New York: G. P. Putnam's Sons.

Mathis, S. B. (1975). *The hundred penny box.* New York: Viking.

Mattox, C. W. (1989). *Shake it to the one that you love the best.* El Sobrante, CA: Warren-Mattox.

McDermott, G. (1974). *Arrow to the sun.* New York: Puffin.

McDermott, G. (1975). *The stone-cutter.* New York: Puffin.

McDermott, G. (1986). *Anansi the spider.* New York: Henry Holt.

McGovern, A. (1984). *A pilgrim's first Thanksgiving.* New York: Scholastic.

McGovern, A. (1987). *The defenders.* New York: Scholastic.

McGovern, A. (1991). *If you sailed on the Mayflower.* New York: Scholastic.

McKeown, M. (1969). *Linda's Indian home.* Portland, OR: Binford & Mort.

McKissack, P. (1985). *Aztec Indians.* Chicago: Children's Press.

McKissack, P. (1986). *Flossie and the fox.* New York: Dial.

McLain, G. (1990). *The Indian way.* Santa Fe, NM: John Muir.

McLean, V. (1987). *Chasing the moon to China.* New York: Redbird.

McLean, V., & Klyce, K. (1989). *Kenya! Jambo!* Memphis, TN: Redbird.

Mendez, P. (1989). *The black snowman.* New York: Scholastic.

Miles, M. (1971). *Annie and the old one.* Boston: Little, Brown, & Co.

Mohr, N. (1979). *Felita.* New York: Bantam Skylark.

Mohr, N. (1986). *Going home*. New York: Dial.

Mora, P. (1992). *A birthday basket for Tia*. New York: Macmillan.

Moran, T. (1987). *A family in Mexico*. Minneapolis, MN: Lerner Publications.

Morimoto, J. (1990). *My Hiroshima*. New York: Viking.

Morninghouse, S. (1992). *Habari gani? What's the news? A Kwanzaa story*. Seattle, WA: Open Hand.

Munsch, R. (1986). *Love you forever*. Buffalo, NY: Firefly Books.

Musgrove, M. (1976). *Ashanti to Zulu: African traditions*. New York: Dial.

Myers, W. (1988). *Scorpions*. New York: Harper Keypoint.

Myers, W. (1991). *The legend of Tarik*. New York: Scholastic.

Myers, W. (1993). *Malcolm X: A biography*. New York: Scholastic.

Norman, H. (1987). *Who-paddled-backward-with-trout*. Boston: Little, Brown & Co.

O'Dell, S. (1960). *Island of the blue dolphins*. New York: Dell.

O'Dell, S. (1989). *Streams to the river, river to the sea*. Boston: G. K. Hall.

Ortiz, S. (1988). *The people shall continue*. San Francisco: Children's Book Press.

Paek, M. (1988). *Aekyung's dream*. San Francisco: Children's Book Press.

Paterson, K. (1990). *The tale of the mandarin ducks*. New York: G. P. Putnam's Sons.

Paulsen, G. (1985). *Dogsong*. New York: Bradbury.

Perl, L. (1977). *Mummies, tombs, and treasures*. New York: Clarion.

Perrault, C. (1985). *Cinderella*. New York: Dial.

Polacco, P. (1988). *The keeping quilt*. New York: Simon & Schuster.

Polacco, P. (1990). *Babushka's doll*. New York: Simon & Schuster.

Prusski, J. (1988). *Bring back the deer*. San Diego: Harcourt Brace Jovanovich.

Ringgold, F. (1990). *Tar Beach*. New York: Crown.

Ringgold, F. (1992). *Aunt Harriet's underground railroad in the sky*. New York: Crown.

Rohmer, H., & Achondo, M. (1982). *The legend of food mountain*. San Francisco: Children's Book Press.

Rohmer, H., & Anchondo, M. (1988). *How we came to the fifth world*. San Francisco: Children's Book Press.

Rohmer, H., Chow, O., & Vidaure, M. (1987). *The invisible hunters*. San Francisco: Children's Book Press.

Rose, D. (1990). *The people who hugged the trees*. Niwot, CO: Roberts Rinehart.

Roth, S. (1988). *Fire came to the earth people*. New York: St. Martin's Press.

Roth, S. (1990). *The story of light*. New York: Morrow Jr. Books.

Sakade, F. (1958). *Japanese children's favorite stories*. Boston: Charles E. Tuttle.

Sales, F. (1989). *Ibrahim*. New York: J. B. Lippincott.

San Souci, R. (1978). *The legend of Scarface*. New York: Doubleday.

San Souci, R. (1987). *The enchanted tapestry*. New York: Dial.

San Souci, R. (1987). *The talking eggs*. New York: Dial.

Say, A. (1990). *El chino*. Boston: Houghton Mifflin.

Say, A. (1991). *Tree of cranes*. Boston: Houghton Mifflin.

Seattle, Chief. (1991). *Brother eagle, sister sky*. New York: Dial.

Seeger, P. (1986). *Abiyoyo*. New York: Macmillan.

Siberell, A. (1982). *Whale in the sky*. New York: Dutton.

Simon, S. (1988). *Volcanoes*. New York: Morrow Jr. Books.

Simon, S. (1992). *Animal fact-animal fable*. New York: Crown.

Sneve, V. D. (1989). *Dancing teepees: Poems of American Indian Youth*. New York: Holiday House.

Speare, E. (1983). *The sign of the beaver*. New York: Dell.

Spier, P. (1990). *People.* New York: Doubleday.

Stanek, M. (1989). *I speak English for my mom.* Morton Grove, IL: Albert Whitman.

Stanley, D. (1988). *Shaka, king of the Zulus.* New York: Morrow Jr. Books.

Stanley, F. (1991). *The last princess: The story of Princess Ka'iulani of Hawaii.* New York: Four Winds Press.

Steptoe, J. (1988). *Mufaro's beautiful daughters.* New York: Lothrop, Lee & Shepard.

Stolz, M. (1988). *Storm in the night.* New York: HarperCollins.

Strickland, D. (Ed.). (1982). *Listen children: An anthology of black literature.* New York: Bantam.

Surat, M. (1983). *Angel child, dragon child.* Madison, NJ: Steck-Vaughn.

Tadjo, V. (1989). *Lord of the dance: An African retelling.* New York: HarperCollins.

Taylor, M. (1975). *Song of the Trees.* New York: Dial.

Taylor, M. (1976). *Roll of thunder hear my cry.* New York: Bantam Books.

Taylor, M. (1981). *Let the circle be unbroken.* New York: Bantam Books.

Taylor, M. (1987). *The friendship & the gold cadillac.* New York: Bantam Books.

Taylor, M. (1987). *The gold cadillac.* New York: Dial.

Taylor, M. (1990). *Mississippi bridge.* New York: Dial.

Taylor, M. (1990). *The road to Memphis.* New York: Puffin.

Terrell, J., & Terrell, D. (1974). *Indian women of the western morning.* New York: Dial.

Toye, W. (1969). *The mountain goats of Temlaham.* New York: Oxford University Press.

Toye, W. (1979). *Fire stealer.* Toronto: Oxford University Press.

Troughton, J. (1979). *How rabbit stole the fire.* New York: Bedrick/Blackie.

Tsuchiya, Y. (1988). *Faithful elephants.* Boston: Houghton Mifflin.

Tune, S. C. (1988). *How Maui slowed the sun.* Honolulu: University of Hawaii Press.

Turner, G. T. (1989). *Take a walk in their shoes.* New York: Cobblehill.

Uchida, Y. (1981). *A jar of dreams.* New York: Atheneum.

Uchida, Y. (1983). *The best bad thing.* New York: Macmillan.

Uchida, Y. (1985). *The happiest ending.* New York: Atheneum.

Velarde, P. (1989). *Old father story teller.* Santa Fe, NM: Clear Light.

Vidal, B. (1991). *The legend of El Dorado.* New York: Knopf.

Vuong, L. (1982). *The brocaded slipper.* New York: J. B. Lippincott.

Wallace, I. (1984). *Chin Chiang and the dragon dance.* New York: Atheneum.

Wallin, L. (1984). *In the shadow of the wind.* New York: Bradbury.

Waters, K., & Slovenz-Low, M. (1990). *Lion dancer: Ernie Wan's Chinese New Year.* New York: Scholastic.

Weinstein-Farson, L. (1988). *Wampanoag.* New York: Chelsea House.

Wells, R. (1992). *A to zen: A picture book of Japanese culture.* Saxonville, MA: Picture Book Studio.

Wilbur, K. (1978). *The New England Indians.* Chester, CT: Globe Pequot.

Williams, K. L. (1990). *Galimoto.* New York: Lothrop, Lee & Shepard.

Winter, J. (1988). *Follow the drinking gourd.* New York: Knopf.

Winter, J. (1991). *Diego.* New York: Knopf.

Xiong, B. (1989). *Nine-in-one grr! grr!* San Francisco: Children's Book Press.

Yarbrough, C. (1979). *Cornrows.* New York: Coward-McCann.

Yee, P. (1990). *Tales from gold mountain: Stories of the Chinese in the new world.* New York: Macmillan.

Yep, L. (1975). *Dragonwings.* New York: Harper Trophy.

Yep, L. (1977). *Child of the owl.* New York: HarperCollins.

Yep, L. (1979). *Sea glass.* New York: HarperCollins.

Yep, L. (1989). *The rainbow people*. New York: HarperCollins.

Yolen, J. (1972). *The girl who loved the wind.* New York: Crowell.

Young, E. (1989). *Lon po po : A red-riding hood story from China.* New York: Philomel.

Zim, J. (1975). *My shalom, my peace.* Tel-Aviv, Israel: Sabra Books.

Zinn, H. (1980). *A people's history of the United States.* New York: Harper & Row.

Index

READER RESPONSE SURVEY

The authors and editors of *Multicultural Literacy: Mirroring the Reality of the Classroom* would like to know what you think of the ideas presented in our book and how useful you find the theory and teaching practices. Your comments will be used to improve future editions of our text, and can also be used to initiate a reader network through Internet if names and addresses are provided. Please do not feel compelled to comment on the entire text, you may just comment on certain portions of text as well. Thank you for your interest and commitment to multicultural literacy.

1. Name (optional):

2. Address (optional):

3. How did you learn about this book?

4. If you are a preservice teacher:

    a. What is the name of the course in which this book was assigned?

5. If you are a school practitioner:

    a. Was this book assigned to you in a course you are taking?

       (YES/NO)   If yes, which course:

    b. What is your role in the school?   Circle one:

       Teacher (grades taught _____)

       Administrator/Supervisor   Parent   Other

6. If you are teacher educator:

    a. What is the name of the course in which this book will be used?

    b. Will this be a primary or supplementary text (Circle one)?

7. Please identify the portions of the book you find most meaningful.

8. Has the book helped to increase your knowledge of culturally responsive instruction?

    a. (YES/NO)   In what ways?

    b. What additional suggestions do you have?

9. Has the book increased your knowledge and sensitivity to cultures?

   a. (YES/NO)   In what ways?

   b. What additional suggestions do you have?

10. Has the book increased your knowledge of Multicultural Children's Literature?

   a. (YES/NO)   In what ways?

   b. What additional suggestions do you have?

11. Did you find the bibliography of Children's Literature useful?

   a. (YES/NO)   In what ways?

   b. What additional suggestions do you have?

12. In what ways are you applying the information presented in your own classroom?

13. What are your suggestions for improving this book?

14. Other Comments.

Please return to:
    Laura McKenna
    Senior Editor, Education
    Longman Publishers USA
    10 Bank Street
    White Plains, NY 10606-1957